THE POLITICS
OF ASSIMILATION

THE POLITICS
OF ASSIMILATION

A STUDY OF THE
FRENCH JEWISH COMMUNITY
AT THE TIME OF THE
DREYFUS AFFAIR

BY

MICHAEL R. MARRUS

OXFORD
AT THE CLARENDON PRESS
1971

Oxford University Press, Ely House, London W. 1

GLASGOW NEW YORK TORONTO MELBOURNE WELLINGTON
CAPE TOWN SALISBURY IBADAN NAIROBI DAR ES SALAAM LUSAKA ADDIS ABABA
BOMBAY CALCUTTA MADRAS KARACHI LAHORE DACCA
KUALA LUMPUR SINGAPORE HONG KONG TOKYO

PRINTED IN GREAT BRITAIN
AT THE UNIVERSITY PRESS, OXFORD
BY VIVIAN RIDLER
PRINTER TO THE UNIVERSITY

TO MY
MOTHER AND FATHER

PREFACE

ALTHOUGH this book deals with the assimilation of Jews in France at the end of the nineteenth century, developments which are discussed in these pages will bear similarities to those in other communities at other times. Readers will, I hope, find analogous themes and personalities to indicate that the patterns followed by French Jewry were by no means unique, and that the questions of assimilation which fill the following chapters are neither peculiarly French nor Jewish. My own discussion, however, has necessarily been less ambitious, and I have been chiefly concerned with describing the problems of a particular community at a particular time. Yet in so doing I have undoubtedly drawn, as every historian must, upon my own experience and upon sources which are not, strictly speaking, related to the subject at hand. The years which I spent as a graduate student at the University of California at Berkeley in the middle 1960s were particularly fruitful in this respect; I owe a great deal, more than I can acknowledge, to the spirit of that time. This was a turbulent, hopeful, and creative period, and one in which many of the basic social questions raised here were discussed in a much more passionate and less historical context. It was also, of course, a contentious period, and I am acutely aware of the fact that many who have helped me would not agree with everything that I have written.

The research for this book was done mainly in Paris, during the academic year 1966-7, and during the spring and summer of 1969. I am grateful to the Woodrow Wilson Foundation and to the Canada Council whose fellowships enabled me to carry on this work in an atmosphere which constantly evoked the memory of the *belle époque*. A fellowship from the University of California permitted me to do much of the writing in the rich and stimulating environment which I have described. During my stay in Paris a number of people graciously accorded me interviews to discuss their family histories and, on occasion, their own recollections of the Dreyfus years. I am indebted to them for their hospitality, their insights, and their assistance in my research. The staff of the library of the Alliance Israélite Universelle were particularly kind to me, and made available their outstanding facilities for work in this field. I would also like to thank MM. Gérard Nahon and Maurice Moch for permitting me to examine material in the archives of the Consistoire Central and the Consistoire de Paris.

In the course of preparing this study I have benefited from the advice and suggestions of a number of scholars. Among the many who have aided me I would especially like to thank Professor Carl E. Schorske, Dr. Nelly Wilson, Mr. Heinz Warschauer, and Mr. Zosa Szajkowski. Several of my colleagues at the University of Toronto offered their encouragement during the final stages. My friend and teacher Professor Seth L. Wolitz first proposed this subject to me over three years ago, and he has since provided the intellectual friction from which, I hope, some light has been generated. Above all I would like to express my gratitude to Professor Richard F. Kuisel, who read an earlier draft of the manuscript with great care, and whose criticisms helped me to clarify my ideas, both for the reader and for myself. The index was prepared by Mrs. Susan Klement, whose concentration and patience far exceeded what I could have brought to the task. A final note of thanks is due to Mr. Michael Bergot and Mr. Charles Pachter who saved me from a number of errors.

Paris, July 1969

CONTENTS

LIST OF PLATES

Thanks are due to the following for permission to reproduce these plates:
H. Roger Viollet, Paris, for Plates I*a*, IV*a* and *b*; The Bibliothèque Nationale,
Paris, for Plates I*b*, II*a*, *b* and *c*, III*a*, *b*, IV*c* and *d*.

ABBREVIATIONS AND SHORT TITLES
USED IN FOOTNOTES

A.C.C.	Archives of the Consistoire Central
A.C.P.	Archives of the Consistoire de Paris
Actes	*Actes et conférences de la Société des Études Juives*
A.I.	*Les Archives Israélites*
A.I.U.	Archives of the Alliance Israélite Universelle
A.N.	Archives Nationales
Annuaire	*Annuaire des Archives Israélites pour l'an du monde* . . .
Annuaire S.E.J.	*Annuaire de la Société des Études Juives*
A.P.P.	Archives of the Préfecture de Police, Paris
B.N.	Bibliothèque Nationale
É.S.	*L'Écho Sioniste*
J.E.	*The Jewish Encyclopaedia* (12 vols., New York, 1901–6)
Journal officiel, Chambre	*Journal officiel de la République française, Débats, Chambre des Députés*
J.S.S.	*Jewish Social Studies*
R.E.J.	*Revue des Études Juives*
U.I.	*L'Univers Israélite*
U.J.E.	*The Universal Jewish Encyclopaedia* (10 vols., New York, 1939–43)

NOTE: The Société des Études Juives published its *Annuaire* until 1886. From 1886 the annual lectures given before the Société and which made up this publication were printed in the *Actes*, along with a general review of the year and other business. The latter was usually bound together with the *R.E.J.*, but its pagination is in roman numerals.

CHAPTER I

INTRODUCTION

A SENSE of tragedy hovers about any historical study of European Jewry in the late nineteenth century. Tragedy clings to the subject because the reader knows that the historical path was leading ultimately to the Nazi extermination of European Jews. During the course of modern Jewish history there have been many moments in which the future seemed dark, and the fate of Jewish communities seemed to hang in the balance. But hardly ever, until the decades preceding the First World War, had presentiments of impending holocaust been so widespread among certain groups of Jews, or had prophetic statements been so relevant to what actually occurred. In analysing the causes and effects of Jewish activity during this period, in describing the character of Jewish thought, the historian cannot insulate himself from the knowledge of what was to come only a few decades later.

With French Jewry the story is subject to a particularly bitter irony. For in no other country was optimism stronger, was there greater confidence in what the future would bring. Although there were a few French Jews whose prescience matched that of Theodore Herzl and eastern European spokesmen, the majority were faithfully wedded to the official, optimistic creed of the Third Republic. There was a general belief that France was leading Europe and the world to a higher stage of civilization.

This book describes the community of Jews at a moment when cracks were emerging in their ideal portrait of the future. We enter their bright world of optimism during the *belle époque*, just as anti-Semitism was making its appearance in France as an organized mass movement. Inevitably, perhaps, feelings about the sequel to our story have seeped into the chapters which follow, and have given our judgements a cast with which all might not agree. In our view the chief spokesmen for French Jewry, the men who celebrated French ideals as the *summum bonum* for Jews the

B

world over, were tragically blind to the implications of the anti-Semitic campaign of which they were the victims. The historian cannot ignore his feelings about his subject; he can only attempt to balance these with a judicious evaluation of the evidence, and make clear to his readers the basis upon which his historical judgements are made. In the final analysis, of course, the reader must decide for himself whether the description is fair, and whether justice has been done to the men of the past.

Our title is 'The Politics of Assimilation: a Study of the French Jewish Community at the Time of the Dreyfus Affair'. A word should be said to clarify the nature of the subject-matter and to set forth the general approach of the chapters which follow.

Assimilation, we have found, lies at the heart of our problem. Any effort to describe the Jewish community in France at the end of the nineteenth century faces the fact that the Jews of France were highly assimilated into French life and that, at the same time, their assimilation was never complete and was thus a continuing problem. By 'assimilation' we are referring here to the process by which individuals of Jewish background assumed an *identity* which is essentially French. Such identification may take a number of different forms: Jews may intermarry with other Frenchmen, may accept the basic civil allegiance demanded of French citizens, may engage in extensive social interaction with other Frenchmen, and may otherwise move towards a situation in which, in the expression of the time, they were 'Frenchmen like any other'. Assimilation has many different forms and degrees, and we shall not enter here into a full discussion of this problem.[1] Rather we have a particular manifestation of assimilation in mind.

The particular object of our inquiry is 'the politics of assimilation'. By this we mean the way in which French Jews translated their identification with France and with French life into perspectives upon and activity in public affairs. Largely excluded from this discussion is any analysis of the personal behaviour of

[1] For a useful analysis of assimilation see Milton M. Gordon, *Assimilation in American Life: the Role of Race, Religion, and National Origins* (New York, 1964), chs. iii–vi.

individual Jews, their modes of social intercourse, and their private responses to various aspects of French life. Where such questions are relevant to individual biographies they will be discussed, but our central purpose is to highlight Jewish thought and activity on broader, public questions. Attention is therefore directed towards issues of national political concern, specifically politics, public policy, and, of course, the important issue of anti-Semitism.

It is difficult to define the 'French Jewish community' with any precision. Some of these Jews, as we shall see, arrived in France from eastern Europe in the wake of the Russian pogroms of the 1880s. Others could refer to generations of ancestors born in France, and had, indeed, no other pole of loyalty. All of these Jews, however, whatever their background, considered themselves, and were considered by the French community at large, to have *some* Jewish identity. As we shall point out in the chapter which follows, the end of the nineteenth century imposed a vaguely racial definition of Jewishness which was largely accepted by Jew and non-Jew alike, and which defined the quality of being Jewish in a manner distinct from religious belief or cultural identification. Generally speaking, this was a time when 'Jewishness' was widely applied, and could not easily be removed. We have chosen to follow this contemporary 'racial' definition in referring to 'Jews', and thus we shall consider as Jewish those whom the French community at large, both Jews and non-Jews, considered as such.[1]

There remains the problem of the extent to which such an agglomeration can be considered to have formed a 'community'. We live in an age which has seen the progressive dissolution of communities, and in a sense our study offers another example of this modern phenomenon.[2] It is here assumed, however, that there

[1] See Louis Lévy, 'L'espèce juive et ses variétés', *U.I.*, 6 Oct. 1897, pp. 86–7; R.T., 'La vitalité d'Israël: comment et pourquoi nous restons juifs', *U.I.*, 2 Dec. 1898, pp. 325–6. For a fascinating discussion of this problem see Jean-Paul Sartre, *Réflexions sur la question juive* (Paris, 1954), pp. 83–4, *passim*. French Jews use the designation 'Juif' and 'Israélite' when referring to a Jew. Traditionally, 'Israélite' has been employed to avoid the supposed pejorative connotation of 'Juif', and assimilationist Jews have tended to prefer the former. On this point see Zadoc Kahn, *Sermons et allocutions* (3 vols., Paris, 1894), ii. 264.

[2] On the breakdown of community see Robert A. Nisbet, *Community and Power* (New York, 1962). For a discussion of the general question of 'Jewish community'

was some community of interest and common behaviour among French Jews which permits us, for some purposes at least, to refer to them as a community. Part One of our study investigates this problem, and examines the extent to which a 'Jewish community' did exist in France during this period.

Although the discussion is intended to include the entire community of Jews in France, our focus is clearly upon Paris. Problems peculiar to provincial Jews, such as their municipal politics, for example, have not been treated here. Paris was, as will be explained, the centre of Jewish life in France, the directing force of Jewish activity which the far smaller provincial communities tended to follow.[1] In Paris there was a Jewish press, and the governmental organs of the Jewish community. And in Paris the Jewish community articulated its response to the great upheaval in French society in the course of the Dreyfus Affair. For these reasons we have decided to concentrate upon the French capital.

The Dreyfus Affair was a time of crisis in French society, and a period of particular distress for the French Jewish community. This was the moment when the tide of anti-Semitism rose higher in France than at any other time in the nineteenth century, a moment when violence in the streets, brutal press attacks, and the threat of proscription forced Jews to re-examine the nature of their allegiance both to France and to the older community of which they were a part. For some Jews who lived through those years the fine hopes which had been built by the Revolution of 1789 were cast in the dust; yet for most the tradition of assimilation into French society provided sufficient comfort and adequate security. 'The time of the Dreyfus Affair', then, is an appropriate setting for this study, for it was at that time that many of the problems in which we are interested were consciously faced and openly discussed.

Speaking of the Jewish response to the Dreyfus Affair, one leader of the Jewish community at the time mused that it would

see Salo W. Baron, *The Jewish Community: its History and Structure to the American Revolution* (3 vols., Philadelphia, 1942), i. 3–30.

[1] See Zadoc Kahn, op. cit., iii. 62; Prague, 'Le culte en province', *A.I.*, 11 Aug. 1898, p. 258; Jules Bauer, 'Le judaïsme de province', *U.I.*, 12 Mar. 1897, pp. 790–1.

'take well over a century to unravel this complicated [*mystérieuse*] story, if it ever is unravelled'.[1] Having attempted just such an unravelling, the author can appreciate Salomon Reinach's caution in analysing the Jewish community in France during this historical period. Documents on the subject are scarce, and it is only with difficulty that the available sources give answers to the questions asked. With the exception of some material in a recent history of the Alliance Israélite Universelle, there is no extensive study of French Jewry at that time, and no general survey of the problem of Jewish assimilation in France.[2] Moreover, there is no adequate history of the Jews in France, and there are few detailed biographical works on important leaders of the Jewish community.[3] There is, of course, the magnificent novel by Marcel Proust, whose insights into the activities of French Jews at the time of the Affair are breathtaking in their perception. But Proust was interested in the psychological dimensions of social change; our problem here, as we have indicated, is somewhat different.

There are two basic reasons why there is such a paucity of literature on French Jewry during the modern and early modern periods. For one thing, there were never many Jews in France compared with other European countries. After long years of persecution the Jews were finally expelled from France in 1394, and though small numbers were periodically readmitted, they generally lived a precarious existence from that time until the emancipation decrees of 1790 and 1791. Up to the time of the French Revolution, and even for some time afterwards, these Jews were scattered about the country in various settlements, each with

---

[1] Salomon Reinach, 'Conférence de M. Salomon Reinach', *Bulletin de l'Association amicale des anciens élèves des Écoles Halphen et Lucien de Hirsch*, vol. i, no. 2, Apr. 1908.

[2] André Chouraqui, *L'Alliance Israélite Universelle et la renaissance juive contemporaine, 1860–1960* (Paris, 1965). A number of books on peripheral subjects have, however, been useful or suggestive. See Michael A. Meyer, *The Origins of the Modern Jew: Jewish Identity and European Culture in Germany, 1794–1824* (Detroit, 1967); Raymond F. Betts, *Assimilation and Association in French Colonial Theory, 1890–1914* (New York, 1961); Charlotte Roland, *Du ghetto à l'Occident: deux générations yiddiches en France* (Paris, 1962).

[3] An important exception for our purposes is Julien Weill, *Zadoc Kahn, 1839–1905* (Paris, 1912).

its own history and its own special problems.[1] Such a community
is not easily described. Another problem arises as one approaches
the nineteenth century. For after the emancipation brought by the
Revolution, with the accession of Jews to full political rights, the
process of assimilation was enormously accelerated. And with
assimilation, as one historian of anti-Semitism has recently noted,
it becomes extremely difficult to study the Jews in any systematic,
historical sense.[2] With the loss of corporate identity recognized
by law, not only did the notion of Jewish distinctiveness diminish,
but much of the institutional structure of a separate community
was dismantled. While the consciousness of being Jewish certainly
persisted, this consciousness is often difficult for the historian to
extract and analyse. Problems such as these are particularly acute
for the historian of the Jews in France, where emancipation came
so early, and where the basis for Jewish life in the period before
emancipation was generally so weak.

Hannah Arendt has been one of the few writers to probe deeply
into the implications of Jewish assimilation in western Europe at
the end of the nineteenth century. Her work provides us with a
brilliant and sometimes bewildering commentary on the history of
Jews who were the first to be faced with the forces of modern anti-
Semitism. She contends that the fate of these people was bound
up with the societies in which they lived, that as French Jews
assimilated into a corrupt and degenerating Third Republic they
assumed some of the vices of that society, and were unable to face
the larger political implications of the struggle against anti-
Semitism. She is concerned with the 'disintegrating' effects of
assimilation, and with the corresponding disintegration of European society. Ultimately, it seems to us, she is concerned with the
terrible breakdown of community in our time.[3] Her work, more
than that of any other, has influenced the chapters which follow.

[1] See Arthur Hertzberg, *The French Enlightenment and the Jews* (New York,
1968), chs. ii, vi, vii, *passim*.
[2] Léon Poliakov, *Histoire de l'antisémitisme*, vol. iii, *De Voltaire à Wagner* (Paris,
1968), p. 10.
[3] Hannah Arendt, *The Origins of Totalitarianism* (Cleveland, 1958), chs. ii–iv;
id., 'From the Dreyfus Affair to France Today', *J.S.S.*, vol. iv, no. 3, July 1942,

This book consists of three parts. In the first we shall consider
the extent to which Jews formed a community in France; three
chapters will explore the various elements which associated men
who to varying degrees identified themselves as Jews. Part Two
describes the political dimension of Jewish assimilation in the
period immediately preceding the Affair; separate chapters will
discuss the political theory and the politics of the Jewish community. Part Three is concerned with the Dreyfus crisis itself,
and with its political ramifications for the Jewish community.
It contains a chapter on Bernard Lazare, probably the most
seminal Jewish thinker in France at the time, another on the
response of the Jewish community to the Affair, and finally a
chapter on the Zionist movement in France as it arose during this
period.

The study as a whole, it is hoped, will provide a picture of a
community of Jews, unsure of itself and divided on certain vital
issues, facing a period of crisis. Perhaps too it will offer some basis
for criticism of the politics of assimilation, criticism from which
we may judge that the French Jewish community was less prepared than it might have been for the impending tragedy.

pp. 195–240; id., 'The Jew as a Pariah: a Hidden Tradition', *J.S.S.*, vol. vi, no. 2,
Apr. 1944, pp. 99–120; id., 'Privileged Jews', *J.S.S.*, vol. viii, no. 1, Jan. 1946,
pp. 3–30.

PART ONE · COMMUNITY

W A S there a community of Jews in France? Did French Jews, who for the most part considered themselves to be devoted citizens of the Republic, have any sense of allegiance to their fellow Jews? To what extent, if any, did the old communal bonds of ghetto life persist into the era of emancipation? No answers, of course, can be conclusive in dealing with elusive questions such as these. The essence of community, what we have loosely defined as community of interest and common behaviour, is rooted as much in subjective conceptions as in institutions. Indeed, the relationship between these is a highly complex and dialectical one. Subjective conceptions influence institutions; institutions in turn influence subjective conceptions. Factors such as these make the identification of communities difficult. In the three chapters which follow we have chosen to highlight certain features which seem to us significant in explaining the character of the Jewish community in France. The first of these chapters demonstrates how the vocabulary of race was adopted within the Jewish community as a convenient means to express existing feelings of community among Jews. Following this, we shall approach the problem through the consideration of various 'ties' of community—forces which operated both in the minds of men and in their daily activity, forces which, to varying degrees, provided for Jewish identification and Jewish action.

CHAPTER II

RACE AND COMMUNITY

JEWS and non-Jews used the language of race in order to define the Jewish community at the close of the nineteenth century. One of the most interesting features of the Jewish community in France at this time is the way in which Jews subscribed to a definition of themselves which the larger French community had provided. Before emancipation, before they achieved formal equality, Jews had been excluded from full participation in French society, and bore the heavy burden of being a people kept legally apart from the other subjects of the French king. But the Jews had never been commonly considered separate in a physical or biological sense. This latter notion took hold in the century after the French Revolution, as biology and anthropology moved to provide the basis for a distinction which French law no longer permitted. The facts about *la race juive* were never settled with any precision; the public was unable to follow the learned disputes of the initiated, and anthropologists themselves appeared continually at odds when it came to schemes of racial classification. Yet a consensus was reached that some racial identity existed among Jews. It is important to recognize that the idea of a Jewish racial type was not a simple product of the anti-Semitic propagandist. Rather the racial category was a common and universal assumption, held by Jews and non-Jews, impervious to the occasional detractor, resisting periodic assaults by science, and steadily working its way into everyday language. Race, in fact, provided Jews with the means to express their sense of a distinct Jewish identity, a sense which was difficult to define in other terms, and which they themselves were not always prepared to admit.

Philology built the original academic foundation for the idea of a Jewish race during the first half of the nineteenth century, and the chief architect of this conception in France was Ernest Renan, perhaps the most famous man of letters of his day. Renan drew upon the studies of German scholars of the time, men whose investigation of languages appeared to open the way to important new discoveries about the history of mankind. These linguists painstakingly explored the origins of languages, classified them into two main groups, and speculated imaginatively on the cultural implications of this division. The first of these groups had linguistic roots in Sanskrit; the peoples who once spoke these tongues were classified as Aryans or Indo-Europeans. The second group sprang from the ancient Hebrew; the family of languages was designated by the term Semitic, and the people who spoke these languages, Semites.[1] With these assumptions, further speculation could proceed.

Renan's main contribution to this end was a long and detailed study of the history of Semitic languages, first published in 1855. Here the new philology paraded confident generalizations about Aryans, Semites, and Jews. Renan faced the issue of Semitic inferiority squarely: 'I am . . . the first to recognize that the Semitic race, compared to the Indo-European race, represents essentially an inferior level of human nature.'[2] In the work of Renan the Jewish religion continued throughout history to provide the core of Semitic beliefs, and the Jews were viewed as the Semitic people *par excellence*. This was certainly the impression given in Renan's most popular and influential work, the *Vie de Jésus* (1863).[3] Renan

---

[1] Jacques Barzun, *Race: a Study in Superstition* (New York, 1965), pp. 97–8; Salomon Reinach, 'La prétendue race juive', *Actes* (1903), *R.E.J.*, vol. xlvii (1903), p. v; id., *Les Origines des Ariens: histoire d'une controverse* (Paris, 1892); James Darmesteter, *Prophètes d'Israël* (Paris, 1892), pp. 247–8; Hannah Arendt, *The Origins of Totalitarianism* (Cleveland, 1958), pp. 158–84; Léon Poliakov, *Histoire de l'antisémitisme*, vol. iii, *De Voltaire à Wagner* (Paris, 1968), pp. 321–34.

[2] Ernest Renan, *Histoire générale et système comparé des langues sémitiques* (Paris, 1855), pp. 4–5.

[3] This work, in the view of one modern writer, was probably the most popular book in France in the nineteenth century next to the Bible. See Dora Bierer, 'Renan and his Interpreters: a Study in French Intellectual Warfare', *Journal of Modern History*, vol. xxv, Dec. 1953, p. 381. The following passage is typical of Renan's method of generalization throughout: 'Un des principaux défauts de la race juive est son âpreté dans la controverse, et le ton injurieux qu'elle y mêle presque toujours. Il n'y eut jamais dans le monde de querelles aussi vives que celles des juifs entre eux. C'est le sentiment de la nuance qui fait l'homme poli et modéré.'

claimed that from the *physical* point of view Semites and Aryans formed a single race, the white race. From this one might gather that 'race' was used in his work as a purely cultural term.[1] He did, however, recognize that the Semitic race presented 'a very pronounced [physical] type', that Jews and Arabs were visibly recognizable everywhere.[2] At one point, moreover, he even seemed to consider 'race' as a socio-economic category.[3] In general, Renan moved with remarkable ease past the fine distinctions of race, people, physical type, and linguistic group. Indeed, his facility served to render the term virtually meaningless to a critical reader. He scattered racial terminology somewhat recklessly about his writings, yet he did so in such a manner as to imply the existence of a distinct, identifiable Jewish race.[4] Like another famous French speculator on the differences between races, Count Arthur de Gobineau, Renan implied that the racial element was of crucial importance in human history; yet again like Gobineau, he never managed to present his ideas on this subject with any consistency. For Renan, as for most of his contemporaries who, it appears, were equally careless, race was a convenient designation which avoided a more precise definition of the nature of the ties among

Or, le manque de nuances est un des traits les plus constants de l'esprit sémitique.... Jésus, qui était exempt de presque tous les défauts de sa race, et dont la qualité dominante était justement une délicatesse infinie, fut amené malgré lui à se servir dans la polémique du style de tous.' Ernest Renan, *Vie de Jésus* (1863) (new edn., Paris, 1965), pp. 335–6. Cf. ibid., p. 89.

[1] See Renan, *Histoire des langues sémitiques*, p. 491.
[2] Ibid., p. 490.
[3] See, for example, Renan, *Vie de Jésus*, p. 219.
[4] See Bierer, op. cit., p. 376; and Théodore Reinach in *Actes* (1893), *R.E.J.*, vol. xxvi (1893), pp. xiv–xvi. It is surely difficult to accept, in this context, the judgement of Robert F. Byrnes (*Antisemitism in Modern France*, vol. i, *The Prologue to the Dreyfus Affair* (New Brunswick, New Jersey, 1950), p. 48) that Renan 'represents the scientific, positivistic, materialistic second half of the nineteenth century at its very best'. Byrnes further remarks that Renan's *Histoire du peuple d'Israël*, published between 1887 and 1893, 'could not be used by the antisemites, even indirectly, against their chosen enemies'. The influence of the much more popular *Vie de Jésus* and even of the *Histoire des langues sémitiques* should certainly also be considered in relating Renan to French anti-Semitism. Moreover, Renan's work was used for other related purposes such as the tendency to think in terms of racial categories and to establish a qualitative difference between races. See, for example, Barzun, op. cit., p. 106, n. 5.

peoples and which betokened, at the same time, the existence of a powerful tie—far-reaching and of great social importance.

Beginning in the 1860s, anthropologists made a serious effort to clarify this vague racial terminology and to express human differences in physical terms. In 1859 Paul Broca founded the Anthropological Society of Paris; before long studies of racial characteristics, their origins and development, became popular in academic circles. However, despite the precision of the various skull measurements, despite the impressive scientific apparatus brought to bear on the problem, the matter of the Jewish race was not settled. Paul Broca omitted the Jews from his list of the human races; another scholar, Pruner-Bey, included them. Other respected anthropologists like Quatrefages made little attempt to resolve the issue; the tendency was to be tentative in areas of dispute, and to print differing tables side by side. Some of these named the Jews a race, others did not.[1]

By the 1890s the naturalists' zeal for classification, measurement, and speculation had fixed itself in the public consciousness. On the popular level the earlier philological themes were simply added to what were now assumed to be the biological branches of humanity. What emerged was a strange and potent mixture—a concoction of science and literature prepared for the public by scholars and cranks alike. Everyone had a hand in the matter of race. According to one journalist in a fashionable Paris daily, the whole question of races and religion was à la mode: 'There are newspapers, books, even salons where one is automatically labelled as Aryan, Arab, Slav, or Semite. A whole bourse of races rises and falls with certain types.'[2] In 1872 Renan had written that he was becoming more and more impressed with the viewpoint of 'historical ethnography'—the explaining of historical development by reference to racial characteristics.[3] Twenty years later the

---

[1] A. de Quatrefages, The Human Species (New York, 1879), pp. 370–3. Cf. Salomon Reinach, 'La prétendue race juive', pp. viii–ix; Raymond F. Betts, Assimilation and Association in French Colonial Theory 1890–1914 (New York, 1961), ch. iv.

[2] Georges Thiébaud, 'Questions de races', Le Gaulois, 4 June 1893.

[3] Ernest Renan, La Réforme intellectuelle et morale de la France (1872) (new edn., Paris, 1967), p. 57.

French public was equally impressed; it devoured books on national character, popular psychology, and race. Popular writers incorporated the tentative conclusions of naturalists, linguists, and historians, and spoke with the authority of science.

Probably the best known of these was the physician and sociologist Gustave Le Bon. With Le Bon the scientific drive for definition was transferred boldly to the study of mankind. 'What is most clear to me', he wrote, '. . . is that each people possesses a mental constitution as fixed as its anatomical characteristics.' Scientific thinking involved the analysis and classification of these fixed 'mental constitutions'. From them one could derive 'great permanent laws which direct the general march of each civilization'. 'The life of each people, its institutions, its beliefs and its arts are only the visible traces of its invisible soul.'[1] Another well-known social theorist reached similar conclusions with respect to national character. The latter, wrote Alfred Fouillé, was 'intimately related to temperament which is itself related as much to heredity and ethnic traits as to the physical environment'.[2] While Fouillé warned against a tendency to mix questions of national character and race, others, such as Le Bon, were far less cautious.[3] For Le Bon 'race' and 'people' were frequently interchangeable terms. Vagueness was considered a fault not of terminology, but of inadequate knowledge about the mysteries of the human spirit. The Jews, considered from this point of view, were clearly a race, a distinct physical and psychological type separated from the French race by the immutable laws of culture and ethnography.

Anti-Semites invariably armed themselves with weapons forged in the 'scientific' studies of philology or biology. Édouard Drumont began his massive *France juive* with a discussion of the traditional battle between the Semitic and Aryan races. He mustered

---

[1] Gustave Le Bon, *Lois psychologiques de l'évolution des peuples* (Paris, 1894), pp. 5–6, 11.

[2] Alfred Fouillé, *La Psychologie du peuple français* (Paris, 1898), p. i. Cf. id., 'La psychologie des peuples et l'anthropologie', *Revue des Deux Mondes*, 15 Mar. 1895, pp. 365–96.

[3] Fouillé, *La Psychologie du peuple français*, p. i. Cf. Robert K. Merton's introduction to Gustave Le Bon, *The Crowd: a Study of the Popular Mind* (New York, 1960), p. xxxviii.

Renan himself in support of the contention of Semitic inferiority.[1]
Another anti-Semite, the Belgian socialist Edmond Picard, claimed
that 'the Aryano-Semitic struggle' arose in society because of the
conflicting 'psychologies' of the two peoples.[2] Racism was, in the
observation of one perceptive columnist, at once the basis for
accusing Jews of separatism and the means to isolate them:
'Judaism, in effect, one can never repeat it too often, is not a religion: it is a race. The Jews, whatever the country to which they
belong, have retained too many ties, too much cosmopolitanism.
They remain sincere blood brothers across all national limits. . . .
If the French Jews are French, they are only so in a certain measure,
as much as they have assimilated into our race, and one must admit
that in general they have assimilated only slightly. Race only forms
itself through a long atavism [sic].'[3]

But anti-Semites were not alone in making social assumptions
on the basis of race. Everywhere in French society during this
period there existed some form of the racist concepts outlined
above. Thus with the best of intentions the scholar Anatole Leroy-
Beaulieu defended the Jews before a Catholic audience, speaking
'as a Christian and as an Aryan'.[4] Leftists of the time like Georges
Clemenceau could, in political argument, refer to the Jews as 'a
race distinct from the Celts', while the venerable vice-president of
the Senate, Scheurer-Kestner, once alluded to some distasteful
quality of a Jewish deputy as 'a defect of his race'.[5] Both Scheurer
and Clemenceau defended Alfred Dreyfus and did so at considerable expense to themselves; neither was considered hostile by the
Jewish community, and neither considered himself a 'racist' in any
way.[6] The same was true of Fernand Labori, defence counsel for
both Dreyfus and Zola. Labori was simply using a common frame

[1] Édouard Drumont, *La France juive: essai d'histoire contemporaine* (2 vols.,
Paris, 1886), i. 12-13.
[2] Henri Dagan, *Enquête sur l'antisémitisme* (Paris, 1899), pp. 1-2.
[3] Léonel de la Tourasse, 'Juif et Allemand', *La France nouvelle*, 9 Jan. 1895.
[4] Anatole Leroy-Beaulieu, 'L'antisémitisme', *Revue bleue*, 10 Apr. 1897, p. 449.
[5] Georges Clemenceau, 'Au-dessus de la race et de la religion', *L'Aurore*, 10 June
1898; Robert Gauthier (ed.), *'Dreyfusards!'; souvenirs de Mathieu Dreyfus et autres
inédits* (Paris, 1965), p. 200.
[6] Cf. 'Les Juifs', *La France républicaine*, 6 Aug. 1892.

of reference when he referred unfavourably to 'the Semitic spirit' in contrast with the 'pure idealism' of Aryans.[1] Similarly Jules Ferry, attempting to respond to an anti-Semitic charge, praised the Jews from the standpoint of race. 'The virtues of this race', Ferry wrote to a Jewish correspondent, 'are immediately apparent. Its defects or its vices, which tend to disappear, to fade day by day, are the remains of a long servitude.'[2]

French Jews, being an integral part of French society, shared in its ideas on race. Jews commonly spoke of *la race juive*.[3] So long as the idea of a Jewish race did not imply an attack upon themselves, the designation was accepted, commented upon, and used freely in Jewish circles.

In 1868, for example, a non-Jew, Alfred Legoyt, presented a *mémoire* on the 'biostatic immunities of the Jewish race' to the Central Committee of the Alliance Israélite Universelle, the largest Jewish philanthropic organization in France. Legoyt spoke with some authority; he was an important government statistician and had made a careful study of the literature dealing with the Jewish race.[4] His main conclusion was not remarkable; following anthropological notions of the day he claimed to have demonstrated that Jews had a lower death-rate, acclimatized better around the world, and were in general more adaptable to changing conditions than the surrounding populations.[5] Unlike his work of 1865 where he pointed to sociological reasons for this vitality, Legoyt now judged that it was due to a 'privilege of race'.[6] This was the aspect of the investigation which most interested Jules Caravallo, the Alliance official who made a report on the *mémoire* to the Central Committee. Caravallo noted that various authorities agreed on the fact

[1] Gauthier, op. cit., p. 248.
[2] 'Jules Ferry, ami des Juifs', *U.I.*, 1 Apr. 1892, p. 422.
[3] See Théodore Reinach in *Actes* (1893), *R.E.J.*, vol. xxvi (1893), p. xviii. Reinach describes 'cette vieille et banale opinion [of the Jews constituting a race] non moins répandue chez les Juifs eux-mêmes que chez leurs ennemis . . .'.
[4] Narcisse Leven, *Cinquante ans d'histoire: l'Alliance Israélite Universelle (1860–1910)* (2 vols., Paris, 1911), ii. 338.
[5] Alfred Legoyt, *De certaines immunités biostatiques de la race juive* (Paris, 1868).
[6] Ibid., p. 78. Cf. id., *De la vitalité de la race juive en Europe* (Paris, 1865), p. 23.

that the Jews constituted a distinct racial type.[1] Further, the Jewish cranial dimensions which helped to produce this conclusion were 'without exception superior to the dimensions of the corresponding Christian cranium . . .'.[2] While one had to be somewhat cautious about these results, observed Caravallo, it seemed reasonable to accept 'a superiority of the Jewish heads over the Christian heads'.[3] The Jews were, when viewed in Darwinian terms, a race 'strongly organized for struggle', one of 'the militant races'. The Jewish race was created by God 'to live, to struggle, to triumph definitively one day by the physical privileges of race, by its cerebral development, and by the privileges of a well-tempered spirit'.[4] Caravallo cautioned sternly against arrogance on this account: 'If God has given us a brain more vast, He has imposed upon us the duty to perfect it by greater meditation, by more work, by a firm and courageous march towards the triple pole, the supreme goal of our activity: the beautiful, the true, the good.' Legoyt's *mémoire* was accepted by the Alliance. It awarded him a gold medal, had the work printed and distributed in the schools of the Alliance, and had three hundred copies sent to various libraries.[5]

The theory of a Jewish racial quality which enabled the Jewish people to thrive in diverse environments proved durable, among both Jews and non-Jews. Here, when examined in historical perspective, was a racial explanation for the physical survival of the Jews. Here too was a useful weapon to use in response to charges of Semitic 'inferiority'. The theory found its way into Quatrefages's popular textbook on human races, and was repeated at a statistical congress by an important demographer named Lagneau, a member of the Academy of Medicine.[6] Isidore Weil, the Grand Rabbi of Colmar, considered, as a variant of this quality, a distinctly Jewish faculty for assimilation as an 'atavism'.[7] 'There always flows in our veins', he wrote, 'the blood of our fathers who,

---

[1] Jules Caravallo in Legoyt, *De certaines immunités biostatiques*, pp. 9–10.
[2] Ibid., p. 10.   [3] Ibid.
[4] Ibid., p. 15.   [5] Ibid., p. 16.
[6] A. de Quatrefages, *L'Espèce humaine* (8th edn., Paris, 1886), p. 161; 'La vitalité juive', *U.I.*, 1 Nov. 1889, p. 107.
[7] Isidore Weil, 'La caractéristique d'Israël', *U.I.*, 16 Jan. 1890, p. 261, and *U.I.*, 1 Feb. 1890, p. 294.

distinct from the other peoples of Asia that all suffer in servitude, were never in the service or pay of the great or the conquerors of the moment.' These servile Asian peoples, unlike the Jews, were never able to survive the process of human selection imposed by a world of struggle.[1]

Although the notion of a Jewish race was subjected to a barrage of academic criticism at the end of the century, Jews for the most part stood by its basic premiss of some biological tie among the Jewish people. In 1893 the Société des Études Juives, a sophisticated society devoted to the study of Jewish history and philology, entertained the anthropologist Victor Jacques who spoke on the question. Jacques based his researches upon various indices of racial measurement, taken from both the living and the dead; he examined crania, the shape of the nose, hair colour, eye colour, and height. Of course, he admitted candidly, there were a number of distinct Jewish types. But this was to be explained by virtue of the mixture of races in ancient Palestine; contemporary Jews stood in direct descent from these, as the science of ethnography had shown, and as the various body measurements had demonstrated.[2] While the Société, a distinctly highbrow organization of notably moderate views, did not necessarily endorse Jacques's conclusions, it certainly accepted his perspective as a legitimate one in the light of existing knowledge, and published his arguments in its *Revue*. The members seemed impressed.

Elsewhere, Jews often combated anti-Semitic racism with racial information of their own. 'The Jewish race', wrote one columnist in a Jewish year-book, 'is not an ordinary race [*une race banale*], let us admit it. It is endowed with a certain number of diverse characteristics, *sui generis*, which make it the most noticed and most envied of human families.'[3] These characteristics, it was claimed, included the Jews' 'distinct physiognomy', 'their shifty looks', 'the liveliness of their gestures', but also 'moral virtues',

---

[1] 'Les tempéraments serviles, les héros d'obédience passive, n'ont jamais passé, que nous sachions, pour la sélection de l'humanité.' Weil, 'La caractéristique d'Israël', *U.I.*, 16 Mar. 1890, p. 388.

[2] Victor Jacques, 'Types juifs', *Actes* (1896), *R.E.J.*, vol. xxvi (1896), pp. xlix-lxxx.

[3] Ben Mosché, 'Ce que disent les noms israélites', *Annuaire 5654* (1893-4), p. 58.

'intellectual qualities', 'a few significant defects', and other 'uncommon physical or ethnic qualities'.[1] Some 'defects' of the Jewish race were said to be due to mental inactivity caused by centuries of oppression and isolation during which Jews 'did not find use for their marvellous cerebral faculties'.[2] The popular psychologist Max Nordau claimed that 'thousands of years' of ghetto life had prevented generations of Jews from getting proper physical exercise and had thus weakened the Jewish stock in modern Europe.[3]

Jews who wished to indicate that they were Jews by birth alone usually expressed this fact by reference to race. Proust, whose mother was Jewish, wrote with unmatched sensitivity about the identity problems of highly assimilated Jews at the end of the nineteenth century. It is not surprising that racial conceptions fascinated Proust and figured prominently in his portraits.[4] One of his most poignant sketches is of the old and sick Swann, an assimilated Jew. Here Jewish racial characteristics reveal themselves in Swann's physiognomy and are intimately related to a sense of Jewish identity:

> Swann's punchinello nose, absorbed for long years in an attractive face, seemed now enormous, tumid, crimson, the nose of an old Hebrew rather than of a dilettante Valois. Perhaps too in him, in these last days, the race was making appear more pronounced the physical type that characterises it, at the same time as the sentiment of a moral solidarity with the rest of the Jews, a solidarity which Swann seemed to have forgotten throughout his life . . . had revived.[5]

There were many who, like another of Proust's characters, Bloch, considered that there was indeed some ingrained quality of

[1] Ibid.

[2] Albin Valabrègue, 'Le juif de demain', Le Figaro, 16 Sept. 1893.

[3] Max Nordau, Écrits sionistes (Paris, 1936), p. 112. Cf. id., 'Le sionisme et l'antisémitisme', Le Siècle, 9 July 1899. Nordau was a Zionist leader of Hungarian origins and a close lieutenant of Theodore Herzl. On Nordau see pp. 265–7, below.

[4] On the question of Proust's views on race see Siegfried E. van Praag, 'Marcel Proust: témoin du judaïsme déjudaïzé', Revue juive de Genève, no. 49, June 1937, pp. 388–9, and Cécile Delhorbe, L'Affaire Dreyfus et les écrivains français (Paris, 1932), pp. 232, 246–7.

[5] Marcel Proust, Remembrance of Things Past, tr. C. K. Scott Moncrieff (2 vols., New York, 1932–4), ii. 67. Cf. ibid., p. 77.

Jewishness which was built deeply into their nature, which passed
from generation to generation, and which could only properly be
described in the language of race.[1] A case in point is the Radical
deputy Alfred Naquet, whose parents were Jewish but who had
given up religious practice after his thirteenth birthday and
had married a Catholic. Naquet declared his affiliation in an article
written for a Jewish periodical in 1886: 'I am a Jew by race, I am
no longer [a Jew] by religion . . .'.[2] Others, like Daniel Halévy,
less at ease with their family's past, less familiar with their Jewish
background, could make abrupt reference to 'the tainted idiosyn-
crasies of my race'.[3]

Learned opinion was moving, by the 1890s, towards rejecting
the concept of a Jewish race. Renan had changed his emphasis
sharply in the decade before, and now took the position that there
was no distinctly Jewish racial type.[4] The lengthy article on race
in the *Grande Encyclopédie* which dates from this period drew a
sharp distinction between race and ethnic group. The Jews, the
implication was, were the latter.[5] Paul Topinard, one of the best-
known French anthropologists of his time, put the matter clearly
in his textbook: 'The Jews are only a religious federation, an
ancient dispersed people, very mixed today as at their origins. . . .
From their beginnings . . . the Jews cannot be considered a race.'[6]
In 1891 Madame Clémence Royer, the French translator of Dar-
win, refuted the idea of a Jewish race before the Anthropological
Society of Paris.[7] There was still room for controversy on the subject, and there was still much scholarly opinion to the contrary,

[1] Marcel Proust, op. cit., i. 565.
[2] Alfred Naquet, 'Les juifs', *U.I.*, 16 Aug. 1886, p. 725.
[3] Quoted in Alain Silvera, *Daniel Halévy and his Times: a Gentleman-Commoner in the Third Republic* (Ithaca, New York, 1966), p. 91.
[4] See Ernest Renan, *Le Judaïsme comme race et comme religion* (Paris, 1883), and id., *De l'identité originelle et de la séparation éventuelle du judasîme et du christianisme* (Versailles, 1884). Cf. 'M. Renan et l'antisémitisme', *Le Figaro*, 30 June 1892.
[5] J. Deniker, article 'Race' in *La Grande Encyclopédie* (31 vols., Paris, n.d.), xxviii. 13.
[6] Paul Topinard, *Éléments d'anthropologie générale* (Paris, 1885), p. 212.
[7] See Salomon Reinach, 'La prétendue race juive', pp. viii–ix.

particularly on the part of German theorists and naturalists.[1] In
general, however, French anthropologists were unhappy with the
misuse of their work by vicious and unscholarly anti-Semites such
as Drumont.

The publication of a number of anti-Semitic works, beginning
with *La France juive* in 1886, made it clear to some leaders of the
Jewish community, long before the paroxysm of the Dreyfus
Affair, that the concept of race could be an extremely effective
anti-Semitic weapon. Salomon Reinach, the Jewish archaeologist
and classical scholar, attacked current notions about an Aryan race
and Aryan superiority in a series of lectures at the École du Louvre
in 1891.[2] At the Société des Études Juives Renan delivered a lecture on the misuse of the term 'race' in relation to the Jews. His
talk was published in the *Revue* of the Société and in pamphlet
form; it was constantly used by Jews in refuting anti-Semitic con-
tentions. The Jewish scholars Isidore Loeb and James Darmesteter
popularized Renan's attack on anti-Semitic racism.[3] Loeb, a rabbi
and professor at the Jewish Seminary in Paris, summarized all of
the literature on the subject. He cited Topinard to the effect that
unity of race was in no way necessary for nationhood. Further,
he disputed the contention that the Jews constituted a single race
in direct descent from the Jews of ancient Palestine. In fact, he
said, there was no 'pure' race existing anywhere in the world. All
races were mixed, and had been so from pre-historic times.[4] Darmesteter cast the ultimate discredit upon the idea of a conflict
among races: it was, he said, a vicious crusade launched by the
Germans from across the Rhine, bringing confusion and barbarism
where there should have been national unity and strength.[5]

Yet the idea of a Jewish race had struck deep roots by the 1890s.
Scholarly refutation did little, even within the Jewish community,
even among those Jewish scholars who themselves refuted anti-
Semitic racists, to eliminate all elements of racial thinking. Thus

[1] See Barzun, *Race*, chs. vi, vii.
[2] Salomon Reinach, *Origines des Ariens*.
[3] See above, p. 20, n. 4; James Darmesteter, *Prophètes d'Israël*, pp. 262–77, and
id., *Notice sur la vie et œuvre de M. Renan* (Paris, 1893); Isidore Loeb, *Réflexions
sur les juifs* (Paris, 1894).
[4] Ibid., pp. 8–10.   [5] Darmesteter, *Prophètes d'Israël*, pp. 269–75.

Loeb, in showing that there was no 'pure' Jewish race, declared
that 'Jewish blood has received infusions of Aryan or other blood
which has profoundly modified it'.[1] In his article devoted in part
to disproving systematically the idea of a Jewish race, we find the
following sentence: 'All nations are composed of different races,
[and within each of these nations] the Jewish race can find its legitimate place.'[2] Clearly the concept of a Jewish race died hard.
Darmesteter appeared to salvage the idea of race and the Darwinian
framework which usually went with it even as he denounced the
whole conception as a German plot. 'A race', he wrote, 'only
manifests its own genius, in all of its brilliancy and health, when it
mixes with an element of a foreign genius.' This did not happen in
Germany where the races were kept strictly apart and where the
'productive struggle of contrary forces' did not take place. In
France, on the other hand, 'each [of the races] brings to the melting
pot the quality of its own metal, the one its resistance, the other its
brilliance . . . .'.[3] Darmesteter's confusing imagery which served to
obscure the question of race, along with Loeb's retention of the
racist notions of blood and its mixing, illustrates the degree to
which it was still common to write and speak in terms of
race. This was, moreover, the academic level of argumentation.
Confusion rises as one examines more popular discussions of the
matter.

We may consider, for example, the article 'Anti-Semitism and
the Question of Race' written by Louis-Germain Lévy for the
Jewish weekly publication L'Univers israélite.[4] Lévy began by
stating how anti-Semites were now using 'scientific' arguments
on race to justify their position. His article was offered as a refutation of these arguments. 'It has been demonstrated a thousand
times', he wrote, 'how contrary it is to the facts of history to
establish compartments between the races.' This was especially
true in France where, in the Middle Ages, 'much Jewish blood
entered by way of forced or voluntary conversions into the body

---

[1] Loeb, op. cit., pp. 11–12.   [2] Ibid., p. 13.
[3] Darmesteter, op. cit., pp. 275–6.
[4] Louis-Germain Lévy, 'L'antisémitisme et la question des races', U.I., 1 Apr.
1895, pp. 459–62.

of the nation and where, consequently, Jews form a constituent part of society'. But this mixing was apparently insufficient to justify in Lévy's mind the abandonment of the concept of a distinct Jewish or Semitic race. Designed to combat racism and racial compartmentalization, his article tended instead to argue for the *equality*, or at least the potential equality, of the Jewish and Aryan races. The article was never clear on this issue. At times it appeared that Lévy was refuting entirely the idea of biologically distinct races of Frenchmen. From this it would follow that Jewish characteristics were historically determined and changed with historical circumstances. Yet at other times Lévy seemed in spite of himself to have accepted the common notions of Aryan superiority and Semitic inferiority along with ideas of biologically inheritable characteristics. The fundamental confusion of his position is apparent in the conclusion of the article, where Lévy spoke optimistically of the future chances for equality. These chances were high because the Jews could still progress, while 'the peoples of the Occident' were at such a high level of civilization that additional progress was extremely difficult:

One can then believe that the Semites, thanks to their intelligence and their facility for adaptation, thanks to stasis reached by Aryan civilization owing to its maturity, that these Semites will not take long to strip themselves of their horrible faults and to rejoin their Aryan cousins on the heights where they bask in a glorious light of purity and holiness.[1]

It is striking to note the degree to which Jews relied upon the doctrines of race even while combating the men whom they charged with racism. In a heated exchange in the Chamber of Deputies in 1895, Alfred Naquet delivered a blistering attack on anti-Semitism which was praised in a Jewish publication and reprinted for distribution by the Jewish Consistory.[2] Naquet contended that modern French Jews were the equal of other Frenchmen; in the course of time they had clearly lost that 'inferiority which I find in all Oriental people', an inferiority from which the Jews had once suffered, but from which they had been freed due

---

[1] Ibid., p. 462.
[2] La Rédaction, 'À M. Alfred Naquet', *U.I.*, 1 June 1895, p. 581.

to the action of what he called 'Aryan fertilization'.[1] As noted
above, Naquet continued to refer to himself as a 'Jew by race', and
he did so despite his own arguments of racial mixing.

This was essentially the position of Camille Dreyfus, a free-
thinker and the political editor of the daily *La Nation*. Dreyfus wrote
a series of articles against anti-Semitism in the beginning of 1890.
His position was that anti-Semites were attempting to import into
France a 'war of races' begun in Germany; anti-Semitism singled
out the Jews, a race with some faults, but whose deficiencies were
largely due to past maltreatment. In any case, the Jewish race had
'blended into the great French family, little by little, through
mixed marriages'. Moreover, the Jews had brought to this family
'the contribution of a race of remarkable energy and tenacity'.[2]
Two days later Dreyfus apparently regretted this use of racial
language: 'I spoke of the Jewish race; I fear I made a blunder: Is
there still a Jewish race? Is there even any distinct race within the
modern French race on French soil? A long time ago wars and
conquests reduced the purity of race to the state of a metaphysical
entity, that is to say, to nothing.' The last comment, we may
assume, was added in deference to Dreyfus the free-thinker. However, the matter did not, as one might expect, end there. Dreyfus
continued to believe that there had once been an important racial
distinction between Jews and non-Jews; this belief entered into
his argument and distorted it. He admitted that the Jews, by virtue
of their enforced isolation, might have escaped this racial mixing.
As his articles succeeded one another, it became clear that race
was to him something more than a 'metaphysical entity'. The journalist in him finally got the better of Dreyfus: 'Were those grand-
mothers so chaste, that a drop of blue Aryan blood never mixed
itself with the cursed blood of the Semites which flows in my
veins?' It was all, then, a question of degree. Mixing had occurred,
at least to some extent, and yet racial distinctions of some sort
remained. 'The Jewish race', he concluded, 'subsists today less

---

[1] Alfred Naquet in *Journal officiel, Chambre*, 27 May 1895, p. 1493.

[2] Camille Dreyfus, 'Pour les juifs', *La Nation*, 21 June 1890; C[amille] D[reyfus],
'Procès en diffamation', *La Nation*, 19 Jan. 1890; id., 'Les fils des croisés',
La Nation, 22 Jan. 1890.

through the absence of mixture as through memory and the solidarity from former persecutions.'[1] 'Racial' differences were thus tacitly admitted; the framework of races was never fully abandoned, and, in the end, Dreyfus was unable to drop the vocabulary which he inherited from the philologists and naturalists. Three years later he admitted candidly to an interviewer that he was a 'juif de race'.[2]

What can we conclude from all of this confusion over the matter of race? Camille Dreyfus, Louis-Germain Lévy, and Alfred Naquet did not, to be sure, mean by 'race' the same thing as did Drumont or Quatrefages. It is apparent that they did not study the question carefully, and it is certain that they did not accept the jumble of cranial measurements and nasal indices. Indeed, to them 'race' was not a precise term at all; their attempts to achieve precision collapsed in hopeless contradiction. By 'race' they meant, to varying degrees, a sense of community with other Jews, a sense of some common historical fate, a 'solidarity of origin with men who were the co-religionists of my fathers', as Dreyfus put it.[3] Almost invariably this sense of solidarity, this identification with other Jews linked the living and the dead; almost invariably it joined men who had no religious bond in common; and almost invariably it was associated with a historical tradition which transcended national boundaries and went beyond human memory. This was what Proust meant when he looked for the primary cause of some ideas in 'Jewish blood'.[4] It was what the rationalist Julien Benda saw, as he contemplated the formative influences of his youth; it was what the free-thinker Naquet meant when he declared: 'I am a Jew by race myself, and far from being ashamed of it, I am proud, for it is always glorious to have as ancestors men who struggled, who suffered unjustly, and who include numerous martyrs.'[5]

[1] Camille Dreyfus, 'La race juive', La Nation, 23 Jan. 1890. Cf. C[amille] D[reyfus], 'La question juive', La Nation, 24 Jan. 1890; id., 'Filles des juifs et fils des preux', La Nation, 26 Jan. 1890.

[2] 'Propos d'un juif', Vérité, 30 July 1892.

[3] Camille Dreyfus in Journal officiel, Chambre, 25 June 1892, p. 919.

[4] Proust, op. cit., i. 669.

[5] Julien Benda, La Jeunesse d'un clerc (Paris, 1936), pp. 35–6, 66; Alfred Naquet, 'Les juifs', U.I., 16 Aug. 1886, p. 925.

This tie, moreover, often linked to a personal sense of honour as in the case of Naquet, was strong enough to reach even those for whom Jewishness was a mark of inferiority, or for whom the hold of religious tradition was a vestige of superstition.[1]

It becomes clear that for Jews the physical tie was largely an afterthought, an attempt on their part to validate in a scientific way what their experience and emotions told them was true—that there was some basic Jewish identity. Jews expressed this feeling of Jewish identification by resorting to the familiar vocabulary which biology had recently provided.

In the France of the 1880s and 1890s men were conscious of their roots in the nation and in the past. Jews too were conscious of these things; Jews too considered their roots. But this sense of a deep emotional or ethnic tie binding together from birth the members of what was nominally a religious group received no sanction in the national culture; it did not fit the normally accepted pattern of allegiance in French society. France was a Catholic country in which the Catholic faith, and by transposition other religious faiths, were traditionally defined by clearly delineated religious practices. The secular spirit which was supplanting Catholicism in many areas of French life did not differ on this—a religious group was considered united in the exercise of a particular religion. The Jews, however, were an exception, and considered such by Jews and non-Jews. The Jewish identity was something about which some Jews were proud, others indifferent, and still others ashamed; it was something which was never clearly defined, which was looked upon with an element of suspicion by the outside world and with misunderstanding everywhere. Only the biological terminology of race provided a semantic framework within which all Jews could express these feelings of Jewish identity. Only race offered the excuse for a lingering Jewishness among men who had renounced their religion. Race, moreover, was fashionable. The term was frequently used in reference to emotional or cultural ties; it had entered through the works of a number of French

---

[1] As was probably the case with Julien Benda. See Robert J. Neiss, *Julien Benda* (Ann Arbor, 1956), pp. 18–19. Cf. Lothar Kahn, 'Julien Benda and the Jews', *Judaism*, vol. vii, no. 3 (Summer 1958), pp. 248–55.

writers into common speech. The term responded so well to the needs of Jews that they were unable to eliminate it from their vocabulary even when men of goodwill began to expose it as dangerous. By the 1890s it had so deeply penetrated the Jewish consciousness that it resisted refutation by Jews and non-Jews alike. In some manner this testifies to the strength of a sense of community among French Jews.

CHAPTER III

THE TIES OF COMMUNITY: 1. SUFFERING

IN his sermon delivered on the festival of Purim, on 1 March 1885, the Grand Rabbi of Paris, Zadoc Kahn, reflected on the ties which held the Jewish community together. In the past there had been what he called a 'community of suffering', a cohesiveness formed under the steady pressure of oppression emanating from a hostile environment. This oppression bound Jews together for their own protection, it drew them into what he called an 'indissoluble union'. In time, however, oppression lessened, and it remained to be seen what other ties could hold the Jewish people. There was, of course, the common religion. 'But religious sentiment weakened, indifference made visible progress', and, as the nineteenth century progressed, religion proved increasingly to be a source of division rather than union. What was left, according to Zadoc Kahn, was a sentiment of 'Jewish solidarity' which could be activated through philanthropic organizations, specifically the Alliance Israélite Universelle whose twenty-fifth anniversary was being celebrated that Purim.[1] Zadoc Kahn was aware that there were powerful forces tending towards the dissolution of the Jewish community in France; his sermon was a frank recognition that the experience of modern Jewry called into question the very existence of a Jewish community, and that the future of that community was by no means secure. The Jewish community then, by the admission of one of its most respected and perceptive leaders, was in a precarious position.

This chapter and the one which follows take up Zadoc Kahn's analysis, broadening his categories in order to describe something of the structure of the Jewish community in France. Throughout, the emphasis will be to determine what forces were contributing to the disintegration of the community, and what forces were keeping it together.

[1] Zadoc Kahn, *Sermons et allocutions* (3 vols., Paris, 1894), ii. 218-19.

'Our history, over the centuries, is simply a lamentable spectacle of an immense holocaust which constantly begins anew and which never ends.'[1] Suffering has always been considered an integral part of Jewish history, and Zadoc Kahn's pessimism, quoted here from his sermon on the eve of the Jewish New Year in 1876, recalled a theme which was sufficiently powerful to trouble the conscience of a Jewish community even in the country of emancipation and in the era of progress. The Jews formed a small community in France, a community dwarfed by the large Jewish populations of eastern and central Europe, a tiny and therefore vulnerable minority in a Catholic society. At the time of the Dreyfus Affair these Jews could look back upon only a hundred years of citizenship, scarcely a century in which the Jew had been officially considered the equal of other Frenchmen. And anti-Semitism still existed. Despite social progress, despite the steady assimilation of the Jewish community, some vestige of the old malignancy remained, sometimes hidden by a thin film of gentility, protected from view by the smugness of a society which believed that it had finally achieved human equality. Less frequently, anti-Semitism was as it had once been—overt, strident, and brutal.

A rough estimation of the Jewish population of Europe at the end of the nineteenth century, based on the work of four statisticians at the time, showed over five million Jews in Russia, almost two million in Austria-Hungary, 600,000 in Germany, about 180,000 in England, and 100,000 in the Netherlands. France, according to the same source, had only 86,000 Jews out of a total population of about thirty-nine million.[2] By all estimates the Jewish community in France was one of the smallest of the major European countries. In France the Jewish minority was further overshadowed by the existence of well over half a million Protestants.[3] This fact of being a tiny minority particularly impressed foreign Jews whose interest in the French Jewish community was

[1] Ibid., p. 33.
[2] Alfred Nossig (ed.), *Jüdische Statistik* (Berlin, 1903), p. 448. See ibid., pp. 430–52.
[3] *Statistique de la France* (1872), 2nd ser., vol. xxi (Paris, 1873), p. xxvi.

aroused at the time of the Dreyfus Affair.[1] It was a factor to be considered in view of the strength and importance of anti-Semitic pressure which was building up from the 1880s.

Most estimations of the Jewish population of France, however, were necessarily inaccurate. In 1872 the French government adopted the view that religious affiliation was a private matter and, in consequence, information on it was no longer collected by government census.[2] At that time the French Jewish population was officially listed as 49,439 (not including the portions of Alsace and Lorraine recently ceded to the German Empire), of whom 24,319 lived in Paris or its vicinity.[3] But since the 1872 census there had been important demographic changes. Large numbers of Jews moved from the German occupied territories into France; others came from various parts of central or eastern Europe. These Jews invariably flocked to Paris; while in the rest of France the Jewish population declined or remained stationary, in Paris it continued to rise.[4] Although there was no government census of French Jews after 1872, the Ministre des Cultes periodically asked the Consistoire Central, the government-sponsored administration of the Jewish community, for an estimate of the numbers. The consistorial census for 1897 declared that there were 71,249 Jews in metropolitan France, of whom 45,000 lived in the Paris area. In addition, there were estimated to be almost 45,000 Jews in Algeria. Significantly, no city in France had even a tenth as many Jews as Paris which accounted for well over three-fifths of the total.[5] Historians have frequently noted that the Jews are 'the most urbanized people in the world', and have traced this in large measure to the background of restrictions which had always kept Jews from the

[1] See, for example, Paul Bettelheim, 'The Jews in France', *The Nineteenth Century*, vol. xlvii, Jan. 1900, p. 116.

[2] See Zosa Szajkowski, 'The Growth of the Jewish Population in France: the Political Aspects of a Demographic Problem', *J.S.S.*, vol. viii, no. 4, Oct. 1946, p. 297.

[3] *Statistique de la France* (1872), 2nd ser., vol. xxi (Paris, 1873), pp. xxvi, 34–5.

[4] S. Debré, 'The Jews of France', *Jewish Quarterly Review*, vol. iii, Apr. 1891, pp. 372–3.

[5] A.N. F¹⁹ 11024.

land.[1] It is important to recognize that the Jews avoided most cities in France apart from the capital. Jews in France were not only urbanized, they were heavily concentrated in Paris. Marseille had 3,500 Jews according to the Consistoire, Bordeaux 2,110, Nancy 1,849, and Lyon 1,370. The next largest communities were Bayonne with 865, Besançon with 763, Lille with 663, and Reims with 640.[2] However, these figures too are unreliable; in some cases, as with Paris, they are rough estimates, in others they represent only those Jews who had ties with the departmental *consistoire*. Théodore Reinach judged that there were, about this time, 40,000 Jews in Paris (fewer by 5,000 than the estimate of the Consistoire) and 72,000 in all of France. Reinach obtained his figures for Paris from calculations based upon the number of Jewish burials a year.[3] But these statistics indicated only those burials presided over by a consistorial rabbi and did not, therefore, include either many eastern European Jews who had their own rabbis or Jews who had secular funerals. Further, there was always, in Paris, a large group of Jews in transit to London or America whose number could not be determined either through burial statistics or through consistorial ties. It seems reasonable to estimate that because of the continued immigration of Jews and because of the large transient population, there were somewhat more Jews in France than the consistorial estimate. It is probably safest to accept the round figures commonly cited in Jewish year-books: about 80,000 Jews in all of France, and 50,000 in Paris.[4]

As we have noted, what is most significant about the distribution of the Jewish population is the extent to which Paris was the centre of Jewish life in France. This was clearly a nineteenth-century development and deserves some explanation. Before 1800, when the effects of emancipation had not yet fully been felt,

---

[1] Robert F. Byrnes, *Antisemitism in Modern France*, vol. i, *The Prologue to the Dreyfus Affair* (New Brunswick, New Jersey, 1950), p. 94. Cf. Louis Wirth, *The Ghetto* (Chicago, 1956), p. 19.

[2] A.N. F[19] 11024. Cf. 'Statistique: le chiffre de la population israélite en France', *Annuaire 5646* (1885-6), pp. 24-5.

[3] Théodore Reinach, article 'Juifs' in *La Grande Encyclopédie* (31 vols., Paris, n.d.), xxi. 272.

[4] 'Statistique', *Annuaire 5646* (1885-6), pp. 24-5.

70 per cent of the Jewish population resided in Alsace where Jews had lived in large numbers ever since their expulsion from France at the end of the fourteenth century. The remainder of the Jewish community at the beginning of the nineteenth century was concentrated in Lorraine, on the west coast of France around Bordeaux and Bayonne, and in the south about the former papal sanctuaries of Avignon and Comtat Venaissin. Fewer than a thousand Jews lived in Paris before the Revolution.[1] The smaller Jewish communities in the south and west of France were Sephardic, mostly descendants of Spanish and Portuguese Jews who had fled the expulsion edict of the Spanish monarchy in 1492. These were French-speaking, generally successful and well established in the communities in which they lived.

The Jews of Alsace and Lorraine were Ashkenazim, German-speaking Jews who were far less integrated with the surrounding population, and far less advanced economically than their co-religionists in the west and south. These Ashkenazim were among the poorest and socially most backward of western European Jewry. They lived, for the most part, in small villages scattered throughout the countryside, engaging in petty commerce away from the larger cities. The predominance of this *élément campagnard* prevented the formation of an intelligentsia and contributed to their isolation from the surrounding community.[2] With economic expansion and the weakening of small-scale rural commercial enterprise following the Revolution, the isolation began to break down, strong competition from the towns appeared, and, as a result, many of these Jews were ruined. They began to leave the countryside and moved gradually towards the larger commercial centres such as Strasbourg, Metz, and Mulhouse.[3] This experience of leaving

[1] Zosa Szajkowski, 'The Growth of the Jewish Population in France: the Political Aspects of a Demographic Problem', *J.S.S.*, vol. viii, no. 3, July 1946, pp. 180–3. According to another estimate, Paris in 1809 contained 2,733 Jews, of whom 1,324 were born there. Léon Kahn, *Les Juifs de Paris depuis le VIe siècle* (Paris, 1889), p. 100.

[2] André Neher, 'La bourgeoisie juive d'Alsace', in *La Bourgeoisie alsacienne: études d'histoire sociale* (Strasbourg, Paris, 1954), pp. 436–7; Howard M. Sachar, *The Course of Modern Jewish History* (New York, 1958), pp. 54, 57.

[3] E. Schnurmann, *La Population juive en Alsace* (Paris, 1936), pp. 12, 143.

the small communities was often profoundly disturbing to the fixed pattern of Jewish life. Further, a strong tradition of anti-Semitism in Alsace continued to plague their existence during the first half of the nineteenth century, and anti-Jewish outbreaks were not uncommon. To some extent these Alsatian Jews became *déracinés*, uprooted from a traditional form of existence, 'like castaways tossed by the waves churned up by urban life', as one writer puts it.[1] Many of these Jews left Alsace entirely and moved to Paris.[2] During the Second Empire Alsatian Jews continued to go west. But the great movement of Jews away from this area took place in the years immediately following the Franco-Prussian War. At least five thousand Alsatian Jews chose to remain French and left the annexed territory, escaping German military conscription and an economic depression from which Alsace had suffered for some time. Patriotic reasons and a feeling that there would be less anti-Semitism in France also played a significant part in this decision.[3] Some of these Jews, such as the family of André Maurois, for example, moved to small industrial towns in the north of France, to Normandy or the Nord; some remained in the east, in French Lorraine or what little of Alsace was still left under French sovereignty. Others, including the family of Alfred Dreyfus, came directly to Paris, often leaving behind one member of the family to manage a family business within the German Empire.[4] Sooner or later, however, most of these Alsatian refugees felt the attraction of Paris; Jewish businesses moved to the capital, and Jews came there for an education and government service. No other group of Jews settled in Paris in such numbers. By the end of the nineteenth century the Alsatian element of the Paris Jewish population was clearly predominant.[5]

[1] Schnurmann, op. cit., p. 144.
[2] See Paul Lévy, *La Langue allemande en France: pénétration et diffusion des origines à nos jours* (2 vols., Paris, 1952), ii. 5, 13, 17.
[3] Isidore Cahen, 'Les exilés volontaires', *A.I.*, 1 June 1872, pp. 332–8; 15 July 1872, pp. 439–40; 1 Dec. 1872, pp. 722–4; 15 Dec. 1872, pp. 754–6; Szajkowski, 'Growth of the Jewish Population', pp. 308–9; Neher, op. cit., p. 439.
[4] Maurois was born Émile Herzog. See André Maurois, *Mémoires*, vol. i, *Années d'apprentissage et années de travail* (Paris, 1948), pp. 9–11, *passim*; Robert Gauthier, 'Les Alsaciens et l'Affaire Dreyfus', *Saisons d'Alsace*, no. 17 (Winter 1966), p. 58.   [5] Article 'Paris' in *J.E.*

This steady movement of Jews from Alsace to the capital was not the only trend which contributed to the pre-eminence of Paris within the Jewish community. Jews from Provence gravitated towards Paris during the course of the century, deserting one of the oldest and best-established Jewish communities in Europe.[1] The trickle of immigrants from eastern and central Europe before 1882 also tended to move towards the capital, and their numbers swelled as time went on and as conditions became more difficult under the tsars. Between 1876 and 1901, according to one estimate, 4,000 Russian Jews came to Paris, along with 1,000 from Galicia and 3,000 from Rumania.[2] As the largest community of Jews in France, Paris was the natural haven for eastern European refugees. It was there that philanthropic organizations were the most highly developed and that a centre existed where relatives who arrived at different times were able to meet.[3] In Paris these Jews usually moved to the Marais, behind the Hôtel de Ville and in the centre of the city. There the immigrant felt less alone, less uprooted than in the provincial towns.

Further, Paris became the centre of Jewish institutional life. The impressive synagogue of the Rue de la Victoire in the ninth *arrondissement* was opened to the public in 1875 and, as the seat of the Grand Rabbi of France, it became the religious focus of the country.[4] The École Rabbinique de France, the centre for the training of rabbis, moved to Paris from Metz at the end of 1859. Metz had been one of the oldest Jewish centres in France, and the move, considered only a realistic administrative decision by officials in Paris, was keenly resented in Alsace.[5]

[1] See Zosa Szajkowski, 'The Decline and Fall of Provençal Jewry', *J.S.S.*, vol. vi, no. 1, Jan. 1944, pp. 31–54.

[2] Michel Roblin, *Les Juifs de Paris: démographie, économie, culture* (Paris, 1952), p. 66. Cf. Mark Wischnitzer, *To Dwell in Safety: the Story of Jewish Migration since 1800* (Philadelphia, 1948), for a general discussion of this subject.

[3] Maurice Lauzel, *Ouvriers juifs de Paris: les casquettiers* (Paris, 1912), pp. 13–14.

[4] Julien Weill, *Zadoc Kahn 1839–1905* (Paris, 1912), p. 71.

[5] Jules Bauer, *L'École Rabbinique de France 1830–1930* (Paris, n.d.), pp. 101–2, 125; cf. L.-M. Lambert, *Précis de l'histoire des Hébreux depuis le patriarche Abraham jusqu'en 1840* (Metz, 1840), p. 416 n.; Pierre Aubery, *Milieux juifs de la France contemporaine à travers leurs écrivains* (Paris, 1957), p. 124.

In general, however, Jews preferred Paris not only because of its inherent opportunities, but because they had few roots elsewhere in France. Traditionally urban, they chose as a new home the city which dominated French life and whose magnetic appeal was particularly strong at this moment in French history.[1] The older Jewish communities in France, always small, now ceased to grow and often slipped into stagnation.

In Paris this Jewish population had done remarkably well. From being a people of outcasts and even renegades at the time of the Revolution, the Jews had, in less than a century, worked their way into all layers of French society. The rapidity of this advance is particularly striking. André Neher notes that the Alsatian Jewish community was held, through oppression, discrimination, and unfavourable economic conditions, in a poor and backward condition until around 1860.[2] Yet by the 1890s the success of the Alsatian Jewish community in Paris, but recently arrived, was generally apparent. Not everyone was successful, of course; yet a general trend is discernible. Jews had made their mark not only in banking and commerce, but in manufacturing, the liberal professions, and the civil service. As artists and workers, aristocrats and revolutionaries, scholars and politicians they had demonstrated how eager they were to emerge from the close communal patterns of ghetto life. The long period of isolation was over. Anti-Semites spoke frequently of an 'invasion' of Jews into French life; Jewish leaders spoke with pride of the avidity with which Jews climbed the social ladder; in essence they were both referring to the same thing. By the time of the Dreyfus Affair the social divisions of the Jewish community were almost as complex as those within the rest of French society.

What follows is a brief description of these social divisions, considering as a basis for discussion the extent to which the old community of suffering persisted. It should be stressed, at this point, that the evidence for this kind of discussion is very limited and that judgements must often be based upon an assessment of contemporary observations.

[1] Byrnes, op. cit., p. 96.   [2] Neher, op. cit., p. 437.

A titled aristocracy constituted the highest social layer within the Jewish community, in terms of esteem and probably wealth. Here the undisputed leaders came from the Rothschild family. Secure in their fortune, their international reputation, and their Austrian title, the Rothschilds were, as will be seen, at the same time acutely aware of their ties to the Jewish community. But Jewishness did not prevent the titular heads of Jewish society from tasting the fruits of French social life. After 1830, with close ties to the French monarch Louis-Philippe, the family had a reputation of mild loyalty to the Orleanist cause; yet with the advent of the Emperor Napoleon III several decades later, the Rothschilds maintained and even enhanced their social position. On at least one occasion the Emperor was entertained at Ferrières, the Rothschild country estate which featured a private synagogue.[1] But while within the Jewish community they dominated the aristocratic stage, they were not alone. A number of Jews whose nobility was equally of foreign derivation bore important titles—the Counts Camondo and Cahen d'Anvers, and the Barons Koenigswarter, Léonino, d'Almeida, and Menasce.[2] Moreover, there was a floating society of extraordinarily wealthy Jewish noblemen who resided on occasion in Paris, who had large homes, often in the *banlieue*, but who were frequently abroad. Such were the Baron Maurice de Hirsch, who at various times resided in London, Vienna, and Paris, and the Baron Horace de Günzberg, head of one of the largest investment banking systems in the Russian Empire.

These noblemen were the heirs of the court Jews of the eighteenth century. Sometimes, as in the case of the Rothschilds, they were literal heirs; sometimes, as in the case of de Günzberg, they served in a similar capacity a century later. Always, however, their role was comparable to that of their Jewish predecessors: to serve the governments of the day by providing loans and other financial services; to take up, through their privileged status, a certain leadership within the Jewish community; and simultaneously to

[1] Jean Bouvier, *Les Rothschild* (Paris, 1960), p. 184; Frederic Morton, *The Rothschilds: a Family Portrait* (New York, 1961), p. 137.

[2] See Ben Mosché, 'Les titres nobiliaires et les juifs', *Annuaire 5647* (1886–7), p. 57.

wear their Jewishness lightly, confident in the protection provided by the most powerful men in Europe.

Prominent leaders in banking and international finance, they conducted themselves as dynastic heads; they married among themselves or with untitled banking families who were engaged in the same sort of activity but who were relatively recently established. The Baron Joseph Léonino was such an aristocrat; born in 1830 in Genoa, he made a fortune in banking there, moved to Paris in the 1860s, and married into the wealthy Oppenheim family. His son, Emmanuel, married Juliette, daughter of the Baron Gustave de Rothschild.[1] The brothers Abraham and Nissim Camondo came to Paris from Constantinople about the same time as Joseph Léonino. As heads of a large and successful banking house in Turkey they had enormous financial resources at their disposal; they rose to importance in the world of French finance and invested heavily in French economic development. Isaac, the son of Abraham Camondo, became, among other things, an administrator of the Banque de Paris et des Pays-Bas, the president of a number of railroad, natural gas, and cement companies, while simultaneously being renowned as an art collector and the composer of several operettas. Another Camondo, Moïse, married the daughter of Count Louis Cahen d'Anvers.[2] Baron Jacques de Reinach, best known for his implication in the Panama scandal, moved in these aristocratic circles. Reinach was a model for anti-Semitic caricatures, and was eventually driven to suicide in 1892; like many Jewish financial magnates he came from Germany and, further adding to his cosmopolitanism, his title was Italian. With many Jews of this social stratum he had established himself in Paris and received his naturalized citizenship during the Second Empire.[3]

The Jewish banking houses, however, were by no means completely in the hands of the ennobled. Fulfilling the same role as the

[1] Obituary of Joseph Léonino, A.I., 28 June 1894.
[2] Obituary of Nissim de Camondo, U.I., 1 Feb. 1889, p. 313; A.I., 31 Jan. 1889; obituary of Isaac de Camondo, A.I., 13 Apr. 1911; obituary of Abraham de Camondo, U.I., 1 Jan. 1890, p. 230; 'Nouvelles diverses', A.I., 15 Oct. 1891, p. 339.
[3] Jean Bouvier, Les Deux Scandales de Panama (Paris, 1964), p. 138.

latter in society, and a part of the same social layer, were a number of extremely wealthy Jews engaged for the most part in finance, and mainly of German origin. In the years following the Franco-Prussian War Paris rivalled London in the volume of capital invested on foreign markets. Paris became the centre of European finance and a number of Jews rose to prominence in this field.[1] Among them the names of Bamberger, Reinach, Stern, Deutsch, Heine, Ephrussi, Goudchaux, Lippmann, Pereire, and Bischoffsheim stand out. The social group of which these Jews formed a part seems to have been formed simultaneously with the expansion of the French economy under Napoleon III and with the concomitant heavy investment in railroads and industry. As we have seen, this was the time when the Camondo brothers, Joseph Léonino, and Jacques de Reinach established themselves in France.

The Belgian banker Louis-Raphaël Bischoffsheim may be taken as typical of the wealthy Jewish bankers who turned towards France during the Second Empire. Born in Mainz, a German city where Jews had lived since Roman times, he was the head of a large banking firm with offices in Brussels, Antwerp, London, and Paris. During the time of Napoleon III, the headquarters of the operation was moved to the French capital. There Bischoffsheim directed his enterprise and rose to considerable importance in the financial world. He financed a number of railways, especially in the south of France, and became a director of the Banque des Pays-Bas, the Crédit Foncier Colonial, the Franco-Egyptian Bank, and the Société du Prince Impérial. His son, Raphaël-Louis, took over from him and was a member of the Chamber of Deputies for a number of years.[2]

Another important name in this connection is Pereire. The Pereire family were the descendants of Jacob Rodriguez Pereire who came to France from Spain at the beginning of the eighteenth century as a Maranno, a secret Jew who had been forced publicly by Spanish authorities to give up the exercise of his faith.[3] His

---

[1] See Herbert Feis, *Europe the World's Banker 1870–1914* (New York, 1965), p. 33.
[2] Article 'Bischoffsheim' in *J.E.* and *U.J.E.*
[3] Article 'Pereire' in *J.E.* and *U.J.E.*

grandsons, the brothers Jacob Émile and Isaac, were financiers and brokers in Paris. They founded the Crédit Mobilier, one of the first investment banks in France in 1852, along with several other members of the Jewish *haute finance*.[1] The Pereire brothers were also known for their support and leadership in the Saint-Simonian movement. Isaac's son, Eugène, a banker and businessman, administered railroads in the Midi, helped to finance other lines in Spain, was Consul General of Persia, and a member of the *Corps législatif* under Napoleon III.[2]

This wealthy bourgeoisie, like the nobility, had its 'floating society'. Members of the Sassoon family, for example, also of Spanish origin, were frequently seen in Paris at the end of the Second Empire. The firm of David Sassoon and Company, based in London and Bombay, was extremely successful in Anglo-Indian trade and commerce; in time the family became known as 'the Rothschilds of the East'.[3]

Wealthy Jews such as these enjoyed at least nominal acceptance in the Parisian world of high society. Though often their ancestors had never set foot in France, or even left the ghetto, their own manners and demeanour were, except to the most pedantic of socialites, beyond reproach. Their luxurious *hôtels*, frequently along the broad avenues of the eighth *arrondissement*, near the Parc Monceau, were host to Jews and Gentiles alike.[4] Perhaps the most celebrated *salonnarde* of them all was Madame Arman de Caillavet, revered by *mondains* and a model for one of the most important of Proust's characters. She was the daughter of Frédérique Koenigswarter and the wealthy Jewish banker from Austria, Auguste Lippmann. Her salon was a glittering affair, attended by Anatole France, the younger Dumas, and a host of other artists and

---

[1] See J. H. Clapham, *The Economic Development of France and Germany 1815–1914* (Cambridge, England, 1961), p. 383; Rondo E. Cameron, *France and the Economic Development of Europe, 1800–1914* (Princeton, New Jersey, 1961), pp. 134–44.

[2] See above, p. 38, n. 3.

[3] Article 'Sassoon' in *J.E.* and *U.J.E.*

[4] See, for example, Raoul Cheron, 'Mondanités', *Le Gaulois*, 5 Jan. 1898; Seth L. Wolitz, 'The Proustian Community', unpublished Ph.D. dissertation, Yale University, 1965, ch. v. Cf. Léon Bailby, *Pourquoi je me suis battu: souvenirs, I* (Paris, 1951), pp. 106–7.

intellectuals.[1] Geneviève, the daughter of the composer of *La Juive*, Fromenthal Halévy, married Émile Straus, a Jewish attorney who handled the affairs of the Rothschilds. She too directed a salon of distinction; among her attendants were Jews and non-Jews, bankers and businessmen, the cream of the intellectual community, the Faubourg Saint-Germain, and the diplomatic corps.[2]

Jews of this social set had broken out of the closely-knit group which had remained a pattern of life for some time after emancipation.[3] Affluent and self-confident, morally supported by the example of Jews who had helped through commerce and finance to build the very structure of modern France, these Jews breathed in an atmosphere which was far indeed from the old community of suffering. As Daniel Halévy, brother of the famous historian, put it when reminded of the suffering of Jews the world over: '. . . how happy I am to have left that hell, to have escaped from Judaism . . .'.[4] It was easy to announce that one had 'escaped from Judaism' when one's culture and education were thoroughly French, as in the case of Halévy, or when one's parents had dined with Louis-Philippe or the Emperor. Moreover, one could follow the Rothschild example and maintain a certain element of Jewishness as a family distinction, an occasionally remembered part of family history which did not, at the same time, commit one to avoiding the anti-Semitic salons of the aristocracy. The world of these Jews was essentially identical to the world of the wealthy bourgeoisie or aristocracy of Catholic origin, and it shared in the prosperity and comforts which nineteenth-century France so generously offered.

Others were less fortunate. On the lower levels of the middle class the majority of Jews, shopkeepers, small-scale manufacturers,

[1] Article 'Caillavet' in *Dictionnaire de biographie française*; Jeanne-Maurice Pouquet, *Le Salon de Madame Arman de Caillavet* (Paris, 1926); André de Fouquières, *Mon Paris et ses Parisiens* (5 vols., Paris, 1953-9), ii. 182.

[2] Fouquières, op. cit., ii. 245-6; George D. Painter, *Marcel Proust, a Biography* (2 vols., London, 1959-65), i. 89; André Maurois, *Proust: a Biography*, tr. Gerard Hopkins (New York, 1958), *passim*; Alain Silvera, *Daniel Halévy and his Times: a Gentleman-Commoner in the Third Republic* (Ithaca, New York, 1966), pp. 45-6.

[3] See Hannah Arendt, *The Origins of Totalitarianism* (Cleveland, 1958), p. 99.

[4] Daniel Halévy, *Carnets*, entry for 4 Jan. 1898.

civil servants, and professional men were probably far less protected from what remained of society's hostile attitude towards
the Jews. These Jews had, of course, less material security; beginning in the 1880s their situation was complicated by depression in
France and by restricted opportunities for newly graduated *licenciés*
and *agrégés*. Times were difficult in both business and professional
spheres. In 1898 *Le Temps* spoke with concern of a new and growing class, 'the intellectual proletariat', a class of university or *lycée*
graduates which was unable to find work commensurate with its
education and ambitions.[1] Among writers and intellectuals, a
growing group in French society, times were equally difficult;
since 1890 the publishing industry had entered a period of severe
crisis with a sharp falling off in the number of books sold and a
consequent hesitancy in publishing the works of new, untried
writers.[2] All of this meant competition, a competition particularly
strong in the liberal professions, in law, in journalism, in medicine
—the very professions into which middle-class Jews were moving
in considerable numbers. Jews of the second generation in France
were gradually discarding the old patterns of petty commerce and
small-scale manufacturing. Adaptation to French life meant
responding to increased social and professional opportunities and a
reluctance to continue in many family businesses.[3] Despite what
has been described as a general poverty among Jews of this new
professional class, there were remarkable successes in professional
life. Despite the competition, Jews did well. It was calculated in
1895 that 7 out of 260 members of the Institut were Jews.
There were Jewish army officers, five listed as generals in 1889,
Jewish municipal councillors in Paris, Jewish deputies, senators,
and important civil servants. Léon Blum, Paul Grünebaum-
Ballin, and André Spire were among the first Jews to enter the
Conseil d'État, the centre of the French administrative system.
Jews achieved prominence in academic life, at the Sorbonne, at

[1] 'Le prolétariat intellectuel', *Le Temps*, 25 Jan. 1898.
[2] Robert F. Byrnes, 'The French Publishing Industry and its Crisis in the 1890s',
Journal of Modern History, vol. xxiii, Sept. 1951, pp. 232–42.
[3] I. Déhalle, 'L'assimilation des Israélites français', *U.I.*, 30 Aug. 1901, p. 754;
6 Sept. 1901, p. 785.

the Collège de France, the École Polytechnique, the École Normale Supérieure, and most particularly the École Pratique des
Hautes Études. Only the careers of diplomacy and the Cour des
Comptes, the most important court for financial matters, were
considered beyond the reach of Jews.[1] 'In the theatre, in literature,
and in literary criticism, in the press, in scholarship, in law and
medicine, and in Republican politics, this was a glorious and
golden age for French Jewry, which produced a number of leaders
in these particular fields out of proportion to the relative number
of Jews in France.'[2]

However, this success was purchased at the cost of the revival
of many antagonisms; against the Jews there was arrayed a force
of newly awakened jealousies, secret suspicions, and old fears.
Among Jews who were a part of this struggle up the ladder of
French society, competition frequently left its mark in terms of
some consciousness of Jewish community.

'Whatever we do', wrote the editor of a Jewish weekly publication, 'we are bound to provoke... recriminations... [and] discontent.' Hippolyte Prague felt that Jews were subjected to a pitiless
scrutiny by the surrounding community; their slightest gestures
and their most inconspicuous activities were open to complaint
and attack.[3] Unlike the Jewish aristocracy, high financiers, or others
of considerable wealth, most middle-class Jews felt some degree of
hostility towards them in the world in which they lived. This was
particularly so in a competitive business or professional environment. The response suggested by Théodore Reinach was typical
of that evoked by middle-class Jews: 'Let all our businessmen be
prudent, all our millionaires simple and charitable, all our scholars
modest, all our journalists patriotic and disinterested.'[4] Prague referred to the same solicitude when he spoke of 'a constant anxiety

---

[1] See Léon Kahn, op. cit., pp. 183–9, for a list of Jews in public life at the time of
publication. See also 'Les juifs à l'Institut', A.I., 24 Oct. 1895, p. 339; H. Prague,
'L'égalité en France plus d'un siècle après la Révolution', A.I., 27 June 1901,
pp. 202–3.

[2] Byrnes, *Antisemitism in Modern France*, i. 97.

[3] H. Prague, 'Causerie', A.I., 14 Jan. 1892, p. 9.

[4] Théodore Reinach in *Actes* (1887), R.E.J., vol. xv (1887), pp. cxxxii–
cxxxiii.

not to attract hatred [and] not to awaken passions' which had entered into the Jewish mode of life.[1]

Yet along with this sensitivity, middle-class Jews placed a high value upon individual successes in French society; these achievements were viewed with pride by Jews and considered an example for young people. The critic Julien Benda reported that a whole section of the Jewish bourgeoisie held up the Reinach brothers as models for their sons. The Reinachs achieved spectacular success in everything they undertook, carried off the top academic prizes, and were seen as a credit to the Jewish community.[2] The Jewish press followed diligently the various *concours*, the annual competitions for admission to the civil service and the *grandes écoles*.[3] Other awards were carefully watched: the annual distributions of the Legion of Honour, awards by the Académie française, military promotions, political successes, etc. Even 'honourable mention' was considered, on occasion, worthy of publication. Each week

---

[1] H. Prague, 'La désolation du peuple juif par M. l'abbé Soulier', *A.I.*, 12 Mar. 1891, p. 81. Cf. id., 'Si Turpin avait été juif', *A.I.*, 7 June 1894, p. 178; I. Déhalle, 'L'assimilation des Israélites français', *U.I.*, 16 Aug. 1901, p. 683.

[2] Julien Benda, *La Jeunesse d'un clerc* (Paris, 1936), p. 43. But Benda had grave reservations about the Reinachs' success, reservations which tell as much about Benda (and perhaps his own family's pressure upon him) as they do about the social conditions of the time: 'Le triomphe des Reinach au concours général me paraît une des sources essentielles de l'antisémitisme tel qu'il devait tonner quinze ans plus tard. Que les juifs s'en rendissent compte ou non, de tels succès étaient sentis par les autres Français comme un acte de violence. . . . La justice voulait sans doute que les Reinach eussent tous les prix si leurs copies étaient les meilleures; mais l'intérêt politique, et celui des juifs tout le premier, voulait qu'on ne leur donnât que quelques-uns. Le bon goût le voulait peut-être aussi, qui, lui encore, est autre chose que la justice.' Ibid., pp. 43-4. Cf. the following statement by the Rabbi of Avignon in 1889: 'Efforçons-nous toujours d'arriver au premier rang, parmi les travailleurs honnêtes et loyaux, dans toutes les carrières ouvertes à notre activité. . . . Offrons l'exemple de toutes les vertus civiques et sociales. Ne cessons d'être d'irréprochables citoyens. Soyons, en un mot, les dignes enfants de la France!' Benjamin Mossé (ed.), *La Révolution française et le rabbinat français* (Paris, 1890), p. 194.

[3] See, for example, B.-M., 'Les carrières libérales', *U.I.*, 20 Aug. 1897, pp. 677-9, where it is noted that a large number of Jews, 'plus nombreux que ne le comporterait une stricte proportionnalité', have done well in the *concours*. B.-M. also points out what was considered a relevant factor: 'Le judaïsme ne connaît pas ce qu'on appelle vulgairement les fils de famille; les enfants de nos millionnaires conservent le goût du travail et ne se croient pas en droit de mener une existence désœuvrée, inutile et frivole.' Ibid., p. 678.

the *Archives israélites* and the *Univers israélite* included this kind of information in a column 'Nouvelles diverses'. Each year the *Archives israélites* drew up an honour roll for its year-book which summarized Jewish appointments, promotions, and other successes during the previous year.

This Jewish drive for accomplishment, seen by anti-Semites as an incorrigible Jewish urge for domination, criticized strongly by others who had less malice, was the natural response of a group whose members had been denied for centuries the right to participate in society and who, as full citizens, now felt a need to justify their newly won status. Further, Jews came well equipped to do well in the French system of *concours*, the competitive foundation of the intellectual establishment. With a long tradition of valuing intellectual pursuits, Jews now found themselves able to achieve through intellectual activity the recognition which had been kept from them by law and custom. And, understandably, they proceeded to do so. Middle-class Jews at this time, according to Benda, wanted 'to prove that we were not an inferior race as our detractors claimed, but on the contrary a race of the first order...'[1] The statement illustrates how success was often viewed collectively; success was 'Jewish' because serious pressures against a Jewish collectivity had existed in the past and to some extent persisted in the present. Failure too was 'Jewish' because it cast aspersions upon an entire people. A sense of a Jewish collectivity was, in this way, a reaction to the past and present hostility of the surrounding population. Jewish consciousness flowed from prejudice against the Jews.

To be sure, the above remarks must be carefully qualified. Not all middle-class Jews reacted in the same way to their environment. Some were as comfortable in their position as were the members of the Jewish aristocracy. Some, no doubt, felt little trace of hostility towards the Jews. The evidence is extremely thin for these kinds of judgements. Yet it would appear likely, on the basis of scattered statements, the tone of the Jewish press, and the testimony of such acute observers as Benda, that within the Jewish middle class there did exist a certain Jewish consciousness based directly

[1] Benda, op. cit., p. 43.

upon negative outside pressures. This seems to distinguish them from the upper social levels of the Jewish community. As we shall see, moreover, these class distinctions within the Jewish community prevented any possibility of this particular consciousness from becoming generally shared throughout that community.

According to Michel Roblin's careful study of the matter, a Jewish working class did not exist in Paris prior to 1880. Until that time the Jewish population of the capital was made up for the most part of *petite bourgeoisie*.[1] Yet three different sources from the Dreyfus period estimated the number of Jewish proletarians at 20,000.[2] No sudden mass immigration took place to account for these figures, and there is clearly a discrepancy here which calls for explanation. The problem seems to be largely one of definition. The three writers referred to considered as proletarian the large number of salesmen, cabinet-makers, tailors, shoemakers, hat-makers, etc., who were almost all poor, who were mostly foreign-born, but only some of whom worked for wages, and many of whom were capitalists on a very small scale. Little is known about these Jews; they had no newspapers of their own, and practically no separate means of contact within the larger Jewish community. Whether or not they can properly be described as 'proletarians', these Jews had a good deal in common which warrants considering them as a social group distinct from the 'Jewish middle class' discussed above.

They were virtually all poor. Many were artisans, working and often living in small apartments or ateliers in Paris. These jobs were rapidly learned and provided a bare subsistence. Others, the majority according to one observer, were petty merchants or pedlars, with establishments ranging from sidewalk stands and horse-drawn wagons to small stores. The necessary capital to begin such enterprises was often available from Jewish philanthropic organizations. Living on the margins of the French

[1] Roblin, op. cit., pp. 60–1.

[2] Paul Pottier, 'Essai sur le prolétariat juif en France', *Revue des revues*, 1 Mar. 1899, pp. 482–3; Henri Dagan, 'Le prolétariat juif mondial', *Revue blanche*, 15 Oct. 1900, pp. 264–5; Alfred H. Fried, 'Das jüdische Proletariat in Frankreich', in Nossig (ed.), *Jüdische Statistik*, p. 386.

economy, the Jews who constituted this social group frequently had little contact with the rest of French society, and, unlike the Jewish middle class, presented no competitive threat to other elements in French life. Generally, these Jews lived together in a section of the fourth *arrondissement*, on either side of the Rue de Rivoli, particularly along the Rue des Rosiers, the Rue Saint-Paul, and other streets nearby where a virtual ghetto was formed in the centre of Paris. Here the presence of many immigrants recalled the atmosphere of the eastern European *schtetl*; on the 'Pletzl' on the Rue de Rivoli not far from the Hôtel de Ville, newly arrived Jews could have letters and newspapers translated for a few centimes. Yiddish was heard on the streets; signs in Hebrew script were in the windows; and immigrants could be seen walking about in the caftans and fur hats of Jews from Russia, Poland, or Rumania.[1]

Suffering, of course, was a principal part of the life of these Jews. Most were born in eastern or central Europe and bore still fresh memories of pogroms. For these refugees who did not speak French when they arrived, who had left behind them everything, including the comforts of a close and protective Jewish community, life was hard indeed. Upon arriving in Paris they were often, unless they had the good fortune to have relatives who were already well established, at the mercy of a Jewish intermediary who was supposed to find them work. Frequently they were exploited by the Jewish *patrons* who gave them employment; the immigrants had no trade unions with which to defend themselves and, because of the steady stream of new arrivals, they were in a weak position before their employers—they could always be replaced. In time the 'collar of misery' tightened; bitterness rose; and the frustrations of a people long oppressed came to the surface.[2] At times this found expression in hostility towards the wealthy Jewish com-

---

[1] Pottier, op. cit., pp. 484–5; J. Tchernoff, *Dans le creuset des civilisations*, vol. iv, *Des prodromes du bolchévisme à une société des nations* (Paris, 1938), pp. 276–8. Cf. Charlotte Roland, *Du ghetto à l'Occident: deux générations yiddiches en France* (Paris, 1962). See Viviane Issembert-Gannat, *Guide du judaïsme à Paris* (Paris, 1964) for a brief historical guide through Jewish districts of Paris.

[2] Pottier, op. cit., p. 486; Fried, op. cit., p. 387; Dagan, op. cit., p. 266; Lauzel, op. cit., p. 20.

munity. 'The question of race', one Jewish worker told the columnist Henri Dagan, 'is a hoax. Everything boils down to self interest. . . . What a farce, this Jewish solidarity. . . . Everyone is
interested in his own skin, and that's that.'[1] Often too, this misery
led to the formation of mutual aid societies among these Jews in
similar circumstances: the Amicale d'Odessa, the Amicale Russe,
the Amis Solidaires, etc.[2]

Yet the suffering which these Jews experienced in France derived essentially from their social and economic position in French
society and not from their Jewishness. There is no evidence that
their poor condition heightened their sense of community with
other Jews in France. Class differences within the Jewish community were too sharp for this. As with the Jewish aristocracy and
the Jewish *haute finance*, their world was shaped by the society
around them in such a way as to break down the concept of a
single united Jewish community bound by the ties of anti-Jewish
hostility. What difficulties they experienced in their daily lives
came not from a French movement against the Jews, but rather
from the predicament of the immigrant or the proletarian in any
industrializing society. In this respect they differed from the
Jewish bourgeoisie whose Jewishness was relatively more of a
handicap in France and who, in a sense, bore the brunt of French
anti-Semitism.

Jewish students from Russia, living and studying in Paris during
this period, constituted a small but important social group which
deserves some attention. There were perhaps as many as five hundred of these young people in Paris in 1894, and their number had
augmented considerably in the years before the Dreyfus Affair.
Many had arrived in the wake of the tremendous famine which
swept Russia in 1891–2. Forbidden by the *numerus clausus* from
attending a university in their mother country, they came to Paris
to study in a number of faculties, medicine being the most popular.
Usually they came from middle- or upper middle-class Russian
Jewish families which had been able to afford some secondary

[1] Dagan, op. cit., p. 266.
[2] Tchernoff, op. cit., iv. 278, n. 1.

COMMUNITY

education for their children. They survived on tiny allowances from home, with help from a student mutual aid fund, and by odd jobs, doing translations or teaching Russian. Their existence was precarious; living expenses in Paris were high; the exchange rate on the rouble was low, and lodging difficult to obtain.[1] It seems reasonable to assume with Pierre Aubery that their 'material conditions of existence appeared infinitely more insecure and unhealthy in France . . . than in Russia'.[2]

Typical of these students was Jehudah Tchernoff, whose memoirs portray with remarkable vividness the life of this group in Paris in the early 1890s. Tchernoff was from Nizhni Novgorod in central Russia; he came to Paris as a young student in 1892, with his Jewish religion stamped in his passport, a strong fear of the Okhrana (the Russian secret police), and painful memories of the bloody pogrom of 1884 which ravaged the Jewish community of his native city.[3] Many of the Jewish students with whom Tchernoff associated were revolutionaries. These young people were 'animated by a common hatred of the [Russian] autocracy'; in Paris they reconstituted, to some extent, the splintered and divided sects of the nascent revolutionary movement at home.[4] To a large degree these preoccupations with revolution and with Russian political developments reinforced the isolation of the students from the community at large. Furthermore, according to Tchernoff, the students had by and large broken with traditional Judaism ever since their education in the Russian *lycées*.[5] What Jewishness remained did not provide much of a tie with the Jewish community of France.

In Russia the Jewish stamp was the mark of a political category, the sign of a brutal and physical oppression for which there was no real equivalent in France. In France the condition of the Jews

---

[1] 'Colonie d'étudiants israélites russes à Paris', *A.I.*, 13 Dec. 1885, p. 400; G. Schleier, 'Coup d'œil sur les étudiants israélites russes', *A.I.*, 19 Apr. 1894, pp. 124–5; 'Les réfugiés russes', *L'Éclair*, 28 Sept. 1896.

[2] Aubery, op. cit., pp. 61–2.

[3] Tchernoff, op. cit., vol. iii, *De l'Affaire Dreyfus au dimanche rouge à Saint-Pétersbourg* (Paris, 1937), pp. 95–6; ibid., iv. 163.

[4] Ibid., vol. ii, *Le Destin d'un émigré* (Paris, 1937), p. 16.

[5] Ibid., p. 130.

was so different from that in Russia that there existed no possibility of a shared experience between the two groups of Jews. Tchernoff testifies to his feelings about French Jews: 'My intellectual and moral being differed from theirs. . . . I could only find affinities with people who had known the same suffering, felt the same torments, had shared my view of life, my ideas of social justice. The mentality of free Jews, born in a free country, emancipated by the Revolution, seemed to be very far from that of the Jewish masses and created a gulf between me and them . . .'[1] These students, like the immigrant workers, were close to suffering and were preoccupied with the difficulties of an uprooted and outcast Jewish people. But, like the 'Jewish proletariat', their suffering separated them from middle- and upper-class Jews; it provided divisions, not unity, resentment, not the sense of a Jewish solidarity before a common historical assault.

Thus, though traces remained here and there, the old 'community of suffering' was no more. Jews in France were still able to feel the hot breath of their assailants and to experience the cold rejection of certain elements of French society. Although few in number, the Jews received more than their share of attention. Yet time had done its work in mitigating the effects of anti-Jewish attacks. French Jews had emerged from the ghetto and were scattered throughout the French social structure. They no longer perceived life in the same way as before and they differed fundamentally in the kind of life they led. As might be expected, they experienced social pressures, even the pressures of anti-Semitism, differently. Oddly enough, Jews at both extremes of the social scale seem to have been less likely to experience anti-Jewish hostility in their daily lives than Jews in the middle ranges of society. Jews who suffered heavily in French society were apparently less likely to suffer from being Jewish than from being members of a commonly downtrodden social or economic group. Suffering might still, under extraordinary conditions, be the basis for

---

[1] Ibid., iv. 246–7.

cohesion. But in France at least, in the period before the Dreyfus Affair, a Jewish community held together by the force of outside hostility was impossible. Divisions based upon class were too great, and the kind of action carried on by anti-Semites was too selective in its application.

CHAPTER IV

THE TIES OF COMMUNITY: 2. RELIGION AND ORGANIZATION

THE religious tie which traditionally bound the Jewish people together operated at two levels. Theoretically the Jews considered themselves chosen by God to fulfil a specific function on earth. 'The fact of being chosen by God for His service meant that Israel had been singled out from the ranks of the other nations and had been assigned a position *sui generis*.'[1] Because one was a Jew, then, one had to follow the will of God and remain to some extent distinct from the surrounding society. On the practical level there was the Mosaic Code, a host of biblical injunctions which provided the Jew with a complicated rule of conduct. From this law an elaborate system of ritual and ceremony was constructed which virtually necessitated for its fulfilment a closely tied community. During the Middle Ages the Jewish ghetto arose, partly due to coercive regulations imposed from the outside, but partly also, as the sociologist Louis Wirth argued, in response to Jewish traditions. 'To the Jews the geographically separated and socially isolated community seemed to offer the best opportunity for following their religious precepts, of preparing their food according to the established religious ritual, of following their dietary laws, of attending the synagogue for prayer three times a day, and of participating in the numerous functions of communal life which religious duty imposed upon every member of the community.'[2] To be sure, the medieval period was one in which separate communities of all sorts, particularly occupational groups, tended to live together in some form of segregation. But with the Jews, because of their religion, the separation was particularly intense. Moses

[1] Jacob Katz, *Exclusiveness and Tolerance: Studies in Jewish–Gentile Relations in Medieval and Modern Times* (New York, 1962), p. 13.
[2] Louis Wirth, *The Ghetto* (Chicago, 1956), p. 19.

Mendelssohn, the Jewish philosopher of the Enlightenment, pointed to the important social function of this system of religious regulation:

The ceremonial laws of the Jews, aside from other causes we cannot discover, seem to have as a secondary purpose to set this nation visibly apart from all the rest and remind it constantly, through the performance of many religious acts, of those holy truths which should be unforgettable for all of us.[1]

Thus religious tradition became a corner-stone of a Jewish community which for hundreds of years preserved a sharp degree of independence from society at large.

During the course of the nineteenth century in France this communal tie, the tie of religious belief and practice, lost most of the strength which it had had in the years before emancipation. Indeed, with the arrival of eastern European Jews and with the constant reminder for French Jews of an earlier tradition of piety and belief, religion became a mildly divisive force within the Jewish community. The faith of the fathers in this way lost most of its power to create a community; as indifference spread among those who called themselves Jews, the danger grew that the inner strength of Judaism, a force which had helped to keep a people together for so many centuries, would be lost.

The erosion of religious belief in an age of science and positivism was profound in France and struck at the foundation of all religions. Generalizations about this trend are difficult to apply throughout the country. It may be that the Catholic foundation of the nation remained firm in the provinces, in the small peasant communities which were to a large extent isolated from urban intellectual and cultural developments. But change was perceptible in the larger cities, especially in the capital, among many sections of the middle class, among the educated élite of the country—in those very areas of French society where the Jews were concentrated. Here a faith in progress, through human

---

[1] Quoted in Michael A. Meyer, *The Origins of the Modern Jew: Jewish Identity and European Culture in Germany, 1749–1824* (Detroit, 1967), p. 38.

accomplishment and under the direction of science, was supplanting patterns of religious commitment.

Moreover, in France there was always, when it came to religion, an important political question. In the first decades of the Third Republic the Catholic Church found itself in a distinctly political stance, in clear alignment with those forces which wanted to destroy the Republic and restore a social system whose roots were in the pre-1789 period. As the prominent Catholic monarchist Albert de Mun once put it: 'The Church and the Revolution are irreconcilable, either the Church must kill the Revolution or the Revolution will kill the Church.'[1] The Ralliement, an attempt formally to reconcile the Church with that revolution and with the existence of the Republic, met mostly with failure. Serious political repercussions arose from this confrontation between the Catholic Church and the French political establishment. During the 1870s and 1880s the battle turned on the *question scolaire*, the control of educational institutions. Further conflict arose over the attempt to ban some religious orders and other systematic efforts on the part of political groups to institutionalize secularization in France. With bitter legislative battles the anti-religious mood became reinforced and its impact could not be limited to Catholicism. Political disputes such as these, the intransigence of certain elements within the Catholic Church, and a general intellectual climate hostile to revealed religion produced within French society a turning away from all religious teaching and a rejection of formal religious affiliation.

The Jewish community was severely affected by this anti-religious atmosphere. By the time of the Dreyfus Affair, according to an editorial in the *Archives israélites*, the growth of religious indifference posed a greater threat to the future of Judaism in France than the public campaign of the anti-Semites.[2] This 'crisis of irreligion', coinciding with the 'crisis of anti-Semitism', was seen

[1] Adrien Dansette, *Religious History of Modern France*, tr. (2 vols., New York, 1961), ii. 33. See Alexander Sedgewick, *The Ralliement in French Politics* (Cambridge, Mass., 1965).

[2] H. Prague, 'Les devoirs et les consistoires', *A.I.*, 1 Oct. 1896, p. 322. Cf. id., 'Coup d'œil sur l'état présent du judaïsme en France', *A.I.*, 10 Sept. 1896, pp. 298-9; id., 'Contre la décadence', *A.I.*, 21 Jan. 1897, pp. 17-18.

COMMUNITY

to be 'in the course of undermining the Jewish faith, of reducing its beliefs to the status of legends and ruining its institutions . . .'.[1] Young people, it was observed alarmingly, were growing up in ignorance of their religion, its history, its literature, and its accomplishments.[2] The Grand Rabbi of France referred to this tide of religious indifference in his Yom Kippour sermon in 1899; in his judgement the situation was worse in France than in the United States, England, or Russia.[3] 'Incredulity', he said on another occasion, 'no longer shows any reserve and holds its head high. The expression of a sincere faith arouses indecent laughter. It takes courage to dare openly to believe in anything but brute force or science . . .'[4]

Several factors placed Judaism in a particularly vulnerable position. As we have noted, the Jewish population of France concentrated in those very areas of the country where the trend against formal religion was the strongest. The Jewish community of Paris, the community which had been called by the Grand Rabbi 'the standard-bearer of Judaism, the beacon whose light spreads far and wide', was located in the darkest centre of the anti-religious movement. Many of the points raised in the late 1850s against moving the rabbinical seminary from Metz to Paris had been related to the feeling that the capital was a 'séjour des plaisirs et des séductions', a frivolous place where religious fervour was no longer possible, where modernity and an easy life made a public mockery of an ancient religious community.[5] These arguments carried even more force in the 1880s and 1890s. On the other hand, except for the communities of what remained of Alsace and Lorraine, Judaism suffered even more from indifference in the provinces than in Paris. Away from the capital the size of the communities was very reduced, attendance at religious services low, and the synagogues,

[1] H. Prague, 'Le culte en province', A.I., 11 Aug. 1898, p. 258.
[2] 'Les étudiants israélites et l'histoire juive', A.I., 13 Sept. 1899, p. 298.
[3] L. L., 'Le sermon du Grand Rabbin de France lors du jour de Kippour', U.I., 22 Sept. 1899, p. 9.
[4] Zadoc Kahn, Sermons et allocutions (3 vols., 2nd edn., Paris, 1903), ii. 233.
[5] L.-M. Lambert, Précis de l'histoire des Hébreux depuis le patriarche Abraham jusqu'en 1840 (Metz, 1840), p. 416 n.; Jules Bauer, L'École Rabbinique de France 1830–1930 (Paris, n.d.), p. 101.

unlike the sumptuous and imposing edifices of Paris, were small and modest. These communities had very meagre resources; the towns of the provinces had few affluent Jewish families and there was a constant tendency for successful Jews to move to Paris.[1] Thus in Bayonne, as reported in the *Univers israélite*, it was becoming impossible to recruit boys for the choir, and the use of young girls, not sanctioned by Jewish tradition, was being considered.[2] Elsewhere it was difficult to get together a *minyan*, the ten men necessary for a religious service, either on the sabbath or even on holidays. 'In Paris', it was noted, 'this morbid work of decomposition is less striking. In the midst of a numerous population it is only necessary to have religious activity among a few believers and practising [Jews] to give the illusion for the whole.'[3] Another factor in the decline of religious commitment among Jews was the growing tendency for Jews to enter the liberal professions. Indifference, it was generally agreed, was higher among professors, teachers, doctors, lawyers, engineers, etc., than among other careers which required less academic preparation. The notable success of Jews in the arts, in letters, and in science was said to have set up a process of 'selection in reverse' by which Judaism was losing its most gifted sons.[4]

While the Consistoire maintained three Jewish schools in Paris, which taught a total of about 700 pupils, these schools were largely attended by the children of the poor; other Jewish children received little or no specifically Jewish education.[5] Parents who could afford it sent their offspring to Catholic schools or to the better-known state institutions. Within the Jewish quarter of the fourth *arrondissement* there were at least six state-supported schools whose students were predominantly Jewish. But there was no effort made to teach Judaism in these schools, and the curriculum was basically

[1] Jules Bauer, 'Le judaïsme de province', *U.I.*, 12 Mar. 1897, pp. 790–1.

[2] *U.I.*, 19 Nov. 1897, p. 282.

[3] H. Prague, 'Le culte en province', *A.I.*, 11 Aug. 1898, p. 258.

[4] R. T., 'Les carrières libérales et la religion', *U.I.*, 29 Jan. 1897, pp. 594–6; 12 Feb. 1897, pp. 657–8.

[5] 'L'enseignement religieux à Paris', *U.I.*, 21 Feb. 1896, pp. 688–9; L. L., 'Le sermon du Grand Rabbin de France lors du jour de Kippour', *U.I.*, 22 Sept. 1899, p. 9.

designed to adapt the pupils to French life.[1] For these reasons leaders of the Jewish community worried about the commitment of the coming generation to Jewish beliefs. Hippolyte Prague spoke of 'the poison of scepticism which corrodes the heart of young people of the *lycées* and *universités*'; France, even when compared with Germany, was considered particularly deficient in this respect.[2] Four synagogues, commonly known by the name of the street on which they were located, served the religious needs of the Jewish community of Paris. The largest of these, on the Rue de la Victoire in the ninth *arrondissement*, had a clear pre-eminence, and was the congregation of the Grand Rabbi of France. The three others were the synagogues of the Rue Notre-Dame de Nazareth, the Rue des Tournelles, and the synagogue of the Sephardic rite on the Rue Buffault. Together these synagogues had a seating capacity of just over five thousand. In addition there were a number of very small *oratoires*—chapels and religious meeting-places, mostly in the Jewish quarter, where eastern European and other Orthodox Jews met. The synagogues were filled, if ever, only on the High Holy Days, for the important festivals of Yom Kippour (the Day of Atonement) and Rosh Hashanah (the Jewish New Year). These were the two occasions on which Jews who had only the most nominal connections with Judaism might attend a religious service. If one estimates very roughly, on the basis of French population statistics, that about one-fifth of the Jewish community was either under the age of thirteen or too infirm or otherwise unable to attend a religious service, then it appears, remarkably, that there was room for only about one-eighth of the total Jewish population of Paris which could be expected to attend a religious service.[3]

---

[1] Paul Pottier, 'Essai sur le prolétariat juif en France', *Revue des revues*, 1 Mar. 1899, p. 488.

[2] H. Prague, 'L'éducation juive: à propos d'un nouveau roman', *A.I.*, 14 Oct. 1897, p. 323; see also 'Les étudiants israélites et l'histoire juive', *A.I.*, 13 Sept. 1899, p. 298.

[3] I have found no evidence of auxiliary services held elsewhere in Paris during the High Holy Days. The synagogues and their seating capacities are listed in *Annuaire 5658*, pp. 67–8. The *Annuaire* estimated the Paris Jewish population at about 50,000. According to the *Statistique générale de la France* (1891) (Paris, 1894), p. 189, for every 100,000 Frenchmen there were 17,498 under fifteen years of age.

PLATE I

b. Synagogue of the Rue Notre Dame de la Nazareth

a. Rothschild Wedding 1876. Synagogue of the
Rue de la Victoire

Moreover, during the 1890s Jews were noticeably absent from the synagogue even on the High Holy Days. The difficulty was that these days, coming in the early autumn, often coincided with the *villégiature*, the period during the year when middle-class Parisians flocked to the beaches and resort areas. If the weather was warm in September many Jews preferred to remain in the country and extend their summer vacation rather than return to the city. When according to the Jewish calendar the High Holy Days came too early in the autumn, attendance was likely to be low. 'Piety', in one rather cynical observation of the time, 'will depend on the calendar.'[1] Sabbath services, traditionally held on Saturday mornings, had fallen off drastically by the late 1870s; most men worked on Saturdays and, it was noticed, the ladies did not get up in time. As a result Saturday afternoon services, known in Hebrew as *mincha*, were introduced. With this change the congregation in the synagogue of the Rue de la Victoire was sufficient to fill the entire ground floor and even some of the galleries. But by 1897 people no longer came even for *mincha*; generally only one or two hundred, still mostly ladies, were present each week. Wealthy Jews, according to the same source, did not attend these services, only 'les milieux plus modestes'.[2]

The French Jewish community continued to observe the Bar Mitzvah, the religious initiation ceremony for boys thirteen years of age. Yet during our period the institution was in decline. Before each Bar Mitzvah it was the custom to have a rabbi examine the candidate to determine if he was sufficiently prepared in his knowledge of Hebrew and the Scriptures. By the middle of the 1890s this examination had become a simple formality with virtually no one being rejected. The ceremony itself was considerably reduced in length; often it consisted only of the recitation by heart of five verses from the Pentateuch.[3]

---

[1] R. T., 'Les revenus des synagogues', *U.I.*, 2 July 1897, p. 454; Jules Bauer, 'Villégiature', *U.I.*, 25 June 1897, pp. 428–9; *A.I.*, 31 Aug. 1899, pp. 290–1.

[2] R. T., 'L'office du samedi après-midi', *U.I.*, 10 Dec. 1897, pp. 357–8; Simon Debré, 'The Jews of France', *Jewish Quarterly Review*, vol. iii, Apr. 1891, p. 410.

[3] 'L'examen de la bar-mitswa', *U.I.*, 20 Nov. 1896, p. 267; H. Prague, 'Le culte en province', *A.I.*, 11 Aug. 1898, p. 258.

A number of ceremonies and customs practised by the Jewish community were either heavily influenced by Catholic ritual or adopted outright from Catholicism. One of the latter, a religious initiation for boys of thirteen and girls of twelve, was patterned on the Catholic First Communion. The dress for this ceremony was the same as that of the Catholic rite; in the words of one French rabbi describing the practice to English readers, there was an 'odour of Christianity' about it.[1] Another such ritual was the bringing into the synagogue of newly born children to be blessed: '. . . the resemblance of this ceremony to the ceremony of baptism', according to the same source, 'has, perhaps, contributed to its becoming . . . completely [accepted] in higher Jewish social spheres.'[2] Other rituals borrowed from Christianity were the collection-plate passed around during marriage ceremonies, the summoning of a rabbi to the bed-side of the dying, the covering of coffins with flowers and garlands, and the use of the organ during religious services.[3] The official dress for French rabbis, adopted at a rabbinical conference in 1856, was the same as that of a Catholic priest, with a slight difference, the collar-band being white.[4] In 1896 the Grand Rabbi of France considered, as a way of solving the problem of low attendance at sabbath services, the institution of a sabbath service on Sunday mornings. The idea, however, met with no success. Yet the fact that a figure such as the Grand Rabbi could have made such a proposal (although the original suggestion was in an unsigned article) tells something of the mood of the Jewish community.[5] Simon Debré, the rabbi quoted above, offered some elaboration on the nature of this borrowing. The chief reason for it was the small size of the Jewish community which made it impossible not to feel the influence of Christian forms of worship. While it was often done unconsciously, there was no strong inclination on the part of French Jews to resist the adoption of these customs and ceremonies. 'Not only do the large majority . . . see no harm in borrowing from a religion . . . but it may be said that the very resemblance to the ceremonies of

[1] Debré, op. cit., p. 412.   [2] Ibid., p. 416.
[3] Ibid., p. 417.   [4] Article 'France', J. E.
[5] Julien Weill, Zadoc Kahn, 1839–1905 (Paris, 1912), p. 175.

Christian ritual is generally an excellent recommendation in France for every innovation.'[1]

Out of the entire Jewish population of France, in the view of an editorialist for the *Univers israélite*, there were probably only five hundred or so in 1898 who were worthy of being called Orthodox.[2] These Orthodox Jews, however, were conspicuous. In Paris, where most of them lived, they worshipped in the *oratoires* in the shabby district of narrow streets around the Hôtel de Ville. Mainly from eastern Europe, and having come from a community in which religion was an integral part of their lives, they saw, for the most part, only 'a certain worldly snobbery' in the religious forms of French Jewry. Theirs was a religion of commitment and passion, of devotion and 'mystical ardour' which distinguished them sharply from the rest of the Jewish community.[3] They were, of course, much more faithful to traditional practices than Jews born in France. At least one-quarter of all the Bar Mitzvahs in Paris during this period were from immigrant families and usually the fraction was much higher.[4] Unable to accept or to understand the ceremonies of the greater French community, they tended to remain apart, particularly on the High Holy Days when they could not be seated in the consistorial synagogues. In consequence they founded tiny *shuls* for worship in private apartments, small shops, or rooms rented for the purpose.[5]

The existence of a substantial number of Orthodox Jews in Paris somewhat troubled the established Jewish community. The latter felt uneasy in the presence of Jews whose religious practice seemed to lend substance to the caricatures of anti-Semitic propagandists. Settled French Jews considered that the removal of ancient political and social disabilities imposed upon Jews the

[1] Debré, op. cit., pp. 416–17.

[2] R. T., 'La vitalité d'Israël: comment et pourquoi nous pratiquons', *U.I.*, 16 Dec. 1898, p. 390.

[3] See J. Tchernoff, *Dans le creuset des civilisations*, vol. iii, *De l'Affaire Dreyfus au dimanche rouge à Saint-Pétersbourg* (Paris, 1937), p. 15.

[4] The Bar Mitzvah statistics are listed in 'Un peu de statistique', *U.I.*, 5 Feb. 1909, p. 657, and 'Le nombre des "bar mitswa" de 1896 à 1910', *U.I.*, 26 Jan. 1912, pp. 624–5.

[5] Tchernoff, op. cit., vol. iv, *Des prodromes du bolchévisme à une société des nations* (Paris, 1938), pp. 277–8.

obligation to present before the world a public image of modernity.

Typical of this position was an article written in 1900 by the archaeologist Salomon Reinach entitled 'The Interior Emancipation of Judaism'.[1] Reinach declared that 'ritualism', as he put it, was a fetter which Jews placed upon themselves, a burden which was becoming increasingly oppressive in the modern world. 'At a time when the progress of science and consciousness has done everything to bring men together, the ritualism of the Jews isolates them; it digs around them a trench deeper than that of prejudice and hatred; it gives credit to the deceitful idea that the Jews are strangers among the nations.' Reinach wanted above all to remove the basis of isolation, what we have seen as the community building force of the Jewish religion. 'The true religion', he claimed, 'was an affair of sentiment, not of practices.' From this it followed that Jews were obliged to free their religion of the trammels of a ritual which kept them apart from the surrounding population. All educated Jews had an obligation to point the way to this 'interior emancipation'. Ritual, in Reinach's view, was thus a divisive force within the Jewish community, a sign of backwardness which marked the vast majority of eastern European Jews and which distinguished them from their enlightened brethren of western Europe.

It is significant that despite the repugnance which many French Jews felt towards traditional ritual and the details of Jewish worship, relatively few took the final step of renouncing their religion and converting to Christianity. While little is known about the number of Jewish conversions, there seems to be general agreement that the number was low.[2] There were essentially two reasons for this. First of all, the condition of the Jews in France was such that, unlike in Heine's Germany (or, one might add, Disraeli's England), one obtained the ticket to assimilation not

[1] Salomon Reinach, 'L'émancipation intérieure du judaïsme', U.I., 26 Oct. 1900, pp. 172–5. Cf. the criticism of Reinach's article by R. T., 'L'émancipation intérieure du judaïsme', U.I., 2 Nov. 1900, pp. 197–200.
[2] L. Cazé, 'Ce que sont devenus les israélites convertis au xixᵉ siècle', Revue des revues, 1 Sept. 1896, pp. 430–6; Debré, op. cit., p. 393.

through baptism but rather, in part at least, through an avowed transcendence of formal religious beliefs. Most of France during this period, as we have seen, was moving gradually towards secularization. In society, in the world of business, in government, and in the professional world, to be *laïc*, to have no formal religious connection, was hardly ever a hindrance, and often an advantage. There were even, in the opinion of one writer, special advantages for those who were born Jews. In an anti-clerical atmosphere 'the Jewish origin of an initiate . . . seemed even to constitute an *a priori* warrant of loyalty and a certificate of republicanism, by virtue of the absence of the "clerical complex" stamped on others by their education'.[1] Jews were, in fact, much more an integral part of French society than were Jews in Germany. There was, in society, a large degree of indifference when it came to questions of religion, because the level of religious commitment in many areas of French life was so low. Thus it was possible to give an airy comment, as did Madame Straus (*née* Geneviève Halévy) when asked about the possibility of her conversion: 'J'ai trop peu de religion pour en changer.'[2] Secondly, the nature of the anti-Semitic campaign in France was such that there was no real possibility of escaping through conversion. If anti-Semites could attack Gambetta or Jules Simon as Jews, there was little hope for those who publicly announced a change of religion to be fully accepted as Christians.[3] If Jewishness was, as we have noted, really considered in large degree a matter of race, a Jew who renounced his faith was still looked upon as a Jew. Indeed, Jews who did convert were generally considered to have done so by reason of cowardice and were thus exposed 'to the contempt of all honest men' from their families, their former Jewish compatriots, and the rest of society.[4] This was the difficulty that Raïssa Maritain, who came from Russia with her Jewish parents, encountered at the time of her conversion to

---

[1] Arnold Mandel, 'French Jewry in a Time of Decision: Vestigial Remnant or Living Continuity?', *Commentary*, vol. xviii, no. 6, Dec. 1954, p. 539.

[2] Moshé Katan, 'La famille Halévy', *Évidences*, Mar. 1955, p. 11.

[3] See Édouard Drumont, *La France juive: essai d'histoire contemporaine* (2 vols., Paris, 1886), *passim*; Robert Launay, *Figures juives* (Paris, 1921), p. 28.

[4] B.-M., 'Un baptême', *U.I.*, 7 Nov. 1902, p. 198.

Catholicism.[1] The universal assumption in these cases was that the convert had left his religion to join another, not out of sincere religious belief, but out of moral weakness.[2] In most cases, then, the negative reactions of society, both Jewish and Gentile, made conversion more trouble than it was worth.

The question of conversion touches upon an aspect of the Jewish affiliation related to the above remarks which is important to consider. For many Jews there was an element of personal honour involved in their continued identification as Jews. Often this was the strongest argument against making the final, irrevocable break with the Jewish community. Indifference was possible, even common; complete separation was another matter. This was so particularly among members of the highest social strata, among those families such as the Rothschilds or Camondos whose members had long been leaders of the Jewish community. For these Jews their religion was the mark of 'a part of their patrimony which [was] also part of their family prestige'.[3] This feeling, however, also existed elsewhere, among Jews of the middle class who, despite the rational perspective of unbelievers, continued at least nominal practice of Judaism as one necessary part of their identity. Pierre Abraham, a young boy at the time of the Dreyfus Affair, recalls the viewpoint of his father who, though intellectually a rationalist, continued to be faithful to Jewish traditions:

He saw religion only in the light of a traditional tie which bound us to the previous generations of Jews. Since in the past the Jews suffered from humiliations, persecutions, massacres, it seemed to him necessary not to cut his bonds of sympathy with a history woven with grief and injustice. The sole means in his power to prove to himself his devotion to his ancestors was to continue the ritual practices which had belonged to them. That is why, his whole life long, he went to synagogue for Rosh Hashanah, he celebrated Passover at home, he fasted strictly on

---

[1] Raïssa Maritain, *We have been Friends Together* and *Adventures in Grace*, tr. (Garden City, New York, 1961), p. 237.

[2] H. Prague, 'A propos de récentes conversions', *A.I.*, 20 May 1897, p. 154; R. T., 'La France aux Français!', *U.I.*, 18 Feb. 1898, pp. 679-80.

[3] Mandel, op. cit., p. 537.

Yom Kippour, and he had a religious education for his children up to their Bar Mitzvah . . .[1]

Abraham sees his father as an exception in this regard. Clearly he was, considering the strictness of observance. Yet there is sufficient testimony along similar lines to conclude that there were many Jews who at least shared these feelings and who, as a result, continued some Jewish practices such as attendance at the synagogue on the High Holy Days. Often a related reason for such observance was the unwillingness to break a family custom or to upset parents.[2] In any case, it is apparent that outward forms of Judaism continued to have social relevance and importance which went beyond their religious function, and were kept alive by many Jews for precisely that reason.

The issue of intermarriage, forbidden by Jewish law, involved a similar approach by Jews. Once again, there is no statistical information available, but given the high degree of assimilation of French Jews, the incidence of marriage between Jews and non-Jews seems to have been rather low.[3] The official organs of the Jewish community roundly disapproved of intermarriage and brought public pressure to bear against it in specific cases.[4] In many cases, this pressure seems to have been successful. As with the practising of Jewish rites, what mattered here was not so much the acceptance of a religious duty but rather some recognition of an individual obligation to continue the communal practices of one's forefathers when the religious basis for those practices had long since lapsed.

With this perspective on the matter of religious tradition, a perspective widely held in the French Jewish community, it may be asked why the question of Reform Judaism, so vexing and often divisive an issue in Germany and elsewhere, never became significant in France. Simon Debré gave three reasons for the lack of a French Reform movement.[5] In the first place, a substantial

---

[1] Pierre Abraham, 'Mon père, juif', Europe, no. 93 (Summer 1953), p. 27.
[2] See Pierre Aubery, Milieux juifs de la France contemporaine à travers leurs écrivains (Paris, 1957), p. 76.
[3] R. T., 'La France aux Français!', U.I., 16 June 1898, p. 679.
[4] See U.I., 16 June 1892, p. 598.   [5] Debré, op. cit., pp. 386–92.

amount of 'reform' had already been carried out by our period
through the agency of the Consistoire Central and an assembly of
French rabbis in 1856. The decision had already been taken for
such changes as a modern dress for rabbis, having sermons delivered in French, etc. After 1856, moreover, rabbis were given considerable latitude in making revisions in ritual where they saw fit,
and they occasionally did so. Secondly, it was observed that
indifference was so widespread within the Jewish community that
few people had sufficiently deep religious convictions to mount
and sustain a modernization movement against established tradition. In fact, practices such as the strict observance of the sabbath
and the dietary laws, normally the objects of 'reform', had already
gone quietly into disuse. Finally, there were few Orthodox Jews
in France and, as a result, little force behind a defence of old traditions. Perhaps because the Orthodox Jews remained apart, there
was an easy spirit of toleration between all parties and thus little
reason for the breaking away of any section of the Jewish community. After the period of the Dreyfus Affair, the Union Libérale
Israélite, a Reform-type congregation, was launched in Paris under
the leadership of Théodore Reinach.[1] But this congregation never
succeeded in being the basis for a larger movement and was never
a centre of controversy comparable to the large-scale developments which took hold somewhat earlier in Germany and in
America.

   There was still, then, something of a religious tie within the
Jewish community, just as a weakened tie based upon the old
'community of suffering' persisted in some social groups. What
kept these ties effective, however, what translated them into action
was a well-organized system of administration involving rabbis
and laymen, the government-sponsored apparatus, and a large
network of charitable organizations. As we have argued, divisive
elements too remained: the memories of oppression were short in
some social strata, quite dead in others; religious devotion lost
most of its binding force, yet curiously lived on as a mark of

---

[1] Michel Roblin, *Les Juifs de Paris: démographie, économie, culture* (Paris, 1952),
pp. 140-1.

Jewishness. But for all of its weakness, the Jewish community in France had a continuing life of its own, a life which was not entirely dependent for its definition upon government statutes, the beliefs and prejudices of the average Frenchman, or the accusations of the anti-Semites. The remainder of this chapter will explore the administrative organization of the Jewish community which permitted this continued existence.

No discussion of the administrative organization of the Jewish community is possible without an understanding of the role which the Rothschild family played in that community's administration.[1] Their role was extraordinary, as was their position in French society and virtually everything the family did. A word should be said first of all about the basis of the Rothschild position.

The Paris branch of the Rothschild family was founded by James, youngest of the five sons of Mayer-Amschel Rothschild who together emerged from the Frankfort *Judengasse* and, during the first part of the nineteenth century, established their family as one of the arbiters of European finance. The Rothschild Frères, their Paris branch, was founded in 1812; by the time of the Restoration, James (who was created an Austrian baron in 1822) was dealing with the heads of government in France, was an important figure in the world of international affairs, and, with his brothers, was achieving a real pre-eminence in European banking. The Rothschild enterprise developed into a fine example of what was referred to as the *haute banque*—a group of private institutions whose capital came from a single family or close associates, which were hidden from public scrutiny, which were cosmopolitan, which dealt with heads of government, and which eschewed business undertakings or small-scale operations. Within the *haute banque* the Rothschilds were among the most powerful. During the first half of the nineteenth century, according to the bank historian Jean Bouvier, the Rothschild fortune was many times the capital of the Bank of France.[2] The wealth of the family became a legend in France; for competitors such as the Crédit Mobilier during the Second Empire or the

---

[1] On the Rothschilds see especially Jean Bouvier, *Les Rothschild* (Paris, 1960).
[2] Ibid., p. 48.

Union Générale in the early 1880s, Rothschild Frères was the implacable enemy which held French finance in an iron grip; for socialists of whatever stripe the bank became a sort of capitalist Bastille, a symbol of the power of money and the privilege of wealth.[1] James died in 1868 and was succeeded at the head of the Paris branch by his eldest son Alphonse. With his brother Gustave and some help from a younger brother Edmond, Alphonse de Rothschild exercised a masterful control over the family fortune. They built railways, controlled the important Chemin de Fer du Nord, were directors of the Banque de France, and helped to guarantee France's staggering war indemnity in 1871. The three brothers, moreover, fitted easily into French high society; whereas James had been essentially a German Jew who spoke execrable French, Alphonse, Gustave, and Edmond were thoroughly Parisian and much more polished. In their own way, the Rothschilds had become a part of French life.

The Rothschild family continued to feel a deep commitment to the Jewish community in France, a commitment which coexisted curiously with their obligations to the salons of the aristocracy and the fashionable charities of the *haut monde*. James's sons were raised in a home which was faithful to Jewish practices, received a thorough Jewish education, and were instructed, in a tradition of *noblesse oblige*, to be leaders of the Jewish community.[2] Devotion to Judaism, Alphonse once said, was a proud family tradition, 'a legacy which he had received from his father and grandfather'.[3] The family remained generous, both with their time and with their money. Each year during our period the Rothschilds gave about 84,000 francs in public donations to the Jewish community of Paris.[4] Rothschild baronesses were chairmen of three out of six

[1] See, for example, Isidore Singer, *Anarchie et antisémitisme* (Paris, n.d.), pp. 12–13.

[2] Zadoc Kahn, *Souvenirs et regrets: recueil d'oraisons funèbres prononcées dans la communauté israélite de Paris 1868–1898* (Paris, 1898), pp. 2–10; Israël Margalith, *Le Baron Edmond de Rothschild et la colonisation juive en Palestine 1882–1899* (Paris, 1957), pp. 64–5.

[3] S. H., 'Cinquantenaire consistorial de M. le baron Alphonse de Rothschild', *U.I.*, 30 May 1902, p. 333.

[4] This calculation is based upon weekly entries of donations in *U.I.* for the Jewish calendar year 1896–7.

ladies' charitable committees listed in a Jewish year-book of 1897, and members of another two. Rothschild barons were chairmen of at least four other committees. Rothschild patronage was instrumental in building the synagogue of the Rue de la Victoire, in founding the Société des Études Juives in 1879, and in setting up a Jewish hospital, a home for the elderly, an orphanage, a Hebrew primary school, and a number of scholarships for the needy.[1] The Rothschilds engaged in Jewish philanthropy with a certain *panache*, in a manner which became distinctive in style and generosity. No one could make donations in quite the same way. In 1881, for example, on the occasion of the Bar Mitzvah of his son, Alphonse gave 10,000 francs to public charity in his *arrondissement*, 50,000 francs to the Jewish community, and promised 1,000 francs to each Jewish boy whose Bar Mitzvah would occur on the same date in the future.[2]

But most important of all of this participation was the role played by the Rothschilds in the Consistoire Central and the Consistoire de Paris, the two most important of the government-sponsored organizations set up to run the Jewish community in France. Like their illustrious father James, the two senior members of the family's French branch took their leadership seriously. Alphonse entered the Consistoire Central in 1850, when he was only twenty-three, and held office as its president from 1869. Gustave was elected to the Consistoire de Paris in 1852 at the age of twenty-two, and within six years was elected its president, a post which he held until 1910.[3] Thus at the time of the Dreyfus Affair the heads of the Rothschild family in France had been the officially designated leaders of the Jewish community since the days of Napoleon III. The importance of this long-standing control over the governmental agency of the Jewish community is obvious; the views of the Rothschild family had to

[1] See *Annuaire 5658* (1896–7).

[2] Léonce Reynaud, *Les Juifs français devant l'opinion* (Paris, 1887), p. 275.

[3] S. H., 'Cinquantenaire consistorial de M. le baron Alphonse de Rothschild', *U.I.*, 30 May 1902, p. 332; 'Le Jubilé consistorial de M. le baron Gustave de Rothschild', *A.I.*, 1 Jan. 1903, pp. 4–5, and 8 Jan. 1903; article 'Rothschild', *J.E.* and *U.J.E.*; Léon Poliakov, *Histoire de l'antisémitisme*, vol. iii, *De Voltaire à Wagner* (Paris, 1968), pp. 354–63.

be considered in virtually all decisions, and their policies had critical advantages for implementation. In the course of time the community came to depend upon both their donations and their decisions. Their prestige and wealth had made them leaders to whom the other leaders of the Jewish community necessarily deferred.

One can perhaps understand how the anti-Semites were able to cast the Rothschilds as 'kings of the Jews'. When Robert de Rothschild, the young son of Gustave, was slightly injured while leaving school one afternoon, it was reported carefully in the Jewish press; when Baron Arthur de Rothschild's new yacht *Eros* put in at Nice, it was blessed by the Grand Rabbi of France who happened to be in the vicinity.[1] When some elements within the Jewish community wanted to spend community funds in commemoration of the Revolution of 1789, the royalist-oriented Rothschilds objected and the matter was peremptorily closed. 'Without the Rothschilds,' complained one critic, 'without their effective support, nothing much can be done.'[2] But with constant Rothschild support, it might be added, French Jews were 'not accustomed to exert themselves'.[3] Decisions were in large measure left to those who were paying the bills. It would be wrong, however, to consider that this power was continually being employed; the Rothschilds did not exercise a tyranny over their fellow Jews. Rather the Jewish community hardly required a firm policy-making authority; as will be seen, it was administered, not governed, and the influence of the Rothschild family made itself felt through that administration.

The administrative machinery to which we have been referring dated for the most part from the time of Napoleon I, and it bore the characteristic stamp of French bureaucracy established during the Empire. The Napoleonic mark was distinctive: a rigid hierarchy, tight centralization in Paris, and firm state control. With the blessing of the Emperor the Jewish religion had been designated a *culte reconnu*, an officially recognized religion whose

[1] 'Nouvelles diverses', *U.I.*, 22 Jan. 1897, p. 578; 'Le monde et la ville', *A.I.*, 4 Feb. 1886, p. 38.   [2] Ranc in *Le Matin*, 15 Sept. 1892.
[3] Max Nordau, 'The Decadence of Judaism in France', *Jewish Chronicle*, 18 Jan. 1907, p. 10.

adherents agreed to accept the ecclesiastical and administrative organization imposed by the State.[1] In return for this acceptance the State had granted a number of legal privileges to the Jewish religion and even provided, after 1831, for the payment of Jewish rabbis. The State set up a Consistoire Central located in Paris, composed of the Grand Rabbi of France and one lay member supposedly representing each departmental *consistoire* in France and Algeria. The laymen of the Consistoire Central were in fact to be elected from among Jewish notables residing in Paris. There were nine departmental *consistoires* in metropolitan France, the most important being that of Paris. Others were set up in Bayonne, Besançon, Bordeaux, Épinal, Marseille, Lille, Lyon, and Nancy. Beneath each departmental *consistoire* there was a unit in the provinces known as the *communauté*, but this was of minor importance and need not concern us here. The chief organ of government was, of course, the Consistoire Central whose members, apart from the Grand Rabbi of France, were elected for eight-year terms, and half of whom stood for re-election every four years. To qualify as an elector a Jew had simply to make some donation to a recognized Jewish charity or to rent a seat in a synagogue. The Consistoire Central was the official intermediary between the Ministre des Cultes and the departmental *consistoires*, had some authority over the rabbinate, and was 'charged with the over-all supervision of the interests of the Jewish religion'.[2] Most importantly, the Consistoire Central made financial decisions which concerned both the granting and the spending of money at the departmental level. An annual budget was voted upon by each *consistoire* and then approved by the Consistoire Central. The departmental *consistoires* were elected in a fashion similar to that of

[1] A good account of the administrative structure of French Judaism may be found in the article by Eugène Hepp, 'Cultes non-catholiques', in Léon Say (ed.), *Dictionnaire des finances* (2 vols., Paris, 1889–90). The relevant statutes may be found in Penel Beaufin, *Législation générale du culte israélite* (Paris, 1894), or in Isaac Uhry, *Recueil des lois, décrets, arrêtés, règlements et circulaires concernant les Israélites 1850–1903* (Bordeaux, 1903). An earlier collection is by Achille-Edmond Halphen, *Recueil des lois, décrets, ordonnances, avis du Conseil d'État concernant les Israélites depuis la Révolution de 1789* (Paris, 1851).

[2] See, in any of the above collections, *Ordonnance du roi portant règlement pour l'organisation du culte israélite, du 25 mai 1844*, Article 10.

the Consistoire Central. Their job was one of local administration, with some authority over rabbis and with some responsibility of reporting periodically to the local prefect. Each year the State granted over 160,000 francs to pay the salaries of Jewish religious officials, to support the Jewish seminary, and to help keep up repairs on synagogues. In addition to these receipts the *consistoires* received money from private donors, the largest of whom were, of course, the Rothschilds. (The family each year gave publicly at least half of the sum provided annually by the French government.) Other income came from the sale of kosher meat, funerals, and various property revenues.[1] Most charitable donations within the Jewish community appear to have been made directly to the *consistoires* which then allocated funds to the various Jewish charities.

Napoleon had intended this elaborate system to serve as 'a kind of police force over Jewish morals, under the cold and unsympathetic supervision of the Ministry of Religion'.[2] As it turned out, the consistorial structure proved somewhat less than energetic in its regulatory role and, not surprisingly, less a police force than a conscientious body of *fonctionnaires*. Judaism was not the potentially subversive force which the Emperor had believed it to be, and as a result its official organs had little real police work to do. Instead, they fitted easily into the less glamorous administrative habits of the French bureaucracy. By the end of the nineteenth century it was apparent that the apparatus set up for repressive control had become a smoothly running and unimaginative bureaucratic machine. Editorials in the Jewish press were full of charges to this effect: '. . . the most complete immobility', said the *Univers israélite*; 'passivity' and 'inertia', accused the *Archives israélites*. A number of specific complaints were offered: the *consistoires*, it was said, were constantly deferring to what they believed to be the wishes of the State—the result was that they were slow to act and excessively conservative in their decisions. The Consistoire Central held itself aloof from the Jewish community —it did not publish its deliberations, a summary account of its

[1] See 'Le régime financier du culte israélite', *Le Temps*, 18 Mar. 1893.

[2] Howard M. Sachar, *The Course of Modern Jewish History* (New York, 1958), p. 64.

activities, or even its budget.[1] Perhaps the most telling of these complaints was that the Consistoire had become a sort of Académie française of French Judaism, a body to which election was a fine honour but little else, a highly presentable group of distinguished gentlemen whose job was less to provide a leading or dynamic force within the Jewish community than to be a showcase of Jewish achievements in various fields.[2] Thus in 1898 the lay members of the Consistoire Central consisted of a Regent of the Bank of France (Alphonse de Rothschild), the first honorary president of the Cour de Cassation (G. Bedarrides), two important bankers (Eugène Pereire and Henry Deutsch), a retired general (Abraham Sée), a senior municipal official of Paris (Henri Aron), the Inspector-General of the Ponts et Chaussées (Maurice Lévy), and several well-known doctors and lawyers.[3]

Certainly the *consistoires* were at fault. Yet, as one older member of the Jewish community pointed out, much cause for the over-all lethargy and high-handedness could be traced to the indifference and apathy of those who were supposed to elect the *consistoires*. Both the Consistoire Central and its departmental counterparts took their cues from the Jewish communities which elected them. Few Jews seemed willing even to make the nominal contribution necessary to become an elector.[4] Abstentions were normally very high during elections; by statute at least one-third of those eligible had to vote on the first round for the election to be final and, as voting was generally not nearly so heavy, a second *tour* was usually necessary. In 1897 there were only 3,911 Jews qualified to vote in elections for the Consistoire de Paris, and less than one-third participated on either round.[5] Moreover, the community appeared as a

[1] B.-M., 'Élections consistoriales', *U.I.*, 9 Oct. 1896; H. Prague, 'Quelques réflexions de circonstance sur le Consistoire Central', *A.I.*, 20 Aug. 1896, p. 274.

[2] H. Prague, 'L'organisation du culte israélite en France', *A.I.*, 10 Sept. 1897, p. 290; id., 'Quelques comptes rendus', *A.I.*, 10 June 1897, p. 177; 'L'élection consistoriale du 31 octobre', *A.I.*, 21 Oct. 1897, p. 331; Prague, 'Quelques réflexions de circonstance sur le Consistoire Central', *A.I.*, 20 Aug. 1896, p. 273; Debré, op. cit., p. 373.   [3] *Annuaire 5658* (1897-8), p. 64.

[4] Un vieux membre de la communauté, 'Les élections consistoriales', *U.I.*, 25 Sept. 1896, pp. 14-16.

[5] See 'Élections consistoriales', *A.I.*, 15 Oct. 1896, p. 339; A.C.P., Sér. 1 C[8] for Oct. and Nov. 1897; H. Prague, 'Une création nécessaire', *A.I.*, 30 Sept. 1897, pp. 305-6.

rule uninterested in consistorial affairs and little inclined to make
suggestions, to provide pressure or even the support for reform.

 These deficiencies were dramatically set forth in the spring of
1897 when an unusual candidate, a certain Doctor Metzger, ran
against Henri Aron for a seat on the Consistoire Central. Metzger
was a radical who based his campaign on the need to renovate
drastically the consistorial machinery. The members of the Consistoire, he charged, were 'excellent bureaucrats, almost all
decorated. Unfortunately, they are all chained to their desks when
we need men of action, and the least . . . man of the people who
had a little energy would be incontestably superior.'[1] Metzger
wanted to extend the consistorial franchise to all Jewish males,
including those too poor to afford a charitable contribution. 'I
want', he declared, 'to be a Jew of progress and of justice.' Specifically, he wanted to democratize the Consistoire and, in addition,
to introduce a number of reforms in ritual. But the voters wanted
no part of 'a Jew of progress and of justice', at least according to
Metzger's definition. When the election was held the results
proved, according to Le Matin, 'the profound attachment of the
Jewish electors to their traditions . . .'. Henri Aron received 1,309
votes, and Doctor Metzger 39. According to one observer, the
turn-out for such an election had never been higher.[2]

    The laws of Napoleon and their subsequent modification also
provided regulations for rabbis.[3] The Grand Rabbi of France was
chosen by a body composed of the Consistoire Central and two
delegates from each departmental consistoire. Other Grand Rabbis,
ranking rabbis of the departmental consistoires, were appointed by
the Consistoire Central according to a rather complex procedure
which need not detain us here. The statutes further declared that
there would be academic requirements for the title 'grand rabbin'
or the lower title of 'rabbin communal'. These requirements were
to be determined by the Séminaire Israélite, the State-supported
seminary in Paris which was administered by the Consistoire de

---

[1] 'Les réformes du culte israélite', La Liberté, 23 Mar. 1897.
[2] Le Matin, 29 Mar. 1897; L'Univers, 31 Mar. 1897.
[3] See p. 69, n. 2 above.

Paris and which was under the ultimate authority of the Consistoire Central. Furthermore, the statutes regulated the authority of rabbis, the position of *ministres officiants* who substituted for rabbis in very small communities, and established modes of discipline for all of these where conflicts arose. Little, in Napoleon's scheme of things, was to be left to the imagination. Salaries were also fixed by statute—the law of 8 February 1831. The Grand Rabbi of France received 12,000 francs a year, the Grand Rabbi of Paris 5,000, other Grand Rabbis 4,000, the *rabbins communaux* between 2,500 and 1,750, and the *ministres officiants* between 2,000 and 600.[1] Practically speaking these salaries, especially in the case of the *rabbins communaux*, were much too low to support their recipients. Communities tended to supplement the incomes of their rabbis by direct donations or by small fees given at weddings or funerals.[2]

As the religious leaders of the Jewish community the rabbis helped to draw that community together, to articulate some of its feelings and aspirations. With the gradual assimilation and with the spread of religious indifference which we have noticed, the role of the rabbi changed; prayer and ritual declined in importance, and with them the function of the rabbi as the learned teacher and judge in matters of conduct. Increasingly rabbis were evaluated and chosen on the basis of oratorical powers. Sermons had become steadily more important in religious services as traditional forms of worship fell into disuse; by the 1890s sermons were delivered nearly every Saturday in the synagogues, and were designed not as the Talmudic exercise they had once been, but rather as 'a series of admonitions' of a general moral character.[3] There were serious implications here for the relationship between the rabbi and his congregation. The Grand Rabbi Simon Debré put it this way: 'At present [1891] it is the duty of the orator above everything not to alienate the kindly disposition of his

[1] There were in France, in 1894, ten *grands rabbins*, two professors at the seminary with that rank, and twenty-six *rabbins communaux*. See Hepp, op. cit.; L. W., 'Le rabbinat français', *U.I.*, 16 Jan. 1894, pp. 266–7.

[2] R. T., 'Les fonctionnaires religieux', *U.I.*, 7 Jan. 1898, pp. 489–92.

[3] Debré, op. cit., p. 399.

hearers, to gain their sympathy, and, lastly, to attract them to the service and make them fond of the synagogue. No more indignant tirades against the caprices of our age, no more barren discussions on questions of dogma or theology—the dominant note is soft and paternal.'[1] With a 'dominant note' such as this rabbis were often reduced to the position of simple moralizers. Rabbis did not dare, it was charged, attack the pillars of the Jewish community, especially those who contributed to its support and to the support of the rabbinate.[2]

Others felt that rabbis had abandoned their functions as teachers and guides to become salaried bureaucrats—*fonctionnaires* who efficiently performed the necessary religious duties, but who viewed their role narrowly and who could not speak out on the most vital and controversial issues facing Judaism.[3] Yet at the same time the emphasis upon public speaking put the rabbi in a position where he was recognized by Jews and by the community at large as a spokesman and leader. Rabbis were interviewed by the press on public questions affecting the Jewish community and, however insipid or circumscribed their statements, they were to some extent a public focus for that community, more generally accepted as leaders, for example, than the far less conspicuous gentlemen who happened to be members of the *consistoires*.

The rabbinate thus changed significantly in character during the nineteenth century, and in the course of this change suffered from other serious problems. French rabbis during the first quarter of the century came mostly from Alsace—they were German- or Yiddish-speaking, unfamiliar with French life and somewhat isolated from the French society in which they lived.[4] With the foundation of the rabbinical seminary at Metz in 1829, with the immigration of Jews into France, and with the moving of the seminary to Paris in 1859, matters began to change. In time the centralization of rabbinical training in the seminary, along with the introduction of French studies into the curriculum, brought

[1] Debré, loc. cit.   [2] *La Vraie Parole*, 7 June 1893.
[3] H. Prague, 'Impressions du culte', *A.I.*, 24 Aug. 1899, pp. 269–70; cf. 'Les rabbins et les administrations israélites', *A.I.*, 21 Feb. 1889, pp. 58–9.
[4] Léon Kahn, *Les Juifs de Paris depuis le VIe siècle* (Paris, 1889), pp. 126–7.

rabbis closer to French life and culture. The seminary's purpose was seen as both religious *and* patriotic; its graduates were no longer the extremely learned and studious scholar-teachers of the ghetto days, but rather modern Jews turned out as, among other things, educated representatives of French civilization. However, the seminary was continually short of funds and often hard pressed to fulfil this new role.[1] More importantly, it was increasingly difficult to recruit candidates for the rabbinate; study was long and difficult and the opportunities outside Paris few and bleak. Alsace and Lorraine had provided by far the largest contingent of students before 1872. After the closing of the border for such travel in that year, the seminary, which always had difficulty in attracting French-born students, looked to foreigners to fill its classes. A scholarship programme to attract French students launched in 1900 by Zadoc Kahn did not succeed, and there was considerable alarm at the prospect of losing that essentially French character of the rabbinate, so recently secured.[2]

As Grand Rabbi of France from 1889 until his death in 1905, Zadoc Kahn dominated the French rabbinate as the Rothschild family dominated the activity of the *consistoires* and other related organizations. Just as the Rothschild influence was present in all important administrative activities of the Jewish community, so was the influence of Zadoc Kahn. His authority, however, flowed not from philanthropic or organizational skills, but rather from his moral force, from his extraordinary energy, and from his devotion to the Jewish community as a whole, in all of its aspects, both material and religious. Anti-Semites frequently referred to Zadoc Kahn as the 'Pope of the Jews'; this was a recognition, to some extent, of his unusual influence.[3] In Salomon Reinach's description, he was 'the great chaplain of Judaism', the leader whose tact and diplomacy extended to the extremes which existed within a much divided community.[4]

---

[1] Bauer, *École rabbinique de France*, pp. 162–3, 182.
[2] Ibid., pp. 169–70. Cf. letter to *A.I.*, 31 Aug. 1888, p. 272; Tchernoff, op. cit., vol. iii, *Affaire Dreyfus*, p. 17; Aubery, op. cit., p. 55.
[3] Abbé L. Vial, *La Trahison du Grand Rabbin de France* (Paris, 1904), p. 28.
[4] 'Conférence de M. Salomon Reinach', *Bulletin de l'Association amicale des anciens élèves des Écoles Halphen et Lucien de Hirsch*, vol. i, no. 2, Apr. 1908.

Zadoc Kahn was born in the small Alsatian town of Mommen-
heim in 1839.[1] He attended the rabbinical seminary during the
years 1856 to 1862, and only six years after graduation was elected
Grand Rabbi of Paris. During his tenure his prestige grew—at a
time when the sermon was becoming increasingly important,
Zadoc Kahn stood out particularly for his oratorical powers and for
his ability to express with force the feelings of the community.
In 1886 his friend and colleague Isidore Loeb paid him the following tribute: '. . . no other Jewish preacher of the present time . . .
has merited in the same degree to represent exactly and to reflect
the ideas, the sentiments, the sympathies, the joys, the grief, the
hope, the aspirations of the community of modern Jews.'[2]

Few activities within the Jewish community escaped Zadoc
Kahn's attention; he presided over meetings of a multitude of
charitable organizations, student groups, and other societies. During the 1880s he gradually took over the duties of Grand Rabbi of
France from the ailing Rabbi Isidor, and in 1889 he was formally
named to that post. In his position as Grand Rabbi of France Zadoc
Kahn attempted to unite the diverse interest groups and social
strata of the French Jewish community—the rich and poor,
Sephardim and Ashkenazim, conservatives and reformers, French
and eastern European Jews. He provided an element of co-ordina-
tion and cohesiveness within the community; he was a member
of the Consistoire Central, honorary president of the Alliance
Israélite Universelle from 1890, honorary president of a Jewish
men's club, the Union Scolaire, and of the Association of Jewish
Students from Russia, in addition to being an ex officio member of
most Jewish charities. He attended meetings regularly, reported
on various activities to the Consistoire, and served as an intermediary between these organizations.[3] In particular Zadoc Kahn
was the trustee of many private donations to different groups;
wealthy families entrusted him to dispense money where he felt

---

[1] For details of the life of Zadoc Kahn see the useful biography by Julien Weill,
Zadoc Kahn 1839–1905 (Paris, 1912).

[2] Isidore Loeb, review of Zadoc Kahn's *Sermons et allocutions, R.E.J.*, vol. xiii
(1886), p. 151.

[3] Weill, op. cit., pp. 245, 265–6.

PLATE II

a. Zadoc Kahn, Grand Rabbi of France
1889–1905

b. Baron Alphonse de Rothschild
1827–1905

c. Baron Gustave de Rothschild
1829–1911

it was needed. He retained the confidence of these philanthropists even when they were hostile or indifferent to Jewish religious practice. Often the Grand Rabbi of France became the personal emissary of Jewish donors, investigating and reporting on needy groups both within and without the Jewish community. He seems to have acted very closely with the Rothschild family in this capacity.[1] Such a role was obviously a difficult one to fill, yet criticism was apparently rare or non-existent, even among the dispossessed.[2] It is clear that Zadoc Kahn was more than the religious leader of French Jewry; he was a community leader whose activity drew together Jews who differed in almost every respect, Jews for whom the 'community of suffering' was only a legend and in whom the spark of religious solidarity was almost extinguished.

In 1888 the French journalist and historian Maxime Du Camp observed in his study of private charities in Paris the critical role which charity played in providing cohesion for a Jewish community divided by both class and interests. Jews of whatever background, of whatever Jewish consciousness, had sufficient memory of the time of persecutions to 'take pity on those who suffer'. Even French Jews, Du Camp claimed, in some sense remembered what they had suffered.[3] Jewish tradition, he contended, instilled a certain view of charity, a view which stimulated action to a degree not common in the surrounding community. The Hebrew word for charity, צרקה (tzedakah), was also the word for justice. Justice and charity were a part of the duty of every Jew; indeed, they were the same duty, the obligation imposed upon Jews to work for the reduction of inequality and the rectification of the iniquities which human will or blind fortune had visited upon mankind. A duty such as this was in the last analysis personal; it was a necessary element in the daily activity of the just man.[4]

---

[1] See A.I.U. (France VI, A 43).
[2] See Tchernoff, op. cit., vol. iii, Affaire Dreyfus, p. 77.
[3] Maxime Du Camp, Paris bienfaisant (Paris, 1888), p. 297.
[4] Ibid. Cf. 'La charité', U.I., 18 June 1897, pp. 407–8: 'La charité juive, la צרקה n'est, comme son nom l'indique, qu'une des formes de la justice, elle est la justice elle-même dans ce qu'elle a de plus élevé, car elle doit tendre surtout

Such, at least, was the theory. As we shall see, the Jewish community appeared to have carried out the traditional injunction and had, in fact, constructed a remarkable system of charitable organizations in Paris.

Yet one should not misunderstand the character of this system and see in it a form of socialism within the Jewish community. There was little stress here upon the Prophetic ideal of social justice. Zadoc Kahn made it clear that the practice of charity was not a thoroughgoing attempt to eradicate poverty or suffering. He considered as 'dangerous illusions' any ideas that it would be better to prevent the evil than to cure it; charity would always be necessary in human society, the rabbi felt, and it could not ultimately change either human nature or the griefs of humanity.[1] A book of prayers commonly used in the Jewish community included a 'prayer for the poor' which counselled resignation and self-help and soberly warned the poor against 'immoderate desires'.[2] Charity, then, was a tradition which drew upon benevolence as its primary motive force. What seems indisputable, however, is the extent to which this benevolence, commonly referred to as 'Jewish solidarity', flowed from all elements of the Jewish community. Charitable associations, particularly in Paris, were the meeting-places for Frenchmen who had nothing in common but their Jewishness. 'Without them', said Isidore Loeb referring to these societies, 'we would be as lost in the vast capital, isolated, dispersed, scattered like dust.' 'It is there that beats the heart of the Jewish community of Paris.'[3]

What were these charitable societies? The largest and most important was the Comité de Bienfaisance, a catch-all organization which, in addition to providing many services of its own, supported many other charitable institutions.[4] The Comité dispensed

à atténuer les inégalités du sort, à réparer les iniquités de l'aveugle fortune. Elle est naturellement austère, parce qu'elle suppose avant tout un effort personnel.' B.-M., 'A propos de la catastrophe du Bazar de la Charité', *U.I.*, 14 May 1897, p. 231.

[1] Zadoc Kahn, *Sermons et allocutions*, ii. 155–7.

[2] Lazare Wogue, *Le Guide du croyant israélite* (2nd edn., Paris, 1898), pp. 423–7.

[3] Isidore Loeb, introduction to Léon Kahn, *Les Sociétés de secours mutuels, philanthropiques et de prévoyance* (Paris, 1887), pp. 6–7.

[4] A list of the various organizations along with a brief description of their activities may be found in each issue of the *Annuaire* and in Debré, op. cit., pp. 427–34.

almost half a million francs annually in monthly distributions to the poor, providing food, clothing, and shelter to the indigent, and small loans to Jewish tradesmen. One of the institutions which the Comité helped to support through an annual subsidy was the Jewish hospital on the Rue Picpus, founded by Baron James de Rothschild in 1852. This hospital was for adults and children, had an out-patients' service, and included a home for the aged. The patients were for the most part poor, and medicines were free. A seaside branch was maintained for purposes of convalescence. There was a Jewish orphanage founded by the Rothschilds, a reform school for boys and one for girls, a society of ladies to visit the bedridden, and a society to give dowries to poor Jewish girls. Each year scholarships, prizes, and awards of several kinds were given to the poor from funds established by donors. Two trade schools were supported by the Jewish community. The first was the École de Travail on the Rue de Rosiers which had about 100 male students. The students lived on the premises and were taught a handicraft. The second was the Institution Bischoffsheim, where girls could learn a lady's profession along with sewing, dancing, singing, and English.

Committees of Jewish community leaders administered each of these organizations. We have noticed that almost all of these committees included a Rothschild and the Grand Rabbi of France, Zadoc Kahn. In addition there was usually the founder or most prominent donor of the particular institution if such existed, and several other laymen. During this period it was fashionable in Paris for ladies of the nobility or the upper middle class to take part in charitable activity, especially in the bazaars which raised money for various organizations.[1] The Jewish community was no exception. Because of the small size of that community, however, there was no hierarchy of charities which distinguished the fashionable from the unfashionable. Committees, in fact, contained a social cross-section of the Jewish community, though perhaps weighted somewhat at the highest social levels. Thus, for example, the Comité des Dames Inspectrices des Écoles for 1894–5, whose

[1] Louis Sapin, 'L'incendie de la charité', in Gilbert Guilleminault (ed.), *Le Roman vrai de la IIIᵉ République: prélude à la Belle Époque* (Paris, 1956), p. 277.

president was the Baroness Gustave de Rothschild, had among
its members four other baronesses (Günzberg, Koenigswarter,
Léonino, and another Rothschild), along with Madame Jules
Ephrussi, wife of the wealthy banker, Madame Zadoc Kahn, and
a number of ladies of modest circumstance.[1] Lip-service, at least,
was paid to the idea of equality. Yet at the same time, the degree
to which Jews participated in these organizations was not high,
according to contemporary writers. One estimate was that only
900 out of a total Jewish population in Paris of 50,000 contributed to the Comité de Bienfaisance in 1898. As a result, it
was reported, the Comité was frequently in financial difficulties.[2]
According to Isidore Loeb all of the works of the community were
supported by only about 2,500 Jews.[3] Moreover, with the influx
of eastern European immigrants and with the migration of Jews
to the capital, the Jewish indigent population was rising rapidly,
more quickly than the rest of the Jewish population and its level
of donations. In addition, the resources of the Jewish community
diminished during this period. Though the population continued
to rise, a number of very large fortunes passed by way of mixed
marriages into the hands of non-Jews.[4] The rumour was that the
Rothschilds took up the slack, and by 1894, it was said, they were
owed about 300,000 francs by the Consistoire.[5]

Another class of Jewish organizations was at least partly self-
supporting. The Jewish community had a scholarly society, the
Société des Études Juives (founded with the help of the Rothschilds), two burial societies, a Jewish men's club, the Union
Scolaire, an association of Jewish students from Russia, thirty-three
mutual aid societies of various sorts for men and eleven for
women. The Consistoire helped to finance a Jewish weekly

[1] *Annuaire 5655* (1894–5), p. 74.
[2] Ben Mosché, 'La charité publique israélite à Paris', *A.I.*, 11 Aug. 1898,
pp. 261–2.
[3] Isidore Loeb, 'La vérité sur la richesse des Juifs', *La Vraie Parole*, 10 Oct.
1894.
[4] Salomon Reinach, op. cit.; H. Prague, 'Des devoirs de la charité juive', *A.I.*,
19 Apr. 1894, pp. 121–2; R. T., 'Les revenus des synagogues', *U.I.*, 2 July 1897,
p. 453.
[5] Singer, 'M. Zadoc Kahn', *La Vraie Parole*, 27 Oct. 1894.

periodical, the *Univers israélite*, and probably aided another weekly, the *Archives israélites*.[1]

By far the best known of all of the philanthropic organizations remained somewhat apart from the other activities of the Jewish community. This was the Alliance Israélite Universelle, a body which had offices in Germany and in Austria but which was founded, directed, and largely financed in Paris.[2] The Alliance was devoted to the betterment of the moral and material condition of Jews outside France, particularly in the Levant; its main means to this end was education—the founding and maintenance of schools for Jewish children in countries where Jews were still a persecuted and underprivileged minority. The Alliance was founded in 1860 by a number of young middle-class Jews, inspired, as one of them later put it, by the spirit of the French revolution of 1848. Their purpose, according to one founder, was 'the union of all free Jews for the emancipation of Jews all over the world'.[3] Their ideals were the sometimes paradoxical ideals of the liberal opposition to Napoleon III: both patriotic and internationalist, both humanitarian and suspicious of humanitarianism dispensed by the machinery of an authoritarian state. The outstanding representative of this tradition was Adolphe Crémieux, the associate of Gambetta and the man most responsible for the emancipation of the Jews of Algeria. Within the Alliance there was a great consciousness of a mission which was peculiarly French. 'This programme [of the Alliance]', said Zadoc Kahn in 1898, '. . . consisted and still consists in carrying abroad what is most noble, most equitable, most liberal, most human in the genius of our country....'[4]

---

[1] See A.C.P., 1 C⁸ sessions 15 and 16 Dec. 1898; A.C.P., sér. B 62, letter L. Bloch to the Consistoire, 1 Dec. 1897. Bloch mentions that the *U.I.* had 691 subscriptions in 1896-7.

[2] On the Alliance see André Chouraqui, *Cent ans d'histoire: l'Alliance Israélite Universelle et la renaissance juive contemporaine 1860-1960* (Paris, 1965); S. Posener, *Adolphe Crémieux: a Biography*, tr. Eugene Golob (Philadelphia, 1940).

[3] Narcisse Leven, 'Un souvenir de la vie d'Eugène Manuel', *Bulletin de l'Alliance Israélite Universelle*, 1901, pp. 19-20. Cf. Zosa Szajkowski, 'Conflicts in the Alliance Israélite Universelle and the Founding of the Anglo-Jewish Association, the Vienna Allianz and the Hilfsverein', *J.S.S.*, vol. ix, Jan.-Apr. 1957, pp. 29-50.

[4] *Discours prononcés aux obsèques de M. Salomon Goldschmidt, président de l'Alliance Israélite* (Paris, 1898), p. 7.

As for the oppressed Jews, he said, 'their eyes turn towards Paris, attracted as if by a ray of light and hope'.[1] More will be said of the Alliance below. For the moment it suffices to mention that it attracted, as did all Jewish philanthropic organizations, Jews of the most varied social backgrounds. Among its leaders, members of its Comité Central, were noblemen like the Count Camondo or the Baron de Hirsch, free-thinkers like Sylvain Lévi, politicians like Joseph Reinach, and academics of stature like Michel Bréal, Adolphe Franck, and Jules Oppert. The Alliance was, as Zadoc Kahn had seen, one of the ties within the Jewish community, but it was at the same time a tie which bound that community even more closely to French society and to the universalistic ideals of republican France.

In this chapter and the one which precedes we have been discussing the ties which operated within the French Jewish community. In part, no doubt, Jews who felt the existence of ties with their fellow Jews were simply reflecting the view generally held in French society that the Jews were a people, united and distinct. As we have noted, the feeling that the Jews had some unity and had some common basis for action and experience found inarticulate expression through the vocabulary of race. Another force for Jewish unity, one which had held the Jews together in the past, was the pressure of anti-Semitism. Yet hostility towards the Jews, as we observed in Chapter III, could not bind a socially differentiated community such as existed in France. Still, sentiments of Jewish community persisted. Although religious ties were in decline, and although a distinct legal tie no longer existed, a 'Jewish solidarity' remained to aid those who were in need. Practically, this was expressed through the agency of Jewish organizations, largely charitable, which existed to allow some Jews to help other Jews.

The existence of these charitable organizations, the existence of the governmental apparatus of the *consistoires*, the rabbinate, and, over all, the ubiquitous Zadoc Kahn and the Rothschild family, seem to have enabled the Jews to maintain an identifiable, though

[1] Zadoc Kahn, *Sermons et allocutions*, ii. 208.

weakened, Jewish community. It is true that active participation, either in the *consistoires*, in religious services, or even in charitable activity, was not particularly high, but we may wonder how high such participation was anywhere in French society.This kind of information, unfortunately, is not readily available to the historian. On the whole it seems that Jewish involvement was sufficient to maintain this framework of common activity, to keep alive the idea of a Jewish community, and to provide the necessary focus for psychological identification. Perhaps it is true that 'if there had not been, since 1880, the successive waves of immigrants, the history of French Judaism would probably be concluded today'.[1] Perhaps philanthropy and vague feelings are supports too weak for a modern community—certainly they are difficult to extract and define historically. Nevertheless, it is apparent that at the end of the nineteenth century Jews in France were not so closely identified with French society that they had broken entirely with an older pattern of identification. This pattern persisted, though in a weakened form; it was a reality, though sometimes ignored; it was a part of life for French Jews, though its importance varied greatly among individuals.

[1] Rabi (pseud.), *Anatomie du judaïsme français* (Paris, 1962), p. 20.

PART TWO · POLITICS AND ASSIMILATION BEFORE THE AFFAIR

THROUGHOUT western Europe the years before the end of the nineteenth century saw the formation of important new political movements. Revolutionary socialism, aggressive nationalism, and imperialism became the objects of political organization, and frequently challenged existing liberal institutions. New political parties, new political passions were floated upon a tide of mass participation. Jews, however, stood apart from much of this. Having been but recently and somewhat incompletely introduced into the life of the nations in which they lived, most of them still hungered for security. Jews resisted radical change, and viewed these menacing new developments with suspicion. They did so not only out of allegiance to the liberal forms of government which had guaranteed their emancipation; they did so also because they were threatened, at this time, in an immediate way. For along with other political changes, the end of the nineteenth century saw the formation of anti-Semitism as an organized political force.

Yet French Jews faced this time of upheaval with a degree of confidence not evident elsewhere among the Jews of Europe. They aligned themselves with the traditions of the French Revolution, articulated a general political perspective which glorified their association with the Third Republic, and expected that they would be safe. Their political theory and their political strategy was that of assimilation. Their approach to a world of change was to accentuate their identification with France, and to prove by their patriotism that they were worthy of respect.

CHAPTER V

THE POLITICAL THEORY OF
ASSIMILATION

POLITICAL theorists during the 1880s and 1890s put a great deal of
emphasis on what Gustave Le Bon referred to as the 'mental constitution' to be found in each people, a fixed set of characteristics
which changed but little over time and space.[1] Academics and
politicians spoke unblushingly of 'the French spirit' or 'the Jewish
soul'. Scientific research, moreover, was generally considered not
to be breaking down such concepts, but to be strengthening them,
making characteristics more clear and identifiable, and providing
increasing evidence for the differentiation of peoples.

Certainly in France men were conscious of a formidable culture
which stood out as distinctively French, unique among the peoples
of the earth. One joined such a culture by assimilating; and after
having done so one was French. There was little room within this
culture for serious differences or for real diversity. 'In France',
wrote the republican politician Yves Guyot, 'we confuse assimilation and uniformity. We are still with the old Platonic idea of
universals. We want to model everyone in our own image, as if it
had attained an absolute perfection and as if all Frenchmen were
alike.'[2] This view of a uniform and permanent French civilization
drew upon certain airy sociological generalizations of the Enlightenment, particularly of Montesquieu, which had been shaped
and given historical expression in the experience of the French
Revolution. The Revolution, it was said, swept away those intermediary bodies, the remnants of feudalism which stood between
the individual Frenchman and the nation and which had been the

[1] Gustave Le Bon, *Les Lois psychologiques de l'évolution des peuples* (Paris, 1894),
pp. 5–6.
[2] Yves Guyot, *Lettres sur la politique coloniale*, quoted in Raymond F. Betts,
Assimilation and Association in French Colonial Theory 1890–1914 (New York, 1961),
p. 8.

guarantors of inequality. In the new France each man was a citizen, free and equal; each was therefore entitled to a share in the national patrimony. The French spirit, or French culture, it was held (at least by republicans), was the essence of this patrimony. It is important to stress that what was involved in this great historical transformation was the universal *sharing* of a national inheritance rather than the encouragement of the free and undirected development of individuals. In France, as a result, the idea of freedom was almost invariably linked to a sense of belonging to the nation, of being a citizen; the possession of citizenship, as everyone recognized, was the true mark of emancipation.

For Jews in France this set of ideas had particular significance. Not only had the Revolution made them citizens, it also provided them with the first opportunity to share fully in that French national culture which was so much esteemed. Citizenship was the sign of emancipation, the guarantee that the Jew was free. Citizenship meant that the Jews no longer formed a rigidly separated group in society and that they were as entitled as anyone to refer to the national culture as their own. Emancipation was thus from the start linked with assimilation; the Jews were freed and, as a part of their freedom, were in some sense obliged to become French. Jewishness might be preserved, but only in a sphere which did not affect the Jew's relationship with the nation. The matter went further than the mere assumption of French culture (acculturation), or even extensive social interaction with other Frenchmen; it affected the character of a man's being. In the words of one assimilated Jew: 'Let there be neither Jews nor Christians, except at the hour of prayer for those who pray! That is what France proclaimed on 26 August 1789, by the Declaration of the Rights of Man. From that day on France recognized only citizens.'[1]

Jews considered themselves singularly qualified to assimilate into French society. According to the editor of the *Univers israélite* the Jews had always in their long history shown a special 'aptitude

---

[1] Ernest Crémieu-Foa, *La Campagne antisémitique: les duels, les responsables: mémoire avec pièces justificatives* (Paris, 1892), p. 12. Cf. Robert Misrahi, *La Condition réflexive de l'homme juif* (Paris, 1963), pp. 29–31.

for imitation' which was stronger than in other peoples.[1] French Jews, it was sometimes said, were in an even more favourable position in this respect than other Jews and could therefore set an example of assimilation for the rest of Europe.[2] The process of becoming French, of securing equality with other Frenchmen, of what Isidore Cahen called 'social fusion', was accepted enthusiastically in Jewish circles, as we shall see.[3] Even before the growth of the anti-Semitic movement, Jews developed a theory of 'Franco-Judaism' which was meant to adapt them fully to French society. By the time of the Dreyfus Affair a generation of historians and social thinkers had prepared the intellectual basis for this fusion, and a series of religious and social agencies had secured its dissemination.

During the nineteenth century historians followed the thinking of their contemporaries and considered the past most frequently in national terms. The Jews, when they appeared in such works, were generally cast in the role of outsiders, aliens whose story was treated as somewhat peripheral to the matter in hand.[4] Jewish historians attempted in the course of that century to rectify the damage thus done to the Jewish past; for the first time histories of the Jews in post-biblical times written by Jews began to appear. The most famous of these scholars was the German historian Heinrich Graetz, whose eleven-volume *Geschichte der Juden* began to appear in 1853. A French translation of this monumental work, considerably abridged, was published between 1882 and 1897. While in France nothing of comparable stature was written, a number of shorter, more popular histories appeared, were widely read, and provided the basis for thought about the Jewish situation in the modern world. These brief historical surveys offered an excellent opportunity for various writers to editorialize on the

---

[1] L. Wogue, 'Fleurs et couronnes', *U.I.*, 16 Mar. 1893, p. 387.

[2] Alfred Berl, 'Le mouvement sioniste et l'antisémitisme', *La Grande Revue*, 1 July 1899, p. 19.

[3] Isidore Cahen, 'Le cinquantenaire des Archives israélites', in *La Gerbe: études, souvenirs, lettres, pensées* (Paris, 1890), p. 9.

[4] See Gavin I. Langmuir, 'Majority History and Post-biblical Jews', *Journal of the History of Ideas*, vol. xxxvii, no. 3, July–Sept. 1966, p. 363.

condition of the Jews in France. From them we are able to discern a coherent theory about the Jewish experience, particularly as concerned with the question of Jewish emancipation.

The earliest of these French histories of the Jews in modern times, published in 1828 by Léon Halévy, set the tone for subsequent works. Halévy hoped that his book would be useful: 'It will certainly be so in so far as I will have proved to the fanatic Christians (if there still remain any) or to the unenlightened Christians (which is more common) that the Jews are not only men, but useful, active men, with a distinguished character [*organisation*], worthy of liberty, and who have done much for it; and to the Jews, that if time grants them new rights, it also imposes upon them new duties.'[1] This double message was an appropriate one for Halévy to deliver; as a Saint-Simonian he admired 'useful, active men', and as a young Jew, born a Frenchman and the son of an immigrant, he felt a natural identification with the country which appeared, at the time, in the vanguard of European civilization.[2] Halévy's father, Élie, had come to Paris from the German town of Würzburg at the end of the eighteenth century, bringing with him a coolness towards traditional Judaism (though he eventually became the cantor of the principal Jewish synagogue in Paris) and an enthusiasm for the France which had emancipated the Jews—'the most beautiful nation, splendour of creation', as he once put it.[3] From this background Léon drew most strongly upon his father's assimilationist inclinations. As a member of the first generation of emancipated Jewish intellectuals, Léon achieved early recognition in the intellectual milieu of the last years of the Restoration. For many young men of the time the intellectual atmosphere was dominated by the thought of the Comte de Saint-Simon. With a number of other Jewish followers of that strangely seductive social theorist, Halévy expressed the conviction that religious orthodoxy was a hindrance to progress and

[1] Léon Halévy, *Résumé de l'histoire des juifs modernes* (Paris, 1828), p. vii.
[2] See Moshé Katan, 'La famille Halévy', *Évidences*, Mar. 1955, p. 10. Léon was the grandfather of the critic and historian Daniel Halévy.
[3] Alain Silvera, *Daniel Halévy and his Times: a Gentleman-Commoner in the Third Republic* (Ithaca, New York, 1966), pp. 1–2.

simply a nostalgic relic of a past that was long since dead. This was a particularly relevant contention in 1828, a time of clerical reaction and of rising liberal opposition to Catholic control of government. With respect to his own people Halévy took great pains to demonstrate that the Jews had indeed been worthy of emancipation at the time of the Revolution.[1] Yet he also felt that Jews had still to make further progress. While he admitted that 'the Jews of France had already done much for their complete regeneration', he considered that much work remained to be done in order to bring them fully into the orbit of modernity. 'Frenchmen by country and by institutions, it is necessary that all [French Jews] become so by customs and language. It is necessary, in a word, that for them the name of Jew become accessory, and the name of Frenchman principal.' One way of accomplishing this end, according to Halévy, was to reform the Jewish religion which was 'too Asiatic for European nations'. The most important general objective, however, was 'the complete and definite fusion of those of the sect of Moses with other Frenchmen'.[2] Clearly, the aim was not only the assumption of French culture, but a more complete and thorough association with the nation.

These propositions became common currency within the Jewish community, and worked their way into a number of histories which were published subsequently. Enthusiastic generalizations about Jewish history seemed to flow easily whenever one came to a discussion of the Jewish situation in France. These tended in every case to illustrate the momentous importance of the French experience in Jewish history as a whole. Thus L.-M. Lambert, the Grand Rabbi of Metz, waxed eloquent over the decision of the French government in 1830 to support Jewish rabbis financially. It was, he said, 'the greatest act of justice that the Hebrews had obtained since the destruction of the Second Temple'.[3]

The focus of the most sweeping historical statements was usually the French Revolution and the emancipation of the Jews. The Revolution of 1789, wrote Isidore Cahen, was 'our second law of

---

[1] Halévy, op. cit., pp. 318–25.   [2] Ibid., pp. 325–6.

[3] L.-M. Lambert, *Précis de l'histoire des Hébreux depuis le patriarche Abraham jusqu'en 1840* (Metz, 1840), p. 416.

Sinai'.[1] According to the historian Maurice Bloch, 'the time of
the Messiah had come with the French Revolution. The time of the
Messiah had come with that new society which substituted for the
old Trinity of the Church that other Trinity whose names can be
read on all the walls: "Liberty! Equality! Fraternity!" '[2] Even the
turgid and pedantic work of Moïse Schwab seemed to reflect some
of this enthusiasm for the process of emancipation: '. . . everywhere
that a little air and liberty has been conceded to it, this superior
and indomitable race [the Jews] has nobly picked up its head and
has paid the debt of hospitality by contributing to the grandeur
of the adopted fatherland by its work in the sciences, letters, and
arts.'[3]

On the hundredth anniversary of the Revolution, in the spring
of 1889, special commemorative services were held in synagogues
throughout France. The sermons delivered on this occasion, subsequently collected and published by the Jewish community, were
a popular expression of these conceptions of the importance of the
French Revolution in Jewish history. Rabbi Kahn of Nîmes, for
example, referred to the Revolution as 'our flight from Egypt . . .,
our modern Passover'.[4] In the judgement of Rabbi Herrmann of
Reims, France 'was designated by Him who directs the destinies of
humanity to work for the emancipation of all the oppressed, to
spread throughout the world the great and beautiful ideas of justice, equality, and fraternity which had formerly been the exclusive patrimony of Israel'.[5] The conclusion to be drawn from such
statements was clear. France had played a very special role in
Jewish history as the 'apostle-nation', the nation which had carried
out the will of God and had performed for the Jews the inestimable
service of liberation.[6] In this way Jewish leaders assigned to France
a semi-religious position in the history of the Jews. Jews in France

[1] I. Cahen, 'Les décrets et les israélites', A.I., 4 Nov. 1880, p. 363.
[2] Maurice Bloch, 'La société juive en France depuis la Révolution', R.E.J.,
vol. xlviii, 1904, p. 20.
[3] Moïse Schwab, Histoire des israélites depuis l'édification du Second Temple jusqu'à
nos jours (2nd edn., Paris, 1895), p. 7.
[4] Benjamin Mossé (ed.), La Révolution française et le rabbinat français (Paris, 1890),
p. 100.
[5] Ibid., p. 94.   [6] Ibid., p. 18.

were told that they owed a historical debt to their country, a debt which was in turn invested with religious significance, which placed a heavy claim upon their loyalties, and even upon their normal, everyday activity. With this in mind, the rabbi of Avignon advised his congregation:

> Let us always strive to reach the first rank of honest and loyal workers in all careers open to our activity. . . . Let us offer an example of all civic and social virtues. Let us never cease to be irreproachable citizens. Let us, in a word, be worthy children of France.[1]

Notably absent from these conceptions of modern Jewish history was any reference to a distinctive 'Jewish soul' or a 'Jewish spirit' as an important historical force. Indeed, the common view of modern Jewish history was that it was essentially passive; the Jewish fate was largely determined by the environment in which Jews lived rather than by their own creative force. Environmental theories of history had emerged from the teachings of Enlightenment *philosophes*; these theorists held that individuals accomplished little in the development of societies, but rather that the physical, social, or political conditions under which men lived were frequently decisive. Such theories proved particularly applicable to the Jewish experience. In his well-known *Histoire des Israélites* Théodore Reinach cited the familiar expression which summed up this perspective: 'Each country has the Jews that it deserves.'[2] The point here was that such negative qualities as Jews were said to possess were in fact negative, but were at the same time the direct result of outside oppression:

> Hatred, persecution, legal restrictions have everywhere engendered in the Jews physical and moral decadence, all of the vices of oppressed and deprived races; tolerance and equality of rights have promptly

---

[1] Mossé (ed.), op. cit. p. 194. Cf. Zadoc Kahn's sermon of 19 Sept. 1876: '. . . la patrie a d'immenses droits sur nous, et jamais nous ne pouvons nous croire quittes envers elle. Il faut, autant qu'il dépend de nous et en tout temps, concourir à sa prospérité, à sa grandeur, à la sécurité de son existence; il faut savoir lui sacrifier notre repos, nos biens, notre vie même, quand l'intérêt l'exige.' Zadoc Kahn, *Sermons et allocutions* (2nd end., Paris, 1903), ii. 28.

[2] Théodore Reinach, *Histoire des israélites depuis la ruine de leur indépendance nationale jusqu'à nos jours* (5th edn., Paris, 1914), p. 315.

remade them into men, worthy to take a place among the best and most useful citizens.[1]

One might gather that, as passive victims of persecution, as a people thus essentially stripped of authority over their own destiny, the Jews might be excused for such faults as the historian discovered. Yet Reinach was inclined to be hard on the Jews for their 'decadence'. In the first edition of his history, published in 1884, speaking of the period 1500–1750, we find the following passage:

... in general the Church attained its goal: as [in] a house whose windows to the outside are closed, Israel was withering away for want of light and air; *it came to deserve the contempt under which it fell [il mérite après coup le mépris sous lequel il succombe]*.[2]

The offending judgement was mildly criticized at the time and was changed in subsequent editions.[3] But the slip, if such it was, reflects the inclination, even among Jews, to view Jewish history as directed from the outside on the one hand, and at the same time to blame the Jews for following certain historical paths.

The assimilation of the Jews flowed naturally from emancipation according to this point of view. France had made citizens of the Jews; implicitly, in Reinach's work, the Jew was obliged to accept a new definition of himself, a definition supplied by the traditions of the Enlightenment and 1789. Such was the law of

[1] Ibid., p. 371. Cf. the similar judgement about Jewish 'faults' by Camille Dreyfus: 'La race? Elle a ses défauts sans doute, mais à qui la responsabilité doit-elle en remonter, sinon à ceux qui pendant des siècles et des siècles ont courbé cette race sous le joug et sous l'ignominie?' 'Pour les juifs!', *La Nation*, 21 Jan. 1890.

[2] Théodore Reinach, *Histoire des Israélites depuis l'époque de leur dispersion jusqu'à nos jours* (Paris, 1884), p. xiii (my italics). Cf. a similar disposition to blame Jews for a condition imposed upon them in a study of anti-Semitism by Rabbi Élie-Aristide Astruc. Speaking of the ostentation and imprudence of wealthy Spanish and Portuguese Jews before their expulsion in 1492 he says: 'C'est donc incontestable: les juifs sont dans leur tort. Ils n'auraient dû oublier qu'ils étaient minorité dissidente; pour mettre toutes les chances de leur côté, ils auraient dû ne commettre aucune faute et, dans cet âge d'or, avoir toutes les vertus.' *Origines et causes historiques de l'antisémitisme* (Versailles, 1884), pp. 48–9.

[3] H. Prague, 'Critique littéraire', *A.I.*, 19 Feb. 1885, p. 60. In subsequent editions the passage became: '... faute d'air et de lumière; la période de renaissance de l'Europe chrétienne coïncide ainsi avec celle de la plus grande dépression d'Israël.' Reinach, *Histoire* (1901 edn.), p. xii.

progress. Once society ceased to persecute, once the Revolution
and the legislation of Napoleon had cleared the way for Jewish
entry into the body of the nation, all reason for separation was
lost:

> . . . the Jews, since they have ceased to be treated as pariahs, must
> identify themselves, in heart and in fact, with the nations which have
> accepted them, renounce the practices, the aspirations, the peculiarities
> of costume or language which tended to isolate them from their fellow
> citizens, in a word cease to be a dispersed nation, and henceforth be con-
> sidered only a religious denomination.[1]

This programme of emancipation, said Reinach, was 'so visibly
conforming with justice, with the march of history and the
superior laws of civilization, that all civilized countries have more
or less accepted it in theory . . .'.[2] It remained for Jews to carry out
their obligations, to follow the example of the Jews of France. For
Reinach, then, the course of Jewish history was fundamentally
tied to the history of human progress, specifically progress as interpreted by modern France. What the Jews thought or did was
always considered in this light, and judged from this viewpoint.

Concrete evidence for this perspective came from the research
of Léon Kahn, an administrative officer of the Consistoire de Paris
who published a number of historical studies of Parisian Jewry
during the 1890s. Kahn's approach was scholarly and detailed; his
chief contribution was a study of the Jews of Paris before and during the French Revolution which drew heavily upon police records
deposited in the Bibliothèque de l'Arsenal. His work was relatively widely read; sections of his histories appeared in the *Archives
israélites* and the *Revue des études juives*. But his themes were familiar. Before emancipation the Jews lived in the abject servility of
the ghetto, where a man 'had no sooner stepped outside than he
felt contempt and aversion weighing heavily upon him; [where]
he walked along his way, head down, bent over . . .' in the traditional pose of self-abasement.[3] With this description Kahn asked
the essentially loaded question:

---

[1] Reinach, *Histoire*, p. 306.   [2] Ibid.
[3] Léon Kahn, *Les Juifs de Paris au XVIIIe siècle* (Paris, 1894), p. 136.

Who could be surprised if, thus abused, vilified, disgraced, unable to distinguish between evil and good after years of this miserable existence, the least energetic succumbed to the human temptation to live in sin [*de vivre dans le mal*]?[1]

Kahn tried to be sympathetic, but he felt that the best defençe of the Jews was not to romanticize ghetto life, but to analyse accurately the consequences of emancipation for them. In the preface to his last work, *Les Juifs de Paris pendant la Révolution* (1898), he reflected upon the culmination of fifteen years of research on Parisian Jews. His work had taken him from the ghetto to emancipation:

After having described the miserable and humiliating life that they led over the centuries, to preside [now] over their entry into the intimate life of the country which up to that time had been completely barred to them, to see their soul ennobled, lifted up in an atmosphere of tolerance and liberty, to feel their hearts beat in the contact with other great hearts. . . . What a striking contrast! And what a seductive task![2]

Contrast came from observing the differences in the character of the Jews before and after the Revolution: before, there was humiliation and servility; after, there was almost a physical transformation—backs straightened, shoulders squared, eyes lifted.[3] The task was seductive because Kahn would have the pleasure of righting the wrong done to Jewish history, would expose the errors of those who had portrayed the Jews as ingrates or exploiters. The Jews, Kahn found, conducted themselves irreproachably during the Revolution, and in so doing, of course, showed that they could be model citizens: they did not 'render themselves guilty of excesses' during the more violent revolutionary episodes, yet, 'when

---

[1] Ibid., p. 137.

[2] Léon Kahn, *Les Juifs de Paris pendant la Révolution* (Paris, 1898), p. v.

[3] Ibid., pp. vi, 353–4. Cf. the similar observation of another writer: 'En sortant de la servitude, Israël s'est dépouillé des mœurs de l'esclave et a revêtu les vertus de l'homme libre. La transformation a été profonde; elle est frappante pour les esprits non-prévenus; il n'a pas besoin, pour la constater, de compulser les annales de l'histoire; il suffit de jeter les yeux sur les sociétés modernes et de comparer le juif libre de France au juif du pays où il vit dans l'oppression.' Joseph Hirsch, 'Le rôle du judaïsme en France', in *La Gerbe*, p. 39.

the fatherland was in danger they were to be seen "on the true field of honour and of military glory . . . shedding their blood in the legitimate defence of the frontiers"; and, finally, when calm was re-established, they were the first to get back to work, contributing by their labour to the wiping away of all traces of the bloody days, . . . seeking by the dignity of their lives to conquer the most persistent prejudices'.[1]

Like Reinach and like most who contemplated the Jewish experience in France, Kahn saw Jewish life in modern times as being largely determined by historical forces outside Jewish control. His concluding generalization about oppressed peoples in his work on the Jews during the Revolution was meant to be applied to the history of the Jews as a whole. The oppressed person, the Jew, he felt, was corrupted:

Oppression debases, liberty enriches his spirit. If stifled, his natural qualities of heart and mind become obliterated, the moral sense becomes dulled. There is room for nothing else in him but hypocrisy, cowardice, and vice. But comes the idea of liberty, of equality, of fraternity, [and] the atmosphere becomes clear, his spirit breathes purely once again [*tous ces miasmes entassés en lui disparaissent sous la pureté du souffle réparateur*].[2]

The work of these historians was the work of assimilation. Not only did their histories point the way to ending the idea of the dispersed nation, not only did they magnify beyond the point of distortion the significance of the Revolution of 1789, they also merged the very history of the Jews with the history of French civilization. 'Every Jew today having heart and memory', wrote Reinach, 'is a son of the France of 1791.'[3] 'The Jews', said another writer, 'are the living and permanent symbol of the principles of tolerance and liberty which the Revolution had spread throughout the world. . . .'[4] Even the Jewish past was no longer to belong to the Jews, was no longer to be kept separate. The significance of these works is that they provided another dimension to the

---

[1] Kahn, *Les Juifs de Paris pendant la Révolution*, p. 355; id., *Les Juifs à Paris depuis le VIe siècle* (Paris, 1889), p. 85.

[2] Kahn, *Les Juifs de Paris pendant la Révolution*, p. 356.

[3] Reinach, *Histoire*, p. 293.

[4] B.-M., 'Antisémitisme et cléricalisme', *U.I.*, 6 Nov. 1896, p. 196.

identification of the Jews with the country in which they lived. Their importance at the time was to assist French Jews in the formulation of a new theory of the assimilation of Judaism in the modern world.

Patriotism, the intoxicating pastime of the populations of the European powers, was the corner-stone of the new, emancipated Judaism. This was, of course, the most overt form of Jewish identification with the country of emancipation. It was a form of identification, moreover, which was particularly logical for western European Jews to adopt during the decades before the First World War, when patriotic feeling rose frequently to a fever pitch. Several Jewish writers argued that the Jews were inclined by nature to be patriotic; Jews had demonstrated this quality in the past and would, simply if given a chance, do so in modern times. The great example of Jewish patriotism, according to Hippolyte Prague, was the Maccabean revolt against the Roman Empire. Two thousand years of exclusion had not been able to eliminate this disposition:

The Jews have been, over long and dreary centuries, deprived of a fatherland; as soon as they found one in countries hospitable enough to permit them entry and to give them civil rights, they felt the blood of the Maccabees surging up in their veins; suddenly those patriotic traditions were renewed which made the Jewish soldiers in the French army in 1870 worthy descendants of Matthias the Asmonian; ready, like him, to defend dearly the native soil and the national colours.[1]

In 1898 Prague pointed to the Spanish-American War, where Jews fought on both sides, as glowing testimony to Jewish patriotism. Jews everywhere, he said, were ready to shed their blood for their fatherland, 'whatever the regime to which they are subject, be it the most Draconian . . .'.[2] This readiness to serve, it was assumed, was deserving of unrestricted praise. At the time Frenchmen took such a notion as axiomatic and few voices could be raised

[1] H. Prague, 'Le patriotisme juif à propos de Hanoucah', *A.I.*, 15 Dec. 1887, p. 396.
[2] H. Prague, 'Le patriotisme juif à propos de la guerre entre l'Amérique et l'Espagne', *A.I.*, 19 May 1898, p. 154.

against this kind of commitment. Jewish spokesmen followed their contemporaries in the virtual sanctification of national loyalties. Both religion and the fatherland, wrote a columnist in the *Archives israélites*, were 'sacred' for the Jews. 'For the one and the other, it is necessary to fight; for the one and the other, one must know how to die.'[1]

Jewish patriotism received sanction and encouragement from the highest Jewish religious officials, Zadoc Kahn, the Grand Rabbi of France, and J.-H. Dreyfuss, Grand Rabbi of Paris. The former told an interviewer from the Paris daily *Le National* in 1892 that the motto of the Consistoire Central, 'fatherland and religion', was the heartfelt slogan of French Jewry. 'All of the energy of their will, the reserves to their intelligence, the whole treasure of qualities created and strengthened by long suffering and which remained without use, are now devoted to the French fatherland with enthusiastic and ardent gratitude.'[2] This brassy rhetoric came easily from synagogue pulpits during the 1890s; it was nourished on the still sharp memories of the Franco-Prussian War, and did not differ from the patriotic pageantry which, at this time, was a common feature of public gatherings in France. Each year the society Souvenir français, an organization devoted to the memory of French soldiers killed in wartime, held a memorial service in the synagogue of the Rue de la Victoire. At such a service in 1898, with the synagogue bedecked with flags, the Grand Rabbi of Paris made an invocation to what was, in France, an important and openly avowed article of Jewish faith:

Holy and rich patriotism, may you be blessed! We salute with full enthusiasm your dazzling light [*ta clarté éblouissante*], for you have torn aside the veils and appear to us in all of your splendour.[3]

Apart from such direct expressions of loyalty and devotion, Jewish writers most frequently gave vent to their patriotism in

---

[1] S. Ackermann, 'Religion et patrie', *A.I.*, 8 Sept. 1898, p. 294. Zadoc Kahn declared in 1889 that patriotism was one of the capital virtues, 'qui remplissent toute l'existence et impriment une direction méthodique à notre conduite'. The other capital virtues were religion, charity, and family. Zadoc Kahn, *Sermons et allocutions*, iii. 184.

[2] Ch. F., 'Chez M. Zadoc Kahn', *Le National*, 22 Sept. 1892.

[3] *A.I.*, 1 Dec. 1898, p. 387. Cf. *U.I.*, 2 Dec. 1898, pp. 337-8.

discussions of anti-Semitism. With remarkable unanimity they agreed upon one point: anti-Semitism in France was a German import. Just as anti-Semitic leaders such as Maurras and Drumont continually associated the Jews with the German Empire, so the Jews were bent upon tracing the origins of the campaign against themselves to the traditional national enemy. Bismarck was seen as the chief villain of the piece, and the roots of French anti-Semitism were followed back to 1871, to the defeat at the hands of the Prussians.[1] From Germany 'the anti-Semitic virus' then spread across the face of Europe—to Russia, to Austria, and even to France.[2] Yet there was an important qualification to be made at this point. Interpretations tended to agree that in France anti-Semitism was an anomaly and did not fit into the life of the nation. This was only natural, it was said, for such a doctrine had no indigenous roots in the country of the Revolution and emancipation.[3] The sociologist Émile Durkheim, the son of an Alsatian rabbi, put this argument clearly to an interviewer in 1898. 'Our anti-Semitism', he said, speaking of France, 'is the consequence and the superficial symptom of a state of social malaise'; by contrast, the anti-Semitism which one found in Germany or in Russia was 'chronic' and 'traditional'.[4] The conclusion to be drawn was that anti-Semitism was unpatriotic, anti-French, and pro-German. Its triumph would mean the destruction of the French soul and her gifts to the world; the victory of anti-Semitism would be the victory of Germany.[5]

[1] E. Lambert, *Les Juifs, la société moderne et l'antisémitisme* (Paris, 1887), pp. 4–5; Daniel Lévy, 'La guerre de 1870–71 et le patriotisme', *A.I.*, 12 June 1890, pp. 187–8; H. Prague, 'Revue de l'année 5654–5655', *Annuaire 5656* (1895–6), pp. 21–2; id., 'Un spectacle consolant: les antisémites et les élections en Allemagne', *A.I.*, 23 June 1898, p. 193; id., 'M. de Bismarck et les juifs', *A.I.*, 4 Aug. 1898, p. 252.

[2] H. Prague, 'La guerre de 1870: ses conséquences morales et sociales', *A.I.*, 12 Sept. 1895, p. 290.

[3] I. Levaillant, 'La genèse de l'antisémitisme sous la Troisième République', *Actes* (1907), *R.E.J.*, vol. liii (1907), p. lxxxiv; Alfred Berl, 'L'éclipse des idées libérales', *La Grande Revue*, 1 May 1900, p. 316.

[4] Émile Durkheim in Henri Dagan (ed.), *Enquête sur l'antisémitisme* (Paris, 1899), pp. 60–1.

[5] Berl, 'Éclipse des idées libérales', p. 316; Marcel Brunschvig, *L'Antisémitisme* (Cahors, 1902), pp. 30–1. Taking a somewhat different approach, the Grand Rabbi of Paris, J.-H. Dreyfuss, offered this extraordinary picture of what he implied to

Still, the patriotism enunciated within the Jewish community steered clear of *la revanche*, of the militant advocacy of a war of revenge against the Germans. On this point, on the point of calling for action, the rabbis were silent in their pulpits and the Jewish columnists remarkably unresponsive. Despite the growing revanchist sentiment in France during the 1890s, despite the heavy Alsatian element within the Jewish population, the patriotism of the Jews tended to be relatively benign.[1] When Zadoc Kahn edited his sermons for publication he prudently omitted those of the *année terrible* which called for revenge.[2] When Julien Benda described the patriotism of his parents, he made a point of saying that it lacked 'any instinctive, carnal, or irrational element'.[3] Perhaps sensing that the inflamed nationalism of the period held a potential danger for the Jews, their spokesmen avoided the most strident statements, and preferred rather to invest the French nation with the sanctity of divine support or to express a general but vague faith in the ultimate victory of French ideals.

Within the Jewish community there was an attempt to go beyond patriotism in identifying French Jewry with France. The product of this attempt was a general theory about the nature of Judaism which may perhaps best be termed 'Franco-Judaism', the union of Jewishness and Frenchness in a coherent theoretical formulation. Franco-Judaism had for its most articulate spokesman the Orientalist James Darmesteter, whose works reflected the thinking of many elements of the Jewish community and who, in

be the common patriotism of Jews and anti-Semites: 'Nous aimons en ce moment la France, notre patrie, de toutes les énergies de notre être, nous l'aimons avec une ferveur extraordinaire. Nous sommes comme des enfants qui, chérissant chacun leur mère d'une affection ardente, se jalousent quelque peu les uns les autres, comme poussés par une sorte de rivalité dans l'expression de leur dévouement envers elle qui est le commun objet de leur adoration: de là une certaine défiance mutuelle qui, en se prolongeant, risquerait de compromettre le charme et la sûreté de nos rapports, d'affliger celle-là même que nous entourons de notre vénération, et ce qui serait plus grave encore, d'affaiblir, par la contrariété de nos efforts, l'efficacité de notre tendresse filiale et de notre dévouement.' *A.I.*, 1 Dec. 1898, p. 387.

[1] See Pierre Aubery, *Milieux juifs de la France contemporaine à travers leurs écrivains* (Paris, 1957), pp. 203–4; Reinach, *Histoire*, p. 375.

[2] Julien Weill, *Zadoc Kahn, 1839–1905* (Paris, 1912), p. 61.

[3] Julien Benda, *La Jeunesse d'un clerc* (Paris, 1936), p. 41.

his zeal to complete the work of assimilation, shaped the essence of Judaism to fit the essence of the France of the Third Republic. Among Jewish intellectuals such as Michel Bréal and Théodore and Salomon Reinach, Darmesteter was admired for his honesty, his scholarship, and his moral earnestness. But most of all these Jews appreciated the synthesis of Jewish and French values, the formal integration of two systems which had been kept apart so long in the popular imagination.

James Darmesteter was born in Lorraine in 1849, the son of a bookbinder whose family had come originally from the ghetto of Darmstadt, but which had been settled in France for several generations.[1] He had an illustrious Jewish background: his grandfather, Calmann Darmesteter, was what was called a *Lamden* in Alsace-Lorraine, a learned biblical scholar and teacher who was not a rabbi; his mother was born Rosalie Brandeis, the daughter of one of the most important Jewish families in Prague which had produced generations of scholars—some even claimed that her family was descended from Rabbi Akiba, the Jewish scholar and nationalist leader of the second century. The Darmesteters were

[1] The biographical material on Darmesteter is taken from the articles in *J.E.* and *U.J.E.*; James Darmesteter, preface to Arsène Darmesteter, *Reliques scientifiques, recueillies par son frère* (2 vols., Paris, 1890), i; Mary Darmesteter, preface to James Darmesteter, *Critique et politique* (Paris, 1895); Gaston Paris, *Penseurs et poètes* (Paris, 1896); André Spire, *Souvenirs à bâtons rompus* (Paris, 1962) and *Quelques juifs et demi-juifs* (2 vols., Paris, 1928), i; Gabriel Monod, *Portraits et souvenirs* (Paris, 1897); Salomon Reinach, preface to James Darmesteter, *Les Prophètes d'Israël* (Paris, 1931), and *James Darmesteter* (Paris, 1932); Théodore Reinach in *Actes* (1895), *R.E.J.* (1895); Michel Bréal, 'James Darmesteter', *Le Temps*, 2 Nov. 1894, and 'James Darmesteter', *Annuaire de l'École Pratique des Hautes Études* (1895), pp. 17–33; H. P. in *A.I.*, 25 Oct. 1894, p. 356. Gabriel Monod's reflection upon Darmesteter's Jewish background and its relationship to the latter's scholarship is an interesting example of a French liberal's view of race: 'Il [Darmesteter] appartient à une race qui est de toutes la plus cosmopolite à la fois et la plus pure d'éléments étrangers; à une race qui a conservé le sentiment vivant de son antiquité et est restée profondément orientale par certains côtés, tout en étant devenue foncièrement occidentale et moderne par autres; à une race qui a été dans le monde la plus puissante et la plus féconde des forces religieuses et qui est aussi l'agent le plus actif de la vie commerciale, qui allie un don remarquable pour l'abstraction au sens le plus concret pour la réalité, qui est comme le symbole vivant de toute une partie de l'évolution historique, philosophique et sociale de l'humanité, et qui unit à la fidélité obstinée à son passé une entière liberté de spéculation.' Monod, op. cit., pp. 159–60.

extremely poor. At the beginning of the Second Empire the family moved to the Marais in Paris and suffered serious privations, struggling at that time, like many Jewish families from the eastern provinces or from central Europe, to adapt themselves to what they felt to be a cold and inhospitable capital. The Darmesteter brothers, James and Arsène, received the education which their father had never had. James attended the local *école primaire*, went for a short time to the Talmud Torah, the Jewish day school run by the Consistoire, and, with the aid of a Jewish charitable foundation, attended the prestigious *lycées* Charlemagne and Bonaparte. His brother Arsène intended to be a rabbi and studied at the Jewish Seminary for a number of years; later, however, dropping his rabbinical studies, he pursued his interests in philology and languages at the École des Chartes. The two Darmesteters, like the Reinach brothers several years later, were brilliant students. Arsène was appointed lecturer in Romance languages at the École des Hautes Études at the age of twenty-six; he soon became a well-recognized authority in medieval French, and taught at the Sorbonne and the Jewish Seminary. James studied at the École Normale Supérieure, and, after a period of indecision spent largely in writing a novel, some plays, and poetry, plunged into the study of ancient Persian culture and language. Unquestionably, he was strongly influenced by Ernest Renan, the leading French scholar in the field at this time. James received his doctorate in 1872, taught at the Collège de France, and eventually became director of the École des Hautes Études. His most important scholarly work, a translation of the Zoroastrian text the *Avesta*, was crowned by the Académie and considered a remarkable achievement in the scholarly community. When James died in 1894 Max Müller, dean of Oriental scholars, called him the *primus inter pares* among French Orientalists.[1]

James and Arsène Darmesteter entered the field of philology with a firm background in Hebrew; both made full use of the Jewish education so carefully provided by their father. Yet in the academic circles in which these young men moved, there was little place for deep religious commitment. There religions were

[1] Paris, op. cit., p. 2.

analysed, not studied for the purposes of propagation; cultures were compared, but always with a measure which was self-consciously 'scientific'. While philological study has traditionally been an important part of Jewish education, the field became widely popular in France only towards the second half of the nine-teenth century.[1] At that time, however, its real importance be-came quickly recognized. The study of Sanskrit and other ancient languages seemed to open the door to remarkable discoveries about the human past, in particular about the origins and relations between the great religions of Asia. A number of Jews, Jules Oppert, Joseph and Hartwig Derenbourg, Michel Bréal, and Joseph Halévy were notably involved in this work in France. It became important for them, as respected members of the academic community, to approach religious questions with particular 'objectivity', as befitted men of science and learning. It is hardly surprising that Bréal, Halévy, and the Darmesteters soon cut most ties with the established Jewish community.

Those who knew him remembered James as a slight man, pale and frequently ill, timid, and often inclined to hide himself either in silence or in irony. In the period following his student days he characterized himself as a hard and inflexible atheist; he was intensely absorbed in his work, devoted to 'science', and alone. But in 1880 the death of his mother in a tragic accident deeply shocked the young academic; from that moment, according to the woman who later became his wife, James 'felt moral perfec-tion growing in him'. At last, he wrote, the revelation came to him 'that religious sentiment, raised to the supreme power, is the very soul of life'.[2] The scientific and ironic unbeliever now felt the need for a personal religious commitment which as a younger man he had carefully avoided. However, to recapture 'religious sentiment', to distil it from the body of practised religion, was a difficult and arduous task for someone in his position. Troubled by unbelief, Darmesteter began painstakingly to explore a region

---

[1] See Christopher Dawson, 'On Jewish history', Orbis, vol. x, no. 4 (Winter 1967), pp. 1249–50; Jacques Barzun, Race: a Study in Superstition (New York, 1965), p. 98.

[2] Mary Darmesteter, preface to Darmesteter, Critique, p. iv.

which he had hitherto shunned. Divorced from traditional Judaism, he became convinced that the complete rejection of the faith of his forefathers had been a profound error. In a poetic reflection Darmesteter described what he believed to be his own predicament in denying his Jewish past:

Woe to the scholar who studies religion [*les choses de Dieu*] without having at the root of his conscience, in the indestructible and most hidden corner of his being, there where sleeps the soul of his ancestors, an unknown sanctuary from which there arises, like clouds of incense, the line of a psalm, the mournful and triumphal cry that as a child he cast up to heaven as his fathers had done, and which puts him in sudden communion again with the Prophets of yore.[1]

There was never any question of returning to the outward forms of the Jewish religion; the scholar and intellectual had gone too far for that. Yet Darmesteter could never again be accurately described as an unbeliever, and as he reviewed the basis of his Jewish education he became more articulate about the nature of his faith.

The core of his belief, he later claimed, was the Bible. He explained his position this way to Salomon Reinach: 'Je suis juif infiniment peu, je suis *bibliste*.'[2] The Jewish religion, however, despite what he considered its faults, despite its association in his mind with a particular level of historical development, still seemed to respond more clearly than any other to his quest for a faith which could be reconciled with the modern world. For though he lived in a France beset with religious turmoil, where the foundations of faith had suddenly been found weak or even destroyed, he felt that there remained grounds for hope. Darmesteter believed that he had discovered a new basis for belief, one which was related intimately both to the Prophets of ancient Judah and to the France which had emerged after 1789.

Appropriately, Darmesteter developed the first suggestion of what his new religious perspective would be like in a historical survey; the historian and scholar began his search for religious meaning in 1880 with a glance at the significance of the Jewish

[1] Paris, op. cit., p. 48.
[2] Salomon Reinach, *Darmesteter*, p. 24 (italicsi n original).

past as a whole. The essay entitled *Coup d'œil sur l'histoire du peuple juif* stressed above all the essentially progressive nature of Judaism: from the dark past of the ghettos to the brilliant achievements of the Jews in modern times, Darmesteter felt that the Jew had been in some sense in the vanguard of civilization. Such a view was in contrast with the standard judgement that the Jews assumed an essentially passive role in modern history. As an oppressed and persecuted victim, he felt, the Jew during the Middle Ages was particularly well placed to be the enemy of the Church and a thorn in the side of an unjust and corrupt society; long before the Enlightenment it was the Jew 'who forged the murderous arsenal of reason and irony which he transmitted from the sceptics of the Renaissance to the libertines of the *grand siècle*'. Indeed, from this point of view, 'that sarcasm of Voltaire is only the last and resounding echo of a word whispered, six centuries before, in the shadow of the ghetto . . .'. The Jews, the people of the Book who had not the physical but only the intellectual power to secure their preservation, were in continual intellectual opposition to the dominant society.[1] Such was their historical role until that great moment of the French Revolution. What the Revolution accomplished was the 'breaking of the barrier between Jew and Christian'; in so doing the task of the Jews could be considered fulfilled and, consequently, the Jews would no longer have a separate history of their own. From the time of emancipation 'there is no longer any place for a history of the Jews in France; there is only from then on a history of French Judaism, as there is a history of French Lutheranism or Calvinism, nothing more and nothing less'. Henceforth there was no longer any place for the traditional Jewish opposition to the established order; henceforth there was no exclusion and no need for the Jews to keep apart from the nation. The message of the Jews was now the message of France. For the first time the thought of Judaism was in accord with the conscience of a significant part of humanity. The Jew could embrace France because France had risen to that higher level of humanity which it had been the task of Judaism to propagate.[2]

[1] Darmesteter, *Prophètes*, pp. 185–6.
[2] Ibid., pp. 192–3.

Finally, in a theoretical *tour de force*, Darmesteter showed explicitly how the ideology of the French Revolution was in fact the ideology of Judaism. The Revolution represented, in the ideological sphere, the substitution of a scientific conception of the world for a mythical conception; in the practical sphere it represented the institutionalization of the notions of justice and progress. For Darmesteter this dual achievement was simply the application to French society of the central principles of Judaism. Since the time of the Prophets Judaism had rested upon two great dogmas, dogmas which stood for the entirety of the religion. These were what he called 'Divine Unity' and 'Messianism'. Each of these dogmas had its roots in an ancient biblical tradition; each of them, however—and this was Darmesteter's special contribution—had direct relevance to the modern world which had been ushered in in 1789. 'Divine Unity', the biblical concept of monotheism, meant 'the unity of law in the world', or, in other words, the recognition that the world was ruled by scientific, lawlike principles, and not myth. Messianism, when applied to the world, meant a faith in the 'terrestrial triumph of justice in humanity', the belief in progress and social betterment which was the mainspring of the Revolution.[1] Divine Unity and Messianism were in this way the central doctrines of the Revolution. Divine Unity and Messianism, the core of biblical Judaism, were seen to be the basis of the modern French state. Thus, in Darmesteter's view, the Jews could live most comfortably in France because France was building a society which reflected Jewish ideals. The Jews, in a sense, had no need to adapt themselves to the culture of France; to some extent at least, on the most profound level, the culture of France had adapted itself to Judaism. The point was that they were essentially the same.

It seems likely that what precipitated Darmesteter's investigation of the relationship between Judaism and the spirit of France was the publication of a study of the life and work of Joseph

---

[1] Darmesteter, op. cit., pp. 193–5. Similar ideas had been expressed many years before by Alexandre Weill, an eccentric Jewish writer and free-thinker who came to Paris in the 1830s. On Weill see Robert Dreyfus, 'Alexandre Weill, ou le prophète du faubourg Saint-Honoré, 1811–1899', *Cahiers de la quinzaine* (Paris, 1908).

Salvador, a Jew of the first generation of emancipation who, Darmesteter claimed, expressed the latter's own thoughts on the subject of the relationship between Judaism and the modern world. Darmesteter's study of Salvador is interesting, for it exposes not only the similarities in the thought of the two men, but a significant difference. Salvador was born in Montpellier in the south of France in 1796, of an old Spanish Maranno family, supposedly descended from the Maccabees. His mother, Elizabeth Vincens, was a Catholic. As Salvador matured he was drawn to his father's religion; he saw in Judaism a 'positivistic, moral, practical, and historical religion' which was not at war with the modern temperament. Christianity, on the contrary, he viewed as 'theoretical, metaphysical', and devoted to the useless task of explaining 'the unknowable and the unverifiable'.[1] The Law of Moses was founded upon 'right reason and natural equity'; socially speaking this meant the absence of classes and special privileges, politically it stood for individual liberty and resistance to oppression.[2] These ideas, the ideas which Salvador described as the ideas of ancient Jerusalem, were the inspiration of the French Revolution in its struggle against what he referred to as paganism. The symbol of this paganism was Rome, in the form of both the universal Roman Empire at the time of Christ, and the universal Church, the 'semi-pagan' religion which had succeeded it. Salvador heralded the era of a new Jerusalem which would supplant the era of Rome, which would be 'everywhere that the biblical and the revolutionary soul prevails' and which would reintroduce the ideas enunciated by ancient Jerusalem. Salvador believed that this new Jerusalem, a 'universal Jerusalem of truth and justice, of science and law', would actually be established in Palestine, and would be the moral centre of the world which was coming into being.[3]

At this point, however, Darmesteter, whose views accorded well with those of Salvador, made his only real objection. As we have seen, Darmesteter's primary loyalties lay with France. The

[1] James Darmesteter, *Joseph Salvador* (Versailles, 1881), pp. 12–13. Cf. Baron Carra de Vaux, 'Joseph Salvador et James Darmesteter', *Actes* (1900), *R.E.J.*, vol. xl (1900), pp. xxiii–xlviii.
[2] Darmesteter, op. cit., pp. 15–16.   [3] Ibid., pp. 52–4.

new capital, he felt, would not be Jerusalem, but Paris. The new spirit, he predicted, would have as its chief source of radiation the French capital which would become 'the moral capital of the world and the light of men's hearts'; Paris would 'be for a long time the holy city, for it has been the first and the greatest spokesman for the sublime new order which is beginning'.[1] With what he believed to be the impending fulfilment of the promise of the Hebrew Prophets, Darmesteter was prepared to dissolve Jewishness in the 'catholic union of the future', to be directed from France; his consolation for this, or perhaps his deference to Jewish history, was a recognition that the 'catholicism' towards which the French were leading the world was in fact the moral equivalent of the ancient Hebrew faith.[2]

Since 1882, when he wrote a patriotic national history for children stressing the 'internal tranquillity' of France, Darmesteter became increasingly sensitive to the fact that all was not well with the Republic.[3] A decade later, after economic depression, Boulangism, and the violent emergence of anarchism, it was impossible to refer to the future so optimistically. Darmesteter believed, however, that the social and political strife could be settled through a 'moral reform', a reform which would affect all layers of society. What was necessary was that men love their country more than their class and more than their own private interests. In a France torn by dissension over the *laïc* laws, in a France where social divisions had begun to threaten a renewal of violence unparalleled since the Commune, and where the great republican hopes at times seemed dimmed, Darmesteter's quest was for a broad reconciliation. This reconciliation, he felt, would involve a general settlement of social disputes through agreement on moral questions, and would lead, as a result, to the establishment of social peace.[4]

---

[1] Darmesteter, op. cit., p. 59.

[2] Ibid., pp. 58, 62.

[3] J.-D. Lefrançais (pseud. for James Darmesteter), *Lectures patriotiques sur l'histoire de France à l'usage de l'enseignement primaire* (Paris, 1882). Cf. James Darmesteter, 'La guerre et la paix intérieures de 1871 à 1893', *Revue des revues*, 15 Feb. 1894, pp. 197–224.

[4] Darmesteter, *Critique*, pp. 240, 250, 292.

In time, almost certainly under the influence of his teacher Ernest Renan, Darmesteter looked to the Hebrew Prophets in defining the essence of Jewish thought and in providing the basis for the reconciliation so urgently required. The Jewish religion, he came to believe, was more than the negative critique of inequality and injustice which he had once held it to be; it was rather a doctrine capable of solving the problems of a modern society. The real problem of the age was that the victory of science (which he equated in some sense with the victory of the French Revolution) had produced bitter disillusionment. France's division, her instability, her occasional attacks of anti-Semitism were symptomatic of the lack of a higher ideal. Science, clearly, was an insufficient guide for the ordering of a new society:

Science arms man but it does not direct him: it enlightens the world for him to the uttermost reaches of the stars, but it leaves darkness in his heart; it is invincible, and indifferent, neutral, immoral.[1]

Catholicism too could not direct mankind in the modern age; it even, in a state such as France, became corrupted in the exercise of its authority. The message of the Hebrew Prophets could give the moral guidance so sorely needed in the contemporary world; it could purify both modern science and French Catholicism, the two warring 'religions' of modern France. It was not necessary to convert both sides to Judaism; it was simply necessary to build a 'communion d'esprit' under the aegis of a progressive, moral influence.[2] The Prophetic tradition, he believed, contained within it the basis for reconciliation upon which all men could agree. Darmesteter knew that Renan, pre-eminent among French philologists and historians of religion, had always recognized the role of the Prophets in providing the core and substance of the Jewish religion. Like Renan, Darmesteter disapproved of Jewish law which stood, in his mind, for Jewish isolation and even obscurantism;

---

[1] Darmesteter, *Prophètes*, p. viii. Ideas such as these were common in intellectual circles at the time, and an extensive controversy on this very subject arose shortly after these words were written. See Harry W. Paul, 'The Debate over the Bankruptcy of Science in 1895', *French Historical Studies*, vol. v, no. 3 (Spring 1968), pp. 299–327.

[2] Darmesteter, op. cit., pp. xiii–xiv.

what was progressive in Judaism, from his viewpoint, what was relevant to the ills of the modern era, was the liberal and universalistic ethical element which he saw in the teachings of the Prophets.[1] The Jewish tradition was thus in the deepest sense patriotic, for it and perhaps it alone could cure the illness of a stricken nation, and could do for Frenchmen what neither science nor Catholicism in their existing form had been able to do.

James Darmesteter, the mild-mannered scholar, built his intellectual faith upon a foundation of ideological reconciliation. He believed that the world as a whole was moving steadily towards 'a higher and more perfect form of being', that the social and political structure of France was essentially sound, and that, because of this, the deep divisions within the nation could eventually be closed through mutual understanding rather than by the radical reconstruction of society.[2] He further believed that Judaism would fit into the general pattern of reconciliation. The religion of the Prophets could be reconciled with science and with Christianity, and could aid in the salvation of the French Republic. Franco-Judaism, the fusion of Jewish traditions with the ideals of the nation, was Darmesteter's ethical ideal. As one contribution to a general reconciliation in France, he hoped to have stilled the voices which cried out on the one hand for a continued Jewish distinctiveness and on the other for the continued exclusion of the Jews from the body of the nation. When he died on 19 October 1894, ten days before the *Libre Parole* announced the arrest of Alfred Dreyfus, Darmesteter almost certainly believed that, for the Jews at least, reconciliation had been largely accomplished.

Darmesteter was not alone as a spokesman for Franco-Judaism. A number of writers attempted, with varying degrees of sophistication and learning, to fuse the essence of Judaism with what they believed was the essence of modern France. But always the theme was the same: Judaism contained within its doctrines, within its

[1] See Ernest Renan, *Histoire du peuple d'Israël* (5 vols., Paris, 1887–93), i. iii; id., *Le Judaïsme comme race et comme religion* (Paris, 1883); id., *De l'identité originelle et de la séparation graduelle du judaïsme et du christianisme* (Versailles, 1884), p. 25; James Darmesteter, *Notice sur la vie et l'œuvre de M. Renan* (Paris, 1893), p. 38.
[2] Darmesteter, *Critique*, p. 71.

history, and even within its practices the seeds of good citizenship and devotion to the French fatherland. 'Trust in us,' these Jews were saying, 'for we cannot be good Jews without being good Frenchmen.'

In his sermon of installation, on 29 September 1891, the Grand Rabbi of Paris, J.-H. Dreyfuss, drew together his impressions of the relationship between the 'French genius' and 'the fundamental spirit of Judaism'.[1] The theme was perhaps to have been expected on that occasion from Dreyfuss who, having just spent a number of years as Grand Rabbi of Belgium, likely felt the necessity to make some broad declaration of loyalty to France. What impressed him particularly, at the time, were the 'moral affinities between the two races', the Jews and the French. While it was never admitted openly, the basis for these 'affinities' was seen as a common sharing of well-accepted middle-class values. Both Jews and Frenchmen, Dreyfuss declared, were 'respectful of family ties and traditions', both were 'permeated with the same ardour for work, the same care for saving money, the same provident solicitude for the future'. Both were 'preoccupied with the development of material resources, less for the legitimate satisfactions of well-being which they allow than for the intellectual and moral enjoyment of which they can be the source and for the good which they make possible'. There was also a broader, more historical level of comparison. A real similarity existed between the 'mission' of Israel and the 'historical role' of France. Dreyfuss referred to the French as 'this elect people of modern times, spreading abroad the blessed notions of liberty, equality, and fraternity'. There was a direct parallel between this elect people and the elect people of the ancient world. Against the French there was arrayed on the international level the same kind of 'jealousy' for having been divinely chosen which Israel had endured. The one and the other had to suffer in bringing their message to the world around them.[2]

[1] J.-H. Dreyfuss, *Sermons et allocutions* (2 vols., Paris, 1908–13), i. 277–83; J.-H. Dreyfuss, 'Le génie français et l'esprit du judaïsme', *La Vraie Parole*, 19 Apr. 1893.
[2] Cf. Zadoc Kahn, *Sermons*, iii. 20–3. Joseph Hirsch listed a series of 'vertus de la race' referring to the Jews which accords well with Dreyfuss's list of 'affinities': 'la ténacité, l'amour du travail, la solidité du lien conjugal et familial, la vivacité d'intelligence, campagne de sobriété.' Hirsch, op. cit., p. 39.

Spokesmen made constant efforts to adapt elements of traditional Judaism, usually held in suspicion by the public at large, in order to make them relevant to the specific context of a modern, liberal France. The idea of the Messiah, for example, had to be stripped of some of its emotive and 'messianic' significance in order to ensure its consistency with good citizenship and devotion to the existing order. As we have seen, Maurice Bloch solved this problem by explaining that the 'time of the Messiah' had already come, had in fact been ushered in by the French Revolution.[1] Isidore Loeb argued that even among the most religious Jews the Messianic ideal was 'a purely theoretical ideal, without any immediate or proximate application'. For most Jews, he emphasized, the ideal was only the vaguest conception, and should be considered as envisioning simply a general 'evolution of humanity, a kind of emancipation of men and peoples through universal charity and fraternity'.[2] The young Léon Blum felt the need to adapt the essence of Judaism to a different set of ideals. Blum was a literary critic with socialist leanings in the years before the First World War; he undertook, in the face of a tradition of anti-Semitism within the French extreme left, to demonstrate that Judaism was perfectly consistent with socialism. 'The Jew', he said, 'has the religion of Justice just as the Positivists have the religion of Fact, or Renan the religion of Science. Only the idea of inevitable Justice sustained the Jews and held them together in their long tribulations.' 'Their Messiah', he claimed, 'is nothing more than the symbol of eternal Justice which, no doubt, can forsake the world for centuries, but which will surely reign one day.' The Jews, however, do not put off to another world this reign of Justice; it is to come in this world, in the here and now if at all possible. 'Is this not', Blum asked, 'the spirit of socialism? It is the antique spirit of the race. If Christ preached charity, Jehovah called for Justice.'[3]

In another direction, the philosopher and logician Adolphe Franck drew the Jewish past into communion with modern France. 'The

[1] See p. 91, above.

[2] Isidore Loeb, *Réflexions sur les juifs* (Paris, 1894), p. 16.

[3] Léon Blum, *Nouvelles conversations de Goethe avec Eckermann, 1897–1900*, in *L'Œuvre de Léon Blum* (6 vols., Paris, 1954–65), i. 266–7.

essence of Judaism,' he wrote in 1886, echoing the familiar phrase, 'as is shown to us by the history not of the kings of Judah and of Israel, but of Moses and the Prophets, was a proud republicanism, a religious republicanism which makes the civil and political liberty of a people depend upon its moral dignity and religious faith.'[1] Implicit, then, in the Jewish religion was an opposition to those powerful forces which threatened the republican institutions so precariously established in the years following the Franco-Prussian War. During the 1880s republicans frequently referred to the movement which threatened these institutions by a single word—'clericalism'. Clericalism, the institutional force of the Catholic Church, was seen by many as the single most subversive, anti-republican force operating within French life. Franck argued that Judaism was implacably opposed to the domination of society by the forces of the Church.[2] In the charged political rhetoric of the early 1880s, the Jews were by definition 'anti-clerical' because they were so sharply excluded from the political orbit of Catholicism. Assimilated Jews such as Heber Marini could thus make the point that Jews displayed a 'natural superiority' to many Frenchmen, not by virtue of any inherently superior personal qualities, but because they had a liberal Jewish background and were thus protected from the 'exaggerated devotion bordering on fanaticism' engendered by a Catholic upbringing.[3]

It was customary to add in such discussions of the Jewish role in republican France that the Jews were good Frenchmen, not only negatively, through their antipathy to clericalism, but positively, through the useful contributions which they could and did make to French life. Thus the historian Maurice Bloch argued that Jews were not only inherently patriotic, but 'have always displayed military virtues of the first order'. Further, he pointed out that Jews had always contributed to the public prosperity of the

---

[1] Adolphe Franck, 'Le rôle du judaïsme dans le mouvement politique contemporain', *A.I.*, 19 Aug. 1886, p. 258.

[2] Ibid.

[3] Heber Marini, *Le Fin Mot sur la question juive* (Paris, 1886), pp. 21–4. Franck believed that Jewish 'superiority' came in part from Jewish education: '. . . la place que tous les peuples chrétiens ont donné ou laissé prendre à l'Église, le judaïsme a donné à la science, à l'instruction religieuse.' Op. cit., p. 258. See p. 61, above.

countries in which they lived. Such warlike and productive citizens were obviously extremely valuable for modern France.[1] The identification of Frenchman and Jew was in this way made virtually complete. There was little indeed left to be said, when Hippolyte Prague reported to his readers the theory of one Irish scholar—that the *Marseillaise* itself came from an old Hebrew song.[2]

Yet in building this identification, in constructing the elaborate system of reconciliation of which Franco-Judaism was the articulation, Jewish thinkers were undermining the basis for a distinctive Jewish existence. This was not easily admitted. One of the few who did so was Théodore Reinach, whose article on the Jews, written for the *Grande Encyclopédie* about 1894, pointed to the logical outcome of the Franco-Jewish doctrine. This outcome was the end of the Jewish religion and, in a sense, of the Jewish people. Judaism, Reinach observed, only asserts itself in response to anti-Semitism and persecution. 'Once emancipation [and] equality penetrate throughout society, not only in laws, but in customs and ideas, Jewish feeling [*le sentiment juif*] will increasingly lose its fervour [*âpreté*] and will end up, no doubt, by extinguishing itself completely.' He viewed Judaism as steadily evolving into a vague humanism which would join with other religions, each freed from the hold of superstition:

The Jews will absorb themselves bit by bit into the mass of their fellow citizens of a different faith and will contribute, with their [Jewish] blood, some of their strong hereditary qualities. Let there be no mistake about it: the future of Judaism is in the hands of the Christian majority, governments, opinion, and those who make it.

Here we see the outcome of the historical and analytical perspective of the assimilationist spokesmen whose words we have examined in this chapter. The Jews were, once again, seen as essentially passive actors—inclined to assimilate if left alone, and ready to join other Frenchmen in the ecumenical spirit of French-inspired liberalism. In the resulting *mélange*, Reinach considered,

---

[1] Maurice Bloch, *Les Vertus militaires des juifs* (Paris, 1897) and *Les Juifs et la prospérité publique à travers l'histoire* (Paris, 1899).
[2] H. Prague, 'Chronique de la semaine', *A.I.*, 4 Feb. 1886, p. 33.

Judaism would have completed its movement from a nationality to a confessional group, and beyond, to become a constituent historical element in the 'humanistic religion' of the future which France will have done so much to build. In that future Judaism 'should consider its "mission" as accomplished, and die without regret, shrouded in its triumph'. The death of Judaism, moreover, was not to be expected as the result of a long historical process, to be completed in some distant Utopia; implicit in the Franco-Judaism of Reinach, and even of Darmesteter, was the view that Judaism was already slowly dying in nineteenth-century France, even as it made its contribution and identified more closely with the fatherland.[1] Franco-Judaism thus proved to be an inherently unstable doctrine; in seeking the identity of the Jewish spirit with the spirit of France, it seemed to be seeking the effacement of Judaism itself.

Most Jews, of course, did not see so far. The link between Judaism and France led not to despair about the future of Judaism, but to a longer chain of confidence and optimism. Most Jews, in fact, recognized only one kind of threat—the loss of their rights as citizens. Protection for Judaism was seen in terms of their maintenance of citizenship and the rights of Frenchmen; and from the late 1880s, as we shall see, Jews had reason to feel the need for precisely such protection. Rabbi Abraham Bloch of Remiremont gave voice to this feeling in 1889 when, speaking of anti-Semitism, he was carried away into a general declaration of faith:

It is not in France . . ., it is not under the Republic that the rights henceforth sacred can be taken away. The principles of 1789 protect us! And we are full of security, full of confidence for the future [on the one hand] because we live in a land of justice and equality, and on the other hand because we are sure that we have done all that has been expected of us.[2]

Security and confidence in the future, then, came not from the Jew's assertion of Jewishness, but from his faithful fulfilment of

---

[1] Théodore Reinach, article 'Juif' in *La Grande Encyclopédie* (31 vols., Paris, 1886–1901), xxi. 256–80.
[2] Mossé (ed.), op. cit., p. 58. Cf. Zadoc Kahn, *Sermons*, iii. 117–18.

the duties of citizenship. Just as Jewish historians had viewed Jewish history as being controlled from the outside, so Jewish commentators (often they were the same) saw Jewish existence defined in terms of categories which were French and not Jewish. Assimilationist doctrine was so successful in its association of Frenchman and Jew that the latter did not, on the whole, fear or regret or even anticipate the loss of a 'Jewish identity' whose meaning was now eroded and whose historical function seemed to have been assumed by modern France. Confidence and optimism were thus eagerly assimilated along with the other orthodoxies of the French Republic. And in the enthusiasm which usually followed an assessment of the situation of the Jews in France, there was little inclination to examine the relationship between assimilation and the possible extinction of Judaism itself.

A number of agencies served to disseminate or to reflect the ideas discussed in this chapter. As we noticed in Chapter IV, the Alliance Israélite Universelle was a vehicle for assimilationist doctrine and for the celebration of the French example among Jews in France and especially abroad. There were, however, several other institutions which were more directly involved in ministering to the Jewish community in France.

Foremost among these was the rabbinate. It should be noted at this point that French rabbis tended in large measure to come from Alsace and were thus, in the French scheme of things, considered to be among those for whom patriotism was second nature. The fact that so many of the Jewish community also came from areas occupied by the Germans put particular pressure upon Jews to accentuate their patriotism, and upon the rabbis, as the religious leaders of the community, to articulate and to appeal to these feelings.[1] During a period when national sentiment ran particularly high, patriotism proved to be a useful ground of communication between the rabbi and his congregation who were frequently slipping apart in other ways. Zadoc Kahn made this clear in his advice to Isaac Bloch at the latter's installation as Grand Rabbi of Nancy in 1890:

[1] See 'Le sentiment français des israélites d'Alsace', U.I., 27 Sept. 1935, p. 11.

The minister of God will preach the love of the fatherland, and for him it will be a sure means to awaken a sympathetic echo in the people he is addressing. . . . How easy it will be for you, my dear colleague, to speak here of patriotism and to communicate to your listeners the flame which burns within you, here [in Nancy], where eyes are constantly fixed upon the other side of the frontier, where we receive with sighs the echo of regrets which nothing can console and of hopes which nothing can destroy. . . .[1]

But it was easy too, in Paris, where in the 1890s *la revanche*, the call to avenge the French defeat of 1870-1, created a new mood of national assertion, where, in 1893, on the occasion of the departure of Jewish conscripts for the army, the Grand Rabbi of France could declare:

Never, my brothers, has the idea of the fatherland shone more brilliantly than in the unforgettable days which we have just seen. I scorn overwhelmingly [*Je méprise trop*] the foolish theories of those wayward souls who rise up against this idea and who insult the flag. . . .[2]

This patriotic disposition among the religious leaders of the Jewish community facilitated the growth of Franco-Judaism by its exaltation of the idea of the fatherland to an irrational, almost religious level. Rabbinical support, moreover, provided the sanction for similar activity in other areas.

Further direction came from three books which were widely used within the Jewish community—a book of prayers and, less importantly, two catechisms intended for children's use. *Le Guide du croyant israélite* was a collection of prayers prepared by Lazare Wogue, an ordained rabbi who held the chair in Jewish theology at the rabbinical seminary for over forty years, from 1851 to 1894. The book first appeared in 1857, and was reissued in a revised edition in 1898 with the *imprimatur* of Zadoc Kahn. Most relevant to this discussion is the 'prayer for France' which offered a good statement of what the Jewish believer was supposed to feel about the relationship between the French Jew and his country.

---

[1] Zadoc Kahn, *Sermons*, iii. 49. Cf. I. Lévy, *Adieu à l'Alsace* (Paris, 1872) and *Alsatiana: échos patriotiques de la chaire israélite* (Paris, 1873).

[2] Zadoc Kahn, op. cit., iii. 247.

'Almighty protector of Israel and humanity!' the prayer began, 'if of all religions ours is the most dear to You, because it is Your own handiwork, France is of all countries the one which You seem to prefer, because it is the most worthy of You.' If Israel had its chosen task 'in the religious sphere', France had her assignment 'in the human sphere'. To accomplish this work the French people had been given special qualities, not dissimilar from those which the Jews had received; France was gifted with 'a superior character [*organisation d'élite*] which reveals itself each day by the most marvellous results, which has made of this country the centre of human civilization, and of its capital the City of Light'. For the Jews France was 'a second Promised Land', where the Jewish people could thrive; it was the country in which they could truly realize themselves. The prayer ended with a patriotic appeal which showed the intimate relationship between the religion of the Jews and their native land:

Let the love of the fatherland walk hand in hand throughout our existence with the love of God. Each of these loves is sacred, they must never either conflict with one another or be mutually exclusive. The one gives us temporal felicity, the other gives us eternal felicity. . . .

Finally, Lord, and it is a wish which cannot offend France, let her not keep this monopoly of tolerance and of justice for all, a monopoly as humiliating for other states as it is glorious for her! Let her find many imitators, and as she imposes upon the world her tastes and her language, the products of her literature and her arts, let her also impose her principles, which, it goes without saying, are more important and more necessary.[1]

The two catechisms to which we referred stressed the importance of the fatherland in the religious life of the Jew. The one called upon Jews 'to unite our interests and our destiny with the common destiny and with the general interest of the country in which we live'; the other pointed out the need to fulfil, each in his station, the requisite duties to the nation.[2] Significantly, both considered

---

[1] Lazare Wogue, *Le Guide du croyant israélite* (2nd edn., Paris, 1898), pp. 515-19.

[2] Salomon Ulmann, *Catéchisme ou éléments d'instruction religieuse et morale à l'usage des jeunes israélites* (Paris, n.d.), pp. 88-9; Michel Mayer, *Tsidkath Elohim: instructions morales et religieuses* (Paris, 1885), pp. 90-2.

the duties which one owed to France as duties necessary not only for good citizenship, but also for being a good Jew. Indeed, these two sides of man were taken as one; virtually by definition in these works, the good Jew was a good citizen of France.

Other efforts furthered and marked the close connection which existed between Judaism and 'the spirit of modern France'. Jewish philanthropists made a number of conspicuous donations to the community at large, partly in an attempt to dramatize Jewish devotion to and association with the fatherland. The donation of a statue of Joan of Arc in 1890 is a case in point. The Jewish poet and nationalist, André Spire, tells us that among the Jews of Lorraine there was something of a cult of Joan of Arc, the patron saint of France who became an object of much attention in patriotic and nationalist circles beginning about 1890.[1] There were essentially two reasons for this adulation: first of all, there was the fact that she had helped to liberate France from the foreigner; and, second, the fact that she had been misjudged by the Church just as the Jews had been.[2] When a Jewish millionaire named Osiris donated a statue of the saint to the municipality of Nancy in 1890, a ceremony was held in the synagogue, attended by 'le tout-Nancy israélite', at which time the French heroine was compared to the biblical Deborah, Queen Esther, Judith, and a certain Jewish lady who had distinguished herself during the Franco-Prussian War.[3] The occasion received wide attention in the Jewish press. Not to be outdone in this connection, Alphonse de Rothschild, the president of the Consistoire Central and head of the Rothschild family in France, donated a statue of Joan of Arc worth 17,000 francs to the Musée de Cluny two years later.[4] Philanthropic donations in this way contributed to the association which had been established in the theoretical sphere.

[1] See G. Valbert, 'Le culte de Jeanne d'Arc', *Revue des Deux Mondes*, 1 Aug. 1890, pp. 688–700.   [2] Spire, *Juifs*, i. 219.
[3] L. W., 'Jeanne d'Arc et Israël', *U.I.*, 16 July 1890, pp. 659–61. For the text of the sermon delivered on the occasion by Armand Bloch, rabbi of Toul, see Armand Bloch, 'Le patriotisme', *La Famille de Jacob*, vol. xxxiii (1890–1), pp. 8–13. Cf. B.-M., 'M. Osiris, un vrai patriote israélite français', *La Famille de Jacob*, vol. xxxii (1889–90), p. 60; G. G., 'Jeanne d'Arc à Nancy', *La Nouvelle Revue*, 1 July 1890, pp. 178–80.   [4] *U.I.*, 1 May 1892, p. 500.

Finally, it should be noticed that the Société des Études Juives served as a sounding-board for Franco-Jewish theory both in providing a forum for speakers and in helping to publish their work. This organization, founded largely with the help and leadership of the Rothschilds, and with an ample treasury, was devoted to the development of studies related to Jewish history and literature, especially in France.[1] The general direction in which most of these articles tended was hinted at by Théodore Reinach in 1895 when, in an address to the society, he said: 'The Société . . . has nothing to do with the present trials of Judaism, however poignant they may be. It occupies the more serene levels of history, and it is only in dissipating the errors accumulated in respect to Judaism of long ago that it can contribute indirectly *to rehabilitating or consoling the Judaism of today.*'[2] Avoiding controversy and questions of Jewish self-assertion, the Société broadened its membership to include non-Jews, one of whom became its elected president in 1897. The task outlined above translated itself into a series of dry, erudite, and academic articles published in the *Revue.* Partly in response to complaints, the editors inserted a number of articles of a more general character, but always the tone was 'serious', 'scientific', and, as the above quotation might indicate, calculated to show by example that the Jews were capable of 'avoiding any exclusive or sectarian character' in their discussion of the role of Judaism in society.[3] The Société published separately a number of papers by Maurice Bloch, Ernest Renan, and James Darmesteter which have been discussed above, thus contributing to the diffusion of Franco-Judaism throughout the Jewish community.

By the time of the Dreyfus Affair the theoretical association of Judaism and modern France, the intellectual dimension of assimilation, had become the official doctrine of the Jewish community in France. Its propositions were repeated solemnly by Jewish officials on important occasions, and had the backing of the

[1] Session 28 May 1891, in *Actes* (1881), *Annuaire S.E.J.*, vol. i (1881), pp. 278-9.
[2] Théodore Reinach in *Actes* (1895), *R.E.J.*, vol. xxx (1895), p. viii (my italics).
[3] See Zadoc Kahn's address to the assembly of the Société, 26 Nov. 1881, in *Annuaire S.E.J.*, vol. ii (1883), pp. 13-14; and ibid., vol. iii (1884), pp. 12-13; *U.I.*, 16 May 1889, p. 547.

rabbinate, philanthropists, and Jewish intellectuals. Jewish history, Jewish prayers, and contemporary Jewish thought had been mustered in its support. Until the political crisis which shook the foundations of a secure Jewish existence in France, there were no voices raised in opposition to this orthodoxy, there was no school of thought which proposed another direction for Jewish activity, or another pole for Jewish loyalty.

CHAPTER VI

POLITICS AND THE JEWISH COMMUNITY

THE assimilationist theories examined in the previous chapter reached their high point of acceptance in the decade and a half before the Dreyfus Affair. As we have seen, the early period of the Third Republic saw a flourishing Jewish community reflect its close association with the country of emancipation in constructing an elaborate ideology of reconciliation and harmony, of faith in progress and universal improvement. It is paradoxical that during these very years the Jewish community felt the first waves of an attack upon its existence, an attack which was to grow in strength and violence such as no one had predicted and few understood. Throughout this period the political experience of the Jewish community bore the mark of this paradox: Jews found themselves pulled one way by the forces of assimilation and the ideology constructed to reinforce that assimilation, and pulled another way by the forces of anti-Semitism which first made their appearance in an organized, concerted fashion. Assimilation drew the Jews towards France; the anti-Semites constantly reminded the Jews of the fact that they stood outside the French nation. The result was a certain amount of confusion, questioning, and contradictory responses. But the assimilationist tradition was strong, and anti-Semitism relatively weak; the Jews were on the whole comfortable in France, and had lost any other pole of loyalty. The Jewish community demonstrated in its political activity, as it did in its theoretical formulations, that the primary goal of French Jews was to make their association with France complete. And the community did so despite anti-Semitism, which grew to formidable proportions, both at home and abroad.

Since the time of the Revolution French Jews had tended to accept the successive political regimes in France. Jews repeatedly demonstrated their loyalty to the Empire of Napoleon I and, despite effective political disfranchisement, gave at least tacit support to the monarchy of the Restoration. '... Except for a few individual cases,' says one student of the period, 'the Jews as a group participated neither in the republican opposition of the 1820s nor in the Revolution of July 1830, nor in the republican opposition to the July Monarchy. In spite of many anti-Jewish acts during the Restoration, the mass of Jews did not oppose it actively. . . .'[1] With the 1848 Revolution the Jews made their formal entrée into the political life of the nation. In the outburst of solidarity which was generated in February of that year, the Grand Rabbi of the Consistoire Central marched along with Catholic and Protestant clergy under a banner bearing the inscription, 'Union des cultes. Fraternité universelle'.[2] More important, two prominent members of the Jewish community, Adolphe Crémieux and Michel Goudchaux, joined the Provisional Government as Ministers of Justice and Finance respectively. During the Second Empire there was a continuous movement of Jews into France; as we have seen, they participated fully in the economic expansion of the period and achieved notable successes in a number of fields. Politically, they tended to support a regime which a Jewish historian later judged as being 'bien disposé pour les israélites'.[3] Achille Fould, the son of a wealthy Jewish banker, rose to particular prominence in the government of Napoleon III; other Jews such as Léopold Javal, Maximilien Koenigswarter, and Eugène Pereire secured seats in the Corps Législatif.

The beginning of the Third Republic saw an accentuation of this tendency towards acceptance of the existing regime. As always, Jews were attracted by the republican rhetoric which recalled the period of emancipation; further, leaders of the Jewish community had played a vital role in the founding of the Republic. The activity of the Rothschilds, the titular heads of the Jewish community, in

---

[1] Zosa Szajkowski, 'French Jews during the Revolution of 1830 and the July Monarchy', *Historia Judaica*, vol. xxii, Oct. 1960, p. 110.

[2] Léon Kahn, *Les Juifs de Paris depuis le VIe siècle* (Paris, 1889), p. 155. Cf. Zosa Szajkowski, 'Internal Conflicts in French Jewry at the Time of the Revolution of 1848', *Yivo Annual of Jewish Social Science*, vols. ii–iii (1947–8), pp. 100–17.

[3] Salomon Reinach, 'Conférence de M. Salomon Reinach,' *Bulletin de l'Association amicale des anciens élèves des Écoles Halphen et Lucien de Hirsch*, vol. i, no. 12, Apr. 1908.

paying the German war indemnity is well known.[1] It is worth noting, in addition, the extent to which Jews participated in the early governments of the Republic. Foremost among these was Crémieux, the former minister of the Second Republic who became a prominent member of the Provisional Government during the Franco-Prussian War and who resumed his office of Minister of Justice in 1870. Crémieux was at the same time the leading member of the Alliance Israélite Universelle, serving as its president from 1863, with one brief interruption, until his death in 1880. Three other important members of the Alliance, Eugène Manuel, Narcisse Leven, and Léonce Lehmann, served in high-ranking government positions. In the Chamber of Deputies a number of Jews, consistently republican, echoed the sentiment of most politically articulate members of the Jewish community.[2]

It is clear, then, that Jewish identification with France was more than rhetorical. Jews accepted with some enthusiasm the various political regimes which succeeded one another in the period before and during the establishment of the Third Republic. While their preference went in the direction of a republic, it seems apparent that this did not lead them into sharp conflict with the First Empire, the Restoration or Orléanist monarchies, or even the Empire of Napoleon III. A regime which was 'bien disposé pour les israélites' received the political loyalty which Jews considered as proper reciprocation.

While the origins of anti-Semitism in France can be traced to a period far earlier than the 1880s, the movement against the Jews in that country had little mass following before that time. Elsewhere, on the other hand, there were the beginnings of trouble. During the latter part of the 1870s anti-Semitism took root in central Europe as a new political force with considerable popular force behind it. Drawing both upon old animosities and also upon lower middle-class discontent at a time of severe economic depression, anti-Jewish leaders in both the Habsburg Monarchy and

---

[1] See Jean Bouvier, *Les Rothschild* (Paris, 1960), pp. 184–91; Frederic Morton, *The Rothschilds: a Family Portrait* (New York, 1961), pp. 163–5.

[2] See 'Noms israélites ayant figuré au Parlement français', *Annuaire 5647* (1886–7), p. 62.

the new German Empire awakened an ever-present hatred of the Jews. French Jews, however, had felt little organized popular pressure against themselves during the first three quarters of the nineteenth century, and could indeed believe, as does one historian of anti-Semitism in modern France, that Jews 'were protected by the French tradition of tolerance'.[1] Yet tolerance proved to be a somewhat fragile protection, and the situation changed sharply during the 1880s. On 1 January 1881 Lazare Wogue commented on the problem in an editorial for the *Univers israélite*. Looking over the previous year he was troubled by the perceptible growth of anti-Semitism in France, something which he had not noticed the previous year.[2] By the end of 1881 *L'Anti-Juif*, one of the first anti-Semitic papers in France, appeared, published in Montdidier.[3] The following year the sudden crash of the Catholic banking house, the Union Générale, marked the beginning of the popular campaign against the Jews. Polemicists on behalf of the bank, Catholic journalists, and even socialist propagandists agreed on one point: the Jews, led by the Rothschilds, were responsible.[4] After that time the anti-Semitic faction began to build itself into a movement of substantial strength. Thriving upon an extremely liberal press law, the *Loi du 29 juillet 1881*, and upon the protracted economic depression which continued until about 1890, anti-Semitism began an extensive campaign against the Jews of France. The explosion which followed the publication of Édouard Drumont's *La France juive* in 1886 demonstrated that sections of the French public were extremely receptive to the campaign. Significantly, this same decade marked the beginning of an anti-Semitic movement of unparalleled ferocity in the Russian Empire. The repercussions of this movement were soon felt in France, where Jews were only beginning to sense the ambiguities of their own position.

[1] Robert F. Byrnes, *Antisemitism in Modern France*, vol. i, *The Prologue to the Dreyfus Affair* (New Brunswick, New Jersey, 1950), p. 110.

[2] L. Wogue, 'La question juive', *U.I.*, 1 Jan. 1881.

[3] Byrnes, op. cit., p. 96.

[4] Ibid., pp. 131–5; Jean Bouvier, *Le Krach de l'Union Générale, 1878–1885* (Paris, 1960), p. 146; Jeannine Verdès, 'La presse devant le krach d'une banque catholique: l'Union Générale (1882)', *Archives de la sociologie des religions*, no. 19, Jan.–June 1965, pp. 125–56.

This chapter examines the political experience of the Jewish community beset by these first waves of anti-Semitism. It traces the difficult and sometimes painful way in which Jews translated the political theory of assimilation into political action. As we shall see, this political experience accorded ill with the hope and optimism in which the theory was rooted. The events which we shall describe took place against a background darkened not only by a rising anti-Semitic clamour, but also by other ominous examples of political and social unrest—succeeding one another came Boulangism, anarchist bombings, and, on the European stage, the threat of war.

Anti-Semites frequently charged the Jews with being members of a devious political clique or conspiracy working for their own sinister ends. In response, Jews liked to stress that their political preferences did not depend upon their Jewishness, and that Jews were drawn to political parties for the same reasons as other Frenchmen.[1] Hannah Arendt accepts the contention that Jewish political loyalties were diffused, seeing the Jews as acting to a great extent in the service of a corrupt parliamentary system. 'It has been justly observed that at this period of French history every political party had its Jews, in the same way that every royal household once had its retainers.'[2] Certainly this is true in terms of specific political leaders. We find Jewish Radicals like Camille Sée or Camille Dreyfus, Boulangists like Alfred Naquet, and even monarchists like Arthur Meyer. Yet the identification of these individuals should not lead us to ignore certain broad patterns of Jewish political affiliation; as one examines the Jewish community closely such patterns become apparent, and, despite the paucity of evidence, a rationale for Jewish politics is discernible. Indeed, it becomes clear that Jews had somewhat limited political choices in the liberal France of the Third Republic.

Clearly the Jews' tendency to defer to the existing political order in France, strengthened by an acceptance of republicanism as the

---

[1] I. Déhalle, 'L'assimilation des israélites français', U.I., 13 Sept. 1901, pp. 817–19.

[2] Hannah Arendt, 'From the Dreyfus Affair to France Today', J.S.S., vol. iv, no. 3, July 1942, p. 207.

agency of Jewish emancipation, precluded any large-scale association with the parties of the Right after 1870. These political groups were overtly monarchist, rejected the idea of the Republic, and seemed even to reject those Enlightenment ideals which had permitted formal Jewish citizenship. Moreover, the alliance of monarchists and Catholic ultramontanes, an alliance consummated in the bitter fighting against the Commune, further implied the exclusion of the Jews from the political Right. These Catholic leaders were traditionally unfriendly towards Jews, traditionally unwilling to accept the relegation of religion to the private sphere. Their efforts to regulate extensive areas of French life, sweepingly described by republicans during the 1880s as 'clericalism', appeared realistically as a threat to the regime so precariously established in 1875.[1] Very apparently, such an assertion of Catholic political interest was a threat to the Jews. When certain Catholic newspapers, particularly in the provinces, eagerly joined the anti-Semitic chorus after the publication of La France juive, the lines for Jews became even more clearly drawn. By the 1890s the Assumptionist newspaper, La Croix, was, next to Drumont's La Libre Parole, the most important anti-Semitic journal in France.[2] For Jews, as for all republicans, political preference was presented as a stark choice. It was a question of freedom or slavery: freedom, as guaranteed by the Revolution of 1789 and republican institutions; or slavery, with a return to the monarchy and under an ideology of reaction—clericalism.[3] In the republican rhetoric of the 1880s clericalism was a term which designated a whole spectrum of political activity on the Right. Jews could not afford to be associated with such groups which implied an open and standing threat to Jewish existence in France.

In this way Jews found themselves giving broad political allegiance to one of the two sides in the national debate which proceeded with at least verbal violence in the period we are discussing.

---

[1] See I. Cahen, 'La marée montante', A.I., 26 Nov. 1885, p. 382.
[2] See H. Prague, 'Revue de l'année israélite 5651-2', Annuaire 5653 (1892-3), p. 29; Byrnes, op. cit., pp. 181, 194.
[3] See Fernand Crémieux, 'Cléricalisme et judaïsme', in La Gerbe: études, souvenirs, lettres, pensées (Paris, 1890). On 'clericalism' see p. 113, above.

Matters were complicated, however, by the rise of a militant anti-clerical movement which took up the struggle against the Catholic and monarchist alliance. As always, such complications implied difficulties for the Jews.

Jewish leaders perceived a real danger for their community, both in the political turmoil aroused by the anti-clerical *laïc* laws of the 1880s, and in some of the specific measures either passed or discussed. The effort to limit state support for religious institutions, for example, seriously threatened a number of Jewish institutions. Although the *laïc* laws were primarily directed at the Catholic Church, Jewish institutions were unintended victims of this political battle. Successive legislative and government measures cut the budget of the Consistoire, lowered salaries for rabbis, reduced the subsidy for the Jewish seminary, and took away Consistorial power to administer certain trust funds and legacies, and to supervise religious schools. Jewish seminarians lost their military deferments, and in 1890 four students out of a total of ten were called up for service.[1] The attempt to strip cemeteries of their religious character became a serious bone of contention which lasted for over a decade.[2] Further attacks upon 'clericalism' were bound to affect the Jews as other measures were prepared and discussed in government circles. The 'spectre of separation' of Church and State appeared as early as 1886, and threatened the Jewish community with the sudden loss of all government support.[3] However, it appears that these direct assaults upon certain Jewish institutions did not deeply trouble the Jewish community. Only those Jewish leaders directly involved with the institutions affected seemed to be concerned. In the Chamber of Deputies four Jewish members remained silent on the matter; Hippolyte Prague

[1] Jules Bauer, *L'École rabbinique de France (1830–1930)* (Paris, n.d.), pp. 154–5; H. Prague, 'Revue de l'année israélite 5645–6', *Annuaire 5647* (1886–7), p. 24.

[2] 'La promiscuité du cimetière', *U.I.*, 1 Sept. 1881, p. 812; Isidore Cahen, 'Chronique de la semaine', *A.I.*, 10 Nov. 1881, p. 369; H. Prague, 'Revue de l'année israélite 5643–4', *Annuaire 5645* (1884–5), p. 81; L. Wogue, 'Les laïcisations', *U.I.*, 1 Aug. 1881, p. 776; Isidore Cahen, 'La question des cimetières en France', *A.I.*, 9 July 1896, p. 225.

[3] Prague, 'Revue de l'année israélite 5645–6', *Annuaire 5647* (1886–7), p.23.

complained editorially that the Jews as a group seemed indifferent to this real threat to the community.[1]

Yet perhaps indifference was not really the most accurate description, for although there was little public discussion among Jews, there appears to have been much private concern. Jews, in fact, had reason to fear that the campaign against the Catholic Church was leading, in many cases, to a violent attack upon all religious belief. This could lead to increased hostility against the Jewish community, and provide an issue much more serious than the legislative assault upon certain state-supported institutions. Many Jews remained silent during these conflicts in the hope that the controversy would exhaust itself. Isidore Cahen was not alone when he contemplated with apprehension 'the social peace troubled, the germs of religious warfare heated by the fanaticism of a dispossessed clergy, the terrible blow to the spiritualist idea caused by a measure which would cut all ties between religion and the state . . .'.[2] Cahen saw the cutting of such ties as a threat to social stability; like many, he believed religion to be in the service of an orderly society. In the face of radical attacks upon the idea of religion itself, and in view of the resulting moral 'chaos', Cahen was inclined to see the beginning of a larger assault upon the social order in which the Jews, weakened and without allies in the religious sphere, would be the victims.[3] Similarly, while Prague deplored 'the recrudescence of hatred, the attacks of unparalleled violence' of which anti-Semitism was only one dimension, he felt that these were largely due 'to the discontent provoked everywhere by the legislative or governmental measures taken against religious denominations, in particular the expulsion of God from primary-school teaching'.[4] Responding to the open attacks upon all religions, a number of moderates, among whom the most notable was the republican politician and philosopher Jules Simon, founded a League Against Atheism, with a weekly periodical *La*

---

[1] Prague, 'Revue de l'année israélite 5643-4', *Annuaire 5645* (1884-5), p. 81.

[2] Isidore Cahen, 'L'Église et l'État', *A.I.*, 9 July 1885, p. 218.

[3] Isidore Cahen, 'Les cultes en guerre civile', *A.I.*, 1 Jan. 1885, p. 1; id., 'La marée montante', *A.I.*, 26 Nov. 1885, p. 381.

[4] H. Prague, 'Causerie', *A.I.*, 3 Oct. 1889, p. 317.

Paix sociale, in order to combat unbelief and materialism, and to promote the 'grandeur of France'. Jewish leaders, in particular the Academician Adolphe Franck, Zadoc Kahn, and Alphonse de Rothschild, figured prominently in this organization.[1] But it was much more common for Jews to refrain entirely from involvement in the religious issue. Jewish editorialists consistently advised Jews to avoid participation in the debates over the *laïc* laws. Prague attacked Camille Dreyfus, a Radical deputy who was born a Jew but who claimed to be a *libre penseur*, for even bringing up the question of separation of Church and State in 1891. Dreyfus showed a particular 'lack of tact [*maladresse*]', Prague felt, because the issue would only stir up hatred and prejudice against the Jews.[2] Prudence, delicacy, and above all a sense of the need for Jews to keep religious questions out of the realm of public controversy dictated non-involvement in what was the most passionately discussed issue of the 1880s and early 1890s.[3]

Non-involvement, of course, did not mean insensibility. On the contrary, Jews seem to have been considerably affected by the militant anti-clerical campaign. This campaign reveals how unsure the Jews were of their position in French political society. Isidore Cahen explained what he felt were the feelings of the Jewish community: '. . . a religious minority like our own must above all remain on the defensive, and each one of us, while fully exercising the rights of citizenship, must show great reserve when the politi-

---

[1] L. W., 'La paix sociale', *U.I.*, 16 July 1888, pp. 650–1.

[2] H. Prague, 'Un incident à la Chambre', *A.I.*, 5 Nov. 1891, pp. 357–8. Cf. 'Chronique de la semaine', *A.I.*, 18 Nov. 1880, p. 377. 'Nous avons . . . repoussé énergiquement toute solidarité avec les Mayer de la *Lanterne* et les Camille Dreyfus, désignés comme les chefs du mouvement hostile à l'Église.' Ben Mosché, 'Les juifs et le clergé', *A.I.*, 16 Jan. 1896, p. 20.

[3] Apropos the execution of decrees against religious orders in 1880, Isidore Cahen wrote: 'C'est là une de ces questions où nous sommes, nous israélites, et comme tels, absolument désintéressés. . . . Combien plus impérieux n'est pas ce devoir d'abstention, quand la question soulevée n'est pas seulement religieuse, mais politique, quand elle devient une arme de parti, quand les ennemis du Gouvernement et de la Révolution s'en emparent comme d'un drapeau! La Révolution de 1789, voilà notre seconde loi de Sinaï, voilà le seul étendard autour duquel nous, israélites, nous devons nous grouper.' Isidore Cahen, 'Les décrets et les israélites', *A.I.*, 4 Nov. 1880, p. 363.

cal issues in debate touch closely upon matters of conscience.'[1]
'Reserve', in this case, meant reserve with respect to Radicalism,
the extreme Left of French politics during the 1880s. Cahen
referred to Radicalism as the 'sentinelle avancée du nihilisme';
Franck likened it in its fanaticism to the extreme Right of the
Restoration, 'which . . . had forgotten nothing, and learned
nothing'.[2] Unwilling to endanger a still uncertain position by
venturing into political extremism, Jews thus avoided the virulence
of the far Left of French politics.

Jews, then, shunned both political extremes. The Boulangist
episode in the 1880s, when militarist and nationalist elements
shook the foundations of the regime, served to confirm this
tendency. At its inception, the patriotic and anti-republican extremism of the Boulangist movement was masked somewhat, and
support for the General came from widely differing political
groups, united only by their professed patriotism and by a vague
dissatisfaction with parliamentary politicians. A number of Jews,
among them Alfred Naquet, Eugène Mayer, and the Baron de
Hirsch, took part in the political campaign which eventually led
to the collapse of the effort for a radically new political order and
to the suicide of Boulanger. It is interesting to observe the way in
which, as the Boulangist movement grew more openly extremist,
and as it progressively revealed its more dangerous side, Jews were
repelled by its incipient anti-Semitism. By the winter and early
spring of 1889, as the political campaign of the Boulangists was
reaching its height, the movement became associated with the
forces arrayed against the Jews. Boulanger was reported by one
journalist as saying that, if elected, 'he would get rid of the Jews'.[3]
Although the accuracy of the account was contested, it won

[1] Isidore Cahen, 'Les jésuites et les juifs', A.I., 31 Oct. 1889, p. 359.
[2] Cahen, 'La marée montante', A.I., 12 Nov. 1885, p. 365; Franck, 'Le rôle du
judaïsme dans le mouvement politique contemporain', A.I., 19 Aug. 1886, p. 258.
As Franck put it: ' . . . un israélite fidèle à sa religion sera toujours libéral, il ne
sera jamais radical. Jamais il ne viendra imposer ses convictions par la force ou
par la menace.' Ibid.
[3] 'Nouvelles diverses', U.I., 16 May 1888, p. 531; 'Nouvelles diverses', A.I.,
31 Jan. 1889, p. 39; Hippolyte Lévy, 'M. Boulanger et "la juiverie"', A.I., 7 Feb.
1889, p. 43; cf. Frederic H. Seager, The Boulanger Affair: Political Crossroads of
France, 1886–1889 (Ithaca, New York, 1969), pp. 174–81.

credence both in the Jewish press and in the anti-Semitic camp. Drumont announced in *Le Figaro* that he would vote for Boulanger, and anti-Semitic groups from as far away as Budapest began to congratulate the General.[1] Boulangism drew support from the militant Catholic and anti-Semitic *La Croix*, and in 1890 what remained of Boulangism entered into close relations with the newly formed French National Anti-Semitic League. By then the character of the movement had been plain for some time, as was its association with militant anti-Semitism.[2] And for Jews, if such were still needed, another political case could be used to teach the lesson of moderation.[3]

It was only to be expected that the nascent socialist movement of the 1880s and early 1890s found very little support within the Jewish community. As we have seen, extremism, wherever it arose in French politics, seemed to threaten the position of the Jews. Moreover, there was a long-standing tradition of anti-Semitism within French socialism, a tradition which flowed from an early association of the Jews with capitalism.[4] Elements of hostility towards the Jews persisted in the period under examination. Financial scandals, particularly Panama in 1893, provided occasion for anti-Semitic polemics on the part of socialists, and established an anti-Semitic vocabulary which outlasted real hostility towards the Jews. From the Jewish viewpoint, there was a further dimen-

[1] H. Prague, 'Chronique de la semaine', *A.I.*, 21 Feb. 1889, p. 57.

[2] Isidore Cahen, 'Un peu de sincérité', *A.I.*, 21 Mar. 1889, p. 89; 'Les questions religieuses: tremplin électoral', *A.I.*, 28 Mar. 1889, pp. 97–8; Marcus, 'Menus et significatifs incidents de la période électorale', *A.I.*, 19 Sept. 1889, pp. 302–3; L. W., 'Boulangisme et antisémitisme', *U.I.*, 1 Dec. 1889, pp. 163–4; Alfred Naquet, 'Lettre à M. Molina', *U.I.*, 1 Dec. 1889, pp. 164–6; C. D., 'La question juive', *La Nation*, 24 Jan. 1890; Byrnes, op. cit., pp. 232–5.

[3] B.-M., 'Antisémitisme et cléricalisme', *U.I.*, 6 Nov. 1896, p. 198, and 'Anti-sémites et boulangistes', *U.I.*, 30 Apr. 1897, p. 166; Mermeix [Gabriel Terrail], *Les Antisémites en France: notice sur un fait contemporain* (Paris, 1892), pp. 43–4.

[4] On the question of socialist anti-Semitism in France see Byrnes, op. cit., ch. iv; Zosa Szajkowski, *Anti-Semitism in the French Labour Movement: from the Fourierist Movement until the Closing of the Dreyfus Case, 1845–1906* (in Yiddish) (New York, 1948); Edmund Silberner, 'French Socialism and the Jewish Question, 1865–1914', *Historia Judaica*, vol. xvi, part i, Apr. 1954, pp. 3–38; Léon Poliakov, *Histoire de l'antisémitisme*, vol. iii, *De Voltaire à Wagner* (Paris, 1968), pp. 377–91; George Lichtheim, 'Socialism and the Jews', *Dissent*, July–Aug. 1968, pp. 314–42.

sion to socialist activity which made their involvement in it virtually impossible. The socialists were at least nominally revolutionary; their general political goal was the overthrow of the existing order in France. But Jews, as we have seen, made a point of accepting that order, and felt particularly attached to the Third Republic. As one writer explained, the long experience of suffering weighed heavily upon the Jews and prevented them from venturing into the political unknown. Revolution and class struggle were hardly likely to appeal to a people which had only recently found a real measure of security.[1] Far from being revolutionaries, Jews considered themselves model citizens, dedicated to 'law and order'. 'In every country,' wrote Isidore Cahen,

the Jewish masses appear as . . . an element of order and stability. To work to acquire, to spend when one has acquired, . . . that is what characterizes Jewish society. Hard working, firmly committed to social peace and to the idea of the family, believing strongly in property and inheritance, how could it be swayed by those destructive tendencies, by those incitements to violence and confusion which characterize what is called . . . socialism?[2]

Jews who thought differently about such bourgeois matters as 'property and inheritance', who were more inclined by social position to reject the concept of the model citizen proposed by the editor of the *Archives israélites*, were at the same time largely unassimilated, only recently arrived in France, and unlikely to identify with any French political parties, especially revolutionary parties. The large majority of the Jewish community which occupied itself with politics in France was necessarily more assimilated and by social position not inclined to join the still young socialist organizations. Suspicion of socialism remained strong within the Jewish community, and this continued despite the attempts of some to extinguish what remained of socialist anti-Semitism, and despite the progressive remoteness of revolution as a socialist objective.[3]

[1] R. T., 'Les juifs et la presse', *U.I.*, 18 Dec. 1896, p. 406.
[2] Isidore Cahen, 'Le socialisme et les juifs', *A.I.*, 16 Aug. 1885, p. 250.
[3] Alfred Lambert, 'Le socialisme et la cause juive', *A.I.*, 9 Feb. 1893, pp. 43–4; H. B., 'Les juifs et le Parti socialiste français', *U.I.*, 2 Oct. 1895, p. 56. The latter author quotes the socialist leader Jean Jaurès who, when interrupted by a heckler

'... It is an incontestable fact', observed one writer, 'that the mass of Jews leans towards the Opportunists.'[1] This was the most common generalization about the character of Jewish political affiliations during this period: whether the group referred to was called *opportuniste*, or *modéré*, or sometimes *progressiste*, it can roughly be identified as the political centre—solidly republican, and moderately everything else. The political constellation to which we are referring emerged from the split between the followers of Gambetta and the more extreme republicans in the period following the constitutional crisis of *seize mai* in 1877. The former took a relatively moderate position, particularly with respect to the issue of clericalism, the most important political question of the 1880s; the latter became the 'extrême gauche', assumed the banner of Radicalism, and united in a crusade against the Catholic Church. While the Moderates considered the Church too powerful and sought tactical means to limit its influence, the Radicals were much more violent in their attacks and based their opposition on a philosophical hostility towards religion itself.[2] Jews, as we have noted, felt threatened by the virulence of the anti-religious campaign. Their strongest defence, most realized, lay in a general atmosphere of toleration and mutual respect, and in a condition of order and social peace which the Moderates seemed anxious to provide. Popularly, this moderate position was denoted by the term 'libéralisme'. An editorial in the *Archives israélites* put it this way:

If clericalism in its worst sense, the interference of the priests in politics, is the enemy, we can say even more correctly that liberalism, the scrupulous respect for beliefs, the sincere and honest guarantee of the sacred rights of conscience, *voilà l'ami*.

who cried: 'Ce sont les juifs!', replied 'Oh! ne parlons pas des juifs. Il y a bien trop de chrétiens qui sont juifs!' Needless to say, this way of answering anti-Semites was not calculated to appeal to the Jewish community.

[1] R. T., 'Les juifs et la presse', *U.I.*, 18 Dec. 1896, p. 406. Cf. Paul Bettelheim, 'The Jews in France', *The Nineteenth Century*, vol. xlvii, Jan. 1900, p. 118; Alfred Berl, 'Le mouvement sioniste et l'antisémitisme', *La Grande Revue*, 1 July 1899, pp. 44–5; Ernest Renan, *Le Judaïsme et le christianisme: identité originelle et séparation graduelle* (Paris, 1883), pp. 24–5.
[2] See Pierre Sorlin, *Waldeck-Rousseau* (Paris, 1966), pp. 183–5.

The vital political aim, from this point of view, seemed to be 'the triumph of the spirit of moderation and the spirit of pacification in politico-religious matters'.[1] For this reason the *Archives*, and no doubt many Jews, found their political ideal in the Moderate cabinet of Casimir-Périer, formed in December 1893. For one thing, David Raynal, a Bordeaux Jew whose brother had served on the Consistoire de Paris, took the important portfolio of Minister of the Interior. But most important was the policy of Eugène Spüller, as Minister of Public Instruction. Spüller made a serious effort to settle the quarrel over the *laïc* laws; attempting to soothe the violent passions of both sides, to reconcile the Church and the Republic, he called for 'l'esprit nouveau'. Hippolyte Prague, undertaking to speak for his fellow Jews, gave warm and enthusiastic support for this policy.[2]

It is understandable, then, that Jews in France preferred to steer a middle course through the turbulence of French political life. Uneasy with the knowledge that the forces of monarchism and the Church were still powerful, they were driven in one direction; yet fearing political groups which would raise the anti-religious question to the level of a national crusade, they were driven in another. With a memory of the suffering to which they had once been subject, with the realization, since 1882, that anti-Semitism was a force of at least some consequence, Jews had an affinity for security, and a keen sense of their stake in stability.

There is evidence, moreover, that on the eve of the Dreyfus Affair French society was profoundly threatened in its stability, and thus that the insecurities of all groups which depended upon that stability were accentuated. At the end of a decade of depression, the rise of leftist militancy, signalled by the emergence of anarchism, presented a vital threat to the established order in France. As one student of the period has recently put it:

During the ten last years of the century, and more precisely from the municipal elections of 1892 to the legislative elections of 1898, the fear

[1] Prague, 'Causerie', *A.I.*, 3 Oct. 1889, pp. 317–18.
[2] 'M. David Raynal, Ministre de l'Intérieur', *A.I.*, 7 Dec. 1893, pp. 386–7; Prague, 'Causerie', *A.I.*, 8 Mar. 1894, pp. 73–4; id., 'Revue de l'année israélite 5653–4', *Annuaire 5655* (1894–5), p. 31.

of socialism is one of the dominant characteristics of French political life. This remarkable movement of opinion has not yet been studied. Between Boulangism and the Dreyfus Affair, in the time of Panama and the Méline Ministry, France seems to have gone through a period of deep uncertainty [une période creuse]. . . . This . . . masks a profound uneasiness at the rise of the extreme Left.[1]

Did the fear of 'le péril social' accentuate the tendency of the Jews to seek shelter in their traditional political refuge of the centre? Julien Benda, whose first political experience came from this time, says that he had an instinctive horror of 'rowdies [chahuteurs]' which was, perhaps, related to his Jewish background as well as to his experience in Paris.[2] Clearly Jews were sensitive to the violence latent in French society. Isidore Cahen described the darkening political scene which presented itself immediately before the first explosion of anti-Semitism during the Affair:

> Subversive and revolutionary elements of all kinds are bubbling up to the surface of society at this moment: Jews menaced by fanaticism, religion assailed by nihilist doctrine, social bases shaken, furious claims for well-being unmatched by the recognition of moral obligations, unconscious masses discharging the ballast of their traditions, France suffering from the same evils as the majority of nations and Judaism from the same causes of dissolution as other beliefs—what spectacle could be more calculated to sadden and to alarm those who know how to see and especially those who want to see?

Yet it is significant that, for purposes of resistance, Cahen recommended what was a traditional Jewish response: 'it is sufficient to ignore [de ne point se préoccuper] the arrogance of some and the cowardly capitulations of others, to keep illuminated in oneself the flame of truth and of justice, to act firmly according to one's wishes, one's knowledge, and one's love: Providence . . .'[3]

The political career of the Opportunist Joseph Reinach perhaps best exemplifies the middle position taken by most Jews within the French political spectrum. Reinach was born in Paris in 1856,

---

[1] Sorlin, op. cit., p. 358.
[2] Julien Benda, La Jeunesse d'un clerc (Paris, 1936), p. 70.
[3] Isidore Cahen, 'Un livre excellent', A.I., 27 May 1897, p. 166.

of a family originally from the small village of Reinach, near Basel, in Switzerland.[1] His father, Hermann-Joseph, was a successful banker who retired at the age of fifty-three to devote himself to philanthropy and public affairs. Like many Jews who lived through the French experience of 1848, Hermann-Joseph Reinach began his political involvement on the Left. The elder Reinach apparently had extensive political acquaintances. A long-time friend of both Ledru-Rollin and Adolphe Thiers, he was one of the founders of *La République française*, which in time became the militantly republican newspaper of Léon Gambetta.[2]

During the early years of the Third Republic a considerable number of Jews were members of Gambetta's political entourage. Attracted in part by the latter's liberalism and in part by his association in the popular mind with republican patriotism, they supported him as a symbol of the Republic and its resistance to its enemies who were also the enemies of the Jews. Adolphe Crémieux, as we have seen, was Gambetta's mentor during the last years of the Second Empire and his most prominent supporter following the Franco-Prussian War.[3] Isaïe Levaillant, who later became editor of the *Univers israélite*, was a prominent Gambettist, as were Narcisse Leven, the future president of the Alliance Israélite, Léonce Lehmann, a member of its Central Committee for over twenty years, Édouard Millaud, David Raynal, and many others.[4] Anti-Semitic propagandists, led by Drumont, seized upon this connection and made it a weapon in their campaign against the republican cause, going even so far as to claim that Gambetta himself was a Jew.[5]

---

[1] The biographical material on Reinach is taken from the articles in *J.E.*, *U.J.E.*; the *Larousse du xixe siècle*; *La Grande Encyclopédie*; A. F. B., 'M. Joseph Reinach', *Revue de l'histoire contemporaine*, Nov. 1889, pp. 371–3, Dec. 1889, pp. 387–9; Henri Rigault, *M. Joseph Reinach* (Paris, 1889); and obituary in *Le Figaro*, 19 Apr. 1921.

[2] On Hermann-Joseph Reinach see obituary in *A.I.*, 23 Feb. 1899; *U.I.*, 3 Mar. 1899.

[3] See S. Posener, *Adolphe Crémieux 1796–1880* (2 vols., Paris, 1933), *passim*.

[4] See Robert Anchel, 'Le judaïsme et Gambetta: à propos d'un cinquantenaire', *U.I.*, 17 Feb. 1933, pp. 645–7.

[5] Édouard Drumont, *La France juive: essai d'histoire contemporaine* (2 vols., Paris, 1886), i. 549–50, *passim*; Robert Launay, *Figures juives* (Paris, 1921), p. 187; L. Wogue, 'Triple assaut à l'antisémitisme', *U.I.*, 16 Jan. 1893, pp. 261–2.

Joseph Reinach first made himself known in political circles and first drew the attention of Gambetta through the pages of *La République française*. His formal collaboration with the great republican leader began a short period before the formation of the latter's *grand ministère* in 1881, and in this ministry Gambetta named Reinach *chef du cabinet*. In this office Reinach served as a secretary and important political lieutenant of the Premier. Their relationship became increasingly close, and when Gambetta died the following year, Reinach became his political heir. Charged with the responsibility of publishing Gambetta's political speeches and other important documents from the period of the Government of National Defence, Reinach also wrote a popular biography of Gambetta, and a detailed history of the *grand ministère*.[1] In 1886, along with a number of other Opportunists, he purchased and became the editor of the Gambettist newspaper which his father had helped to found fifteen years before. Through its columns, and, after 1889, from his seat in the Chamber of Deputies, Reinach carried on in Gambetta's tradition.

As an assimilated Jew, sensitive to political and social extremism, and as an Opportunist, whose political opponents were as strong on the Left as on the Right, Reinach made a conscious effort to interpret Gambetta in a moderate light. Indeed, he quoted Gambetta's dictum, 'La modération, c'est la raison politique', precisely to help build such an image of the man who was once known in a radically different way.[2] Order was carefully mixed with liberty in his assessment of Gambetta's political accomplishments: Reinach highlighted the manner in which the Gambettist movement was transformed from 'a revolutionary party' into 'a great governmental party', and the way that the achievement of 'necessary liberties' was combined with 'the conclusive demonstration of the need for a strong authority . . .'.[3] Along with most Opportunists of his generation, Reinach decried the violence of the campaign

---

[1] Joseph Reinach, *Léon Gambetta* (Paris, 1884); id., *Le Ministère Gambetta: histoire et doctrine* (Paris, 1884); id. (ed.), *Léon Gambetta: dépêches, circulaires, proclamations et discours 1870–71* (2 vols., Paris, 1886–91); id. (ed.), *Léon Gambetta: discours et plaidoyers politiques* (11 vols., Paris, 1880–5).

[2] Reinach, *Gambetta*, p. 84; cf. id., *Démagogues et socialistes* (Paris, 1896), p. 191.

[3] Reinach, *Gambetta*, p. 181.

against the Church, and posed, with Spüller, essentially as a moderate in the issue.[1] 'Intolerance', he wrote, 'is in itself hateful and mean. Whether it be religious or atheistic, it is equally repugnant to us.' The Radicals, he charged, were 'fanatiques à rebours', and as contemptible in this respect as Catholic extremists.[2]

It is not difficult to interpret Reinach's political liberalism as reflecting, at least in part, what we have seen to be the middle political course preferred by French Jews. His consistent opposition to the socialists in the pre-Dreyfus period was not uncoloured, for example, by his recognition that the parliamentary socialists, even Jaurès, flirted with anti-Semitism.[3] Against the Right his greatest moment prior to the Affair was the Boulangist episode, when his press campaigns took the lead in the struggle against the supporters of the General. Reinach made many enemies during this struggle, and suffered personally from vicious anti-Semitic attacks.[4] One political issue close to Reinach's heart was his proposal to restrict the broad rights granted to newspapers by the law of 1881. This statute had freed the press from a number of important restrictions on inciting attacks on religious and other groups, and was frequently seen, in Jewish circles, as a cause for the rising tide of anti-Semitism during the 1880s.[5] In this courageous effort to control a turbulent and contentious press, as in other political issues in which he took part, Reinach liked to see himself as in the deepest sense patriotic, firmly attached to 'republican idealism', and devoted to the reconciliation of bitterly contending

[1] Reinach, *Essais de politique et d'histoire* (Paris, 1899), p. 9; Mona Ozouf, *L'École, l'Église et la République* (Paris, 1963), p. 180. When Reinach published a collection of his articles from this period, less than four pages out of a total of 376 discussed the *laïc* laws, the most controversial political issue of the time. See Joseph Reinach, *La Politique opportuniste 1880–1889* (Paris, 1890).

[2] Reinach, *Démagogues et socialistes*, p. 125; Rigault, *Reinach*, p. 5.

[3] Reinach, *Démagogues et socialistes*, p. 12.

[4] See, for example, Albert Delpit, 'Les "Nouveaux" ', *Le Figaro*, 12 Nov. 1889; Hippolyte Lévy, 'M. Boulanger et "la juiverie" ', *A.I.*, 7 Feb. 1889, p. 43.

[5] Reinach, *Essais*, p. 13; id., *Mon Compte rendu: discours, propositions et rapports, 1889–1893* (Digne, 1893), pp. 11–30; Penel Beaufin, *Législation générale du culte israélite* (Paris, 1894), p. 108; *U.I.*, 1 Dec. 1889, p. 179; Alfred Berl, 'L'éclipse des idées libérales', *La Grande Revue*, 1 May 1900, p. 298; Hippolyte Lévy, 'Une loi à faire', *A.I.*, 31 Oct. 1889, pp. 351–2.

forces within the nation.[1] 'Neither Radical nor Opportunist,' he declared, describing his political platform to the electors of Digne in 1889, 'but republican and patriot.' For France his prescription was simple: 'religious peace, through tolerance, and social peace, through solidarity.'[2]

Reinach the politician had a great admiration for Benjamin Disraeli, the man whom he considered as a model for Jews participating in public life. In an essay on the British Prime Minister, a Jew who had been baptized as a child, Reinach revealed something of his own political priorities. Disraeli, he wrote, 'did not have in his veins a drop of English blood'. And despite the fact that he was 'doubly a foreigner to England, as a Venetian and as a Jew', yet he was still, 'from the first to the last day of his public life, the most English of the English'. Continuing, Reinach described Disraeli as a fine example of one who had reconciled Jewishness with national traditions:

> He kept all of the faults and virtues of his race; he took all of the virtues and vices of his adopted country. He never ceased in his heart to be a Jew, an Italian, and an Oriental; and there never was a more stubborn Englishman. . . . The purest descendants of the old Saxons appeared as but newly naturalized before him; this son of the Orient . . . had become an integral part of the country around him [*était devenu plus qu'indigène: autochtone*].[3]

Like James Darmesteter, Reinach placed an extremely high value upon this ability to don the garment of a national culture. His constant appeal was to higher interests which would transcend particularism and which would demonstrate the existence of a true French community of which the Jews were a part. His own political ideal was built upon the assumption that France would permit the reconciliation of competing groups, and the reconciliation of all differences in the general interests of national strength and unity.

Such political predispositions, widely held within the Jewish community and exemplified in the career of Joseph Reinach,

---

[1] Reinach, *Essais*, pp. 8, 31, 43–4.   [2] Reinach, *Compte rendu*, pp. 5–6.
[3] Reinach, *Essais*, pp. 108–9.

guided Jews through a number of severe crises in the period under consideration. These crises arose from the growing incidence of anti-Semitism; they reflected the fact that the condition of the Jews was becoming increasingly less secure, both in France and certainly abroad, in central and eastern Europe. The remainder of this chapter will discuss the impact of these crises upon the French Jewish community and the means by which Jews employed the politics of assimilation in their own defence.

One observes, in this connection, a distinct and persistent tendency on the part of Jews to minimize the importance of anti-Semitic outbursts in France and to respond passively to its assaults. Not unexpectedly, the publication and sudden success of the wildly anti-Semitic *La France juive* in the spring of 1886 caught the Jewish community unawares. Drumont's book was a sensational and instantly popular diatribe against French Jews; it was a catalogue of hatred which blamed virtually all of France's misfortunes upon them. Jews bought the book and apparently read it; yet the tendency was to depreciate its significance.[1] No systematic refutation ever came from the Jewish community. One Jewish freethinker sought to organize some form of collective response, but was unable to obtain support from other Jews. A Catholic writer, Léonce Reynaud, published the only extended answer to Drumont.[2] 'It would be only too easy to reply,' said a reviewer in the *Univers israélite*. 'We shall do nothing of the kind; first of all because we would have too much to do, and then, and especially, because pens which are less suspect, of Christian writers, ought to reply.'[3] Similarly, Isidore Cahen explained in the *Archives israélites* that he intended 'neither to discuss such a book in detail nor to undertake an apology for those whom it attacks: it would be to do too much honour to an outpouring as confused and venomous as this . . .'.[4]

[1] See Ernest Crémieu-Foa, *La Campagne antisémitique: les duels, les responsables: mémoire avec pièces justificatives* (Paris, 1892), p. 15; H. Prague, 'Revue de l'année israélite 5647-8', *Annuaire 5649* (1888-9), p. 28.

[2] Heber Marini, *Le Fin Mot de la question juive* (Paris, 1886); Léonce Reynaud, *La France n'est pas juive* (Paris, 1886) and *Les Juifs français devant l'opinion* (Paris, 1887).

[3] L. W., review of *La France juive*, *U.I.*, 1 May 1886, p. 488.

[4] Isidore Cahen, 'Les méfaits de la plume', *A.I.*, 29 Apr. 1886, p. 129. Cf. H. Prague, 'Une œuvre de haine et la presse parisienne', *A.I.*, 29 Apr. 1886, p. 131.

The response to Drumont which best captured the mood of much of the Jewish community was given by the classical scholar Théodore Reinach, the youngest brother of Joseph Reinach, in a lecture given before the Société des Études Juives in December of that year. Reinach declared that the success of Drumont's book was 'ephemeral', though he admitted at the same time that it was a 'disquieting symptom' which could not be ignored. He felt, however, that the Jewish community in France had responded correctly to the book; in the face of calumny it had met Drumont with 'the silence of disdain'. 'The silence of disdain' became the watchword for a certain kind of reaction to anti-Semitism on the part of French Jewry. According to Reinach the situation called for 'prudence and self-discipline [*sévérité*]', an avoidance of controversy about the matter among Jews themselves, and circumspection in their relationships with the community at large. 'Above all,' he advised, 'let us avoid criticizing one another in detail; for with what right, after that, can we complain if we are criticized collectively?' Apart from advising members of the Société to pursue rigorously the study of Jewish history and culture, he proposed no form of action against the anti-Semites which Jews could undertake. Passivity and self-improvement, an effort 'to remove the pretext for calumny' by advancing the work of assimilation—these he considered the Jews' best safeguards in times of difficulty.[1]

During the decade which followed, a continuing discussion over these tactics showed that the issue was not settled so simply for some members of the Jewish community. Zadoc Kahn, for example, had a number of reservations about the policy of 'silence of disdain'. He felt that silence could give credit to certain lies about the Jews, although he was cautious as to the manner of speaking out: 'Judaism . . . has nothing to be ashamed of, either in its past or in the present, and it is well that that be said with frankness and courage, but always with the measure of tact worthy of men who respect themselves.'[2] Hippolyte Prague charged that

[1] Théodore Reinach in *Actes* (1887), *R.E.J.*, vol. xv (1887), pp. cxxxii–cxxxiii. Cf. Léon Simon (ed.), *Selected Essays by Ahad Ha-Am* (Philadelphia, 1912), p. 173, *passim*.
[2] Zadoc Kahn, 'La mission des *Archives israélites* appréciée par le rabbinat', in *La Gerbe*, p. 15.

Jews had too often in the course of their history practised 'this virtue of submission which leads to immolation, to martyrdom'. 'Through a process of atavism', he wrote, Jews were currently too inclined to fall into this response.[1] And Isaïe Levaillant, who in 1896 assumed the editorship of the *Univers israélite* partly in opposition to the policy of passivity, denounced the lack of response which was 'cowardly and guilty, and which considered French Judaism as a sort of sick-room where one is not permitted to move around except by holding one's breath and by walking on tiptoes'.[2]

At the same time, other writers continued to counsel a more passive response. Adolphe Franck, as president of the Société des Études Juives in 1890, drew the following conclusion from the discussion of what response could be offered to attacks upon the Jews: '. . . we have only to continue to fulfil all of our duties to the fatherland, to humanity, to God, and to ourselves, without hiding from the anti-Semites . . . the disgust and the contempt which they inspire in us.'[3] Likewise, Isidore Cahen pleaded for patience:

We have only to await the indispensable protective measures and action on the part of public authority: that is the reason why we rarely turn our attention to the systematic aggressions against our religion, and why we maintain an obligatory silence, deciding to argue only with those who will use the procedures of courtesy and orderly discussion, [and] resolving to leave without response gossip, libel, and slander.[4]

Between these two positions, however, between the advocates of 'silence of disdain' and their critics, there was more agreement than difference, and more common assumptions than they might have admitted. Most noticeably, the proponents of 'action' and of some form of resistance shared with those inclined to silence an optimism about the future of the Jews in France which was based upon an essential confidence in the Republic. The Grand Rabbi of France, who had criticized the 'silence of disdain', set the tone for

---

[1] Prague, 'Causerie', *A.I.*, 30 July 1891, p. 241. Cf. id, 'Examen de conscience', *A.I.*, 4 Oct. 1894, pp. 329–30.
[2] B.-M., 'Un programme électoral', *U.I.*, 16 Oct. 1896, p. 101.
[3] Adolphe Franck in *Actes* (1890), *R.E.J.*, 1890, p. v.
[4] Isidore Cahen, 'Péril social', *A.I.*, 2 June 1892, p. 170.

this optimism in a number of public statements during the 1890s. 'France', he said in 1896,

will not let herself be seduced by unhealthy sophisms, she will remain faithful to her most glorious traditions, she will abandon nothing of her moral greatness in the world and, continuing to ignore differences of origins or of belief, she will only have for citizens devoted sons who have one desire: to see her great, prosperous, and honoured. . . .[1]

On another occasion, in response to an anti-Semitic political meeting, he declared: 'France would not be France, that is, the country of liberal traditions, of ideas of justice and equity, if words such as were spoken the other day had the slightest echo.'[2] Like the spokesmen for a passive policy, those who called for some Jewish response trusted in the rationality of the French public and in the ability of French institutions ultimately to contain hatred and prejudice.[3] Further, both 'resisters' and their more passive coreligionists linked anti-Semitism with a larger assault upon French society. It was frequently asserted, for example, that anti-Semitism was simply a diversion; the real victim, most often, was seen as the Republic itself.[4] From this one could easily deduce that the task of defending the Jews devolved essentially upon others; or, alternatively, that Jews could best defend themselves by being good republicans and by strengthening the existing order in France.

There was a certain comfort to be derived from linking anti-Semitism to a larger enemy which was, in clear intention, the enemy of French society as a whole. During this period, moreover, as 'le péril social' became one of the primary preoccupations of the French bourgeoisie, prominent Jews frequently made the specific indentification of anti-Semitism with the threatening social revolution. Alphonse de Rothschild was questioned on this point by

---

[1] 'Discours prononcés lors de l'installation du grand rabbin d'Épinal', *U.I.*, 16 Oct. 1896, p. 108.

[2] Julien Weill, *Zadoc Kahn, 1839–1905* (Paris, 1912), p. 137.

[3] See L. Wogue, 'Faut-il parler ou se taire?', *U.I.*, 1 Feb. 1890, p. 292.

[4] E. Lambert, *Les Juifs, la société moderne, et l'antisémitisme* (Paris, 1887), p. 8. Cf. Isidore Cahen, 'Péril social', *A.I.*, 2 June 1891, p. 170; Marini, op. cit., p. 14; L. Wogue, 'Ce qui nous manque', *U.I.*, 16 Mar. 1893, p. 395.

an interviewer in 1892. According to the report in *Le Figaro* he said: 'The war against Capital is a foolish and deadly thing; anti-Semitism is foolish and odious. But it's the same gang that wages this double war. . . . If, unfortunately, such insanities become accepted, it will be the definitive ruin of the country.'[1] 'Anti-Semitism', warned the *Archives israélites* after an anarchist bombing attack on the Palais Bourbon in 1893, 'is a school of social disintegration. . . . They begin with the Jews and finish up with parliaments.'[2] The two movements, anarchism and anti-Semitism, were considered the same; they were united in an effort to destroy French society. This connection accounted for the depth of feeling in Jewish circles at the assassination of the President of the Republic by an anarchist in 1894. At a special memorial service held in the synagogue of the Rue de la Victoire, Zadoc Kahn made a passionate plea for order reflecting the feelings of the community:

Society must regain its moral equilibrium, our country must return to her liberal traditions of good sense. . . . firm and energetic leaders must re-establish order in ideas, peace in consciences, and the religious respect for the law.[3]

If anarchism and anti-Semitism were simply differing forms of the same 'péril social', then they had to be fought together. This was Isidore Cahen's conclusion, and on this point he agreed with the advocates of an energetic Jewish response to their attackers: 'The defence of the Jews against a renewal of medieval fanaticism allied

---

[1] Jules Huret, 'Capitalistes et prolétaires: M. le baron Alphonse de Rothschild', *Le Figaro*, 14 Sept. 1892. Cf. Alphonse de Rothschild, 'Une lettre', *U.I.*, 1 Oct. 1892, p. 40; Edmond Le Roy, 'Ce que pensent les Rothschild', *Gil Blas*, 7 July 1892.

[2] H. Prague, 'Anarchie et antisémitisme', *A.I.*, 14 Dec. 1893. Cf. 'Solidarité inéluctible', *A.I.*, 28 Dec. 1893, pp. 409–10; Isidore Singer, *Anarchie et antisémitisme* (Paris, n.d.), p. 3. Arthur Meyer, the Jewish editor of *Le Gaulois*, made the same association: '. . . demandons-nous entre nous si toutes ces attaques passionnées contre les juifs, le capital, les riches, ne sont pour quelque chose dans le déchaînement anarchiste. Demandons-nous si les écrivains se rendent toujours bien compte que, du bout de leur plume sans qu'ils veuillent, sans qu'ils en soient virtuellement responsables, peut partir le fil qui aboutit au détonateur de l'anarchiste.' 'La politique', *Le Gaulois*, 26 Aug. 1895.

[3] Zadoc Kahn, *Sermons et allocutions* (3 vols., Paris, 1894), iii. 379.

with communist fanaticism merges, then, with the defence of society itself. . . .'¹

Finally, both the advocates of resistance and their more passive counterparts had little to propose in terms of a possible Jewish response, and were singularly unable to develop a strategy with which to confront the purveyors of anti-Semitic insults. Discussing the problem of the proper strategy in 1893, Lazare Wogue concluded, as had a number of others, that what was necessary was to reply to Drumont through the press—specifically, to found a newspaper which would be able to compete with *La Libre Parole* for the loyalties of Frenchmen.² Jews had tried the press before. Zadoc Kahn, as the semi-official spokesman for French Jewry, was accustomed to write letters to the major Paris newspapers refuting anti-Semitic charges.³ According to a police report in 1892, the Rothschilds secretly subsidized a number of small Parisian newspapers hostile to anti-Semitism.⁴ But by 1893 something new was being attempted: a Jew named Isidore Singer was preparing to launch a bi-weekly journal which would be the voice of the Jews in opposition to the anti-Semites. It is worth telling the story of this curious journalistic enterprise, and that of another attempted slightly later, for together they illustrate the essential weakness of Jewish defenders during this period.

The name of the first paper put it immediately into confrontation with Drumont—*La Vraie Parole*. Its founder, Isidore Singer, a young Austrian author and editor, had barely mastered the French language, and had been settled in Paris for only three years when he began his journal.⁵ He felt an obligation to take up this task because, he said, the leadership of the Jewish community in France had remained silent for too long, had used their

¹ Isidore Cahen, 'Péril social', *A.I.*, 2 June 1892, p. 170. Cf. id., 'Quelques témoignages', *A.I.*, 23 Apr. 1896, p. 187.
² L. Wogue, 'Ce qui nous manque', *U.I.*, 16 Mar. 1893, p. 396. Cf. Éliézer Lambert, *La Solidarité sociale d'après la morale juive* (Paris, 1899), p. 5.
³ Weill, *Zadoc Kahn*, p. 137.
⁴ A. N. F⁷ 12459, note of 25 July 1892.
⁵ L. W., '*La Vraie Parole*', *U.I.*, 16 Apr. 1893, p. 456; see the articles on Isidore Singer in *U.J.E.* and *J.E.*

'disdain' to obscure the deadly seriousness of the anti-Semitic campaign.[1] The painful truth, however, had to be faced: '. . . the anti-Jewish movement was progressively invading all layers of French society.'[2] Its importance and its dangers could scarcely be underestimated; unless someone took up the Jewish cause, matters would surely worsen. Yet at the same time Singer had confidence in the 'French genius' and in its ability in the long run to secure the triumph of justice and good sense. The motto of *La Vraie Parole* showed how widely he was prepared to cast his net in calling for support: 'With God, for Humanity, for the Fatherland, and for Justice.'[3]

Trouble, however, arose at the outset. Considerable financial support was necessary to launch a newspaper of this nature and, though a socialist of sorts, Singer felt inclined to turn to the rich. In all of France there were about a thousand very wealthy Jews, he announced in the first number; if each of these were able, 'without ruining themselves', to buy twenty copies, twenty thousand could be distributed free of charge. The enterprise, then, would be effectively launched. Singer's scarcely masked irony did not win many of these 'richissimes israélites'.[3] Indeed, it became rapidly apparent that one of Singer's greatest difficulties would be the lack of support from within the Jewish community, and in particular from its wealthiest members. His original capital had been obtained from a bank loan, likely secured through the intervention of Zadoc Kahn. Additional help came from the Baron Edmond de Rothschild and a series of Jewish organizations. But within a short time Singer was complaining loudly that promises made to him were not being kept: the Baron Edmond left abruptly for the Orient without helping the paper as he had agreed, and neither the Alliance Israélite nor Parisian rabbis were helping so much as to subscribe to a single issue.[4] Apparently some

---

[1] *La Vraie Parole*, 29 Mar. 1893.
[2] Singer, *Anarchie et antisémitisme*, p. 10.
[3] *La Vraie Parole*, 29 Mar. 1893.
[4] *La Vraie Parole*, 7 June 1893; I. Singer, 'L'apathie des juifs et la campagne antisémite', *La Vraie Parole*, 28 June 1893; id., 'Lettre ouverte adressée à M. le baron Alphonse de Rothschild', *La Vraie Parole*, 5 July 1893.

of the necessary funds were obtained, for after a brief interval when publication ceased, the newspaper reappeared. But from the end of 1893 its appearance was rather intermittent, the name and size were periodically changed, and, though Singer struggled along, publishing *La Vraie Parole* until the autumn of 1894, the journal never did become a daily as he had hoped, and with more interruptions it eventually disappeared completely in November 1894, just as the Dreyfus Case first burst upon the French public. With this failure Singer left France the following year, and went to New York to begin editing the *Jewish Encyclopaedia*.

What accounts for the failure of *La Vraie Parole* to find support among French Jews? Certainly its content was sufficiently respectable and interesting to have an appeal within the Jewish community. Singer published articles which would attract diverse segments of French Jewry; among his contributors (either with original articles or, more often, in reprinted material first published elsewhere) were James Darmesteter, Zadoc Kahn, Léonce Reynaud, Renan, Salomon Reinach, and Anatole Leroy-Beaulieu. These writers covered a wide range of subjects and did so with considerable skill and presentability. It is possible that the paper's tone was too 'serious' for popular success. And it is further possible that Jews were simply not sufficiently interested in Jewish affairs to support the enterprise—after all, the two Jewish weeklies, the *Archives israélites* and the *Univers israélite*, did not between them sell a thousand copies. However, the problem lay at least in part with Singer himself. The director of *La Vraie Parole* must have sounded to many Jews disturbingly like the anti-Semites the paper was supposed to combat. Singer castigated Jewish bankers, millionaires, rich Jewish merchants, and 'fils de famille' for their inactivity, materialism, and selfishness when it came to matters affecting the Jewish community. As time went on, and as the support for the paper fell off among French Jews, Singer grew more shrill in his denunciations, and more general in his plebeian assault upon the French social system as a whole. By August of 1893 he was denouncing in the most pungent terms the 'insolent plutocrats' who would not help him fight anti-Semitism. His words are best set down without translation:

N'oubliez pas, Mesdames — que vous vous nommiez Stern, Bischoffs-heim, Camondo ou La Rochefoucauld, Lebaudy, Ménier, peu importe — n'oubliez pas que, selon les principes de l'Ancien et du Nouveau Testament, c'est vous qui devriez, au fond, rougir devant les mal-heureuses victimes de notre stupide organisation sociale. . . . Vous n'avez pas le droit, Mesdames du *High Life*, juif ou chrétien, de donner des *five o'clock*, des *garden-party*, des déjeuners dinatoires, des soirées dansantes . . . tant qu'il y aura des millions d'êtres humains qui n'ont pas de pain sec à manger [*sic*].[1]

To the end Singer blamed his failure upon these 'plutocrats' who would not support him financially and who, largely in the persons of the Rothschilds, had a strangle-hold on Jewish organizations. This was the time of the Panama scandal, and it is significant that Singer sharply dissociated himself from the Jewish bankers in-volved in that affair.[2] His stance as a latter-day Amos could not fail to alienate Jews both by his personal attacks and also by his cavalier assault upon the existing social structure; by 1894, for example, the indefatigable editor was claiming to the French public that Karl Marx and Ferdinand Lassalle had 'done more for Judaism than all of our theologians put together'. French Judaism, he argued somewhat unconvincingly, should be a revolutionary force, should march at the head of international Judaism to lead the world towards a revival of religion and social justice.[3] Being somewhat less than revolutionary, the French Jewish community must have been relieved to see Singer safely in New York.

Joseph Aron, a Jewish businessman born in Alsace, made the other attempt to use journalism as a weapon in defence of the Jews. Returning to France after over twenty years spent in the United States, Aron began in 1894 to publish a financial weekly, *L'Homolo-gation*, a paper which made occasional references to anti-Semitism, but which had as its main purpose the defence of small investors threatened with ruin in the wake of the Panama scandal by wealthy speculators and by foreign, especially English, interests.[4] After one

---

[1] I. Singer, 'Programme social de la *Vraie Parole*', *La Vraie Parole*, 19 Aug. 1893.
[2] Ibid.
[3] I. Singer 'Cléricalisme, socialisme et antisémitisme', *La Vraie Parole*, 21 Apr. 1894; id., 'La mission du rabbin', *La Vraie Parole*, 18 Nov. 1893 and 25 Nov. 1893.
[4] See *L'Homologation*, 24 Nov. 1894, 23 Feb. 1895.

other change in name, the paper appeared as *L'Or et Argent* in 1895, devoted now mainly to the protection of small investors in Transvaal gold-mines. The journal was printed on yellow paper, with a somewhat crude typography and a chaotic organization. Articles appeared in French or in English, and included gossip, matters of small interest, business schemes, along with discussions of anti-Semitism. The Paris correspondent of the respected *Financial Post* considered Aron a madman, and yet another representative of the Parisian 'mushroom press'.[1] Whether or not he was 'mad', Aron was clearly even more of a maverick than Isidore Singer. His journalistic venom, however, was mainly reserved for Drumont, who, he felt, would be better and more honestly employed in the defence of the victims of financial speculators. But it is understandable that the Jewish community, and indeed virtually everyone, held Aron at arm's length. His polemical method consisted in printing the statement of his opponent along with his own answer; as a result the pages of his journals often resembled the pages of *La Libre Parole*. Erratic and rambling in his prose, he filled his columns with long open letters to all contenders. Aron could scarcely have been considered a serious competitor for Drumont or anyone else. By the end of 1895 the paper was floundering, and neither Aron nor his octogenarian editor-in-chief was able to save it. The paper finally collapsed in February 1896.

Despite the bizarre character of this enterprise, one cannot wholly dismiss the significance of this attempt to oppose anti-Semitism in the period immediately preceding the Affair. Aron felt that he had to take up the cudgel against Drumont for the same reason as Singer—precisely because no one else seemed willing or courageous enough to do so. The established Jewish press, he charged, preferred passivity, felt inclined to say 'après moi le déluge' when in fact 'le déluge' had already come. It was perhaps understandable then that Aron assumed the guise of a martyr:

Thus I, alone, all alone, I discovered important documents establishing that Drumont was an informer under the Empire, and, still alone,

---

[1] *L'Or et Argent*, 1 Aug. 1895.

I had the courage to print it and to prove it. . . . No one would help me, no one would speak to me about it, no one would propagate this discovery, and the silence of these journals almost made an impostor out of me![1]

It seems likely that the Jewish community was alienated as much by Aron's pugnacious and noisy attacks on anti-Semitism as by his eccentricities. Like Singer, Aron warned that Jews were inclined to underestimate the force of anti-Semitism; he implied, on occasion, that this was due to a certain 'moral cowardice' in the face of insult.[2] Again like Singer, Aron, though patriotically attached to France, ascribed much of the difficulty to a corrupt social system which had to be overthrown; the troubles of humanity, he warned, could only by solved by 'sound financial and social legislation' which would drastically restructure the economic system. Vaguely, his position was a defence of the little man against the rich and powerful; his social prescription—'Réprimons l'excès de l'argent trop puissant.'[3] Though hardly sufficient to make him a social revolutionary, this perspective put Aron with the Radical party on the extreme Left of the French political stage where, as we have seen, few Jews ventured to tread.

Considering these journalistic efforts, we can see that neither of them responded to a wide popular sentiment in France, and that neither was effective enough to win any degree of mass following. But it is most significant for our purposes that even the Jewish community appeared unwilling to support such public efforts by Jews to combat anti-Semitism. One suspects that the increasing alienation experienced by both Singer and Aron came in good measure from the cold response of their co-religionists in France. In a Jewish community devoted to the celebration of French society, to civility, and to the assimilation of the Jews, such crusaders were indeed enemies, and their programme suspect. Some clue to this relationship of Jews to Jewish spokesmen against anti-Semitism comes from an analysis of a more successful attack upon Drumont, at least from the point of view of French Jews.

[1] Joseph Aron, *Questions juives de 1896* (Paris, 1896), pp. 9, 12.
[2] Joseph Aron, *Les Mensonges de Drumont* (Paris, n.d.), p. 5.
[3] Joseph Aron, *La Résurrection de Lazare* (Paris, 1896), p. 15.

During the period immediately before the Affair, Alfred Naquet was one of the most acclaimed Jewish spokesmen against anti-Semitism. A highly assimilated Jew, Naquet was sufficiently atypical within the Jewish community to have married a Catholic and to have been the leading ideologist of the Boulangist movement.[1] His speech before the Chamber of Deputies in 1895 illustrates an approach to the problem of anti-Semitism which received applause in Jewish circles; the speech was reprinted in the Jewish press, and published in pamphlet form by the Consistoire de Paris.[2] His approach differed from that of Singer or Aron: Naquet argued not that Jews must stand together against their enemies, but rather that anti-Semitism was an obstacle to Jewish assimilation and an encouragement to Jewish exclusivism; it had to be destroyed precisely in order to facilitate 'the fusion [of the Jews] with the great mass of French citizens'. 'If', Naquet declared, 'anti-Semitism consisted uniquely in the discussion and refutation of dogma, of the central ideas of the Jewish religion, I tell you very frankly that I would be an anti-Semite myself.'[3] Pressing the point further he declared: 'I believe that the Jews are called upon to disappear . . . and to fuse themselves with the mass of the French nation; but it is on one condition, that liberty and equality subsist, for the day that persecution returns, you will stop the fusion from operating.'[4] Jews more attached to their religion than Naquet, Jews who differed with him on this as on other questions could, no doubt, show their broadmindedness by applauding his statement. Yet there was, at the same time, a way in which Naquet spoke for the Jewish community as a whole, and represented its basic political stance. For the Jewish community had placed a priority upon assimilation which, by the time of the Affair, was so clearly set forward that virtually all acceptable political acts had to be taken within that framework. Naquet's method of response to anti-Semitism was acceptable and popular, while that of Aron and Singer

[1] On Naquet's associations with Boulangism see Seager, op. cit., pp. 73–5, 135, 142, 180.

[2] A.C.P., ser. 3 C (1895). Cf. La Rédaction, 'A M. Alfred Naquet', *U.I.*, 1 June 1895, p. 581.

[3] Alfred Naquet in *Journal officiel, Chambre*, 27 May 1895, p. 1492.

[4] Ibid., p. 1495.

was not, because Naquet's followed this essential criterion for political action.

It was not difficult for the Jewish community to cleave to this political line during this period, at least so far as it concerned purely French developments. Anti-Semitism was, after all, a relatively minor movement until the Dreyfus Affair, however serious its implications might have been. One historian argues that on the eve of that explosion it 'was at its lowest strength since 1886'.[1] The outburst at the time of the Panama scandal, while it caused a great storm in parliamentary circles, does not seem to have threatened the Jewish community as a whole. Thus, from the assimilationist perspective at least, optimism, confidence in the Republic, and the inclination to avoid public controversy in such matters seemed justifiable.

Moreover, at the end of the nineteenth century it was still common in France to view anti-Semitic charges in a personal, as opposed to political, frame of reference. The most common form of opposition to the anti-Semites was not expressed in newspapers or on public platforms, but on the field of honour. Duelling was officially frowned upon in the Jewish community, and yet it was at the same time widely considered, as it was in the French community at large, an acceptable way to settle disputes.[2] The important point, from the perspective of this chapter, is the extent to which duelling reinforced the political attitudes discussed above. It seems clear that such duels, in particular the celebrated *affaire* of Captain Armand Mayer in 1892, to be discussed in another connection, drew energy away from the attempt to construct an organized Jewish opposition to anti-Semitism. Attention was focused, if at all, upon the personal insult; the interested public concerned itself with the confrontation of individuals, with duelling protocol, and with other extraneous personal issues, all of which tended to be clouded in polemic and invective.[3] By

[1] Byrnes, op. cit., p. 337.
[2] Simon Lévy, 'Le duel', *U.I.*, 16 June 1886, p. 609; L. W., 'Un duel', *U.I.*, 16 May 1892, p. 523; R. T., 'Le duel et les juifs', *U.I.*, 26 Nov. 1897, p. 295; Alex Bein, *Theodore Herzl: a Biography* (Cleveland, 1962), p. 89.
[3] Isidore Cahen, 'Quelques observations sur le pamphlet du jour', *A.I.*, 6 May 1886, p. 137.

duelling, Jews showed personal courage and the fact that, unlike the Jews in Germany, they were permitted to assimilate
the code of the French gentleman; meanwhile, anti-Semitism
continued.

For even the most sanguine of optimists, the explosion of anti-
Semitism in Russia in 1881 posed a problem different from the
occasional outburst in France. Public manifestations of anti-
Semitism were as yet rare in France at this time, and Jews were
little troubled by the question of how best to respond to it. When
anti-Jewish riots in the Russian Empire, launched with extraordinary ferocity and with full government complicity, were followed
by large-scale pogroms the next year, the news had a great impact
upon French opinion.[1] Quickly, a Comité de Secours pour les
Israélites de Russie sprang up; its chairman was no less a figure
than the aged Victor Hugo, and among its members were
Gambetta, Waldeck-Rousseau, Jules Simon, Eugène Spüller,
Scheurer-Kestner, and many other notables, including the Cardinal
Archbishop of Paris.[2] Jews of all political persuasions had formed
a committee some time before under the presidency of Alphonse
de Rothschild, and together the two groups now called for public
support. Appeals and protests were published in the popular press;
journals differing as much as the Orléanist Le Gaulois and the
socialist La Lanterne supported the campaign.[3] In 1882 Jewish
solidarity in the face of Russian persecutions posed no problem for
the Jewish community in France; there was a broad basis of sympathy in the community at large, and the vague anti-clerical mood

[1] For details on Russian developments and their impact on western Europe see
Mark Wischnitzer, To Dwell in Safety: the Story of Jewish Migration since 1800
(Philadelphia, 1948).
[2] Zosa Szajkowski, 'How the Mass Migration to America Began', Jewish Social
Studies, vol. iv, Oct. 1942, p. 291.
[3] Zosa Szajkowski, 'The European Attitude to East European Jewish Migration
(1881–1893)', Publications of the American Jewish Historical Society, vol. xli, Dec.
1951, pp. 148–52; 'La solidarité humaine', La Lanterne, 14 May 1882; Victor Hugo,
'Appel', La Lanterne, 19 June 1882; id., 'Un appel', Le Gaulois, 18 June 1882; R.,
'Pour les persécutés', Le Gaulois, 20 May 1882; and other Paris dailies, 20–3 May
1882. See also A. Naquet, 'Les juifs en Russie', Le Voltaire, 15 June 1882; Hippolyte
Millaud, 'Appel aux juifs', L'Indépendant, 22 Apr. 1882.

of the campaign ensured that it would have wide political appeal in Parisian circles.[1]

Matters grew much more difficult, however, as time went on. The late 1880s saw a steadily increasing assault upon Russian Jewry; the terrible famine of 1891–2 worsened their situation, and a current of brutality and murder swept across the face of eastern Europe. As Jews were making their way painfully westwards, escaping from the rule of the tsars, tales of horror began to seep into France. At the same time, however, an increasingly dangerous international situation was slowly drawing France and Russia into a political and eventually military alliance. This *entente*, strengthened by the famous incident in 1891 when Tsar Alexander III had the *Marseillaise* played for French sailors at Kronstadt, was joyously celebrated in France as a great victory for the Republic, a blow against Germany, and a demonstration of French power and prestige.[2] Anti-Jewish elements in France considered that the Jews were particularly vulnerable on the subject of Russia. Early in the course of the alliance anti-Semitic journalists claimed that 'international Jewry' was working to prevent such a *rapprochement* between the two countries; Judeo-German bankers, it was said, were in league with other unpatriotic elements against the interests of France.[3]

Partly in response to such pressures, Jews felt the necessity to trim the sails of their protest against the repression in Russia. There were no more committees of French celebrities to speak out against the pogroms, Hugo and Gambetta were now dead, and with the changed international climate, the fate of Russian Jewry seemed to have been forgotten by the less internationally minded Frenchmen of the 1890s. The most commonly expressed hope in

---

[1] However, Zosa Szajkowski quotes Alphonse de Rothschild as being very cautious, even at this time. Russian Jews, he is supposed to have said, should be helped, 'mais pas de discours politiques — pas de grand appel — pas de meeting. Les journaux pourraient s'emparer de cela. Il s'en suivrait une polémique dangereuse.' 'European Attitude to East European Migration', 148, n. 59.

[2] Jacques Kayser, *De Kronstadt à Khrouchtchev: voyages franco-russes, 1891–1960* (Paris, 1962), pp. 13–19.

[3] Alfred Badaire, 'Rome et Israël', *France et Russie*, 10 July 1891, p. 130; cf. 'Les juifs en Russie', *France et Russie*, 3 Mar. 1891, p. 38.

Jewish circles was now a trust that, due to the *entente*, the 'influence civilisatrice de la France' would cure the Russians of their sickness.[1] Public protest was no longer possible, and caution was the order of the day. '... We know', wrote Daniel Lévy in the *Archives israélites*, 'that any public demonstrations on our part would, even *here*, in certain quarters, be interpreted odiously and would immediately be followed *there* [in Russia] by the most terrible reprisals.'[2] Some Jews now felt the necessity to go even beyond such reticence in the matter of protest. When a Russian naval squadron made a public visit to France in 1893, one Jewish patriot, a well-known actor named Albin Valabrègue, sent the following letter to the major Parisian newspapers:

In other times it would have been sufficient for Jews to associate themselves wholeheartedly with this great demonstration [of welcome for the Russians]. . . . But at a time when an effort is being made to besmirch all of our co-religionists, accusing them of the faults of a few unscrupulous cosmopolitan Jews, it seems to me that we have a duty to show our warm association in a special way. We are not legitimate children of France, we are only adopted children, and as such we have the obligation to be twice as French as the others.[3]

---

[1] Prague, 'Causerie', *A.I.*, 13 Aug. 1891, pp. 261–2.

[2] Daniel Lévy, 'Les persécutions russes et la presse parisienne', *A.I.*, 4 June 1891, p. 178 (italics in original).

[3] Albin Valabrègue, 'Appel aux israélites', *Le Matin*, 14 Sept. 1893, and other Paris dailies. Valabrègue was a member of an old and respected Jewish family from Carpentras, and a close friend of Rabbi Mossé of Avignon. 'Réponse de M. le rabbin Mossé au toast de M. Albin Valabrègue', *La Famille de Jacob*, vol. xxxii (1889–90), p. 39. See also Albin Valabrègue, 'Le juif de demain', *Le Figaro*, 16 Sept. 1893; 'A propos de la question juive', *Le Figaro Supplément*, 27 Sept. 1893. Following this appeal, Valabrègue went on a patriotic speaking-tour. His stance as a Jewish patriot, however, was somewhat marred when after a few weeks he announced that he was the object of 'une révélation intérieure' which told him that 'la religion suprême, la lumière des éternelles vérités, est tout entière dans la philosophie du Christ; le christianisme est allé à droite, le judaïsme à gauche; c'est tout droit qu'il fallait marcher pour aboutir à la fraternité sociale, la religion de l'avenir'. 'Chez Albin Valabrègue', *L'Écho de Paris*, 8 Oct. 1893. Valabrègue's revelation did not stop there, and he eventually converted to Christianity, completing this strange story in 1895. See E. de Kératry, 'Conversion de M. Valabrègue', *Le Figaro*, 19 Feb. 1895; Isidore Cahen, 'Les étapes d'un vaudevilliste', *A.I.*, 28 Feb. 1895.

Valabrègue sought to demonstrate this high degree of Frenchness on the part of these 'adopted children' through a subscription for the Franco-Russian festivities. While no doubt many were embarrassed by this idea, once the project was launched there could be no dissociation; 23,000 francs were collected in less than two weeks, with the Rothschilds contributing 10,000 and the Grand Rabbi of France personally donating fifty.[1]

In this way the French Jewish community drew away from what appeared to be, in 1882, a movement of Jewish solidarity and political protest against injustice. The Jewish community moved instead to a preoccupation with Frenchness and with the political responsibilities of patriotism. Prayers were said in all four Paris synagogues when Alexander III was critically ill in 1894; and when Nicholas II assumed the title of Tsar, Zadoc Kahn called a special service to celebrate the occasion.[2] Questioned on the matter of prayers for Alexander III, Rabbi Israël Lévi offered the following apologetic explanation: '. . . the Tsar, Alexander III, who greatly persecuted the Jews, was a true believer [*un convaincu*], even a fanatic, and he was acting consistently with his conscience in attacking us as rigorously as he did. His character, then, should not be attacked. Finally, and above all, we must remember that he was a friend of France and that in the interest of our fatherland his life is precious.'[3]

Concern for the fate of Russian Jewry moved from the context of protest to the more gentle and politically innocuous realm of charity, and even here activity was carefully limited in the greater interests of patriotism. During this period the steady flow of refugees from Russia, Rumania, and Poland presented organizations of western European Jews with unprecedented problems. Never before in the course of history had emigration proceeded with such magnitude over such an extended period of time; not until the First World War would refugee problems be so severe. Close to 100,000 Jews moved westwards each year about the turn

[1] 'Nouvelles diverses', *A.I.*, 28 Sept. 1893, p. 310.
[2] 'Prières publiques', *L'Éclair*, 21 Oct. 1894; 'Actualité: le service pour le Tsar à la Synagogue', *A.I.*, 11 June 1896, p. 195.
[3] 'Nouvelles diverses', *A.I.*, 25 Oct. 1894, p. 359.

of the century, according to one authority, with the numbers rising still higher after 1903. Jewish committees made up of well-meaning amateurs and philanthropists were woefully unprepared and ineffective in dealing with this increasingly calamitous situation.[1]

As on other occasions, it was Zadoc Kahn who took the lead in France. The Grand Rabbi of France took it upon himself, in a pastoral letter of 1891, to channel Jewish efforts in a charitable direction by aiding refugees, while at the same time emphasizing the patriotic orientation of French Jews on the subject of Russia. The question was extremely delicate. In a key passage, he effectively sacrificed any political implications of the aid to Russian Jews to the higher interests of French patriotism:

On coming to the aid of our brothers in Russia, we are obeying one of the most legitimate of sentiments, we are accomplishing a work of pious solidarity which should not lend itself to any misinterpretation. As French Jews, we are pleased with the recent events [the Franco-Russian *entente*] which have so brilliantly raised the prestige of our country and have crowned twenty years of efforts, of moderation, of wise and fruitful negotiation. But misfortune has its claims upon us, our pity must go out to those who suffer, and we know that an immense population, bound to us by the most sacred ties, is undergoing terrible trials.[2]

Thus, in a short time, Jewish patriotism had taken its toll; for the French Jewish community in the 1890s murder had become 'terrible trials', and 'pity' was substituted for protest.

Refugees from tsarist pogroms first began to arrive in Paris in 1882. The Jewish community's handling of this refugee problem illustrates how their political orientation helped shape their response to a serious social problem. Like assimilated Jews elsewhere, in England, in Germany, and even in America, French Jews were suspicious and ill at ease when faced with their eastern European co-religionists. As the numbers of refugees swelled, as the difficul-

---

[1] Wischnitzer, op. cit., pp. 95–9; Szajkowski, 'European Attitude to East European Migration', pp. 144–7.

[2] Zadoc Kahn, 'Lettre pastorale du Grand Rabbin de France', *U.I.*, 1 Dec. 1891, pp. 163–5; *U.I.*, 16 Dec. 1891, p. 210; Weill, op. cit., p. 141.

PLATE III

a. Russian Jews at Montmartre 1882

b. Installation of Zadoc Kahn as Grand Rabbi of Paris at the Synagogue of the Rue Notre Dame de la Nazareth 1868

ties in securing work for them became more apparent, and as the news from Russia became known in France, they began to attract considerable public attention. These strangely dressed, poverty-stricken Jews, who spoke a tongue which no one understood, and who, because of their dietary laws, refused the food which was offered to them, were received with suspicion and hostility in the non-Jewish working-class quarters to which they first came. The Republican daily *L'Estafette* spoke sarcastically of a 'Semitic invasion' of 'hybrid Jews from the Orient... that the beneficent and humanitarian spirit of Messieurs de Rothschild has recently brought to France'. The socialist *Le Citoyen* feared that the arrival of Jews would mean a loss of work or lower wages for French workers.[1]

Meeting this public feeling, the Alliance Israélite sought to solve the problem by directing the refugees away from Paris to small towns in the provinces. In the autumn of 1882 the Alliance sent a circular letter to Jewish community leaders throughout the country asking them to accept these refugees, and offering a subsidy to facilitate settlement.[2] Of the responses which have been preserved, the communities of Avignon, Ittersviller, Mâcon, Marseille, Roubaix, Sarrebourg, Saverne, Toul, Troyes, and Vichy refused to accept a single refugee; when reasons were given it was generally argued that the Jewish community concerned was too

---

[1] X., 'L'invasion sémitique', *L'Estafette*, 10 Oct. 1882; Partout, 'L'émigration juive', *La Réforme*, 10 Sept. 1882; J. Adrien Martin, 'Les émigrants juifs', *Le Citoyen*, 15 Sept. 1882. Some idea of the popular image of Russian Jews may be gleaned from the following portrait, which originally appeared in *Harper's Magazine* and was reprinted in a French periodical in 1894: 'Il [the Russian Jew] forme une race toute particulière, différente du reste de la population, comme le nègre ou le Chinois des races européennes. On le reconnaît facilement d'aussi loin qu'on l'aperçoive, non seulement à sa physionomie et à sa tournure, mais aussi à certaines particularités de son costume, auquel il tient tout autant que l'Apache à sa couverture et le Mexicain à son sombrero. Le juif russe laisse croître de chaque côté des oreilles une longue mèche de cheveux qui tombe jusqu'au menton; son bonnet en alpaga noir avec sa grande visière qu'il enfonce jusqu'aux oreilles, sa lévite en drap ou en alpaga noir qui tombe tout droit, lui donnent un air de maigreur famélique. Il porte aux pieds des bottes éculées dans lesquelles il enfonce son pantalon; tient d'une main un parapluie et d'une autre une valise, car en Russie le juif voyage constamment pour ses affaires.' 'Le juif russe', *La Revue encyclopédique*, 15 Apr. 1894, p. 131.

[2] The replies to the circular may be found in the A.I.U., VI. D 22.

small or too poor to provide support. At least one official openly admitted that such settlement would contribute to the increase of anti-Semitism and would give the Jewish community a bad name in the judgement of municipal authorities.[1]

As refugees continued to arrive, landing usually in the south of France, provincial officials of the Jewish community grew frantic in their inability to deal with the situation and telegrammed their concern to the central authorities in Paris.[2] By the end of 1893 Zadoc Kahn was writing to an official of the Alliance: 'Our communities ... [illegible] are literally collapsing under their burdens.'[3] Paris proved to be the only possible place of reception, and the Alliance offered the Comité de Bienfaisance in the capital a substantial sum to help pay expenses there.[4]

But Parisian Jews too were reticent about accepting eastern European emigrants. After a considerable anti-Semitic newspaper campaign against the refugees in 1892, a campaign punctuated by genuine fears that the Jews were bringing cholera with them, the Secretary General of the Alliance felt it necessary to stress to an interviewer for Le Matin that in the future the Jews would be diverted to America and would henceforth avoid Paris entirely.[5] Of course, this did not prove to be possible. Perhaps out of a desire to discourage a flood of arrivals, the Consistoire Central did not apply itself energetically to the problem; on the whole, it appears that the eastern European Jews were neither well received nor adequately cared for. The Paris Comité de Bienfaisance even attempted to have eastern European Jews repatriated, and in

---

[1] M. Weil (Saverne) to Comité Central of the Alliance, 30 Oct. 1882, A.I.U., VI. D 22. However, six communities, those of Versailles, Toulouse, Nîmes, Hagenau, Lixheim, and Lille, made a token effort to help. They offered to accept a total of about twenty refugees.

[2] See A.I.U., IX. D 53.

[3] Zadoc Kahn to M. Bigart, 21 Sept. 1893, A.I.U., VI. A 43.

[4] Comité de Bienfaisance to Comité Central of the Alliance, 9 Jan. 1883, A.I.U., III. N 6.

[5] 'L'émigration juive', Le Matin, 28 July 1893; G. S., 'Un encampement', Écho de Paris, 24 Aug. 1892; Félican Pascal, 'Les futurs barons', La Libre Parole, 23 Aug. 1892; 'Les a-t-on désinfectés?', La Libre Parole, 27 Aug. 1892; 'Les juifs russes à Paris', La Gazette de France, 24 Aug. 1892; 'Juifs roumains et russes', Le Paris, 27 Aug. 1892.

addition continually directed them out of France, mostly to America.[1]

It seems clear that the French Jewish community, not unlike Jewish communities elsewhere, was reluctant and unwilling to absorb significant numbers of eastern European Jews. The latter were blamed by some French Jews for undermining the painfully won benefits of assimilation. A popular Jewish novelist, Louis Dollivet, explained how even the small number of refugees had, by their arrival, contributed to the growth of anti-Semitism in France. These unassimilated Jews, he said, understandably struck Frenchmen as being odd and peculiar; had they only been 'filtered out', Dollivet believed, 'no one would have treated the [French] Jews as foreigners'.[2] Julien Benda displayed the common prejudice of French Jews against 'le juif étroitement hébraïque'; this kind of Jew, he wrote was 'asservi par la passion d'un lucre modique et quotidien, patient, craintif, économe, travailleur, conservateur aveugle d'un faisceau de mœurs qui a perdu sa raison d'être'—in short, the traditional picture painted by the anti-Semites. Benda considered that such Jews represented 'a passive resistance in the [forward] movement of our civilization'; by contrast, assimilated Jews had 'broken more and more with the Hebraic tradition' and were thus in the mainstream of modern progress.[3] The implication was that French Jews were obliged to dissociate themselves from their more retrograde co-religionists and to accentuate the progressive elements within Judaism. Salomon Reinach, too, was highly conscious of the 'inferiority' of eastern European Jews, of their political and social backwardness, and of the subtle interrelationship which existed between anti-Semitism and the retention of outdated customs and beliefs.[4] Jews with this perspective saw in the

---

[1] Charles Chincholle, 'La misère en Israël', Le Figaro, 1 July 1892; 'Paris pittoresque', L'Éclair, 25 July 1893; Ch. Formentin, 'Droit d'asile', Le Jour, 25 July 1893; Szajkowski, 'European Attitude to East European Jewish Migration', p. 158.

[2] Louis Lévy, 'Deux conférences', U.I., 1 July 1898, p. 465. Cf. R. T., 'Deux conférences', U.I., 8 July 1898, p. 487; Salomon Lubetzky, 'Les Juifs étrangers et l'antisémitisme', U.I., 15 July 1898, pp. 521–3; 'Antisémitisme sémitique', U.I., 19 Aug. 1898, pp. 695–8.

[3] Julien Benda, Dialogues à Byzance (Paris, 1909), pp. 71–3.

[4] Salomon Reinach, 'L'émancipation intérieure du judaïsme', U.I., 26 Oct. 1900, p. 172.

M

refugees a sudden and disturbing reincarnation of their own pre-1789 condition; this accounts for the discomfort, distaste, and even revulsion experienced. The young André Spire was typical in this respect: '. . . I helped them when they came to my door, but without enthusiasm. Rich and poor, their arrival in France exasperated me.'[1] Finally, one suspects that many Jews had assimilated a sufficient amount of French culture to have accepted much of the anti-Semitic argument. The refugees, who appeared genuinely strange to French Jews, seemed to confirm the validity of caricatures presented in *La Libre Parole*. The point of these French Jews, however, was that the anti-Semites were right only in so far as they referred to unassimilated Jews. French Jews, after all, were 'israélites éclairés', patriotic Frenchmen, and full participants in the life of the nation.[2]

Refugees from eastern Europe were, in a sense, the first victims of the assimilationist politics we have been discussing. French Jews, for the most part, lived through this period without feeling that a crisis was building or that the future of a people was at stake. They steered their middle course carefully, with some apprehension, but certainly without the sense of being seriously threatened. '. . . There is no "Jewish question", at least in France, and we hope there never will be one', wrote Lazare Wogue in 1893.[3] There was, of course, something of an anti-Semitic question, but this was so clearly foreign to French life as to be relatively harmless. 'Jewish questions' were eastern European affairs; Russian pogroms and wide-scale repression elsewhere were to be expected, an unfortunate consequence of retarded development. The spirit of France, however, was something which held even protesters like Joseph Aron or Isidore Singer in thrall. The spirit of France, the French Revolutionary ideal of universal emancipation, was a spirit with which Jews could readily identify. So far from this spirit was anti-Semitism, that Jews could scarcely accept the fact of its continued existence in France; so strong was their belief in French liberalism, that confidence in the politics of assimilation could not be shaken.

[1] André Spire, *Souvenirs à bâtons rompus* (Paris, 1962), p. 37.
[2] Salomon Reinach, 'Émancipation intérieure', p. 175.
[3] L. Wogue, 'Une séance mémorable', *U.I.*, 1 July 1893, p. 611.

PART THREE · THE DREYFUS AFFAIR

WHEN the Jewish staff officer Alfred Dreyfus was arrested and, on the basis of no firm evidence, convicted of espionage at the end of 1894, no one expected that there would be either an 'affair' or a heightened anti-Semitic attack upon the Jewish community in France. For almost three years little was heard of Dreyfus. But behind the scenes men were working for his rehabilitation. Another staff officer, Major Picquart, risked his career to express strong doubts about the evidence upon which the conviction was based; the Dreyfus family was at the same time quietly seeking to secure a revision of the judgement. In the beginning of 1898, however, the storm broke: Émile Zola thundered forth with his *J'accuse*, and the campaign to free Dreyfus became public. Several days later anti-Semitic riots began. Mobs roamed the streets in Nantes, Nancy, Rennes, Bordeaux, and several other cities. They assaulted Jews, sacked their stores, and raided synagogues. Anti-Semitic bands, led by Jules Guérin, paraded in Paris. In Algeria the riots got completely out of hand, and it took several days to restore order.

Here was a test for the politics of assimilation. Here was an occasion when Jews, more than ever before, were forced to consider their relationship to the French community at large. Yet the majority of the French Jewish community lived through the crisis without any significant change in their political outlook. Jews remained committed to the assimilationist ideology which men like James Darmesteter had articulated. Insecure, cautious, and even anxious, they nevertheless declared their confidence in the ideals of the Third Republic. A small group of Jews, however, chose a different path, and rejected assimilation along with the social order which France represented. These Jews were followers of Bernard Lazare; their political perspective was one of Jewish nationalism and, in some cases, Zionism. In the three chapters which follow we shall examine these divergent political positions.

CHAPTER VII

BERNARD LAZARE AND THE ORIGINS OF JEWISH NATIONALISM IN FRANCE

JEWISH nationalism exalted the quality of being Jewish, stressed Jewish distinctiveness, and was committed to Jewish preservation. Unlike the assimilationist creed, Jewish nationalism dictated that the Jews should remain apart; unlike the liberal doctrines of the Third Republic, it did not accept the belief in French pre-eminence. Bernard Lazare, a journalist and *littérateur*, was the unquestioned leader of this movement in France. He was the man most responsible for the public launching of the Dreyfus Affair, and became one of the most persistent critics of the Jewish establishment. Moreover, his personal transition from assimilation to nationalism, completed during the early stages of the Affair, offers a striking illustration of themes which have been discussed in earlier chapters. With Lazare we begin a new perspective on the condition of the Jews in modern France: he provides a reference point from which we can examine once again, in a somewhat different light, the assimilationist position of the majority of French Jews, and at the same time from which we can look ahead to the growth of Zionism, the ultimate rejection of assimilation.

There was nothing in Lazare's background which prepared him for Jewish nationalism. He was born Lazare Bernard in 1865, in the small town of Nîmes, in Provence, where Jews had lived since the seventh century.[1] The Jewish community there had had a

[1] S. Posener, *Adolphe Crémieux 1796–1880* (2 vols., Paris, 1933), i. 3. The biographical material on Bernard Lazare is taken from the articles in *J.E.* and *U.J.E.*; obituaries in *The Jewish Chronicle*, 4 Sept. 1903, *La Revue universelle*, 1 Oct. 1903, pp. 504–5; P.-V. Stock, *Mémorandum d'un éditeur*, vol. iii, *L'Affaire Dreyfus* (Paris, 1938), pp. 30–1; Jean-Maurice Muslak, 'Bernard-Lazare', *R.E.J.*, vol. vi, no. 106 (1946), pp. 34–63; Nelly Jussem-Wilson, 'Bernard Lazare's Jewish Journey: from being an Israelite to being a Jew', *J.S.S.*, vol. xxvi, no. 3, July 1964, pp. 146–68; Baruch Hagani, *Bernard Lazare, 1865–1903* (Paris, 1919).

turbulent history. Made up for the most part of refugees from the Spanish monarchy, the Jews of Nîmes lived for centuries under the protection of the local bishop, but were periodically subject to expulsion, persecution, and pillage. By the second half of the eighteenth century, according to one writer, this ancient community had shrunk to about thirty or forty families.[1] Although the community grew somewhat following the French Revolution, its sons steadily moved to Paris, eventually leaving one of the oldest Jewish settlements in Europe in a state of decline.[2] It is probable that the Bernard family did not have deep roots in the community of Nîmes, having come to Provence from Alsace at the time of Napoleon, along with many other Jews. In any case, the Bernards do not seem to have stood out from the other families of the community. Lazare's father was a modest businessman, a *pratiquant* who faithfully observed Jewish traditions but who at the same time mixed socially with non-Jews, and secured a secular education for his children. His eldest son, Lazare, went through the traditional ceremony of Bar Mitzvah, but it is unlikely that the boy understood the Hebrew words which he uttered on that occasion, or that he felt any strong religious commitment.[3] Completing his secondary studies in Nîmes in 1886, Lazare left for Paris to finish his education, having become an unbeliever, and, like many young Jews of the Midi, having little or no attachment to the religion or the community in which he was raised.

Lazare came to Paris to study at the École Pratique des Hautes Études. However, the distractions of the capital soon proved stronger than his academic aspirations; introduced to a number of literary figures by his cousin, the poet and playwright Ephraïm Mikhaël, he plunged into the exciting and bohemian world of Symbolism. This was the high tide of Symbolist activity in Paris; the

---

[1] Posener, loc. cit.

[2] See Zosa Szajkowski, 'The Decline and Fall of Provençal Jewry', *J.S.S.*, vol. vi, no. 1, Jan. 1944, pp. 31–54; Muslak, 'Bernard-Lazare', p. 362 n. 2.

[3] 'Le théoricien du nationalisme juif: Bernard Lazare', in Lazare papers, box 2, pp. 130–2. This unpublished, unsigned, and undated manuscript (by Jean-Maurice Muslak?) was found among the Lazare papers at the Alliance Israélite Universelle. The material in it seems to have been collected with accuracy and care, and has been verified whenever possible.

unchallenged *maître* was Stéphane Mallarmé, and, after the publication of Jean Moréas's manifesto in *Le Figaro* in 1886, a school
may be said to have been established. The young Jew from Nîmes
abandoned his studies to join with these writers and to devote himself to literature. He now signed his name Bernard Lazare and, in
company with such writers as Maeterlinck, Viélé-Griffin, and
Villiers de l'Isle-Adam, set out to do battle with the literary vogue
of the day, the poetry of the Parnassians and the realism of Émile
Zola. Before long, Lazare became recognized as a critic of some
importance; he contributed a series of articles to *Le Figaro*,
the *Mercure de France*, the *Revue blanche*, and several other reviews.
In 1890 he began to publish the short-lived *Entretiens politiques et
littéraires*, an *avant-garde* journal founded in company with Paul
Adam, Henri de Régnier, and Viélé-Griffin.

During this period Lazare established himself above all as an
independent critic. A pugnacious and belligerent writer, he was
anxious not to be drawn irrevocably into the service of any school
or coterie. Symbolism was still a dominant style of the period and
the style to which he gave most of his allegiance, but it was the
eclectic approach of the *Revue blanche* which attracted Lazare,
rather than the more 'established' *avant-garde* periodical the *Mercure de France*. His criticism was sometimes ruthless and destructive,
but he vigorously defended this as essential for his literary purposes: '... hatred is in literature, as in politics, as in art, a primordial
and indispensable passion; he who does not know how to hate
does not know how to love what is for him beautiful.'[1] A passionate and somewhat violent critical stance was linked to a strong
sense of the artist's responsibility to society. The artist, he felt,
must prepare 'the new morality', the new guide for mankind in
the world which was coming into being:'... the task of the writer,
the task of the artist, the task of *l'art social*, is to teach the man of
today other forms of beauty; it is also to make him suited to
inhabit the world of tomorrow.' In a sense Lazare was concerned with helping to create a new social being. With such a
perspective, there could be no retreat into the aestheticism of *l'art*

[1] Bernard Lazare, *Figures contemporaines: ceux d'aujourd'hui, ceux de demain*
(Paris, 1895), p. iv.

pour l'art: 'For us, the role of the writer is not to play a flute in a tower, contemplating his navel; the artist is neither a hermit, nor an entertainer, and art must be related to social questions [*l'art doit être social*].'[1] Lazare made it clear that for him 'l'art social' was founded upon both a certain fixed view of society and a radically uncompromising political perspective:

The principle of this art must be that life is good and that its manifestations are beautiful. Its ugliness is the product of social conditions. To give to life its beauty it is necessary, then, that art help in its turn to transform society, and it is thus that all social art becomes revolutionary art.[2]

True to this conception, Bernard Lazare made contact with anarchism, ideologically the most revolutionary force in France in the early 1890s. In his earliest flirtations with the anarchist movement, and in his combination of a fervent individualism with an equally strong social consciousness, Lazare did not stand out from most writers of the Symbolist generation. The *Revue blanche*, where the young Léon Blum was the literary critic, was also drawn into this orbit, and became a point of contact between anarchism and Symbolism.[3] But Lazare went beyond flirtation. By 1892, according to Jean Maitron, a historian of the anarchist movement, Lazare's periodical, the *Entretiens politiques et littéraires*, became closely identified with anarchism; about this time he lectured to anarchist societies and contributed to the anarchist newspaper *Les Temps nouveaux*.[4] Deepening his involvement, Lazare testified on behalf of the anarchist leader Jean Grave during the latter's trial in

[1] Bernard Lazare, *L'Écrivain et l'art social* (Paris, 1896), pp. 27, 31.

[2] Ibid., p. 30. Cf. id., 'Histoire des doctrines révolutionnaires', *Le Devenir social*, Jan. 1896, pp. 1–14.

[3] A. B. Jackson, *La Revue blanche 1889–1903: origine, influence, bibliographie* (Paris, 1960), p. 112. Cf. Alain Silvera, *Daniel Halévy and his Times: a Gentleman-Commoner in the Third Republic* (Ithaca, New York, 1966), p. 56; Léon Blum, *Souvenirs sur l'Affaire* (Paris, 1935), p. 20; Eugenia Herbert, *The Artist and Social Reform: France and Belgium 1885–1898* (New Haven, Conn., 1961); George Woodcock, *Anarchism: a History of Libertarian Ideas and Movements* (Cleveland, 1962), p. 305.

[4] Jean Maitron, *Histoire du mouvement anarchiste en France, 1880–1914* (Paris, 1955), pp. 131, 132 n. 5, 434 n. 3.

1893, protested against the celebrated *Procès des trente* which followed the assassination of the President of the Republic, Carnot, and, in the autumn of 1894, joined with the famed geographer Élysée Reclus to help found an anarchist study group in Brussels.[1] Although he always maintained a substantial degree of independence within the anarchist movement, and although as a literary figure he was not associated with the proponents of direct action such as Vaillant or Ravachol, Bernard Lazare had achieved considerable notoriety by the time of the Dreyfus Affair.

Unfortunately, little is known about Lazare's anarchist thought, and it is difficult to tell if it progressed beyond a general but intense hostility to bourgeois, capitalist society. Clearly, however, Lazare considered himself a revolutionary, and, like many artists of his generation, at war with the society around him. French history since the Revolution, in his view, was a continuation of revolutionary struggle, in which 'le peuple' asserted their claims against a bourgeoisie which had betrayed its own revolutionary ideals.[2] The overthrow of the existing order was, in a vague sense, his political objective, and as an artist he viewed his role as helping to prepare the public consciousness necessary for that overthrow.

During these years, the period immediately following the appearance of Drumont's *La France juive*, Lazare did his best to avoid any ties with his Jewish background and indeed displayed a contempt for all religion, especially Christianity. Not long after his arrival in Paris he published, along with his cousin Ephraïm Mikhaël, a short play entitled *La Fiancée de Corinthe*. The theme of this work was the joylessness and suffering brought by the Christian religion; consistent with certain trends within the Symbolist movement, it pointed towards an exaltation of paganism and personal liberation from religious restraint.[3] With most artists and

---

[1] Maitron, op. cit., p. 238; Pierre Bertrand, 'Lettre ouverte à Bernard Lazare', *Les Droits de l'homme*, 30 Oct. 1898; Louis Vauxelles, 'Quelques syndiqués: Lazare', *Les Droits de l'homme*, 24 May 1898; 'Nouvelles diverses', *A.I.*, 18 Oct. 1894, p. 351.
[2] Lazare, 'Histoire des doctrines révolutionnaires', *Le Devenir social*, pp. 1–14.
[3] Bernard Lazare and Ephraïm Mikhaël, *La Fiancée de Corinthe* (Paris, 1888).

writers of the Left, Lazare was steeped in the current anti-clerical and anti-religious mood, and judged himself in conflict with all religious belief. With most Jews of this social group, Lazare considered Judaism as simply one more religion to be opposed. Both Judaism and Christianity were ideologies of the past; both had to be overthrown in the revolution of the future. The publication of *La France juive* did not shake many of them in this regard.

Yet, as we have seen, several issues brought the 'Jewish question' forward for public discussion at this time, and obliged a number of Jews to face more decisively the issues of anti-Semitism. During the late 1880s and early 1890s, as Jewish immigration from eastern Europe increased, and with the growth of anti-Semitism fed by Boulangism, Panama, and various press campaigns, more and more Jews were forced to articulate some view on the situation of the Jews in France. It is probable that the arrival of refugees precipitated Lazare's own interest and concern. In two articles, published in the *Entretiens* of 1890, Lazare discussed the matter for the first time, and, in none too gentle tones, denounced the victims of tsarist persecution.

Lazare first disposed of the Jewish religion, in terms taken from the current, fashionable assault upon positivism. '... For a long time,' he wrote, 'it has fallen into a stupid rationalism; it seems to have borrowed its dogmas from the Declaration of the Rights of Man; it forgets, as does Protestantism, that essential element: that a religion without mystery is like the straw that is sifted out from the grain.'[1] But religious decadence was not, in his judgement, the cause of anti-Semitism. The anarchist and revolutionary declared that the real cause was *social*; its root, moreover, lay in the critical distinction between *juif* and *israélite*. A *juif* was a Jew as portrayed in the traditional anti-Semitic caricature, a person who 'is dominated by the unique preoccupation with making a quick fortune', an individual 'who make(s) money the goal of all life, and the centre of the world'. The *israélite*, on the other hand, was assimilated into French society, was much more refined, 'limited in [his] desires', was either poor or of moderate circumstance, and

[1] Bernard Lazare, 'Juifs et israélites', *Entretiens politiques et littéraires*, vol. i, Sept. 1890, p. 176.

had been settled for a long time in the place in which he lived. French Jews were generally *israélites*; German and eastern European Jews were *juifs*. Lazare felt that anti-Semitic charges were substantially correct when applied to these *juifs*. *Israélites*, he urged, should reject association with these 'moneychangers from Frankfort, Polish bartenders, Galician pawnbrokers, with whom they have nothing in common'. Building upon his anger, he called upon the *israélites* to 'kick out these lepers who corrupt them; to vomit up the rottenness that wants to creep in'.[1] This, Lazare felt, was the way to deal with anti-Semitism erroneously directed against French Jews. In his second article Lazare specifically denounced the 'solidarité juive' which some Jewish agencies called for as a measure of Jewish responsibility towards their co-religionists. What did Bernard Lazare, an 'israélite de France', have in common with 'these coarse and dirty, pillaging Tartars, who come to feed upon a country which does not belong to them'? The Alliance Israélite Universelle, he reported, was helping to receive refugees from eastern and central Europe. But what was the result of this policy?

To welcome these contemptible people to our country, to help them, to patronize them, to implant them in a soil which is not their own and which does not nourish them, in order to facilitate their conquest? For whose benefit is this? For the benefit of the cosmopolitan *juif* who has no ties with any nation, no affection for any nation, who is [like] the Bedouin moving his tent about with complete indifference.[2]

Moreover, the 'israélite de France' was being tarred with the same brush as these wretched foreigners:

... thanks to these hordes with whom we are confused, it is forgotten that for almost two thousand years we have lived in France. . . . What I want to insist upon publicly is that we have nothing whatever in common with these [Jews] who are constantly thrown in our faces, and that we must abandon them.[3]

---

[1] Lazare, 'Juifs et israélites', *Entretiens politiques et littéraires*, vol. i, Sept. 1890, pp. 178–9. Cf. a similar distinction made in a popular article on Russian Jews, 'Le juif russe', *La Revue encyclopédique*, 15 Apr. 1894, pp. 131–2.

[2] Bernard Lazare, 'La solidarité juive', *Entretiens politiques et littéraires*, vol. i, Oct. 1890, p. 230.   [3] Ibid., p. 232.

Anti-Semitism, when directed against French Jews, was the result of a misunderstanding; decent and patriotic *israélites* were confounded with the cosmopolitan *juifs*, and it was only the latter who deserved the opprobrium which Drumont and others somewhat recklessly scattered about.

But to escape from anti-Semitism, Lazare said flatly in 1893, there was only one thing for Jews to do—to assimilate, to vanish entirely, 'losing themselves in the mass of the nation'. Only in this way would Jews be fully accepted by French citizens, and only then would they distinguish themselves fully from the 'invading tribe' of which they had once been a part. Among the 'superior representatives of the race', he wrote, 'the incorporation has [already] been made'. For the others it was only a matter of time, for the Jews 'were destined to disappear totally'.[1]

As we have seen, it was not uncommon for Jews to consider their own disappearance as a people. Lazare, however, went one degree further than most, for he viewed this disappearance as being absolutely necessary in order to destroy anti-Semitism. Non-Jews had come essentially to the same conclusion, though from a somewhat different point of view. Émile Zola, better known as a defender of Jewish rights, declared in an article on the Jews published in *Le Figaro* in 1896 that 'if the Jews still existed', it was the fault of the anti-Semites. Left alone the Jews would have vanished, dissolved, become, in fact, Frenchmen like all others.[2] Lazare, at this point in his life, could see no destiny for the Jews beyond this assumption of Frenchness. In this respect his views did not differ substantially from the middle-class assimilations we have studied. Though professing to be an anarchist and a revolutionary, he had yet to draw the connections

[1] Bernard Lazare, 'La nationalité et les juifs français', *Le Figaro*, 27 Dec. 1893. 'Comment les juifs éviteront-ils cet antisémitisme et cette sorte de tacite réprobation des indifférents à la lutte? Ils ne la pouvaient éviter que d'une seule façon: en disparaissant, en se perdant dans le flot de la nation.'

[2] 'S'il y a encore des juifs, c'est votre [the anti-Semites'] faute. Ils auraient disparu, se seraient fondus, si on ne les avait forcés de se défendre, de se grouper, de s'entêter dans leur race. . . . A force de montrer au peuple un épouvantail, on crée le monstre réel. Ne parlez donc plus d'eux, et ils ne seront plus. . . . Embrasser les juifs pour les absorber et les confondre en nous.' Émile Zola, 'Pour les juifs', *Le Figaro*, 16 May 1896.

between his thoughts about the Jews and his conceptions of French society.

Moreover, Lazare showed himself, at this time, as being singularly critical of his Jewish background and Jewish tradition. In a collection of essays and stories published in 1892, he repeated the traditional image of the Jew as portrayed in much Christian and anti-Semitic literature of the day. He indicated a fascination with the figure of Judas as the model for the Jew since the death of Christ; he repeated the vague imputation of collective Jewish guilt; and he referred to the Jewish condition in modern times as a consequence of divine punishment.[1]

And yet he did more than reflect traditional anti-Semitism. There is an interesting dialogue, in one essay, between Lazare and a Chinese Jew, a 'schismatique', who reports upon the state of their co-religionists scattered about the globe. The Chinese tells Lazare that the Jews, though 'dominated by the basest preoccupations', were at the same time extremely diversified, to be found in all kinds of circumstances throughout the globe. Lazare, in response, agrees, particularly with respect to the 'base preoccupations'. His principal objection to the Jews, however, lay in the fact that they so resolutely remained apart, throughout history, from the societies in which they lived. His most serious ground for complaint, then, was not the 'baseness' of the Jews, for there was baseness everywhere, but rather their obstinate refusal to assimilate. Although he accepted the fact that these societies in which Jews lived were often themselves corrupt, he continued to assume that Jews were obliged to become a part of them.[2] That Lazare admitted the evils of the surrounding societies, that he recognized the corruption of the people who formed them, and that this admission and this recognition meant difficulties for his theory about the need to assimilate, he did not see at the time. It soon became apparent, however, that revolution and assimilation could not be reconciled in this way, and that, for Lazare at least, a radically different perspective on the Jews was necessary.

[1] Bernard Lazare, Le Miroir des légendes (Paris, 1892), passim. Cf. Lazare Prajs, 'Péguy et Israël', unpublished thesis for the doctorât de l'Université, Sorbonne, 1966, p. 33, passim.   [2] Lazare, Miroir, p. 232.

Lazare's interest in Judaism grew. His hostility towards *juifs* in general and eastern European Jews in particular did not prevent him from considering the matter further and from pondering more deeply and in a systematic way the situation of the Jews in the modern world. It may be suggested at this point that one of the factors pressing Lazare towards this study, in addition to the anti-Semitic crisis which was building, was the influence of Maurice Barrès. While the latter became best known as a vicious French nationalist and xenophobe, his following included many whose ideas would lead elsewhere. Among the youth of the literary generation of the 1880s and the early 1890s, Barrès worked a certain magic such as few could escape. 'In the generation of writers which had immediately preceded my own,' wrote Léon Blum, 'he was for me, and for most of my friends, not only the *maître* but the guide; we formed a school about him, almost a court.'[1] Barrès led his followers in a quest beyond the point to which the decadents of the 1880s had taken countless numbers of sensitive young people. His work can be seen as an attempt to escape from the nihilism which pervaded some literary circles, to find some discipline, some certitude upon which to build a rule of life, either in the *culte du moi*, or in an extension of the *moi* to include *le peuple*, or in *la terre et les morts*, or in a mystical union with the Church. Many followed Barrès in this quest, and many worked out, on the basis of his writings, their own personal solution. Bernard Lazare might well have been thinking of Barrès when he wrote, probably in 1892, an essay entitled *Le Passé dans le présent*. Lazare spoke of 'the soul of the past which lies always in the present'; he described his own walk through the Jewish ghetto of Amsterdam, a place with 'an exotic and Oriental aspect', but which at the same time enabled him, as a Jew, to hear 'voices long since dead . . . whose echo . . . reverberates in a mind which is prepared to hear them . . . .'.[2]

[1] Blum, op. cit., p. 86. Cf. Micheline Tison-Braun, *La Crise de l'humanisme: le conflit de l'individu et la société dans la littérature française moderne* (Paris, 1958), i. 137–9; Henri Massis, *Maurras et notre temps: entretiens et souvenirs* (Paris, 1961), p. 24; Pierre de Boisdeffre, *Barrès parmi nous* (Paris, 1952), pp. 202, 205; Paul Gaultier, *Les Maîtres de la pensée française* (Paris, 1921), p. 198; Émile Faguet, 'Un roman de M. Barrès: à propos les *Déracinés*', *Revue bleue*, 20 Nov. 1897, p. 665.

[2] Bernard Lazare, *La Porte d'Ivoire* (Paris, 1897), p. 292. Though this book

Barrès and the literary vogue of the period encouraged writers
and artists to explore the past in this way, and to hear and to cultivate these voices which were a part of an individual's past. Lazare's
preoccupation with the 'Jewish question', which grew steadily
from 1890, reflects at least some fascination with his own cultural
and ethnic background, some effort to cultivate his own *moi* and
to search beneath familiar French traditions for a new basis of
loyalty.

   As early as 1892 Lazare was preparing a study of anti-Semitism
throughout history.[1] The work was published two years later, and
contained within it the seeds of a new perspective on the Jews
which Lazare was soon to develop into a coherent ideology of
Jewish nationalism. This book, which was praised by Drumont
as being 'a fine effort at impartiality', is the point of union of
Lazare's 'anti-Semitic' period and his subsequent development of
a radically different outlook.[2] Significantly, the book was completed before the Dreyfus Affair, and before the explosion of anti-
Semitism which forced many to re-evaluate their views. Lazare's
'conversion', while stimulated and affected by external events,
flowed essentially, as will be seen, from his revolutionary disposition.

   Lazare began his study professing objectivity: 'I am neither an
anti-Semite nor a philo-Semite; it has been my intention to write
neither an apology nor a diatribe, but an impartial study in history
and sociology.' And yet he clearly did 'not approve of anti-
Semitism'; the book was a long and at times disjointed attempt

was not published until 1897, it is listed on the flyleaf of *Le Miroir des légendes*
(1892) as being 'sous presse'. A number of Jewish nationalist writers were influenced by Barrès. See, for example, André Spire, *Quelques juifs et demi-juifs*
(2 vols., Paris, 1928), i. vi–vii, 156; C. Lehrmann, *L'Élément juif dans la littérature
française*, vol. ii, *De la Révolution à nos jours* (Paris, 1961), pp. 84, 104; Frédéric
Empaytaz, 'Barrès et les juifs', *Revue littéraire juive*, May 1928, pp. 408–13; Pierre
Aubery, *Milieux juifs de la France contemporaine à travers leurs écrivains* (Paris, 1957),
pp. 306–7.
   [1] Letter, Bernard Lazare to Vielé-Griffin, 30 Aug. 1892, B.N. n. a. fr. 1375,
p. 310.
   [2] 'C'est un livre fort nourri de faits et dominé, d'un bout à l'autre, par un bel
effort d'impartialité, par la consigne donnée au cerveau de ne pas céderaux impul-
sions de la race. . . . En réalité, il dit ce que nous disons tous les jours, seulement, il
le dit autrement que nous.' Édouard Drumont, review of Bernard Lazare's *Antisémitisme, La Libre Parole*, 10 Jan. 1895.

to account for it.[1] Central to Lazare's argument was the contention, similar to that expressed in his articles of 1890, that 'the general causes of anti-Semitism have always resided in Israel itself'. Throughout history the Jews persisted in being 'unsociable', and 'exclusive', refused to assimilate, and hence isolated themselves from the rest of mankind.[2] This in turn prompted the hostility of the surrounding communities in which Jews lived. Other causes drew their strength from this central fact, and although in the course of time anti-Semitism moved from a religious to a social, and eventually to a 'national' basis, the essential ingredient was always a Jewish distinctiveness which was self-imposed. The Jews remained apart because they were above all a nation which, though containing within it highly diversified elements, had a basic 'unity of sentiments, ideas, ethics'.[3] This Jewish nation retained a national consciousness, drew upon an ancient law and literature, and was fortified by a belief in Jewish superiority. Further, this consciousness was critical for a continued Jewish existence: 'When the Jew ceases to have national consciousness he disappears; so long as he has this consciousness, he continues to be.'[4] Anti-Semitism in the modern period, a period of nationalism, was the reaction of national groups to another nationalism which attempted to exist within the body of the nation; it was the hostility vented upon a group which preferred to remain apart. But here, as Lazare had pointed out before, anti-Semitism revealed its basic contradictions:

..., anti-Semitism was born in modern societies because the Jews did not assimilate, did not cease to be a people, but when anti-Semitism had ascertained that the Jews were not assimilated, it violently reproached them for it, and at the same time whenever possible it took all necessary steps to prevent their future assimilation.[5]

Lazare introduced another theme into his study which was to have great importance in the development of his Jewish nationalism. This was the doctrine of 'the revolutionary spirit of Judaism'.

[1] Bernard Lazare, *Antisemitism, its History and Causes*, tr. (New York, 1903), p. 5.
[2] Ibid., pp. 8–13.
[3] Ibid., p. 248.
[4] Ibid., p. 267.
[5] Ibid., p. 272.

Drawing heavily upon the works of James Darmesteter, Lazare described the Jew's predisposition for the radical transformation of the oppressive societies in which he lived, a predisposition which arose from 'the very essence of the Hebrew spirit.'[1] Even radicals such as Marx and Lassalle, socialists and assimilated Jews, drew upon their Jewish backgrounds in formulating their politics:

... the Jew, even the extreme Jewish radical, cannot help retaining his Jewish characteristics, and though he may have abandoned all religion and faith, he has none the less received the impress of the national genius acting through heredity and early training.[2]

Thus, although the emancipated Jew had lost his religious faith, he was still a part of the ancient tradition, he was still shaped by the 'Jewish spirit' and, in the modern world, as a result, he was 'a veritable breeder of revolutions'.[3] Anti-Semitism was at least in part a reaction to this fact; it was in part, therefore, a movement to defend antiquated traditions by attacking one of the foremost sources of revolutionary spirit.[4]

The conclusion of this study was that anti-Semitism, in all of its guises, was 'everywhere the creed of the conservative class'. Lazare believed, as he had earlier, that anti-Semitism would diminish as assimilation progressed. Assimilation would make progress as the world continued to become smaller, more integrated. Still, the Jews would not necessarily become identified with particular national groups as they became more like the men around them. '... The Jewish spirit is vanishing', he wrote, and with the coming decline of both religious and national exclusivism around the world, a new and cosmopolitan spirit would replace the conservative ideologies of nationalism.[5] Hatred for Jewish capitalists, more-

---

[1] Lazare, *Antisemitism*, p. 277.

[2] Ibid., p. 315.

[3] Ibid., p. 326. Cf. id., 'L'esprit révolutionnaire dans le Judaïsme', *Revue bleue*, 20 Mar. 1893, pp. 622-8. '... les juifs furent mêlés à tous les mouvements révolutionnaires, car ils prirent à toutes les révolutions une part active, comme nous le verrons si nous étudions un jour leur rôle dans les périodes de trouble et de changement.' Ibid., p. 628. Notes and fragments of manuscripts in Bernard Lazare's papers indicate that he was preparing such a study of the role of Jews in revolutionary movements at the time of his death in 1903.

[4] Lazare, *Antisemitism*, p. 329.   [5] Ibid., p. 372.

over, would eventually lead for hatred to all capitalists; 'inflexible laws' were everywhere 'working towards the substitution of communal property for the capitalist regime'.[1]

In his final lines, Lazare the anarchist returned to his revolutionary outlook, and in so doing contradicted one central theme of the book. Anti-Semitism, he observed at the close, was tied to an old order of things, in particular the forces of nationalism and of capitalism. Its central cause, he therefore implied, lay not in Israel itself but rather in the societies in which Jews lived. Its demise in each circumstance was less dependent upon the Jews than upon the degree of social progress that each society achieved. Anti-Semitism would be finally defeated by the forces of social revolution, which were everywhere at work to change the fundamental structure of society:

In every way I am led to believe that [anti-Semitism] must ultimately perish, and that it will perish for the various reasons which I have indicated: because the Jew is undergoing a process of change: because religious, political, social, and economic conditions are likewise changing, but above all because anti-Semitism is one of the last, though most long-lived manifestations of that old spirit of reaction and narrow conservatism, which is vainly trying to arrest the onward movement of the Revolution.[2]

By placing anti-Semitism in its broader social context, and by aligning the cause of the Jews with the overthrow of the existing order, Lazare's perspective on the 'Jewish question' had fundamentally changed. Although he conceded a great deal to the anti-Semitic prejudices of his day, his sympathies were unmistakable; henceforth his own prescription for the Jews could not really be the work of assimilation into a national culture, any more than *embourgeoisement* could be his prescription for the oppressed; what was required was the revolutionary change which would transform all of society and which would in this way eliminate all artificial barriers between men.

The first stage in Lazare's transition to Jewish nationalism was this placing of 'the Jewish question' in a revolutionary social and

[1] Ibid., p. 374.   [2] Ibid., p. 375.

political framework. The second stage, and one which followed quickly upon the first, was his recognition that from the Jewish point of view the most powerful obstacle to Jewish liberation was a psychological one.[1] This obstacle was constructed out of social materials provided by the society in which Jews lived; its character, in western European countries, was less the Jew's cultural backwardness than his profound demoralization which prevented real emancipation.

Lazare first articulated this point of view a few weeks after *La Libre Parole* announced the arrest of Captain Alfred Dreyfus. Lazare knew little about the case at the time, but he chose the occasion provided by the arrest and the excitement which followed to write an article treating some of the broader implications for the Jews of the newly aroused anti-Semitism. The article was entitled 'Le nouveau ghetto'. In it, Lazare appeared to be sceptical as to the possibilities of assimilation in French society as it was then constituted. In the previous few years the anti-Semites had created 'un état d'esprit antisémite' which had had formidable results. The most important of these was that the Jew had been made anew into a 'pariah'; indeed, the situation posed the question of whether the Jewish people was not again excluded from French society as it had been before the Revolution. A new ghetto was being formed in France, Lazare wrote, 'a moral ghetto':

> The Jews are no longer cloistered, the streets in which they live are no longer cordoned off by chains. But a hostile atmosphere is created around them, an atmosphere of suspicion, of latent hatred, of prejudices all the more powerful because unavowed, a ghetto much more terrible than that from which they could escape by revolt or by exile. This animosity is hidden, and yet the intelligent Jew ... can perceive it; he has the impression of a wall that his adversaries have built between himself and those in whose midst he lives.[2]

This conception of a 'hostile atmosphere', of a psychological 'wall', was to loom large in Lazare's nationalist ideology. His subsequent efforts may be seen in good measure as an attempt to

[1] See Hannah Arendt, 'From the Dreyfus Affair to France Today', *J.S.S.*, vol. iv, no. 3, July 1942, p. 239.

[2] Bernard Lazare, 'Le nouveau ghetto', *La Justice*, 17 Nov. 1894.

combat this new ghetto and its consequent demoralization by offering to the Jew a pride in himself, and a consciousness of his own dignity and mission in the world. Inevitably, these had to be conceived in opposition to French society, to the society which, under the guise of emancipation, was subjecting Jews to a more effective and more insidious form of bondage than the one to which they had once been subjected. Since the Jew was being made into a pariah, and since society as it was constituted would not permit Jewish assimilation, the Jew was forced to live upon his own emotional and cultural resources. These Lazare attempted to provide.

What prompted this recognition of the psychological barriers to Jewish emancipation? The Dreyfus Affair, as we have noted, had not yet intruded into the lives of Frenchmen, and the great stimulus which it was to give to all thinking about the Jews was still to come. Lazare, no doubt, was inclined as a literary critic to consider the intellectual and emotional dimensions of anti-Semitism; as he pondered his own experience in the Barrèsian manner, it is possible that he realized the violence of his own former reaction to unassimilated Jews, and that he was led to examine to what a small degree the Jews had in fact been permitted 'to fuse themselves with the French nation'. It is further possible that Lazare had discussed these questions with another assimilated Jew, who had lived in Paris for over three years and who was deeply concerned with the same problems. This Jew, an Austrian correspondent for a famous Viennese newspaper, finished work on a play entitled *Das Ghetto* (and later *Das neue Ghetto*) only nine days before Lazare's article with a similar title appeared in *La Justice*—his name was Theodore Herzl. In many ways, Herzl's thinking ran parallel to that of Lazare; in his play the Austrian journalist and future Zionist leader had considered the plight of the assimilated Jew who, though living in a nominally liberal society, was closely confined in a moral and social ghetto built upon prejudice.[1] It

---

[1] See Israel Cohen, *Theodore Herzl: Founder of Political Zionism* (New York, 1959), pp. 57–8; Alex Bein, 'Un siècle de préhistoire du sionisme français', *La Terre retrouvée*, 15 Nov. 1958, p. 7; id., *Theodore Herzl: a Biography* (Cleveland, 1962), chs. iv–v; Pierre van Passen, 'Paris, 1891–1895: a Study of the Transition in Theodore Herzl's Life', in Meyer W. Weisgal (ed.), *Theodore Herzl: a Memorial* New York, 1929), pp. 37–9.

seems probable that Herzl, who was well acquainted with the Parisian literary world, had some contact with Lazare before the Dreyfus Affair. Whether or not this was the case, the fact that the two men reached similar conclusions is significant. By the beginning of the Dreyfus Affair the pervasive quality of anti-Semitism in French society was apparent to those who were sensitive enough and disposed to look beneath the veneer of liberalism and security. Bernard Lazare, we would suggest, was able to expose the underlying obstacles to Jewish liberation primarily because he was a *révolté*, because he rejected, as could the foreigner Herzl, the assumption that all was well with French society, and that the Jews were proceeding smoothly to full membership in it.

The Dreyfus Affair brought these assumptions of Lazare to full fruition in a doctrine of Jewish nationalism. It is important, before describing the development of this nationalist response, to consider carefully and in a detailed manner Lazare's involvement in the Affair, for it was his experiences and his frustrations during that crisis which coloured his thinking about the Jewish condition as a whole.

P.-V. Stock, the well-known publisher and editor, had a discussion about the Dreyfus case with his friend Bernard Lazare at the very beginning of the Affair. Stock suggested that Lazare and other Jews devoted to public affairs ought to become involved. According to Stock, however, Lazare's reply was negative: 'Why should I? I don't know him or his family. Of course, if he were some poor devil, I would be worried about him soon enough, but Dreyfus and his people are very rich, they say; they will know how to get along very well without me, especially if he is innocent.'[1] Lazare did write two articles denouncing anti-Semitism as the publicity about the case became heated, but the initiative for direct involvement was not his own.[2] It appears that the director of the Santé prison, where Dreyfus was held briefly, heard of Lazare

[1] P.-V Stock, *Mémorandum d'un éditeur*, vol. iii, *L'Affaire Dreyfus* (Paris, 1938), p. 18.
[2] Lazare, 'Le nouveau ghetto', *La Justice*, 17 Nov. 1894, and 'Antisémitisme et antisémites', *L'Écho de Paris*, 31 Dec. 1894.

and recommended him to Madame Dreyfus as an advocate for her convicted husband.[1] Joseph Valabrègue, Dreyfus's brother-in-law, made the initial contact with Lazare in February 1895; Valabrègue was a successful Jewish businessman from Carpentras, a community not far from Lazare's native town of Nîmes, and bore recommendations from many mutual acquaintances in Provence, including the Boulangist deputy Alfred Naquet.[2] Before long Lazare was convinced that there had been a miscarriage of justice: 'The anti-Semitic campaign had enlightened me,' he later wrote, 'and with all the facts which followed, day after day . . . the certitude grew in me that the Affair was the result of an anti-Semitic machination. . . .'[3] Lazare accepted Valabrègue's request, and entered into consultation with Mathieu, the brother of Dreyfus and the latter's indefatigable defender. In this way, the celebrated defender of anarchists and revolutionaries agreed to do everything he could for the wealthy Jewish family.

To his great discomfort, however, his involvement was delayed. Although Lazare wrote his first explosive brochure on the Affair in the summer of 1895, Dreyfus's lawyer Demange apparently prevailed upon Mathieu to maintain a prudent silence for the time being while avenues other than those of public protest were explored. Publication of the brochure was put off for a more favourable moment. Impatient and fretting, Lazare could do nothing. For an entire year, as strings were being pulled and as doors were being knocked upon, he received no information from Mathieu, and was limited in his publication to the most general analyses of the anti-Semitic background of the Affair.[4] Understandably

---

[1] Stock, op. cit., iii. 28. Stock claims that the director of the santé obtained this suggestion from certain anarchist prisoners. Cf. Robert Gauthier (ed.), 'Dreyfusards!' Souvenirs de Mathieu Dreyfus et autres inédits (Paris, 1956), p. 79 n. 1.

[2] Details on this and other aspects of Lazare's involvement in the Affair may be found in a long memorandum which Lazare wrote for Joseph Reinach, for use in the latter's Histoire de l'Affaire Dreyfus. The memorandum is included in the Reinach papers, B.N. n. a. fr. 24897, pp. 209–24, and is printed, in a somewhat shortened version, in Gauthier, op. cit., pp. 84–95. For police reports on Lazare's involvement see A.N. F⁷ 12464.   [3] Gauthier, op. cit., p. 84.

[4] Lazare later wrote, describing his feelings at the time: 'J'ai vécu cette année-là dans l'attente et l'impatience, dans la fièvre d'agir. Je n'ai eu aucun confident de mes actions ni de mes désirs.' Gauthier, op. cit., p. 86.

perhaps, given the restraint which was forced upon him, Lazare's writing took on an acerbic tone. The enemies, of course, were Drumont and the anti-Semites; the problem for the moment, however, was the passivity of French Jews:

There are a great number [of Jews] who have retained a deplorable habit from the old persecutions—that of receiving blows and of not protesting, of bending their backs, of waiting for the storm to pass, and of playing dead so as not to attract the lightning.[1]

The Jews, Lazare wrote, suffered from an 'ancient tradition of humility' and from an 'atavistic pusillanimity': 'They should have arisen, grouped together, not permitted for one minute that their absolute right to live be called into question.' Instead, they did nothing.[2] It seems clear, when considering these passages in their context, that Lazare's experiences with the Dreyfus family gave substance to his views on Jewish passivity. Yet he felt, too, that resistance was coming. Not all Jews, Lazare warned Drumont in a blistering polemic, would be so timid as those Jewish leaders who continually avoided action:

I know of those who have different conceptions. I know of many others . . . who are not so gentle with their opponents. These have had enough of anti-Semitism, they are tired of insults, of calumnies, and of lies, of dissertations on Cornelius Herz and discourses on the Baron de Reinach. And tomorrow they will be legion, and if they take my advice they will openly, gallantly, league together against you and your allies, against your doctrines, and not content with defending themselves, they will attack you; and you are not invulnerable, neither you nor your friends.[3]

Lazare's bitter exchange with Drumont continued into the summer of 1896, and resulted in a duel in which neither man was hurt.[4] Finally, early that autumn, Mathieu decided that the time for publication of Lazare's brochure was at hand. Diversions with

---

[1] Bernard Lazare, 'Contre l'antisémitisme', *Le Voltaire*, 20 May 1896.
[2] Bernard Lazare, *Contre l'antisémitisme: histoire d'une polémique* (Paris, 1896), pp. 6–7.   [3] Lazare, 'Contre l'antisémitisme'.
[4] See Lazare *Contre l'antisémitisme*; 'Une lettre', *La Libre Parole*, 19 Nov. 1896; *Le Peuple français*, 17 June 1896.

Drumont were over. Lazare travelled to Brussels to handle the details and, in the first week of November, the pamphlet appeared in Paris.[1]

Lazare insisted, in this opening salvo, that the anti-Semitic dimension of the Affair was paramount:

> Did I not say that Captain Dreyfus belonged to a class of pariahs? He is a soldier, but he is a Jew, and it is as a Jew above all that he was prosecuted. Because he was a Jew he was arrested, because he was a Jew he was convicted, because he was a Jew the voices of justice and of truth could not be heard in his favour, and the responsibility for condemning this man falls entirely upon those who provoked it by their shameful excitations, by their lies, and by their calumny.[2]

This was to be Lazare's contention throughout the Affair. In a decisive way, the issue now was joined: Lazare henceforth considered himself a defender of the Jews, and a spokesman for the long delayed Jewish resistance. 'From that time on, I was a pariah,' he wrote. 'A long atavism had prepared me for this, [and] I did not suffer morally.'[3] Beginning in the autumn of 1896, the Dreyfusard forces deployed themselves in search of allies. Bernard Lazare hoped to win over a number of important personalities in the political and literary spheres, particularly among those leftists with whom he had been associated. He wrote to Millerand, visited Jaurès, Rochefort, and the anarchist papers *Le Libertaire* and *Père Peinard*. He had interviews with Zola, François Coppée, Scheurer-Kestner, and many others. But virtually everywhere he met with hostility or indifference.[4] In the socialist newspaper *La Petite République* Alexandre Zévaès referred sarcastically to the 'distingué représentatif du *high-life* anarchiste', who was in the pay of 'les journaux de la finance et de la juiverie'.[5] The anarchist journals, though consistently anti-militarist, refused to become involved.[6]

---

[1] Bernard Lazare, *Une erreur judiciaire: la vérité sur l'Affaire Dreyfus* (Brussels, 1896). See notes of 10, 11, 12 Nov. 1896, A.N. F⁷ 12464.

[2] Lazare, *Erreur judiciaire*, p. 9.

[3] Gauthier, op. cit., p. 89.   [4] See ibid., pp. 87–9.

[5] Alexandre Zévaès, 'Une apologie de Dreyfus', *La Petite République*, 9 Nov. 1896. Cf. Clovis Hughes, 'Autour d'une brochure', *La France*, 12 Nov. 1896.

[6] Note of 14 Nov. 1896, A.N. F⁷ 12464; *Le Libertaire*, 6, 13, 20 Nov. 1896; *Père Peinard*, 1, 8, 15, 22 Nov. 1896.

Rochefort, though he promised 'benevolent neutrality' in the Affair, soon broke his word and engaged in vicious anti-Semitic attacks.[1] Zola, against whom Lazare had fought as a literary critic, was scarcely interested at the time; and François Coppée had not even read the brochure. The eminent senator Scheurer-Kestner was highly sceptical when first visited, but once he was won over he wrote to Lazare breaking off all relations 'in the interest of the cause', according to the latter. And it was not only Lazare's anarchism which made Scheurer so prudent. 'I don't wish to appear to have an understanding with the Jews', he told the attorney Leblois in 1897.[2]

Lazare published a second brochure before the appearance of Zola's famous *J'accuse*, but the feeling of the Dreyfusard leadership was that the flamboyant anarchist writer could serve Dreyfus best by remaining silent. Mathieu brought pressure to bear to this effect, and Lazare complied; henceforth his role in the Affair was to be severely restricted.[3]

It would appear that Lazare was treated badly. And yet there was an interesting exception to the ostracism he experienced. Joseph Reinach was one of the first converts Lazare made, and he was a convert who remained faithful during the darkest hours of the Affair. One can imagine how difficult it was for Lazare, a self-proclaimed social revolutionary, to approach the older man, a well-known and wealthy Opportunist politician. Typically, Lazare faced the problem boldly, and in a manner which reflected his feelings at the time: he appealed to Reinach as a Jew. On 28 August 1896, before the appearance of his first brochure, he wrote to Reinach making a formal request for help in the Affair:

We do not agree politically, and our social perspectives differ substantially. . . . Yet [though] a thousand things can separate men, one

---

[1] Mathieu Dreyfus, B.N. n. a. fr. 14379, pp. 98–100. Cf. Roger Williams, *Henri Rochefort: Prince of the Gutter Press* (New York, 1966), ch. ix.

[2] Gauthier, op. cit., p. 94, n. 2; Douglas Johnson, *France and the Dreyfus Affair* (London, 1966), p. 93.

[3] Gauthier, op. cit., p. 95. Joseph Reinach, *Histoire de l'Affaire Dreyfus* (7 vols., Paris, 1901–8), ii. 554, v. 144, vi. 279–80; Jules Renard, *Journal* (Paris, 1935), p. 360; André Fontainas, 'L'antisémitisme et Bernard Lazare', *Mercure de France*, 1 July 1933, p. 55.

PLATE IV

a. Captain Alfred Dreyfus 1859–1935

b. Joseph Reinach 1856–1921

c. Caricature of Alfred Naquet by
André Gill

d. Bernard Lazare 1865–1903

can unite them. We are both attacked as Jews. Monsieur, this is why we can forget our economic or philosophic differences and agree upon the [necessity for a] victorious struggle against anti-Semitism.[1]

Reinach agreed to help. Meetings were held later that autumn, and before long the two men, the anarchist and the Opportunist, became close friends.[2]

It was Charles Péguy's contention, and it has been repeated ever since, that the Jewish community in general held Lazare at arm's length, and was reluctant and unwilling to be associated with him.[3] The reaction of the Jewish community as a whole to the Affair will be considered in the chapter which follows, and we can only, at this point, touch briefly upon this question as it concerns Lazare. And here, of course, it is difficult to establish with any precision the validity of Péguy's charge. Bernard Lazare was hardly known in the Jewish community in 1894. Criticism of Lazare's writing on the Jews had come from the *Archives israélites*, but the journal paid little attention to him until he began to concern himself with the connection between Jewish traditions and revolutionary movements. This theme, increasingly a favourite one with Lazare, was an obvious embarrassment for the greater part of the Jewish community. Hippolyte Prague sharply contested Lazare's association of Jews and subversive activity: such a suggestion, he wrote, 'only reinforces the arguments of our adversaries who portray us as being a seditious people in secret revolt against the established order of things'. Prague agreed that 'in the past, but in the far distant past, under Moses and the Judges', Israel had been 'a fairly indisciplined people, with an irreverent humour and a rebellious

---

[1] Letter, Bernard Lazare to Joseph Reinach, 28 Aug. 1896, Reinach papers, B.N. n. a. fr. 24897, p. 180.

[2] Ibid.; notes, Lazare to Reinach, 18 Oct. 1896, 16 Nov. 1896, et seq.

[3] Charles Péguy, *Notre jeunesse* (1910) in *Œuvres complètes* (Paris, 1916), iv. 108–9, 117–19; Hans Kohn, *L'Humanisme juif: quinze essais sur le juif, le monde et Dieu* (Paris, 1931), p. 60; Hagani, *Bernard Lazare*, p. 28; Muslak, 'Bernard-Lazare', p. 49. But cf. M. Liber, 'Zadoc Kahn et le sionisme', *Écho sioniste*, 10 Mar. 1913, p. 51. Tchernoff suggests that perhaps '. . . Péguy, emporté par son tempérament, pour que la ressemblance fût plus complète entre Bernard Lazare et les prophètes persecutés, a-t-il chargé le tableau'. *Dans le creuset des civilisations*, vol. iii, *De l'Affaire Dreyfus au dimanche rouge à Saint-Pétersbourg* (Paris, 1937), p. 51.

spirit'. Since then, however, 'the horde of freed slaves miraculously became wiser. . . . The evil passions were stifled under the weight of laws, and the pernicious instincts were slowly extinguished.'[1] It is easy to see how Jews, concerned as they were with demonstrating their loyalty and support for the existing regime in France, were reluctant to be reminded of such 'pernicious instincts', and found such a spokesman as Lazare awkward to say the least. Moreover, as the latter became even more interested in the Jewish question, and as he explored more deeply those characteristics which he classified as peculiarly Jewish, other Jewish writers felt it necessary to oppose this viewpoint, and to stress once again the typically French character of French Jews.[2]

The early stages of the Dreyfus Affair dramatized Lazare's position as a champion of the Jewish cause. As we have seen, he spared nothing in identifying himself as a Jew and in highlighting the anti-Semitic character of the Affair. With Lazare there was little grace or tact in such matters. Many Jews, no doubt, were embarrassed to see such issues raised, particularly by one with so dubious a reputation as Lazare. One of his former collaborators on the newspaper Le Voltaire, a Jew of Alsatian descent, Louis-Lucien Klotz, declared that anti-Semitism was in no way involved in the case; making a sneer at a fellow Jew in order to disassociate himself, Klotz described Lazare's brochure as bearing 'un certain cachet cosmopolite'.[3] (The brochure was printed in Belgium.) It was such Jews as Klotz to whom the editor-in-chief of La République française referred when he wrote in response to Lazare's first pamphlet:

The effort of M. Bernard Lazare has completely and pitifully failed, and it was certainly in vain that he tried . . . to give the Dreyfus question

---

[1] Prague, 'Causerie', A.I., 13 July 1893, p. 217; cf. Isidore Cahen, review of Lazare's Antisémitisme, A.I., 6 May 1897, pp. 137–8.

[2] See Kimosch, 'La nationalité française et les juifs', A.I., 4 Jan. 1894, pp. 2–4, 11 Jan. 1894, pp. 10–11.

[3] L.-L. Klotz, 'A Bernard Lazare', Le Voltaire, 10 Nov. 1896. Daniel Halévy, who strongly disliked Lazare, wrote the following in his notebook to describe the latter's activity in the Affair: 'B. Lazare, habile comme agent d'affaires, intermédiaire entre les intellectuels et l'argent juif qui va évidemment peser beaucoup sur la politique en donnant aux partis avancés.' Carnets, entry for 26 Dec. 1898.

a confessional character. Intelligent Jews are the first to recognize that the military court martial decided the case well; they are unanimous in condemning the crime of the ex-captain, and it is easy, in any case, to understand that in a certain measure they are themselves the victims of the treason of their co-religionist. . . . Thus they are the first—and they are quite right in doing so—to regard M. Bernard Lazare's brochure as an unforgivable blunder [*une insigne maladresse*].[1]

In Jewish circles it was apparently the common view that Lazare's first brochure could only have the immediate effect of aggravating the lot of Dreyfus, of giving new substance to the legend of a 'Jewish syndicate' made up of traitors and *sans-patrie*.[2] Few, however, expressed as much in print, for that would have worsened the situation as they perceived it. We must accept in large measure the testimony of others whom we have cited, and Lazare's own analysis which concurred. Indeed, Lazare's exasperation towards his fellow Jews became almost overpowering during this period, and his feelings seem to have had substantial justification. His response, however, was not a rejection of Jewishness, but on the contrary a development of Jewish nationalism.

Under the impact of personal vilification and an increasingly violent anti-Semitic press, Lazare revised somewhat his assessment of anti-Semitism. It was even more serious than he had feared. Lazare admitted that he had been naïve in his former, mildly socialistic interpretation of anti-Semitism. Not only were the anti-Semites the defenders of 'Catholic capital', they were working towards the reconstitution of a theocracy which would mean a total submission of all aspects of life to the Church.[3] The French bourgeoisie were attempting, by sacrificing the Jews, to save themselves from reaction.[4] What was at stake was more than a quarrel within French capitalism; what was at issue was the very shape of French society itself. French anti-Semitism was not an aberration; it was a fundamental part of French society, just as

---

[1] Robert Charlie, 'Insigne maladresse', *La République française*, 11 Nov. 1896.
[2] Julien Weill, *Zadoc Kahn 1839–1905* (Paris, 1912), p. 199.
[3] Lazare, 'Contre l'antisémitisme'.
[4] Bernard Lazare, *Antisémitisme et révolution* (Paris, 1898), pp. 13–14.

Russian anti-Semitism was a fundamental part of Russian society. Everywhere the Jews were persecuted, and France, for all of her pretentions, was no exception. Alfred Dreyfus was the symbol of the persecuted Jew the world over:

> He incarnates, in himself, not only the centuries-old suffering of this people of martyrs, but their present agonies. Through him I see Jews languishing in Russian prisons, striving vainly for a bit of light and air, Rumanian Jews, who are refused the rights of man, those of Galicia, starved by financial trusts and ravaged by peasants who have been made fanatics by their priests. . . . He has been for me the tragic image of the Algerian Jews, beaten and pillaged, the unhappy immigrants dying of hunger in the ghettos of New York or of London, all of those whom desperation drives to seek some haven in the far corners of the inhabited world, a haven where they will at last find that justice which the best of them have claimed for all of humanity.[1]

It was anti-Semitism with its indiscriminate association of the assimilated and the unassimilated, of the Orthodox and the unbeliever, of the French and the German Jew, which reminded everyone of the ties which bound the Jews together. It was anti-Semitism which recalled to the Jews their past of suffering and their continuing struggle for existence. And it was this anti-Semitism which stood for the thorough corruption of French life.

Yet, in his most important shift of emphasis, Lazare argued 'not only that there is no solution for anti-Semitism . . . but that no solution for it must be sought'.[2] Anti-Semitism had existed for as long as Christianity had existed; essentially, it was 'born on Calvary'. Anti-Semitism reflected the degeneracy of French and most of European society. The duty of the Jews was to fight anti-Semitism, not in order to destroy it, but 'out of strict duty towards themselves'. '. . . Every human creature, if he has the will to exist, must know how to resist . . . he must make every effort to maintain his liberty of being, and his liberty of being himself.'[2] What was necessary was for the Jew to ensure his own integrity, his essential quality of being a man and being a Jew. Beside this, the

---

[1] Bernard Lazare, 'Lettre ouverte à M. Trarieux', *L'Aurore*, 7 June 1899.
[2] Bernard Lazare, 'Nécessité d'être soi-même', *Zion*, 30 Apr. 1897, p. 3.

aim of a political victory over the anti-Semites in France was secondary, and perhaps even a diversion. In the face of an implacable attack upon his right to Jewishness the Jew was obliged to exalt his own being; in the midst of a corrupt society he had to cultivate his Jewishness and to perfect it. Only in this sense was resistance worth while, and only in this sense could it truly be successful. The issue, therefore, was not what would become of anti-Semitism, but rather what would become of the Jews.

Lazare's prescription was that Jews had to learn to be themselves. Jews were able to do this by drawing upon their common heritage, their history, literature, and philosophy which one hundred years of emancipation had not been able to eradicate. Because the Jews had this common background and culture they were a nation:[1]

> We have always been the old stiff-necked people, the intractable rebel nation; we want to be ourselves, what our forefathers, our history, our traditions, our culture, and our memories have made us, and we will know well how to win that right which is ours, not only to be men, but also to be Jews.[2]

Unfortunately, French Jews had not recognized this Jewish nationhood; they preferred to assimilate and to become a part of the French nation which appeared to receive them. In so doing they were fatally weakened. Deprived of the defensive strength which came from national solidarity, and tainted by the evils of the French system, they became corrupt, degenerate, and materialistic. French Jews, who considered themselves the élite of the Jewish people, were in fact 'in an advanced state of decomposition'. This élite had 'become rotten in contact with the Christian world, which has exercised the same disrupting influence upon them as civilized peoples exercise upon savages, bringing them alcoholism, syphilis, and tuberculosis'. Instead of resisting this influence, they replied with submission, and thus encouraged further attacks; instead of remaining Jewish they attempted to become Christians, and thus corrupted themselves even more

---

[1] Bernard Lazare, *Le Nationalisme juif* (Paris, 1898), pp. 1–4.
[2] Lazare, 'Nécessité', p. 6.

rapidly than those around them.[1] Assimilation, then, could never be a solution to Jewish problems. The solution of the 'Jewish question', from the Jewish point of view, could only be found in Jewish nationalism:

> Give back to the Jews who no longer have it, reinforce in those who do have it, the sense of Jewish nationality. A people knows how to defend itself when it is conscious of itself and it knows how to defend its own who need to be defended. Let the Jewish nation arise and it will find in itself the necessary force to vanquish its enemies and to win its rights.[2]

Jewish 'national consciousness' constituted the substance of Lazare's appeal, and he did his best to define its character in bold and clear strokes:

> I belong to the race of those who, according to Renan, first introduced the idea of justice into the world. It is faith in the reign of this justice that has animated my people from the time of the Prophets and the poor poets who sang the psalms, to those who, like Marx and Lassalle, have asserted the rights of the proletariat, to those humble martyrs of revolution who paid for their belief in the ideal of equity in Russian dungeons, under the knout, or on tsarist gallows. All, all of them, my ancestors and my brothers, desired, fanatically, that each man be granted his rights, and that the scale never be tipped in favour of injustice. For that they cried out, chanted, shed tears, suffered, despite outrages, despite insults and public contempt.[3]

It was an anti-Semitic myth that the Jews were a people of capitalists and merchants; it was a common distortion to consider the history of the Jewish bourgeoisie as the history of the Jewish people. On the contrary, said Lazare, 'no people has a larger proportion of poor than the Jews'.[4] This was why the wealthy artillery captain could stand for poverty-stricken Jews throughout the world. If one considered numbers, the Jews were overwhelmingly

---

[1] Lazare, *Nationalisme juif*, pp. 7-9.

[2] Bernard Lazare, 'Solidarité', *Zion*, 31 May 1897, p. 26.

[3] Lazare, 'Lettre ouverte à M. Trarieux'.

[4] Bernard Lazare, 'La conception sociale du judaïsme et du peuple juif', *La Grande Revue*, 1 Sept. 1899, p. 615. Cf. id., 'Le prolétariat juif devan tl'antisémitisme', *Le Flambeau*, Jan. 1899, pp. 3-14.

an oppressed and degraded proletariat. If one looked carefully at Jewish traditions, at the Bible and the Talmud, one could find no Jewish traditions of usury and trade. Jews had taken their capitalism from the societies in which they lived; most often it had been forced upon them. Everywhere one looked, in New York, in London, in Paris, and in eastern Europe, the Jews were suffering and crying out for relief. The Jews, in effect, were the proletarian people *par excellence*. '. . . The Jewish proletariat is the most miserable of all,' Lazare added, 'having against it not only its own rich, but also the rich and the poor of the people among whom it lives.'[1] Jewish national consciousness was thus above all a consciousness of the necessity for social justice for an oppressed people, a consciousness deeply embedded in Jewish roots and in Jewish traditions, but also a consciousness with universal applicability. In fighting for themselves, and in struggling against their own oppression, Jews were 'soldiers of justice and human fraternity' for all mankind.[2]

It was necessary for Lazare to stress this last point, for at the time of the Dreyfus Affair the term *nationalisme* was a frequent epithet designating the right wing forces opposed to Dreyfus. Lazare himself had condemned 'national exclusiveness' and predicted its demise, along with other aspects of nationalism, in his book on anti-Semitism published in 1894.[3] Three years later, however, he was arguing somewhat differently: nationalism, he now implied, differed from 'national exclusiveness' and blind chauvinism; it was really the liberty to develop one's own cultural personality and one's own resources, without being forced into obsequious conformity or the imitation of a foreign culture. 'Nothing seems more necessary for humanity than variety', he wrote. The former literary critic described humanity as essentially as much an aesthetic as an anthropological or economic expression; and variation was essential for its well-being.[4] Governments everywhere

---

[1] Lazare, 'Conception sociale', p. 617.
[2] Lazare, *Nationalisme juif*, p. 16. Cf. id., 'Nationalisme et émancipation', *Kadimah*, 15 Aug. 1898. [3] Id., *Antisemitism*, p. 372.
[4] Lazare, 'Nécessité', p. 4. 'Maintenir une nation c'est contribuer à garder intégrale la beauté universelle dont les facettes sont faites de mille beautés particulières communicant toutes dans le tout.' Ibid., p. 5.

attempted to stifle originality and peculiarity. They wanted 'subjects as much alike as children's lead soldiers'. This almost military unification of peoples, this asssault upon human differences, served the general interests of oppression and control.[1] This had to be opposed. Jews could best work for humanity by being themselves, by remaining true to their traditions. Jewish nationalism could thus enrich the community at large at the same time as it asserted itself. Indeed, as he explained it: 'A people only lives when it works for all of humanity.'[2]

In Lazare's vision humanity would organize itself as a free confederation of groups, not as under capitalism, where groups were related to one another on the basis of inequality and suppression. Jewish nationalism had as its ultimate justification that it was helping to prepare one of these groups, that it was preparing one element of society for the brighter world of the future.[3]

Significantly absent from Lazare's Jewish nationalism was any specifically religious commitment. According to his close friend Péguy, Lazare was a non-believer, and remained so all his life.[4] As a child of the generation of Frenchmen which had fought so bitterly against Catholic influence, Lazare's formative years had been spent in reaction against theocratic tendencies within French society. His subsequent analysis of the role of Christianity in the history of anti-Semitism reflected this concern with the damaging effects of religious interference in secular affairs. Just as he considered the Jews to be the special victims of capitalism, so he came to see them as being especially a prey to Christianity:

For centuries the Jew has been demoralized by the Christian. It is the Christian who has made him a trafficker, a usurer; it is the Christian who has searched out the Jew, to make him a businessman, to make his [Christian] city progress, to enrich his capital, to exploit him for his own benefit, without risk. . .[5]

---

[1] Lazare, 'Le prolétariat juif', p. 12.
[2] Quoted in André Fontenais, 'Antisémitisme et Bernard Lazare', p. 57.
[3] Lazare, 'Nécessité', pp. 4–5.   [4] Péguy, op. cit., p. 120.
[5] Bernard Lazare, Le Fumier de Job: fragments inédits précédés du portrait de Bernard Lazare par Charles Péguy (Paris, 1928), p. 97. This work contains fragments of a study on Jewish thought and history which Lazare was preparing at the time of his death for publication in Péguy's Cahiers de la quinzaine.

Christianity, he felt, lent itself to such persecution; Judaism, on
the contrary, based its secular teaching upon reason, equity, and a
freedom from dogma. Ritual was an important part of Judaism,
but Lazare did not see it as fundamental; he recognized that the
outward forms of religious practice were falling into disuse, and
though he apparently regretted this with some nostalgia, his emphasis was upon the compatibility of Jewish tradition with the world
of the future which was to be built upon a foundation of reason:

As soon as the Jew rejects the ties of ritualism, when he ceases to prac-
tise the dietary laws, when he abandons the sabbath, nothing more
remains in him: no troublesome residue litters his mind, no precon-
ceived metaphysical or dogmatic idea gets in his way; once the rite is
forgotten, he remembers only one thing, which the scholars of Judaism
have given to him as an invariable precept: to exercise reason and always
to call upon it. A religion whose rabbis have refused, even before their
God, the right to have an unexamined truth imposed upon them,
cannot be irremediably dangerous.[1]

Thus the Lazare who had in 1890 denounced the 'stupid rationalism' of the Jewish religion was now much more sensitive to the
harmful effects of religious myths. The Lazare who now castigated
the French bourgeoisie had nevertheless adopted the latter's
liberal notions of religious practice. Always an eclectic, he had
learned much from the Dreyfus Affair. With practical political
experience behind him, Lazare had clearly abandoned the indul-
gence of his Symbolist period.

Jewish nationalism, then, did not draw upon religion. Its roots
were historical, and its essence was the revolt of a long-suffering
people:

What things has the Jew not felt in the course of history? What has
he not experienced? What shame is there to which he has not been subjected? What grief has he not suffered? What triumphs has he not
known? What defeats has he not accepted? What resignation has he
not shown? What pride has he not felt? And all of that has left profound traces in his soul, just as the flood waters leave their traces on the
valley floor.[2]

[1] Bernard Lazare, preface to Alphonse Lévy, *Scènes familiales juives* (Paris, 1902).
[2] Lazare, *Fumier de Job*, p. 97.

The aim of Jewish nationalism was to instil a sense of pride and confidence in Jews who were the victims of the societies in which they lived. But its message went further: to 'Christian barbarism' it offered resistance, to oppressed peoples everywhere it offered an example, and to those Jews who sought peace through self-effacement it offered the bitter reminders which were strewn across centuries of torment and disillusion.

Lazare developed and articulated his doctrine of Jewish nationalism between 1897 and 1899, at the height of the Dreyfus Affair, when, as we have seen, pressure from the more cautious Drey-fusards constrained him to remain apart from the battle for revision. He collaborated in a number of Jewish periodicals founded at the time, lectured extensively before Jewish community groups, and, most importantly, became deeply involved in Zionist activity. Lazare's place in the Zionist movement, his following and his practical politics, will be discussed in Chapter IX. In this chapter we have been concerned with the origins of Jewish nationalism as propounded by Lazare, and with the relationship between this doctrine and the Dreyfus Affair. It is important to recognize that although the roots of Jewish nationalism lay in the pre-Dreyfus period, its basic inspiration came from the heroic struggle begun in 1895 and 1896. When few knew anything about Dreyfus, and when French Jews wanted nothing more than silence, Bernard Lazare took up the cause. But for Lazare it was always the Jewish people as a whole whose future was at stake, and he never let anyone forget that during the Affair he spoke as a Jew:

...je veux qu'on dise que le premier j'ai parlé, que le premier qui se leva pour le juif martyr fut un juif, un juif qui a souffert dans son sang et dans sa chair les souffrances que supporta l'innocent, un juif qui savait à quel peuple de pariahs, de désinhérités, de malheureux, il appartenait, et qui puisa dans cette conscience la volonté de combattre pour la justice et pour la vérité.[1]

Bernard Lazare died of cancer on 2 September 1903. He was thirty-eight years old, and left no fortune. Zadoc Kahn discreetly

---

[1] Lazare, 'Lettre ouverte à M. Trarieux'.

began a collection to support his widow and a handful of wealthy Jews made generous contributions.[1] A small monument to Lazare was erected by friends in his native Nîmes; the monument was damaged by members of the Action Française in 1909, and destroyed by the Germans during the Nazi occupation.

[1] Letter, Zadoc Kahn to Joseph Reinach, 8 Oct. 1903, Reinach papers, B.N. n. a. fr. 13578, pp. 199–200.

CHAPTER VIII

THE DREYFUS AFFAIR AND THE POLITICS OF ASSIMILATION

A RELATIVELY minor *affaire* which unfolded two years before the arrest of the Jewish captain provided a preview of the Jewish community's reaction to the anti-Semitic upheaval during the Dreyfus Affair. In the summer of 1892 Jews witnessed the duel between another Jewish officer, Captain Armand Mayer, and the notorious anti-Semitic agitator, the Marquis de Morès. During the emotional outburst which followed Mayer's death at the hands of his opponent, leaders of the established Jewish community reasserted their faith in assimilation, their confidence in the Third Republic, and their devotion to the fatherland. As we shall see, the loyalties thus declared on the occasion of Mayer's funeral proved sufficiently durable to withstand the far more deadly assault which came a few years later. Indeed, the lessons which Jewish leaders drew from the Mayer *affaire* helped to strengthen the assimilationist politics which we have been studying in preceding chapters. Thus prepared, thus made ready for a fundamental challenge to their citizenship and their right to exist as Jews, members of the Jewish community were able to respond to the Dreyfus Affair with a reassertion of their long-standing policies towards the French nation. In this way the Dreyfus Affair proved to be not a turning-point in the history of the Jews in France, but rather a momentous landmark in their steady march towards the goal of assimilation.

This chapter considers the response which most French Jews made to the anti-Semitic crisis of the Dreyfus Affair. As will become apparent, the majority of Jews relied upon the assimilationist tradition when faced with a threat to their existence; what they did, in response to attacks upon their Jewishness, was to assert their Frenchness and their devotion to the Republic. A small minority, however, made up of Jews who were already sceptical of the virtues of assimilation, took the opportunity to reject entirely the assimilationist ideal, and to lay the foundations of Zionism in France. Their response to the Dreyfus Affair will be considered in the chapter which follows.

A series of violent articles attacking Jewish army officers, published in *La Libre Parole* in May 1892, prompted several duels, the last of which led to the death of Armand Mayer.[1] Duelling, as we have noted, was at this time a commonly accepted mode of settling disputes among gentlemen, and French anti-Semites (unlike their German counterparts, for whom a Jew was *nicht-satisfaktionsfähig*, or socially unacceptable for combat) frequently engaged Jewish challengers who chose to consider anti-Semitism as a personal insult.[2] In the spring of 1892 the issue posed by the articles in Drumont's newspaper involved the honour of a French officer, something which traditionally was not to be tampered with. André Crémieu-Foa, a Jewish cavalryman and a captain of Dragoons, was outraged by the articles, and sent his challenge to Drumont. In the resulting engagement both combatants were slightly wounded. (Ironically, Walsin Esterhazy, the commandant who it seems certain was the real traitor in the Dreyfus Case, served as one of Crémieu-Foa's seconds.) But tempers were heated and the matter did not end there. Two more duels followed disputes arising from the first; in the second of these, Mayer, a comrade of Crémieu-Foa, faced an infamous anti-Semite, the Marquis de Morès.[3] In this encounter the young Jewish officer, a Polytechnician and the nephew of the rabbi of an important synagogue in Paris, was killed.

The shock of this event affected not only the French Jewish community, but a wide segment of French opinion. In a rare

[1] For details on the duels see Ernest Crémieu-Foa, *La Campagne antisémitique: les duels, les responsables: mémoire avec pièces justificatives* (Paris, 1892).
[2] See, for example, Simon Lévy, 'Un duel', *U.I.*, 16 June 1886, pp. 609-10; *U.I.*, 1 Feb. 1890, p. 311; L. W., 'Un duel', *U.I.*, 16 May 1892, p. 523; André Spire, *Souvenirs à bâtons rompus* (Paris, 1962), pp. 36, 58-9; Arthur Meyer, *Ce que mes yeux ont vu* (Paris, 1911), pp. 251-3.
[3] On Morès see Steven S. Schwarzschild, 'The Marquis de Morès, the Story of a Failure', *J.S.S.*, vol. xxii, no. 1, Jan. 1960, pp. 3-26.

gesture of agreement, the major Parisian dailies joined in condemning the campaign which had attempted to plant discord among the
true servants of France and which had led to the tragedy. Pictures
of Mayer appeared everywhere draped in black, poems dedicated
to his memory were published in the newspapers, and in the
National Assembly the Minister of War declared solemnly that
the French army recognized no distinctions of religion among its
officers. Mayer's funeral, on a Sunday afternoon, was a spectacular
demonstration of public sympathy. Estimates of the crowd varied
from 20,000 to 100,000; according to Le Matin such a cortège had
not been seen in Paris since the death of Gambetta ten years before.
Mayer was buried with full military honours; high-ranking
officers, a company of infantry, a military band, and a troop of
students from the École Polytechnique in full dress uniform
accompanied the casket; Jewish generals, members of the Consistoire, and other dignitaries from the Jewish community attended.
With cries of 'Vive l'armée!', muffled drums, and the brilliantly
arrayed military units, the event was a patriotic pageant which any
French nationalist would have admired.[1] 'Never has the national
consciousness affirmed itself with greater force,' said Zadoc Kahn
in his eulogy, 'never has the holy unity of the fatherland more
dramatically manifested itself, recognizing equally all of its beloved
sons who defend its flag and who are inspired with its spirit.'[2]

The Jewish community, as a headline in the Archives israélites
proclaimed, recognized a martyr. Mayer, it was noted, came from
Alsace-Lorraine and hence was 'doubly French'; as a Jew, moreover, he stood above all as a symbol of Jewish devotion to the
nation.[3] So attractive was his cause, it was felt, so warm was the
public response to the tragedy, that the general view persisted
that his death would be redemptive in the fight against anti-
Semitism. The Grand Rabbi of France gave voice to these hopes
at Mayer's funeral:

[1] See La République française, Le Matin, Le Siècle, the New York Herald Tribune,
and other major dailies, 27 June 1892.
[2] Zadoc Kahn, Souvenirs et regrets: recueil d'oraisons funèbres prononcées dans la
communauté israélite de Paris 1868–1898 (Paris, 1898), p. 330.
[3] Isidore Cahen, 'Un martyr!', A.I., 30 June 1892, pp. 201–2; 'Une victime
de l'antisémitisme', A.I., 30 June 1892, pp. 202–5.

The sacrifice of his life which he has made will not have been useless for the causes which were dear to him if it serves to dissipate the fatal misunderstandings, and lets shine forth, through the veil of mourning which covers it today, the flag of France, this glorious and immortal symbol of justice, of concord, of fraternity.[1]

One week later Hippolyte Prague noted with satisfaction the general and overwhelming 'upsurge of indignation' which the event had produced in French opinion. In an emotional editorial he set a mood of optimism within the Jewish community:

[We say] No! to anti-Semitism: this Germanic import will not take root in our land! No, France will not deny the work of the Emancipation and the French Revolution! No! the nation which has been justly called the soldier of right and justice will not go back on her word, on her mission![2]

The editorial board of the *Univers israélite* repeated the common view that anti-Semitism had suffered a defeat from which it would probably never recover. But it warned its readers that 'the enemy had not yet disarmed', and that the danger was still serious.[3] Few Jewish leaders, however, were prepared to echo this warning.

In a hastily called session immediately following the Mayer funeral, the Consistoire Central met to decide upon what action to take under the circumstances.[4] The conclusions drawn from this discussion are significant, for the policy thus set down provided the basis and the rationale for consistorial inactivity several years later during the Dreyfus Affair. Alphonse de Rothschild, the president of the Consistoire, indicated that he had called the extraordinary meeting at a time of serious anti-Semitic attacks to decide upon a policy for the official representatives of French Judaism. But in the discussion which followed the members of the Consistoire concluded that their hands were tied and that little, in fact, could be done. The problem, it was generally agreed, lay

[1] Zadoc Kahn, op. cit., p. 332. Cf. Joseph Reinach, 'Sang perdu', *La République française*, 25 June 1892.

[2] H. Prague, 'A la barre de l'opinion', *A.I.*, 7 July 1892, p. 611.

[3] La rédaction, 'La quinzaine tragique', *U.I.*, 1 July 1892.

[4] A summary of this discussion may be found in A.C.C., pr. verb., 28 June 1892.

in the law of 29 July 1881 which precluded any possibility of legal action against anti-Semitic journalists. To blame the government for anti-Semitism would thus be misdirected, for it too was bound by the law. To attempt to change the law was also useless, for such an effort would meet with 'certain defeat', and, more importantly, would subject the Jewish community to an intensified press campaign against itself. More hopefully, the Consistoire observed that in the wake of Mayer's death 'a favourable reaction has been manifested, ideas of appeasement have made perceptible progress, and it can be hoped that the attacks which have been made against us will give way to more healthy and more equitable opinions'. In the end the Consistoire, fortified by this anticipation, decided upon no action at all beyond a letter of condolence sent to Mayer's family.

The Mayer *affaire* has been discussed at some length because it helped to set a mood within the Jewish community, a mood which was of great importance during the Dreyfus Affair. It seems clear that the death of the captain had an enormous impact upon the Jewish community, and the memory of the incident is kept alive in some Jewish families even to this day. Jews seem to have concluded, in agreement with the Consistoire, that their best hope was to do nothing provocative, and to trust in the healing and unifying force of French opinion. Patriotism and devotion to the fatherland were the constant themes of Jewish rhetoric at the time. About the right to be different little, if anything, was said. In his eulogy Zadoc Kahn had set the tone by avoiding any explicit reference to anti-Semitism; his condemnation was directed against those who 'excite hatreds and sow divisions among citizens, all of whom love [the fatherland] equally'.[1] He was praised for his moderation in this respect; as *Le Matin* put it: 'in response to abominable calls for civil war, he has pronounced only the words of peace and pardon [*l' oubli*].'[2] The Jewish community, writes his biographer, received the words of the Grand Rabbi with great enthusiasm and sent hundreds of letters to him expressing its

---

[1] Quoted in Julien Weill, *Zadoc Kahn 1839–1905* (Paris, 1912), p. 147.

[2] *Le Matin*, 27 June 1892. Cf. 'Le duel Mayer–Morès', *La République française*, 26 June 1892.

thanks.[1] Moreover, during the entire *affaire* Jewish leaders held
up the French Army as a magnificent example of tolerance—'a
single family', said Zadoc Kahn, 'having only one passion in its
heart: to assure the glory and the grandeur of the fatherland and
to preside over its good name'.[2] And thus, when Jewish seminarians were conscripted in the autumn of that year, the Grand Rabbi
of France could make a declaration whose militarism approached
that of even the most zealous chauvinist. It was in the army, he
said,

more than in any other place, that beats the heart of France; it is there
that are blended, as in a crucible, the sentiments which are the soul of the
nation; it is there that a lively and joyous youth, devoted to life, seeing
it in its seductive colours, learns contempt in the face of death; it is there
that are formed those brave lads who if necessary will die upon distant
shores to defend the honour of France and to safeguard her interests.[3]

Finally, Jewish faith in the ability of France to protect Jewish
citizens from insult and injury was strengthened by the *affaire*.
Hence their optimism. Jews believed, with some justification, that
the death of Mayer had united French opinion against anti-
Semitism and had decisively demonstrated the reserve of good
feeling upon which the unjustly persecuted could rely. Several
years later, when Jews attempted to draw upon this reserve, their
mistake became apparent.

One historian has recently referred to the common ruling
impulse on each political side in the Dreyfus Affair as being a
volonté de paix, a desire for the peaceful settlement of a disturbed
public order.[4] This view takes issue somewhat with the oft-repeated
interpretation of the Affair as a titanic struggle between the 'two
Frances', the one progressive, liberal and republican, and the other
reactionary, highly nationalist and monarchist. Instead it stresses,

[1] Weill, op. cit., pp. 147–8.   [2] Zadoc Kahn, op. cit., p. 331.
[3] Zadoc Kahn, *Sermons et allocutions* (3 vols, Paris, 1894), iii. 238–9.
[4] Jean-Pierre Peter, 'Dimensions de l'Affaire Dreyfus', *Annales: économies,
sociétés, civilisations*, vol. xvi, no. 6, Nov.–Dec. 1961, p. 1165. Cf. R. D. Mandell,
'The Affair and the Fair: some Observations on the Closing Stages of the Dreyfus
Case', *Journal of Modern History*, vol. xxxix, no. 3, Sept. 1967, pp. 253–65; Hannah
Arendt, *The Origins of Totalitarianism* (Cleveland, 1958), p. 115; Douglas Johnson,
France and the Dreyfus Affair (London, 1966), pp. 212–13.

perhaps excessively, the similarities to be found among the main contestants. On the one side the forces of the Right attempted to mobilize opinion in defence of certain representatives of social authority such as the army, the Church, and the judicial system, which they considered essential for the preservation of a threatened society. On the other side the *aristocratie républicaine*, the solid middle-class defenders of the Third Republic, were similarly devoted to the maintenance of established French institutions and the social peace for which they stood. These two sides, which had so much in common, did not oppose one another until the activity of a vociferous but tiny minority precipitated a crisis. It was only when the revision of the judgement against Dreyfus appeared itself as a defence of an all too fragile public order, as in fact the last way to avert a virtual *coup d'état*, that the division in French opinion became critical, that all political elements were forced to take sides, and that the crisis appeared capable of resolution in favour of the Dreyfusards. But until the trial of Émile Zola, in February 1898, it seems clear that the proponents of revision were a small and embattled coalition of idealists and relatives of Dreyfus, whose persistent and resolute agitation alone was able to keep the cause alive. Before then there was no real division over the matter in French political life, and a consensus existed against causing trouble by contesting the judgement. Until they were able to win over the forces of republican moderation, the parliamentary supporters of law and order, the Dreyfusards were clearly cast in the role of challengers to that order which had the support of articulate political opinion.

This interpretation of the struggle over the Dreyfus Affair seems reasonable in view of the political atmosphere at the time. Pierre Sorlin has described the way in which, from about 1892, the French bourgeoisie was increasingly sensitive to what was called *le péril social*, a threat to established society brought on by the decline of the Opportunists and *ralliés*, the growing power of the extreme Left, and the rising tide of industrial strikes.[1] Society, it seemed, was threatened in a fundamental way during this period, and its 'establishment' was consequently not likely to treat kindly

[1] Pierre Sorlin, *Waldeck-Rousseau* (Paris, 1966), pp. 355-64; see pp. 135-6, above.

a group of agitators and journalists who challenged the integrity of one of the most revered of French institutions—the army. When we consider that both Dreyfusards and anti-Dreyfusards were appealing ultimately to a public devoted to the preservation of a certain kind of order, their common efforts to express themselves in nationalist rhetoric becomes understandable. Patriotism, appeals to national history and to French traditions were the means naturally used by both sides to escape charges of divisiveness and to defend a society which they considered to be in critical need of defence. This is not to minimize the differences between the two; these differences were important, became progressively more so, and at times indicated radically different conceptions of what French society should be like. But it is important not to be confused by what became sharply differing perspectives on Dreyfus, and to recognize this shared *volonté de paix* which so permeated French political life.

As we noted in Chapter VI, Jews were particularly devoted to the preservation of order in French society. Never quite secure in their emancipation, never quite able to escape from the threat of anti-Semitism, Jews tended consistently to defer to the established authority in France. The Dreyfus Affair precipitated a profound crisis in the Jewish community because it posed the possibility that this established authority, its respected institutions and its parliamentary leaders, might be willing, in the very interests of order, in the very name of social peace, to make a sacrifice of the Jews. Until the Affair had reached a climax, anti-Semitism was able to clothe itself in the garb of order, to pose as the defender of French society against an 'invasion' of outsiders. For a long time, and during the darkest hours of anti-Semitic violence, it was the Dreyfusards who were threatening an order which gloried in the majesty of deference to *la chose jugée* and the dignity of the army. Little wonder, then, that Jews, caught between the Dreyfusards who were assaulting their old fortress of security and their attackers who assumed the mantle of authority, were often uncomfortable, even disoriented, and hoped that the protagonists would exhaust themselves and thus enable the old order to reassert itself.

Evaluations of the Jewish response to the Affair have differed substantially. An American observer, Mark Twain, felt that 'the Jews did wisely in keeping quiet during the Dreyfus agitation'.[1] Bernard Lazare, as we have seen, persistently condemned Jews for their inactivity. The most frequently cited analysis along these lines came from the pen of the renegade Catholic Charles Péguy. He felt that the great majority of Jews were then motivated by what he called the Jewish *politique*, a policy based upon a realistic assessment of self-interest, and to the detriment of the Jewish *mystique*, the idealistic and selfless dimension of Judaism. In general, Péguy observed sadly, the bearers of the *mystique* would be betrayed and overwhelmed by the force of the *politique*. Most Jews, he felt, kept silent about Dreyfus and about anti-Semitism because they feared trouble. This majority, he wrote, 'fears disruption. It fears, it fears perhaps more than anything else, to have things upset. Its preference is for silence, tranquillity in a low key.' To this end Jews were prepared to make all kinds of compromises on issues of principle, even to commit betrayal.[2] Péguy was sensitive to the class differences within the Jewish community and considered this factor to be highly significant. What is important in this connection, however, is to recognize that Péguy judged the Jewish *politique* to be the decisive political force within the Jewish community of the time and the best general description of the Jewish response.[3]

---

[1] Letter to Simon Wolf, 15 Sept. 1899, in Simon Wolf, *Some Presidents I have known* (Washington, 1918), p. 149.

[2] Charles Péguy, *Notre jeunesse* (1910) in *Œuvres complètes* (Paris, 1916), iv. 101–2. 'Ils ont peur des coups. Ils en ont tant reçu. Ils aimeraient mieux qu'on n'en parle pas. Ils ont tant de fois payé pour eux-mêmes et pour les autres. On peut bien parler d'autre chose. Ils en ont tant de fois payé pour tout le monde, pour nous. . . . Mais toute la mystique d'Israël est qu'Israël poursuive dans le monde sa retentissante et douloureuse mission. De là des déchirements incroyables, les plus douloureux antagonismes intérieurs qu'il y ait eu peut-être entre une mystique et une politique. Peuple de marchands. Le même peuple de prophètes. Les uns savent pour les autres ce que c'est que des calamités. . . . Je connais bien ce peuple. Il n'a pas sur la peau un point qui ne soit pas douloureux, où il n'y ait un ancien bleu, une ancienne contusion, une douleur sourde, la mémoire d'une douleur sourde, une cicatrice, une blessure, une meurtrissure d'Orient ou d'Occident. Ils ont les leurs, et toutes celles des autres.' Ibid., pp. 103–4. On Péguy see Lazare Prajs, 'Péguy et Israël', unpublished thesis for the *doctorat de l'Université*, Sorbonne, 1966.

[3] See Charles Péguy, *Un poète l'a dit* (Paris, 1953), p. 151.

Somewhat opposed to this point of view, a number of contemporaries stressed that the tremendous assault upon French Jewry, far from encouraging general passivity, had stimulated the community into unified feeling and prompted self-help. Hippolyte Prague considered in March 1898 that French Jews had finally been made to see the error of their ways:

> This grave crisis of anti-Semitism . . . this awakening of the most odious passions which we have just witnessed, has had for an effect to tear away from their satisfied indifference, from their beatific optimism a whole group of people who have been used to consider democratic institutions as a shelter. . . .[1]

Anti-Semitism, indicated an editorialist in the *Univers israélite*, had drawn the Jews much more tightly together than they ever had been before, and had strengthened their community.[2] A modern authority on the history of the Jews in France tends to agree, seeing the Jewish community during the Affair as being united in support of justice and its own honour.[3]

It is impossible fully to resolve these sometimes differing observations, and it is perhaps unwise to attempt to do so. We can only note that within the Jewish community there was a broad spectrum of opinion, with certain similarities of style and belief. We can, however, observe the reactions of representative individuals, and of specific organizations such as the *consistoires*, and attempt to assess the significance of their activity. We can finally, in the chapter which follows, examine the small but significant minority within the Jewish community which took a very different position from the rest, and which, standing with Bernard Lazare and the young militants from eastern Europe, began a revolution in Jewish thought and behaviour. In so doing, it is only fair to add, it appears that the weight of evidence seems to lie with those who believed that the predominant Jewish response was a passive one, and that Jews tended in good measure to refrain from any involvement at all.

---

[1] H. Prague, 'Le péril actuel', *A.I.*, 10 Mar. 1898, p. 73.

[2] R. T., 'La vitalité d'Israël', *U.I.*, 16 Dec. 1898, p. 391. Cf. B.-M., 'La crise ministérielle et l'Affaire Dreyfus', *U.I.*, 23 June 1899, p. 427.

[3] Rabi (pseud.), *Anatomie du judaïsme français* (Paris, 1962), p. 77.

It is difficult to determine exactly when this crisis began. From the moment that the arrest of Alfred Dreyfus was announced to the public, in the autumn of 1894, anti-Semitic journalists began a systematic campaign against the Jews which focused upon the accused captain. Little more than a week after the news that a Jewish officer had been arrested on charges of treason, La Libre Parole was claiming that 'toute la Juiverie' considered itself in solidarity with the traitor.[1] No hint was thought too insignificant, no connection too tenuous, to be offered as decisive proof that the Jews were leagued together in a vast conspiracy to defend Dreyfus and to further the work of espionage. On 2 December 1894, Gaston Méry announced 'the Jews' plan' in Drumont's newspaper. The Jews, he claimed, were hard at work, drawing upon their vast network of international influence to persuade the government to keep the affaire quiet and eventually to save the accused.[2] Before long suggestions were being made to purge all Jews from the army and government offices.[3] The anti-Semitic deputy Théodore Denis made a formal interpellation in the Chamber early in 1895, asking the government about 'measures which it can take to eliminate the predominance of Jews in several branches of the French administration'.[4] Such agitation was almost always made defensively; the object of the purge, it was held, was to protect French society from the 'invasion', from being taken over by an alien race.

Had it not been for the publication of Lazare's first brochure, however, the Affair itself might gradually have been forgotten. As we have seen, this publication raised the issue of anti-Semitism and its connection with the condemnation of Dreyfus. Lazare insisted that Dreyfus was innocent, and that he had been arrested, prosecuted, and convicted for no other reason than that he was a Jew. Anti-Semites lost no time in responding to the charges. In

[1] Gaston Méry, 'Haute trahison', La Libre Parole, 9 Nov., 1894; ibid., 2 Nov· 1894; ibid., 4 Nov. 1894.

[2] Gaston Méry, 'Le plan des Juifs', La Libre Parole, 5 Dec. 1894.

[3] See Léonel de la Tourasse, 'Juif et Allemand', La France nouvelle, 9 Jan. 1895.

[4] 'Liberté de conscience', Le Temps, 13 Feb. 1895; Journal officiel, Chambre, 25 and 27 May 1895, pp. 1472 ff.

a vicious interpellation on 18 November 1896, the Nationalist deputy André Castelin described, to the applause of the extreme Left, the machinations of 'a syndicate of espionage or corruption'.[1] This 'syndicate', of which much was to be heard in the course of the Affair, was seen to be made up in good part of 'the co-religionists of Dreyfus', of Jews who preferred solidarity with the traitor to their duty towards the fatherland. 'La grande société israélite toute entière' was involved, Castelin declared, and together they were behind the campaign for revision.[2] Feeding upon the efforts of the Dreyfus family for revision, anti-Semitic journalists exploited each revelation and each incident to attack the Jews as outsiders, German agents, and the leaders of a vast international conspiracy. The fatherland, some were beginning to say, was in danger.

In many quarters, interest in the Jews mounted to a veritable obsession. By the spring of 1897, according to one Catholic review, 'the Jewish question' was 'the order of the day. Newspapers, reviews, books, discuss it in all of its ramifications. Each [contribution] brings its share of information, often inaccurate, almost always impassioned, which is scarcely calculated to appease the feelings aroused and incline them to a solution conforming with the principles of justice and real wisdom.'[3] This writer, with whom many would have agreed, was one of the new group of 'Jewish experts' who reviewed anti-Semitica for an increasingly interested public.

As the preoccupation with the 'Jewish question' spread, the images of the Jew so carefully cultivated by Drumont and others received the wide public attention which had always been denied them in the popular press. Certain Catholic newspapers in particular aided the anti-Semitic effort. In L'Univers of 2 April 1895, François Veuillot defined the Jews as 'strangers, occupying the soil of any country at all in order to exploit it'; in 1896 La France

---

[1] Ibid., 18 Nov. 1896, pp. 1613-14.

[2] See Édouard Drumont, 'L'interpellation Castelin et le syndicat Dreyfus', La Libre Parole, 17 Nov. 1896; Ad. Papillaud, 'Le syndicat Dreyfus', ibid., 19 Nov. 1896; Lucien Millevoye, 'Le syndicat de trahison', ibid., 19 Nov. 1896; Albert Monniot, 'Les complices de Dreyfus', ibid., 20 Nov. 1896.

[3] Fr. M. J. Belon in Le Moniteur bibliographique, 25 Mar. 1897, p. 77.

catholique made reference to the long-discredited legend of Jewish ritual murders.[1] Moreover, even those newspapers which were indifferent to the fate of Dreyfus contributed to the movement against the Jews. The anarchist journals *Le Père Peinard* and *La Sociale* freely used such derogatory epithets as *youtre* or *youpin* when referring to a Jew.[2] Anti-Dreyfusard cartoonists outdid one another in their caricatures, striving to portray those features which were characteristically 'Jewish' in the most grotesque and obscene manner. Much worse, however, was to come. When survivors of the Dreyfus period refer today to the Affair, they frequently describe the emotional experience as being similar to the world wars, or what it must have been like to have lived through the French Revolution. When describing the Affair in this way they are drawing attention not only to the great issues involved, but also to the immediate proximity of violence.[3] For Jews, of course, against whom much of this violence was specifically directed, this perception was particularly acute.

Anti-Semitic riots began in Algeria, in the spring of 1897, after a minor incident in the town of Mostaganem got out of hand and led to wild outbreaks throughout the colony. Mobs pillaged Jewish stores and sacked synagogues, as rioting flared in all major cities, particularly Oran.[4] Fully reported in Paris, the Algerian disturbances helped to create a climate of violence against the Jews which, under the circumstances of the Dreyfus Affair, emerged in full fury in the beginning of 1898.[5] During the third week of January in that year, immediately following the publication of Émile Zola's *J'accuse*, there were anti-Jewish uprisings in virtually

[1] See Patrice Boussel, *L'Affaire Dreyfus et la presse* (Paris, 1960), pp. 91–2.

[2] Ibid., pp. 62, 104. Cf. 'Lettre au journal *Le Temps*', *U.I.*, 28 Feb. 1896, pp. 726–7.

[3] See, for example, Jules Isaac, *Expériences de ma vie*, vol. i, *Péguy* (Paris, 1959), pp. 144–5, 151–4.

[4] See Algerian newspapers, 18–19 May 1897; Michel Ansky, *Les Juifs d'Algérie: du décret Crémieux à la libération* (Paris, 1950), p. 58; Claude Martin, *Les Israélites algériens de 1830 à 1902* (Paris, 1936), pp. 276–7.

[5] See 'L'antisémitisme en Algérie', *Le Matin*, 22 May 1897; Paul de Cassagnac, 'Contre les juifs', *L'Autorité*, 26 June 1897; Le Paysan, 'En Algérie', *La Croix*, 26 May 1897.

every city in France. Not only were Jewish stores and places of worship attacked and burned, but Jews were assaulted on the streets. The police seemed to be either ineffective or in league with the rioters. 'A vague odour of a *coup d'état* and of Saint Barthélémy hung in the air', Théodore Reinach later wrote.[1] According to police reports the crowds were not only crying slogans related to the Dreyfus Affair, but also 'Death to the Jews!'.[2] In Paris the mob burst out of its traditional battleground in the Latin Quarter to attack Jewish stores on the Right Bank. In Nantes, it was reported, a number of soldiers joined in the demonstrations, and in Bordeaux pitched battles were fought in the vicinity of the main synagogue. Significant outbreaks were reported in Marseille, Lyon, Nancy, and Versailles. Even smaller towns, Clermont-Ferrand, La Rochelle, Poitiers, Angoulême, and Saint-Flour had incidents of violence and anti-Semitic demonstrations. In Algeria, where for several days the police did nothing to prevent the clashes, the riots were particularly bloody; several people were beaten to death in what could only be described as a pogrom.

Although the level of violence eventually subsided in late February, sporadic incidents against the Jews continued throughout the course of the Affair. Jews were always in danger and always faced the possibility that the provocative language of the anti-Semites would be translated into brute force. In addition, there were persistent, though not entirely successful, attempts to boycott Jewish stores and businesses. Anti-Semitic groups grew enormously in strength and, as Hannah Arendt has observed, with their para-military organization they provided an ominous precedent for modern totalitarian movements.[3] The fact that this anti-Semitic violence drew upon an obvious reservoir of mass support made believable what anti-Semites contended—that, in the words of Paul de Cassagnac, the violence represented a vast popular

---

[1] Théodore Reinach, *Histoire sommaire de l'Affaire Dreyfus* (Paris, 1904), pp. 109–10; cf. Joseph Reinach, *Histoire de l'Affaire Dreyfus* (7 vols., Paris, 1901–8), iii. 538–42.

[2] A.P.P. B A/1043.

[4] Arendt, op. cit., p. 112.

'insurrection against the Jews'.[1] French society appeared, as the Affair reached a climax in terms of popular violence, to be isolating the Jewish community and to be in the process of uniting against it.

Matters were not improved by the ambivalence of the extreme Left. On 20 January 1898, as the violence which we have described tightened its grip on the cities and towns of France, the socialist deputies in Parliament, including Jaurès, Viviani, Guèsde, Millerand, and Rouanet, published their first manifesto dealing with the Affair. Not only did they not speak out against the violence, they hardly referred to it. Instead, they denounced the Affair as a 'struggle between two factions of the bourgeoisie' which, like anti-Semitism, was a diversion from the true path of opposition to the capitalist system. Their argument, moreover, showed that the socialists still maintained some of their earlier heritage of anti-Semitism. Thus they contended that the campaign on behalf of Dreyfus was being waged by Jewish capitalists who were trying, in rehabilitating Dreyfus, to gain public support for their own misdeeds and 'to wash out . . . all the stain of Israel'.[2] It was not until several months later that Jaurès came out in favour of Dreyfus and became explicit in his condemnation of the attacks upon the Jews.[3] And even then French Socialism remained divided.[4] It was significant that during this critical moment in the history of the Jews in France, as the violence and feeling against the Jews spread, the official spokesmen of the working class remained apart from the struggle. To the end their opposition both to capitalism and to bourgeois liberalism made them vulnerable to persuasion by anti-Semitic arguments and prevented them from fully espousing the Jewish cause. As the nominally revolutionary elements in

---

[1] Paul de Cassagnac, 'Contre les juifs', L'Autorité, 26 June 1897.

[2] 'Le manifeste', La Lanterne, 20 Jan. 1898.

[3] See Harvey Goldberg, 'Jean Jaurès and the Jewish Question: the Evolution of a Position', J.S.S., vol. xx, no. 2, Apr. 1958, pp. 67–94; Georges Clemenceau, 'Au-dessus de la race et de la religion', L'Aurore, 10 June 1898.

[4] Léopold Lacour, 'Socialistes byzantins', Les Droits de l'homme, 5 Aug. 1898. See Edmund Silberner, 'French Socialism and the Jewish Question, 1865–1914', Historia Judaica, vol. xvi, Apr. 1954, pp. 3–38; George Lichtheim, 'Socialism and the Jews', Dissent, July–Aug. 1968, pp. 325, 339–40 n. 30.

French society slipped into the background or appeared vaguely hostile to the Jews, and as in the name of *la patrie* the forces of the Right mobilized against them, the fate of French Jewry seemed to hang in the balance.

Some sense of the Jewish reaction to this crisis can be gleaned in a study of the two main periodicals of the Jewish community, the *Archives israélites* and the *Univers israélite*. Appearing weekly through most of the Affair, they provided a forum for a number of differing points of view, and described in some detail the reactions of French Jews. Other periodicals, representing the viewpoint of a militant minority and of Zionist orientation, were founded during the Affair and have left eloquent testimony to the divisions which rent the community. Here and there we find other traces of Jewish response: memoirs, letters, and published writings give us hints, tell of individuals, and relate bits of gossip. But in the end a complete analysis must elude the historian of the Affair. Individuals responded not only as Jews, but also as Frenchmen; the historian cannot easily distinguish between these two dimensions. Jewish organizations tended in large measure to abstain from involvement, and this itself tells us something about the Jewish response. But for the historian passivity is much more difficult to describe and analyse than activity, and once again we are faced with a historical record which is inadequate. We can best proceed using the two main periodicals as the chief expressions of Jewish opinion, venturing elsewhere when the historical record permits.

With the first, shocking news of the arrest of Alfred Dreyfus, Jews must have realized that the incident had serious implications for their community. In solemn tones the *Archives israélites* and the *Univers israélite* reported the details to their readers, implicitly relating the developments to the existing climate of anti-Semitism.[1] At the time, however, there was little reason for Jews or the public at large to doubt Dreyfus's guilt; the incident, it was felt, particularly after judgement was rendered late in December, was

[1] L. Wogue, 'Le capitaine Dreyfus', *U.I.*, 1 Nov. 1894; Isidore Cahen, 'Un grave incident', *A.I.*, 8 Nov. 1894.

best forgotten.[1] Commenting on the atmosphere at the close of 1894, Isidore Cahen noted that the year 'was ending sadly for Judaism, for France, and for civilization'. Yet he told his readers that he would not comment upon the Affair or the judgement: 'If silence were not imposed upon us by propriety, out of respect for the mourning of two respectable families [the Dreyfuses and Alfred Dreyfus's in-laws, the Hadamards], it would be by the precarious position in which the dreadful campaign waged by anti-Semitism places not only our Jewish minority, but all minorities....'[2] Léon Blum noted in his memoirs on the Dreyfus Affair that Jews in general at this time avoided discussion of what was undoubtedly one of the most talked-about questions of the day:

> They did not talk of the Affair among themselves; far from raising the subject they studiously avoided it. A great misfortune had fallen upon Israel. One suffered with it without a word, waiting for time and silence to wipe away the effects.[3]

Underlining this urge to avoid the Affair and to take refuge in silence was a basic feeling of insecurity with respect to the position of the Jews. Jewish editorialists sensed that the anti-Semitic exploitation of the Dreyfus trial was likely to have considerable popular appeal, and they were anxious to avoid a confrontation over the issue. With the exception of Bernard Lazare (whose articles were recommended to the public in the *Univers israélite*) no one bothered to refute once again the anti-Semitic charges that the Jews were a community of traitors.[4] Lazare Wogue worried over 'the hostile prejudice which always slumbers in people', although he hoped that better impulses would carry the day.[5] Isidore Cahen, writing several weeks later, was much less sanguine: '... we judge that, thanks to the provocations by which the immense majority of honest Frenchmen are terrorized, our

---

[1] Peloni, 'Un mouvement d'opinion', *A.I.*, 13 Dec. 1894, p. 411.
[2] Isidore Cahen, 'Sommes-nous défendus?', *A.I.*, 27 Dec. 1894, p. 423.
[3] Léon Blum, *Souvenirs sur l'Affaire* (Paris, 1935), p. 25.
[4] 'Encore Dreyfus', *U.I.*, 1 Jan. 1895, p. 271.
[5] Wogue, 'Le capitaine Dreyfus', p. 127.

interests are threatened, our rights are disregarded, and our future security is insufficiently protected.'[1]

As it happened, both Isidore Singer and Joseph Aron, whose somewhat quixotic campaigns against anti-Semitism we discussed in Chapter VI, were publishing their newspapers as the Dreyfus Affair became known to the public. Both journalists, as we have seen, were patriotic defenders of a certain ideal of France; both made it abundantly clear, now with the issue of treason before them, that Dreyfus should be shown no mercy whatever. Although there was no death-penalty for treason or espionage at the time, both felt that, if convicted, the traitor deserved to be executed; Aron believed that he should be shot, and Singer that he should be subjected to 'the pitiless penal code of Moses'— death by stoning, with the Grand Rabbi of France casting the first stone.[2]

As might be expected, then, French Jews hoped that the Affair would soon blow over, and that Dreyfus would be quickly forgotten. Like most Frenchmen, Jews believed, with some exceptions, in Dreyfus's guilt.[3] If there were serious doubts here and there, as seems likely, such doubts were stilled by the stronger feeling of the need not to make an issue of the Affair. If there was some sense that anti-Semitism was playing a sinister part in the business, there was also the necessity, as the *Univers israélite* noted, to defer to the judgement of the court.[4] Nothing could be done, and the best advice seemed to be that of Isidore Singer: to avoid dispute, to cut Dreyfus off from the Jewish community, to dissociate him from French Jewry, and in so doing to rededicate the community to the patriotic exercise of its duties.[5] This was the *volonté de paix* which was to exert its influence within the Jewish community persistently during the Affair.

[1] Cahen, 'Sommes-nous défendus?', p. 423.

[2] Joseph Aron in *L'Homologation*, 8 Nov. 1894; I. Singer, 'La trahison du capitaine Dreyfus et la légende de la solidarité juive', *La Vraie Parole*, 10 Nov. 1894. Cf. Edmond Magnier, 'Le traître', *La Vraie Parole*, 10 Nov. 1894.

[3] I. Déhalle, 'L'assimilation des israélites français', *U.I.*, 16 Aug. 1901, p. 683. Cf. Georges Delahache (pseud.), 'Juifs', *Cahiers de la quinzaine*, no. 5, ser. 3, 1901, pp. 21–2.

[4] 'Encore Dreyfus', *U.I.*, 1 Jan. 1895, p. 271.

[5] Singer, 'La trahison du capitaine Dreyfus et la légende de la solidarité juive'.

Among Jews, virtually the only people who felt differently
about the matter at this time were a small group about the Dreyfus family, and with this in mind it is convenient to consider here
the reaction of the latter from the perspective of the French Jewish
community. The Dreyfus family, it has been frequently noted,
was highly representative of the assimilated Jewish Alsatian bourgeoisie. The family owned a very prosperous spinning-mill in
Mulhouse, and was known to be quite wealthy. After 1871, when
that city fell under German control, Dreyfus's father Raphaël
and three of his sons retained their French citizenship. While the
eldest son Léon remained in Mulhouse to manage the family
enterprise, the others moved to Paris. There, as one observer put
it, the family 'incarnated in the eyes of the Jewish bourgeoisie...
[an attitude of] nationalist *raideur*, French puritanism, [and] a distant manner of disdain towards their parvenu co-religionists'.[1]
The family had few ties with the Jewish community; their social
perspective was entirely taken up with the desire to assimilate into
French society and to eliminate the barriers which might separate
them from their fellow citizens.[2] It is much less well known, however, that the Dreyfuses were themselves parvenus of sorts, or at
least that their assimilation was of very recent development. While
Alfred Dreyfus and his brothers were only nominal Jews, his
father was a *pratiquant*, faithful to Jewish tradition. Dreyfus's
grandfather was a poor Jewish merchant from the village of
Rixheim in Alsace. The latter's brother and several other close
relatives were rabbis.[3]

Understandably, Dreyfus's arrest on charges of treason came as
a severe shock to this family, so recently assured a position in Parisian society, and so dedicated, particularly following the Franco-

[1] André Foucault, 'Un nouvel aspect de l'Affaire Dreyfus', *Les Œuvres libres*,
no. 205, July 1938, p. 310.
[2] 'Leur volonté de s'inféoder absolument à la coutume gauloise, de vivre en
intimité avec nos vieilles familles, d'occuper les charges les plus honorables de
l'État, le mépris qu'ils affichaient pour la Juiverie trafiquante, pour les « pollacks »
de Galicie fraîchement nationalisés, leur donnaient presque figure de traîtres à la
race.' Ibid.
[3] Dr. Mayer in 'Zeitungnachrichten und Correspondenzen', *Der Israelit*
[Mainz], vol. xxxix (1898), p. 276.

Prussian War, to French patriotism. They found it unbelievable
that Alfred, a conscientious officer and a thoroughly dedicated
Polytechnician, could in fact have sold military secrets to the
Germans. Madame Hadamard, Dreyfus's mother-in-law and the
wife of a wealthy Jewish diamond merchant, expressed this feeling in a number of newspaper interviews: How, she asked, could
such a rich and devoted family man have committed such a
crime?[1] Led by Mathieu Dreyfus, the 'frère admirable', in Joseph
Reinach's words, the family resolved to help to prove his innocence.

Yet despite the monstrous and incredible nature of the accusation, the family conducted itself with considerable caution, and held
back in every possible way from making the case a *cause célèbre*.
To some extent at least, their caution mirrored that of the larger
Jewish community. Hannah Arendt has offered a stern commentary upon their tactics: 'In trying to save an innocent man they
employed the very methods usually adopted in the case of a guilty
one. They stood in mortal terror of publicity and relied exclusively
on back-door maneuvers.'[2] Mathieu handled matters with
great secrecy and discretion, working tirelessly behind the scenes,
drawing extensively upon the family fortune, and attempting to
win support in high places.[3] Instead of facing the issues involved
through a campaign of public protest, through a campaign based
upon basic issues of human rights, the Dreyfus family preferred
for two years to keep the matter largely out of the public view.
And during this entire period, with publicity carefully managed
and kept to a minimum, fears grew in the army and elsewhere
that a secret 'Hebrew mobilization' was being prepared, and that
Jewish gold was being used to undermine French institutions. It
is entirely possible that these fears were related to the family's
mode of operation.

At the time there was some criticism of these methods. We have
seen how Bernard Lazare was straining at the leash placed upon
him by Mathieu from the beginning of 1895 to the autumn of

---

[1] Johnson, op. cit., p. 26.   [2] Arendt, op. cit., p. 105.
[3] Robert Gauthier (ed.), '*Dreyfusards!*' *Souvenirs de Mathieu Dreyfus et autres
inédits* (Paris, 1965), pp. 52–3, *passim*; Johnson, op. cit., pp. 60–2.

1896.[1] The Jewish historian Arthur Lévy pressed the Dreyfus family from the very beginning to take open and immediate action. At a meeting at the Hadamard home shortly following Dreyfus's degradation, he suggested a public protest, to be circulated for signatures without delay. The meeting, however, decided firmly against his plan. It was said that such public action would merely be 'beating the air', and that 'it might irritate the government'. Lévy concluded that the Dreyfuses were acting far too timidly and with excessive prudence.[2] Léon Blum, looking back over the tactics employed, considered them to have been mistaken for much the same reason, although he felt they were understandable given the circumstances. For one thing, there was a general expectation that once the facts were fully divulged, the public would be won over immediately; for another, the family and their close friends always wanted to keep open the paths to the government in the hopes of official intervention in the case.[3]

There were many reasons, both social and personal, which might have disposed Mathieu and the Dreyfus family to conduct their campaign in this manner. Among them, however, it seems reasonable to conclude that their position as assimilated Jews in French society played a significant part. Mathieu, of course, had little to say about this. And yet he was always sensitive to the place which anti-Semitism had in the movement against revision, and of the way in which his Jewishness served to isolate him. For example, when he first entered the offices of *L'Aurore*, he sensed in Clemenceau and in other members of the staff of the newspaper a certain 'reserve' which he must have felt on many other occasions: 'I was the brother of him whom the country called "the traitor". I was also "a Jew". . . .'[4] Haunted by the constant charges that the Jews were outsiders, that they were traitors who represented vast cosmopolitan interests, the Dreyfus family strove to avoid militancy and to work within the established institutions of French government and society. To a certain extent

[1] See pp. 181–2, above.
[2] Arthur Lévy, memorandum in Reinach papers, B.N. n. a. fr. 24897, pp. 247–50.
[3] Blum, op. cit., pp. 45–51.   [4] Gauthier, op. cit., p. 184.

they too felt the *volonté de paix*. Only when they were hopelessly frustrated in their efforts at using inside influence did they turn to the field of public protest. And when they finally did so, the Dreyfus Affair slipped out of their hands, and other campaigners, Lazare, Clemenceau, Zola, and eventually Jaurès, came to the forefront. One member of the Dreyfus family in particular had nothing to do with this strategy. In a letter to his wife shortly before his conviction the bewildered captain wrote:

To have worked my entire life for a single goal, the goal of *revanche* against the infamous ravisher of our dear Alsace, and to see myself accused of treason against this country—No, my dearest, my soul refuses to comprehend this![1]

Alfred Dreyfus clung to this position throughout.

With the 'Jewish traitor' safely exiled and prevented from further undermining the French nation, the anti-Semitic press found itself without an immediate object of attack. Presently, however, it uncovered a new scandal, and one with appropriate anti-Semitic overtones. Early in 1895 Isaïe Levaillant, a former Gambettist who had been active in the Alliance Israélite Universelle, was accused of using his government office (Trésorier-Payeur Général of the department of the Loire) to intervene with the magistrates on behalf of a bankrupt firm of fellow Jews, Schwob Frères.[2] Levaillant's public career, which had been a distinguished one, was now ruined.

Devoting himself thenceforth to Jewish causes, Levaillant began to work for the *Univers israélite*, becoming its editor-in-chief in 1896.[3] Since Levaillant did not sign his name to the leading editorials (he generally used the initials B.-M.), one cannot be absolutely sure when his authority fully made itself felt. But it

[1] Alfred Dreyfus, *Lettres d'un innocent* (Paris, 1898), p. 23. In an interesting *éloge* of Dreyfus one columnist closed his article with the following: 'On serait tenté, si on écrivait l'histoire de la tragique affaire qui s'achève, de lui donner pour titre: « Alfred Dreyfus, le plus fidèle des soldats, le plus patriote des Français et le meilleur des chrétiens».' Frédéric Passy, 'Pas tant de foi en Israël', *Le Siècle*, 28 Sept. 1899.
[2] See P. de L., 'Entre juifs', *L'Autorité*, 8 Feb. 1895; 'M. Levaillant révoqué', *Le Matin*, 10 Feb. 1895.
[3] See obituaries, *U.I.*, 27 Oct. 1911, pp. 205–8; *A.I.*, 26 Oct. 1911, pp. 340–1; article in *U.J.E.*

seems virtually certain that the new format of the periodical, from September 1895, was due to his influence. The *Univers israélite* changed from a bi-monthly to a weekly, aimed its appeal at a wider public, and devoted more attention to current political issues. Its subscribed circulation rose from 544 in 1895–6 to 691 in 1896–7; its readership was certainly larger still. Its influence within the Jewish community was considerable.[1]

The most important aspect of this change, which was itself an indirect result of the Dreyfus Affair, was a new editorial policy for the journal. Hitherto a modest advocate of Jewish opinion, it now took a more critical stance, and ventured into controversial territory. The journal now condemned what it considered the dominant inclination of the Jewish community—to remain quiet and passive in the face of anti-Semitism. What Théodore Reinach had once approvingly called the 'silence of disdain' now came under severe attack:

> Silence, even in the eyes of the most intelligent, often passes for an admission of guilt, disdain for a convenient excuse, and certain falsehoods, by dint of being repeated, end up by imposing themselves upon honest men if they are never opposed and nullified.[2]

Specifically, when Dreyfus appeared briefly in the news in the autumn of 1896, Levaillant referred to the 'systematic silence' which Jews had imposed upon themselves since the beginning of the Affair, 'obeying I cannot imagine what feelings of confusion and fear of accepting the dishonourable solidarity which people attempted to impose upon them'.[3] From that time on Levaillant spoke out against this disposition, one which he frequently located in the other important Jewish periodical, the *Archives israélites*; he accused Jews of ignoring the anti-Semitic forces which had exploited the Dreyfus Affair, and reminded them that these forces had to be reckoned with in some way by the Jewish community.

---

[1] Letter, L. Bloch to Consistoire de Paris, 1 Dec. 1897, A.C.P. B 62.
[2] La rédaction, 'Notre programme', *U.I.*, 27 Sept. 1895, p. 6. Cf. H. Prague, 'Le silence du dédain', *A.I.*, 18 Apr. 1895, pp. 121–2.
[3] B.-M., 'A propos des révélations de *L'Éclair*', *U.I.*, 25 Sept. 1896, p. 9.

As we noted in the previous chapter, Bernard Lazare's first brochure on the Dreyfus Affair, appearing in November 1896, posing squarely as it did the anti-Semitic implications of the conviction of the Jewish officer, was received with a certain discomfort in the Jewish community. Yet it would be mistaken to consider that the community was as yet very much involved. The matter received only brief notice in the *Archives israélites*, where Isidore Cahen once again emphasized that Jews were in no way implicated in the Affair.[1] Somewhat less evasive, Levaillant recognized cautiously that some vital issues of judicial procedure might have been at stake; however, he made no reference to anti-Semitism and only passing mention of Dreyfus himself.[2]

What strikes one, in considering the reticence of the two periodicals, their reluctance to pursue the question with any compelling interest or energy, is the ingrained respect which they had for *la chose jugée*.[3] Once the military tribunal had decided, so the argument went, it was incumbent upon all Frenchmen to defer obediently to that decision. Indeed, so strong was this deference that Levaillant had considered it an effective rejoinder to the anti-Semites to charge that it was *they* who had kept alive doubts and hesitations about the judgement, and *they* who had, by endlessly discussing the Affair, 'ended up by compromising the work of justice itself'.[4] In this, of course, Jews did not differ from most Frenchmen, and the difficulty which the Dreyfusards experienced in winning over the public at large stems in large part from this kind of widespread deference. (Here, one might add, was another argument against Mathieu Dreyfus's policy of waiting: the longer the public campaign for revision was delayed, the greater seemed to be the legitimacy of the court's judgement in 1894.)

But for Jews the price paid for this deference was much higher than that of the surrounding community. However much

---

[1] Isidore Cahen, 'L'Affaire Dreyfus: brochures et interpellations', *A.I.*, 26 Nov. 1896, p. 385.

[2] B.-M., 'La Brochure de M. Bernard Lazare', *U.I.*, 13 Nov. 1896, pp. 228–31.

[3] Ibid., p. 230. Cf. Weill, op. cit., p. 166.

[4] B.-M., 'Les Révélations de *L'Éclair*', *U.I.*, 25 Sept. 1895, p. 11. Cf. id., 'L'interpellation Castelin', *U.I.*, 27 Nov. 1896, p. 297.

they insisted upon dissociating themselves from 'the traitor', however much they declared that Jews were no more in league with
Dreyfus than Catholics were with 'their' traitor, Bazaine, French
Jews were haunted by the Affair, particularly as Mathieu began
gradually to release important evidence on the case.[1] The dilemma
was inescapable: to pursue the matter, along with a handful of
Dreyfusards, would be to question the majesty of the law and to
raise in a dramatic and belligerent way, as Lazare had done, the
issue of anti-Semitism; yet to remain silent would be no escape,
for Jews continued to suffer the continual opprobrium of the anti-
Semitic press which used Dreyfus as the symbol of Jewish disloyalty. Until the Affair decisively entered the public arena with
the publication of Zola's *J'accuse*, in January 1898, it seems certain
that most Jews chose the latter course. Thinking of it always, to
paraphrase Gambetta, they spoke of it never. Making the best of
a difficult situation, they chose to rely, as Jews always had, upon
the moral strength of the French nation; they took refuge in
optimism, believing that the spirit of 1789 would eventually
reassert itself. Yet the difficulties remained, and silence did not
seem to help. 'Whether we like it or not,' wrote Levaillant in
November 1897, 'the Dreyfus Affair touches us deeply, it calls
into question our interests and our honour':

Who among us has not suffered from it? Who among us can say that
it has not altered profoundly our social relations with our fellow citizens
of other religions? Have we not all noticed, as we meet socially with
non-Jews, that the conversation falls off suddenly because one has just
mentioned the Dreyfus Affair? What Jewish officer and what Jewish
official has not wondered at any given moment whether the condemnation of the ex-captain would hinder his own career . . .? Truly, this
lamentable story weighs heavily upon the situation of the Jews in
France.[2]

[1] See Isidore Cahen, 'L'Affaire Dreyfus: brochures et interpellations'. 'Mais
à chaque instant de la vie quotidienne, dans leurs relations mondaines ou dans
leurs rapports d'affaires surgissaient à propos du procès certaines allusions qui
leur faisaient voir qu'on établissait une sorte de solidarité entre eux et le traître
condamné.' I. Déhalle, 'L'assimilation des israélites français', *U.I.*, 16 Aug. 1901,
p. 683.
[2] B.-M., 'M. Scheurer-Kestner et l'Affaire Dreyfus', *U.I.*, 12 Nov. 1897,
p. 230.

Moreover, if one can believe the statements and recollections which Jews made during or after the Affair, the number of Jews who believed in Dreyfus's innocence from the very beginning was considerable. To some extent, of course, one must discount such statements as being due to the distortions of memory caused by the enthusiasm subsequently built up around Dreyfus. Still, however weak their reasoning may have been, in 1894 a number of Jews estimated that they were particularly able to judge how dubious were the charges because they knew something of Dreyfus's background. Michel Bréal was a Jewish scholar, also from Alsace, who had no religious ties whatever with the Jewish community; he had always believed, he later wrote, that Dreyfus, as an Alsatian Jew, could never be guilty of treason.[1] Zadoc Kahn, who was distantly related to the Dreyfus family by his daughter's marriage, was also convinced of the captain's innocence from the very beginning.[2] For these Jews, and for others who had doubts about the judgement, the long period dominated by *la chose jugée* must have been particularly painful.

Yet the very forces which imposed silence upon the Jews during this period induced many of them to regard the beginning of the campaign for revision with a certain mistrust. This was what Léon Blum referred to as he considered the reaction of the Jewish community:

The dominant sentiment could be translated into the following formula: 'That is something in which the Jews must not get mixed up....' In that complex sentiment all of the elements were of unequal value. There was, to be sure, patriotism, and even a very touchy patriotism, respect for the army, confidence in its leaders, a reluctance to consider them as either partial or weak. But there was also a kind of selfish and timid prudence which could be judged harshly. The Jews did not want it believed that they were defending Dreyfus because he was a Jew. They did not want their attitude imputed to any distinction or solidarity

[1] Michel Bréal, 'Encore un témoignage', *Le Siècle*, 20 Aug. 1898.
[2] Letter, Leo Wise to Zadoc Kahn, 9 June 1899, A.C.P. B 64; Weill, op. cit., pp. 163–6; Salomon Reinach, 'Conférence de M. Salomon Reinach', *Bulletin de l'Association amicale des anciens élèves des Écoles Halphen et Lucien de Hirsch*, vol. i, no. 2, Apr. 1908. Cf. Isidore Cahen, 'Un grave incident', p. 369.

of race. Above all they did not want, in going to the defence of a Jew, to offer any encouragement to the anti-Semitic passion which was raging at the time with a very considerable intensity.[1]

In short, the Jews made the connection between the Dreyfus Affair and anti-Semitism, but feared that the former was feeding the latter, rather than vice versa. In their view the beginning of a campaign on behalf of the Jewish officer could only worsen matters, without securing his release and, more importantly, without lessening any of the feeling against the Jews. Indeed, agitation promised only to harden and to spread hostile opinion.

Such misgivings could only have been considered justified when, immediately following Zola's manifesto which brought Dreyfus inescapably before the public, there ensued an anti-Semitic outburst the like of which France had never seen. The two main Jewish periodicals reflected the horror of the community as it faced violence in every major town in France. 'The mask is off!' said a headline in the *Archives israélites*; anti-Semitism and *le parti clérical* were showing themselves with their truly murderous intentions.[2] Levaillant declared that he had always, in the past, preserved 'a certain confidence in the good sense, the moderation, the sentiments of equity in a country which had taught tolerance to the world'. Now, however, he saw that he had been wrong: '... anti-Semitism has invaded all parts of the country and has penetrated the most basic levels of the population.' Anti-Semitism, in fact, was popular.[3] As a result, perhaps for the first time in the history of the Jews in France, members of the established Jewish community publicly cast doubts upon the fatherland. 'Aujourd'hui,

---

[1] Blum, op. cit., pp. 25–6. Daniel Halévy described the Jews' reaction in a similar manner: 'On ignorait, et un prudent instinct conseillait de toujours ignorer. La sentence était rendue, on la tenait pour bonne. On croyait, mais faiblement, étant mal exercé à croire. Il est probable que nombre de juifs, mieux exercés à connaître les coups de l'antisémitisme, pensaient différemment. Ils n'en disaient rien, épargnant à des amis, même intimes, l'expression d'un avis qui eût ennuyé, déplu. Le procès Dreyfus était exclu, par un très curieux, tout silencieux accord, de ces conversations parisiennes qui n'excluent rien.' Daniel Halévy, 'Apologie pour notre passé', Cahiers de la quinzaine (Paris, 1910), p. 23.

[2] H. Prague, 'Le masque est tombé', *A.I.*, 27 Jan. 1898, p. 28.

[3] B.-M., 'L'opinion publique et l'Affaire Dreyfus', *U.I.*, 7 Jan. 1898, pp. 486–9.

hélas et trois fois hélas! il nous faut déchanter', wrote Louis Lévy in the *Univers israélite*:

> France is no longer herself or at least does not seem to be herself any longer. . . . She has lost what was her originality. She has borrowed from other countries principles diametrically opposed to hers.

And yet this writer, as was characteristic within the Jewish community, still clung to the optimism which, as he himself had once noted, was part of the Jews' 'politique d'autruche':

> We are convinced that France will soon pull herself together, will be ashamed of the deviation which she has let herself take, will shake herself free of her error. . . .[1]

Levaillant too revealed the same mixture of feelings. If the Affair had shown 'the mob' letting itself be drawn into criminality, at the same time, he wrote, 'the élite of the country remains firmly attached to the ideas of justice and tolerance. And this is precisely what permits us not to despair.'[2] As we shall see, these two strands, of continued optimism and loyalty on the one hand, and of disenchantment bordering on despair on the other, were to be found in various strengths throughout the Jewish community.

Throughout the Affair, Zadoc Kahn was one of those who placed continued emphasis upon a basic devotion to France. Typical of his position was a statement which he made for *Le Siècle* expressing his feelings for the New Year 1899:

> With all my heart, I wish for our dear France that she remain faithful to her natural genius, so wonderfully made up of reason, good sense, loyalty, and generosity; that she abandon nothing of her glorious traditions which have won for her the gratitude and love of the oppressed, that she always strive to be in the first rank among the nations in the defence of the principles of justice, humanity, and social solidarity, in order to be strong and respected without, and united and prosperous within.[3]

---

[1] Louis Lévy, 'L'antisémitisme et la France', *U.I.*, 25 Feb. 1898, pp. 715-16; cf. id., 'Les fautes passées et le devoir présent', *U.I.*, 21 Jan. 1898, pp. 552-6.
[2] B.-M., 'Pas de découragement', *U.I.*, 28 Jan. 1898, p. 583.
[3] 'Quelques vœux d'intellectuels', *Le Siècle*, 1 Jan. 1899.

In the face of persistent vilification and fantastic charges which were stimulated against him by the excitement over the Affair, he held firm to his convictions.[1] In 1897 he had declared before a Jewish audience that anti-Semitism was showing signs of decomposition and decline; two years later, with all of the hatred and violence which had been uncovered, he still remained unshakeable in his faith that all would soon be well with France, and that she would soon reveal her former spirit.[2] Perennially optimistic, the Grand Rabbi of France lived through the Dreyfus Affair articulating the historic Jewish faith in the French Republic. Generously though discreetly supporting the movement for revision, he had the fullest confidence that the Jews and Dreyfus would in due course be welcomed into the community of Frenchmen. Continually he condemned anti-Semitism as a divisive element in French society. Even the verdict against Dreyfus given at Rennes in 1899 did not dampen his spirits. His biographer, who knew him well and who shared his viewpoint, commented upon his reaction at that moment: 'The reparation was only delayed. Like many others, Zadoc Kahn had ardently hoped that it would be procured quickly and in a pacific manner. The enormous storm over a Jew went against his natural sense of moderation and proportion. On the other hand he had the feeling that this sublime affair [*la sainte affaire*] could be useful ferment for the ideas of justice and tolerance. . . .' The basis for this hope lay in the confidence in what he saw as the true French spirit—the fraternal spirit of the Republic. 'Jews of France and their [religious] leader could only be sympathetic to manifestations of enlightened republicanism. It was the France of the Revolution which had emancipated Israel in the past; the republican France of today could only follow her generous traditions in taking up the cause of the victim of reactionary passions.'[3]

Apart from his patriotism, Zadoc Kahn's moderation and commitment to French unity during the Affair may be explained by

---

[1] See Abbé L. Vial, *La Trahison du Grand Rabbin de France* (Paris, 1904); Gaston Pollonnais, 'Démission nécessaire', *Le Soir*, 2 Feb. 1899; 'L'Affaire Dreyfus', *L'Éclair*, 2 Feb. 1899, 12, 18 Mar. 1899; 'Respectueusement', *L'Époque*, 19 Mar. 1899.

[2] 'Réunions juives', *U.I.*, 12 Mar. 1897, p. 797.

[3] Weill, op. cit., pp. 211–12.

reference to his position as the official leader of the French rabbinate. As Grand Rabbi, Zadoc Kahn was, after all, a *fonctionnaire*, a paid officer of the State; as such, it was held, he was required to defer first of all to the greater interests of France. His friend and close associate Salomon Reinach appreciated the limitations involved in this office, and expressed this fact in a lecture delivered several years after the Affair: '. . . he was a *fonctionnaire*; he knew that great interests, other than his own, depended upon his discretion. He did what the circumstances permitted, and nothing more.'[1] Zadoc Kahn, of course, was not alone in thus limiting his actions; all other French rabbis were in the same position. The limitations thus imposed troubled Jewish leaders on occasion. One editorialist early in 1898 in the *Univers israélite*, for example, felt that the rabbinate as a whole was showing 'la plus grande réserve' in the face of anti-Semitic attacks. This was due, he felt, to 'their official position [which] restricts their actions significantly'.[2] However, there was little to be done in this connection, so long as one subscribed to the premisses of the French bureaucratic system and so long as the rabbinate was in part a government agency. And no one from the established Jewish community was prepared to challenge these principles during a time of crisis. That religious leaders accepted these limitations upon their actions, and that the Jewish community had to live with such restraints, these were the prices of assimilation.

Most Jews, of course, were not bound by such restrictions, and, when the Dreyfus Affair became a public issue of importance, some of them did join ranks with other Frenchmen both to defend the exiled officer and to condemn anti-Semitism. Foremost among them was Joseph Reinach, who stood out from the very beginning of the Affair both as a principled advocate and as one who was not afraid to appear so in public. In the course of the Affair anti-Semites attacked Reinach mercilessly; he was certainly, next to Dreyfus himself and perhaps Alphonse de Rothschild, the most

[1] Salomon Reinach, op. cit. According to Weill, '. . . Zadoc Kahn risqua l'impopularité auprès de plus d'un de ses coreligionnaires en ne restant pas neutre ou même hostile à l'agitation dreyfusiste'. Weill, op. cit., p. 202.
[2] R. T., 'Les fonctionnaires religieux', *U.I.*, 21 Jan. 1898, p. 551.

widely hated Jew in France.[1] Reinach's position on anti-Semitism, throughout the Affair, was similar to that of Zola and other non-Jewish Dreyfusards. Essentially, the force of his campaign was directed against the wider implications of the anti-Jewish movement. Jews, he felt, were currently being threatened by anti-Semites, but the latter were in fact attempting to destroy the Republic itself and all that it stood for. In coming to the defence of Dreyfus, Reinach emphasized that he was representing the true spirit of France and its institutions. 'It is we who are defending the honour of the army', Reinach told the electors of Digne in the election campaign of 1898.[2] (He was defeated in this campaign and lost his seat in the Chamber.) In the same year he published a short, scholarly study of the *erreur judiciaire* committed against Raphaël Lévy, a Jew accused unjustly of murder in the seventeenth century. The story, it appeared, bore remarkable similarities to that of Dreyfus. Reinach preferred, however, to let the facts of the case make his argument, and he persistently refrained from polemics either here or elsewhere when discussing the implications of anti-Semitism.[3]

Many other Jews took a similar position. Among them was Victor Basch, a young professor of literature at Rennes, who later died at the hands of the *Milice* in 1944.[4] Michel Bréal, Alfred Berl, the Symbolist poet Gustave Kahn, and a number of others were prominent Dreyfusards. In almost every case these Jews made it clear that they were engaging in the struggle, not in order to defend a Jew, but to defend the basic principles of the Republic. In the words of Gustave Kahn, the purpose of the campaign was to protect the idea of 'la France libérale'.[5] The Jew, warned Berl, was the victim of clerical, militarist, and nationalist passions; if he

---

[1] See, for example, Henri Rochefort, 'Les malices de Reinach', *L'Intransigeant*, 11 Jan. 1898; Octave Mirbeau, 'De Moïse à Loyola', *Le Journal*, 26 Sept. 1897; Jean France, *Souvenirs de la Sûreté générale* (Paris, 1936), p. 132; Charles Péguy, *Notre Jeunesse* (1910), in *Œuvres complètes* (Paris, 1916), iv. 226.

[2] Isidore Cahen, 'Une profession de foi', *A.I.*, 21 Apr. 1898, p. 122. Cf. Joseph Reinach, *Histoire*, iii. 542-9.

[3] Joseph Reinach, *Une erreur judiciaire sous Louis XIV: Raphaël Lévy* (Paris, 1898).

[4] See Paul Langevin, 'Discours', in *Victor Basch 1863-1944* (Paris, 1945).

[5] Gustave Kahn, 'L'idée nationaliste', *Revue blanche*, 15 Nov. 1899, p. 403.

were to be defeated, his defeat might extend to the fatherland itself.[1] Thus defending the Jew was in no way to be seen as engaging in Jewish solidarity; rather it was a simple duty of patriotism. The Orientalist Silvain Lévi, in a rare expression of frankness, related in a letter to the League for the Rights of Man the reason for his earlier hesitation in joining the revisionist movement:

> As long as it had to do with Dreyfus alone, I thought that it was my duty to remain silent. The cause of an innocent man had nothing to gain before public opinion by the adhesion of a Jew; it risked [rather] to lose by it. But today [December 1898] silence would be cowardly; protest is a duty. . . .[2]

Typically, the focus of Lévi's attention was the League for the Rights of Man. In supporting this organization many Jews found both the vehicle for the expression of their patriotism and the means to become involved in the Affair without seriously compromising themselves by their Judaism. When the League was first formed, following the terrible anti-Semitic riots of 1898, the *Archives israélites* noted 'with satisfaction' that out of thirty-four members of its executive, only three were Jews. 'This proves sufficiently', the editorial declared, 'that the Dreyfus Affair . . . is in absolutely no way Jewish, but is purely humanitarian.'[3] The Jewish periodicals commended the League to their readers because it seemed to legitimize protest against anti-Semitism, at least in republican circles.[4]

While these Jewish defenders of Dreyfus did not hide from anti-Semitism, they constantly strove to place it in the context of a much larger struggle. This struggle revolved about France, and their persistent effort was to take up sides in such a way as to emphasize their loyalty and devotion. To this extent they continued

---

[1] Alfred Berl, L'éclipse des idées libérales', *La Grande Revue*, 1 May 1900, p. 312.

[2] *U.I.*, 2 Dec. 1898. Cf. J. Tchernoff, *Dans le creuset des civilisations*, vol. iii, *De l'Affaire Dreyfus au dimanche rouge à Saint-Pétersbourg* (Paris, 1937), p. 40.

[3] 'La ligue des Droits de l'Homme et du Citoyen', *A.I.*, 9 June 1898, pp. 179–80. Cf. Henri Sée, *Histoire de la Ligue des Droits de l'Homme 1898–1926* (Paris, 1927), p. 10.

[4] See R. T., 'Ligue pour la défense des droits de l'homme et du citoyen', *U.I.*, 20 May 1898, pp. 261–4; 'Un discours de Zadoc Kahn', *Paris*, 13 Dec. 1898.

to cling to the nation and its established order as their best defence; Jewish interests and French interests were held to be one. In a talk delivered at a Jewish school in July 1898, Théodore Reinach counselled the children not to be unduly upset by the violence and criminality which was raging:

> ... do not confuse France with the foam which tosses wildly, but temporarily, on the surface of the waves. Continue to love her, this France, with all your strength, with all your heart, as you would a mother, even though she be [momentarily] unjust or led astray, because she is your mother, and because you are her children.[1]

Optimism seemed to follow necessarily from this kind of declaration. For the moment, it was held, France was being led astray. But her most fundamental principles, the principles of 1789, provided for the protection of the Jews; it could only be a matter of time before these principles reasserted themselves. From this point of view Jews would win their rights by identifying themselves on an equal basis with the other 'children' of France. All Frenchmen were equal; to claim this equality, Jews had simply to emphasize their Frenchness, their eligibility for fair treatment. The defence of Dreyfus, following this spirit, was to depend in large measure upon the Jewish assertion of patriotism. Patriotism, not 'Jewish solidarity', was to be encouraged among French Jews; France, and not a conspicuous Jewishness, would ultimately aid the cause of Dreyfus and the cause of all French Jewry.[2]

Somewhat different was the response of those Jews who publicly opposed the revisionist campaign. Their typical reaction was to deny the anti-Semitic dimension of the Affair, and to blame their fellow Jews for stirring up trouble. Like Zadoc Kahn, however, and like the other Jewish Dreyfusards, they emphasized their patriotism.

When, for example, the violence against the Jews was reaching its height in the beginning of 1898, a retired Jewish officer, Fernand Ratisbonne, wrote to *Le Gaulois* to 'disapprove energetically

---

[1] Théodore Reinach, 'Discours prononcé à la distribution des prix des écoles consistoriales israélites de Paris', *U.I.*, 25 July 1898, p. 595.

[2] See Cécile Delhorbe, *L'Affaire Dreyfus et les écrivains français* (Paris, 1932), p. 336.

of the current sterile campaign which so profoundly troubles our country and which tends to discredit our army . . .'.[1] Gaston Pollonnais, the editor of *Le Soir*, was another Jewish opponent of revision who avoided facing the issue of anti-Semitism directly. In his view the presence of Jews among the Dreyfusards called into question the loyalty of the entire Jewish community and fed the fires of anti-Semitism. Joseph Reinach, he felt, as the most prominent Jewish Dreyfusard, was mainly responsible for leading his co-religionists astray. 'Let the Jews take heed!' he wrote in 1899. 'Without Reinach they could count once again upon the protection of the fatherland; if, on the contrary, they persist obstinately in following their evil instincts, the God who protects France will abandon them for ever. . . .'[2] Pollonnais expressed his position in a headline of one of his leading editorials: 'A choice is necessary.' Jews, he declared, had to choose between France and 'an abominable solidarity based on religion'. Almost everything which the anti-Semites wrote he accepted; he intimated, however, that their description of Jews applied rather to a group of which Jews were only a part, and which he normally referred to as 'les cosmopolites'. Jews, he insisted, could escape the opprobrium by making a clear choice, by cutting themselves off from 'les cosmopolites' and by adopting French loyalties instead of Jewish loyalties. One could not, he implied, maintain a loyalty to both. Repeatedly, in his articles, Gaston Pollonnais expressed his patriotism in a defensive and highly self-conscious way:

When the audacious leaders of cosmopolitan Semitism dared to invoke the interests of race in order to create a universal solidarity among all the Jews, I refused to enrol in this foreign legion, I refused to desert the flag, I have, faithful to inflexible, unvarying principles, considered that the religion of France was superior to all others, and, called upon to choose between the triumvirate Dreyfus–Zadoc Kahn–Reinach and my country, it was to my country that I had to dedicate all of my energy and devotion. . . . I will defend thirty-six million Catholics against

---

[1] 'Une lettre de M. Fernand Ratisbonne', *Le Gaulois*, 25 Jan. 1898. Cf. 'M. Fernand Ratisbonne', *Le Siècle*, 26 Jan. 1898.

[2] Gaston Pollonnais, 'Belzébuth', *Le Soir*, 12 Sept. 1899; id., 'La main dans le sac', *Le Soir*, 1 Apr. 1899; id., 'Le syndicat', *Le Soir*, 1 Apr. 1899; id., '1894–1899', *Le Soir*, 2 July 1899; id., 'Les aveux', *Le Soir*, 1 Sept. 1899.

seventy-thousand tyrants. . . . I am with the persecuted against the oppressors, for France, and against the sectarian and cosmopolitan oligarchy.[1]

Another self-appointed defender of French Catholics against their Jewish 'oppressors' was the Jewish director of the Orléanist newspaper *Le Gaulois*, Arthur Meyer. Like Pollonnais, Meyer accepted most of what the anti-Semites contended, although he did feel that many of these charges were 'too generalized'. Somewhat more charitable than the director of *Le Soir*, he appeared to make more of an effort to rescue his co-religionists from being sweepingly designated anti-patriotic. The majority of Jews, he wrote, 'have always disapproved and disapproves still of all that goes against the beliefs of the great Catholic nation, which has done them the honour of admitting them, and to which they are devoted and grateful'.[2] For Meyer, 'Dreyfusism meant revolution', a revolution exploited by 'l'anarchie nationale'; he wished above all for 'l'appaisement', for a re-establishment of order in the country. Then, he felt, 'anti-Semitism would disappear, for there would no longer be a Jewish question'.[3]

Life became increasingly uncomfortable for Jewish anti-revisionists. Both Meyer and Pollonnais converted to Catholicism before the Affair was finally settled, thus formally abandoning the 'syndicate', to whose myth they had contributed.[4] Their strategy had been to protect their own and to some extent Jewish interests by identification with the most explicit defenders of order in French society—unfortunately, these turned out to be uncompromisingly anti-Semitic. They had hoped for a peaceful settlement of the Dreyfus Affair, for a settlement which would eliminate the 'Jewish question'—unhappily, the Affair had a remarkably long life. Conversion, in fact, underlined the failure of their approach.

[1] Gaston Pollonnais, 'Il faut choisir', *Le Soir*, 18 Nov. 1899.
[2] Arthur Meyer, 'A bas les Juifs', *Le Gaulois*, 7 Feb. 1895.
[3] A. Meyer, *Ce que mes yeux ont vu* (Paris, 1911), pp. 134, 137–8, 153.
[4] See biographical articles in *U.J.E.*; 'Nouvelles diverses', *A.I.*, 30 Oct. 1902; 'A propos d'une abjuration', *U.I.*, 7 Nov. 1902, p. 202; 'Le juif Pollonnais', *L'Aurore*, 20 Jan. 1898; Raphaël Viau, *Vingt Ans d'antisémitisme* (Paris, 1910), p. 324.

Condemned by Jews, the frequent target of attacks by Clemenceau in *L'Aurore*, and never fully accepted by anti-Semites, Jewish anti-Dreyfusards found it difficult to reply to the inevitable charges of *lâcheté*.[1] Though few in number, these Jews became extremely prominent, and often subject to the polemics of both sides; though they professed their Frenchness at every opportunity, they most frequently found themselves to be the object of universal ridicule.[2]

From what has been said it should be clear that Jews were to be found on all sides during the Dreyfus Affair, representing many different points of view. Common to all of those whom we have discussed, however, was a strong identification with France, a strong feeling that in this moment of crisis for French Jews one of the most important things to be done was to demonstrate one's patriotism. Common too was a recognition that this was a time of crisis, a time when Jewish loyalties were being tested. We may safely assume that the great majority of French Jewry followed suit, taking up positions between the extremes which we have mentioned. Beyond this it is difficult to generalize, and statistical estimates of the Jewish response are impossible. We may, however, investigate the governmental organs of the Jewish community, the *consistoires*, in order to explore this question further.

From the earliest period of the Affair, Jewish columnists blamed the *consistoires* for setting an example of passivity and 'systematic silence' for the rest of the Jewish community. This policy of the *consistoires*, which Prague referred to as 'la politique des bras croisés', was seen to have led to indifference and demoralization;

---

[1] See H. Prague, 'La République, les israélites, le Saint-Siège, et M. Arthur Meyer', *A.I.*, 14 Feb. 1895, pp. 50–1; Georges Clemenceau, 'Au-dessus de la race et de la religion'; id., *L'Iniquité* (2nd edn., Paris, 1899), pp. 164, 352–3, 374–5.

[2] An interesting case was that of the Radical Jewish Deputy L.-L. Klotz, who made the mistake of trying to oppose both Dreyfus and Drumont in a Chamber debate in the autumn of 1898. Predictably, he was attacked by both sides. See *Journal officiel, Chambre*, 14 Nov. 1898, pp. 2197–8; *A.I.*, 17 Nov. 1898; M. Adler, 'Trop malin', *La Cloche*, 1 Nov. 1898; D., 'Un élu: L.-L. Klotz', *Les Droits de l'homme*, 18 May 1898. Cf. the similar experience of an unidentified Jewish army officer: Paul de Cassagnac, 'Réponse à un juif', *L'Autorité*, 31 Jan. 1898.

French Judaism, it was felt, had been 'hamstrung by the consistorial organization which paralyses all of its movements and constitutes the most serious block to its religious and social development'.[1] In the spring of 1897, as we have noted, these issues were dramatized by the protest candidacy of a Doctor Metzger, who ran for a seat on the Consistoire Central with a programme sharply critical of this posture.[2] But Metzger was singularly unsuccessful in this effort, and matters proceeded much as they had before.

Members of the *consistoires* considered it their duty to demonstrate on practically every occasion that Jews were dedicated citizens of the Republic, and that their interests were at one with the interests of France. Yet the emphasis, critics sometimes sensed, was upon the interests of France, and as the Jewish community moved into a period of crisis the weakness of the consistorial system in this respect became progressively more apparent. Some idea of the dominant attitude in the *consistoires* may be drawn from a statement made in October 1897 by Alfred Neymark, an unopposed candidate for the Consistoire de Paris. His speech was delivered at the very beginning of the Dreyfus crisis, and against a background of anti-Semitic violence in Algeria:

More than ever, one must be a good Jew and a good Frenchman. Specifically, one must proclaim one's convictions before the entire world, defend the Jewish cause in all circumstances, claim the rights which are ours, and at the same time place the interests of France above all others, for it is to her that we owe what we are; we must therefore spare her neither our time, nor our property, nor our blood. The good Jew is a good Frenchman, and he who hides his religion does a disservice both to his co-religionists and to his country.[3]

---

[1] H. Prague, 'Les protestants et leurs adversaires', *A.I.*, 25 Feb. 1897, pp. 57–8. Cf. id., 'Réflexions sur le Consistoire Central', *A.I.*, 20 Aug. 1896, p. 274; B.-M., 'A propos des révélations de *L'Éclair*', *U.I.*, 25 Sept. 1896, p. 9; id., 'Élections consistoriales', *U.I.*, 9 Oct. 1896, p. 71; H. Prague, 'L'organisation du culte israélite en France', *A.I.*, 16 Sept. 1897, p. 290; R. T., 'Les fonctionnaires religieux,' *U.I.*, 21 Jan. 1898, p. 552; H. Prague, 'Causerie', *A.I.*, 30 June 1898, pp. 201–2.

[2] See p. 72, above.

[3] L. L., 'La réunion préparatoire pour la prochaine élection consistoriale de Paris', *U.I.*, 22 Oct. 1897, pp. 137–8.

Even such statements as this, however, were impossible a few months later when, with the serious explosion of anti-Semitic violence, to defend 'the Jewish cause' was clearly to be construed as the public defence of the Dreyfusard cause. Realizing this political fact, and accepting their duty as government agencies to remain aloof, the *consistoires*, in effect, did nothing, at least nothing publicly. Here, of course, they drew upon the precedent set by the Mayer incident several years before. At the height of the anti-Semitic disturbances, on 25 January 1898, the issue was raised formally at a meeting of the Consistoire Central. A letter from 'un notable de Paris' requested the Consistoire to approach the government 'about the events which are taking place in Algeria, in Paris, and in certain towns in France'. Although two members of the Consistoire supported this mildly conceived plan, the Consistoire decided firmly to reject the idea.[1] One month later, when the immediate crisis had subsided somewhat, the following brief notice appeared in the *Archives israélites*:

The Consistoire Central has sent to the government a notice of protest against the hostile demonstrations of which Jews, both in France and Algeria, have been the victims and it asks a more effective protection for citizens belonging to the Jewish religion.[2]

Beyond this the Consistoire took no action with respect to the specific events unfolding in France. When the Consistoire de Bordeaux requested, in the summer of 1899, that the Consistoire intervene with a superior authority to protect the Jews of Rennes during Dreyfus's second trial, the request was promptly rejected. And when Rabbi Bloch of Versailles was savagely beaten about the same time, the Consistoire did no more than send him a letter of sympathy.[3]

In fact, the Consistoire Central behaved as if there were no crisis at all, and carried on in the most routine manner possible. Meeting approximately once a month, it did so with many absentees: with the exception of Bedarrides, the vice-president of the Consistoire who hardly ever attended its meetings, the worst attendance

---

[1] A.C.C., pr. verb., 25 Jan. 1898.
[2] *A.I.*, 24 Feb. 1898, p. 63.
[3] A.C.C., pr. verb., 27 June 1899.

record was that of its president, Alphonse de Rothschild.[1] In the absence of Rothschild, Zadoc Kahn usually presided. The Consistoire's limited sensitivity to the crisis may be illustrated with a specific case. With the great flood of anti-Semitic literature in France at the time of the Affair, the Consistoire took exception to one book by Théophile Valentin, *Les Fleurs de l'histoire*. This book, which contained a violently anti-Semitic passage, had been distributed as a prize in a school in the south of France. The Consistoire complained about this fact to the Ministre des Cultes on 26 November 1897. The Ministre des Cultes passed this complaint on to the Ministre de l'Instruction Publique and the Conseil Supérieur de l'Instruction Publique. Much later, in August 1898, the book was finally banned from the schools. And, almost one full year after its original complaint, on 25 October 1898, the Consistoire was advised by the Ministre des Cultes that favourable action had been taken.[2] Considering the fact that anti-Semitism had reached flood proportions, such a success in halting a tiny stream seems to have been virtually of no value whatever, especially in view of the laborious bureaucratic operation necessary to effect it. And there is no record of the Consistoire having attempted anything more ambitious in the fight against anti-Semitism.

The Consistoire Central spent most of its time grappling with the vexed issue of Algeria, and in this connection it confronted more serious problems. The question of Algeria was an extremely complicated one, and cannot be discussed in detail here. In outline, the situation was the following. Since the 1880s anti-Semitic agitation, often led by Radicals or Socialists, focused upon the alleged political power of the Algerian *consistoires*. They had, it was charged, turned themselves into political machines supporting Moderate or Opportunist candidates. A rapidly expanding and increasingly incendiary anti-Semitic press demanded the abrogation of the Crémieux decree of 1870, which had made naturalized French citizens of the Algerian Jews. Beginning in the spring of 1897, this campaign moved from the newspapers to the streets; violent outbreaks became common throughout Algeria, and public

[1] A.C.C. pr. verb., 1897, 1898, 1899. Bedarrides died in mid 1899.
[2] See A.N. F¹⁹ 11031.

order appeared to be breaking down. The uprisings of January 1898 were little short of a pogrom. The elections of 1898 in Algeria worsened matters, and led to the success of a number of anti-Semites, including Drumont. With the establishment of the Brisson ministry in Paris, a new Governor-General, Laferrière, was named to attempt pacification. Somewhat deferential to anti-Semitic pressures, the new governor moved against the Algerian *consistoires*, limiting their authority and splitting them up into smaller units. The situation, however, remained extremely tense.[1]

For French Jews in general, and for the Consistoire Central in particular, the question of Algeria was an extremely sensitive one. Generally speaking, the fate of Algerian Jewry came to the attention of the French community only during moments of grave crisis, and when it did so the violence of the attacks and the depth of anti-Jewish feeling were profoundly unsettling. It is perhaps understandable that the established Jewish community at times considered their Algerian co-religionists something of a nuisance. Unlike the Jews of metropolitan France who could be defended as model citizens of the Republic, the Algerians were in a much more dubious position. For one thing, they were in constant need of material aid. These Jews were extremely poor; in the summer of 1898 the Consistoire Central estimated that out of 19,000 Jews in Oran, Constantine, and Algiers, almost 5,000 were indigents.[2] Moreover, Algerian Jews were in large measure unassimilated; many did not even speak French, were uneducated, and fell into the category of *indigènes*, the indigenous population of the colony which was judged to be of a lower degree of civilization than true Frenchmen.[3] In many ways their situation was comparable to that

[1] See Zosa Szajkowski, 'Socialists and Radicals in the Development of Anti-Semitism in Algeria, 1884-1900', *J.S.S.*, vol. x, no. 3, July 1948, pp. 257-80; C. Martin, *Les Israélites algériens de 1830 à 1902* (Paris, 1936); M. Ansky, *Les Juifs d'Algérie: du décret Crémieux à la libération* (Paris, 1950); A.C.C., pr. verb., 30 Nov. 1899.
[2] Ibid., 5 July 1898.
[3] Ibid., 30 Nov. 1899; B.-M., 'Choses d'Algérie', *U.I.*, 5 Feb. 1899, p. 621. 'Ne rencontrons-nous [pas] tous les jours à Paris des israélites de marque qui, sous l'effet d'un sot orgueil et d'une ignorance présomptueuse ou sous l'empire de sentiments encore moins avouables, trouvent de bon goût et de bonne politique de dauber sur les juifs algériens et d'élever des doutes sur leur moralité, dans l'espoir, sans

of eastern European Jews, and the response of the French community to their suffering was similar.

Fearful that any overt action on its part would heighten charges of consistorial interference in politics, and perhaps reluctant to keep the Algerian question before the public eye, the Consistoire Central avoided taking any strong stand on the question of Algerian anti-Semitism. When it did act on such issues, it did so secretly. When Laferrière's reorganization of the Algerian *consistoires* was prepared in a manner highly damaging to the Jewish community, the plan was submitted to the Consistoire Central requesting its 'observations' within forty-eight hours. The Consistoire, considering the 'special circumstances which prevailed at the time' (i.e. sporadic anti-Semitic outbursts—it was August 1898), did not contest such a high-handed procedure, and made a number of feeble recommendations which left the most damaging effects of the change intact.[1] When the Consistoire d'Alger requested permission to sue the anti-Semitic paper *L'Antijuif* for defamation in November 1898, the Consistoire denied permission, 'because that would give an opportunity for unscrupulous individuals to pursue their campaign of hatred and calumny'. Instead, a decision was taken to write a complaint about the article in question to the relevant government ministry.[2] When a similar request was made the following month to sue *La Libre Parole*, this was also denied.[3] Throughout, the Consistoire Central attempted to avoid pub-

doute, que leur moralité à eux en ressortira par comparaison plus éclatante?' B.-M., 'Le discours de M. Rouanet', *U.I.*, 26 May 1899, p. 299.

[1] A.C.C., pr. verb., 30 Nov. 1899; B.-M., 'La réorganisation des consistoires algériens', *U.I.*, 2 Sept. 1898, pp. 760–2; Martin, op. cit., p. 359.

[2] A.C.C., pr. verb., 15 Nov. 1898.

[3] Ibid., 27 Dec. 1898. One columnist reprimanded the Consistoire in the following manner: '. . . il faut rappeler, à la face du pays, que les israélites sont des citoyens comme les autres. Si nous ne nous défendons pas, on ne nous défendra pas. Envoyer de l'argent aux juifs, c'est bien; mettre un terme aux vexations qu'ils endurent, serait mieux. . . . Si le Consistoire Central intervient en faveur des juifs d'Algérie, il fera bien de donner à son intervention quelque publicité. Pourquoi tenir secrètes des démarches qui ne seraient que trop justifiées? Nous avons intérêt à savoir qu'on s'occupe en haut lieu de faire respecter nos droits, et il faut que la France apprenne que les antijuifs s'acharnent après de modestes employés et de pauvres ouvriers, à qui ils enlèvent leur gagne-pain.' R. T., 'Les juifs algériens et la France', *U.I.*, 10 June 1898, p. 364.

licity over the issue of Algerian anti-Semitism, and to direct the issue into the well-worn channels of the French administrative system. In a similar way the Consistoire de Paris weathered the anti-Semitic storm over the Dreyfus Affair with a minimum of *dérangement*. Meeting less than once a month, the second most important governmental agency within the Jewish community carried on with its normal business as if little of importance were happening. During the entire year of 1898, anti-Semitism managed to intrude into the agenda with only two matters of business. In May the Consistoire agreed, because of the threat of force and violence, to postpone the annual service usually held in memory of French soldiers and sailors *morts pour la patrie*.[1] And, secondly, in three separate meetings the Consistoire debated an administrative *cause célèbre*, a matter of grave principle for the Consistoire which was a caricature of the real issues which raged outside its confines. This matter first arose when, after an unusually violent demonstration in Paris in February 1898, the façade of the synagogue on the Rue des Tournelles was slightly damaged. The Consistoire, arguing that the synagogue was a 'municipal monument', wrote to the Prefect of the Seine asking that it be repaired by the civil administration. Further, at its meeting of 31 March the Consistoire decided to write to the Prefect of Police calling his attention to the fact of what had taken place, and 'declining all responsibility in the past and future for incidents which might take place . . . [*sic*]'. A considerable exchange of correspondence followed. But the Prefecture of the Seine refused to pay for the damages (and, incidentally, scolded the Consistoire by estimating repairs at only 250 francs); the Prefect of Police contested the accusation of inefficient police protection in the past, although he promised the street would be adequately patrolled for Passover. After protesting weakly over having to bear such financial charges ('which are too frequently imposed upon it by the Prefecture . . . which weigh heavily upon its contingency budget, and which mount steadily'), the Consistoire took its medicine.[2] This *affaire* took practically

---

[1] A.C.P. IC^8, 23 May 1898.
[2] Ibid., 31 Mar. 1898, 23 May 1898, 13 Oct. 1898; letters, A.C.P. B 62; A.C.P. BB.

nine months to be played out, and it exhausted the Consistoire's involvement in the Dreyfus Affair.

The Consistoire Central and the Consistoire de Paris, as arms of the French administrative system, behaved as such. Their failure to respond in any significant way to the Dreyfus Affair, to provide any leadership for a threatened community, was noticed, and complaints were not long in coming from those who wanted a more militant or more constructive stance. But from the point of view of the Consistoires, nothing could be done; their mandate was set down by government decree, and this did not extend to the extraordinary. As a part of the French bureaucracy, the Consistoires behaved bureaucratically. Their job was efficient administration, and they could not, they felt, concern themselves with questions of public order, the administration of justice, or even the rights of the Jews. These questions belonged to other agencies. As a result, the Dreyfus Affair and the anti-Semitic crisis hardly touched the Consistoires at all. Members must certainly have discussed the issues of the day at their meetings, but such discussions do not appear in the official *procès-verbaux*. Like many of their constituents, the Consistoires took refuge in what they considered to be their normally prescribed duties.[1]

From the beginning of the anti-Semitic crisis both the *Archives israélites* and the *Univers israélite* had, along with and often as part of their criticism of the official governmental organs of French Jewry, called for an organization of Jews to combat anti-Semitism and to defend Jewish rights.[2] Probably what many had in mind was an organization of Jews such as the already existing American B'nai B'rith or the German Verein zur Abwehr des Antisemitismus. Logically, the agency which might have assumed this task, once it was clear that the Consistoire would not, was the Alliance Israélite Universelle. The Alliance, after all, was an organization

[1] See Weill, op. cit., p. 168.
[2] See H. Prague, 'Défendons-nous', *A.I.*, 3 Jan. 1895, p. 2; Louis Lévy, 'Une création qui s'impose', *U.I.*, 3 Dec. 1897, pp. 331–2; R. T., 'Hanoukka et la liberté religieuse', *U.I.*, 24 Dec. 1897, p. 423; Louis Lévy, 'Les fautes passées et le devoir présent', *U.I.*, 21 Jan. 1898, pp. 552–6; F. Uhry, *A.I.*, 3 Feb. 1898, pp. 38–9; X . . . négociant, *A.I.*, 17 Feb. 1898, p. 50.

devoted to fighting anti-Semitism the world over. And yet, as its historian has noted, during the entire period of the Dreyfus Affair, 'as an organized body the Alliance . . . observed an extreme prudence' with respect to anti-Semitism in France.[1] No doubt the Alliance recognized that the issue of local anti-Semitism was an extremely sensitive one, and it did not wish to endanger its activities abroad by alienating important supporters in France, the centre of its operations. Specifically, the Alliance could not afford to compromise what had been its posture since its inception: an alliance of French Jews devoted to the dissemination of the French ideal of Jewish emancipation and assimilation.

Each year the Alliance listed in its *Bulletin* a series of 'false accusations' against the Jews which had been made in various European countries; its entries for 1897, 1898, and 1899 illustrate the difficulties the organization faced in confronting anti-Semitism in France. In 1897 the publication noted with surprise that 'the country which has filled the universe with the idea of equality and fraternity' should be witness to an anti-Semitic campaign:

France has not ceased to be the country to which Jews the world over are accustomed to turn to receive examples and lessons of morality. It is not possible that she will tolerate this reversion to ideas of the Middle Ages, to a reaction unworthy of her past, her historic glory, her fine and loyal spirit. . . .[2]

When events of the following year belied this statement, the *Bulletin* ignored the problem of French anti-Semitism and the Dreyfus Affair. It chose to do this rather than to change the principles upon which it had based its operations. For the next two years, as anti-Semitism raged, and as the convicted Jewish captain became known to Jews throughout the world, there was no discussion of France whatever in the pages devoted to 'false accusations'.[3]

---

[1] André Chouraqui, *Cent ans d'histoire: l'Alliance Israélite Universelle et la renaissance juive contemporaine 1860–1960* (Paris, 1965), pp. 140–1; Zosa Szajkowski, 'Conflicts in the Alliance Israélite Universelle and the Founding of the Anglo-Jewish Association, the Vienna Allianz, and the Hilfsverein', *J.S.S.*, vol. ix, nos. 1–2, Jan.–Apr. 1957, p. 39.
[2] 'Fausses accusations', *Bulletin de l'Alliance Israélite Universelle*, 1897, pp. 25–6.
[3] Ibid., 1898, pp. 74–88; ibid., 1899, pp. 65–108.

Among existing organizations, the only other candidate for possible action was the Société des Études Juives. But, as we have noted, the Société determined from its foundation that its activities would not be diverted by any involvement in contemporary political issues.[1] It did not change this basic stance during the course of the Affair.

One might have expected, perhaps, that a movement for active Jewish resistance to anti-Semitism would have arisen from one of the numerous salons which aligned themselves with the Dreyfusard cause. But although there were at least two important salons which Jews habitually attended, these social gatherings of upper middle-class and aristocratic socialites were hardly likely to be centres of Jewish community organization. In their Proustian world of *fin de siècle* brilliance, they played out the drama of a society in decline. From all accounts, it appears that Jewish *salonnards* (to use Léon Daudet's phrase) emulated their Christian social peers, and considered the Dreyfus Affair largely from the perspective of their own always tenuous social position. Thoroughly assimilated, at least in their own minds, they were as yet unsure of their status and anxious to meet the demands of high society. Brilliance and wit, poise and elegance mattered more to them than anything else. Interest and discussion focused about the Dreyfus *case*, about the personalities and details of the matter; the Dreyfus *Affair* and the burning issues of anti-Semitism and human rights were decidedly out of place.[2]

No large-scale Jewish organization was ever created in France for the specific defence of Jewish rights during the Dreyfus Affair. Yet a small Comité contre l'Antisémitisme did emerge, although its membership and activity were kept secret at the time. The Jewish leaders who founded this group decided to keep the fact of its existence hidden from the Jewish community at large, and it came into the public eye only in 1902, when the storm had subsided. The nature of its activity tells a great deal about the politics of French Jewry during this period.[3]

[1] See p. 120, above.

[2] On the world of the salons see especially Seth L. Wolitz, 'The Proustian Community', unpublished Ph.D. thesis, Yale University, 1965, chs. iv–v.

[3] Most of the information about the Comité comes from the long letter which it circulated within the Jewish community in 1902. A copy of this letter was found

Zadoc Kahn, the Grand Rabbi of France, seems to have taken the initiative for the formation of this committee. Calling together a group of personal friends immediately following Dreyfus's court martial, he explained his feelings on the need to form such a body. Two weeks later, on 10 January 1895, a second meeting was held, 'of those Parisian Jews who had a reputation in letters, science, law, finance [and] politics . . .'.[1] At that meeting it was decided to go ahead with the idea, and to form a committee of Jews which would act, not secretly, but in the open to defend Jewish interests. Although some of those present disliked the idea of any overt action, and although others wanted to avoid any 'action confessionnelle', there was sufficient support to empower Zadoc Kahn to begin the work of organizing. The latter named Narcisse Leven, a distinguished Jewish lawyer and Moderate politician, to be the committee's president. Among the participants were several members of the Alliance, Isaïe Levaillant, Salomon Reinach, and Henri Aron, a member of the Consistoire Central. However, the committee seems to have been unable to secure much support within the Jewish community, and its efforts, if they continued much at all after 1895, did not come into the open.

From the long letter which the committee circulated in 1902, it would appear that, while remaining hidden from the public view, its work intensified during the critical period of anti-Semitism at the time of the Dreyfus Affair. But its membership was always limited to a very select number of Jews, and its very existence remained an extremely well-kept secret. No mention of the committee was ever made in the Jewish periodicals, and no hint of its presence ever reached the anti-Semitic press. The committee seems to have subsidized the publication of a number of pamphlets and other material against anti-Semitism, and helped in some degree to defeat anti-Semitic candidates during elections. It is probable that it contributed to the support of *Le Journal*

in the Collection Ochs at the Bibliothèque Historique de la Ville de Paris, and is designated D 784. It was also reprinted in *U.I.*, 5 Dec. 1902, pp. 332–7. For anti-Semitic reaction to the Comité see A. de Boisandré, 'Un nouveau syndicat juif contre l'antisémitisme', *La Libre Parole*, 26 Nov. 1902.

[1] Weill, op. cit., pp. 169–71. Neither of these meetings was reported in *U.I.* or *A.I.*

du peuple, a newspaper founded in 1899 to support the Dreyfusard cause.[1]

This mode of operation, relying heavily upon financial aid, upon a small group of prestigious community leaders, upon influence and discussion behind the scenes, was typical of the Jewish community. We have noted that the Dreyfus family preferred to use this strategy for almost two years following the first court martial. We have observed how reluctant were most Jews to expose themselves publicly as defenders of a co-religionist. And we have seen how loath were the *consistoires* to depart from their traditional conduct of business through administrative channels. Old habits and old memories died hard. The politics of assimilation which had arisen in a period of relative tranquillity became the *mot d'ordre* for a community faced with crisis. Jews who had sought protection and security in the past through the mediation of the established authority, who had deferred always to the forces of order, chose now to continue as before. This was, for the Jewish community, the meaning of the *volonté de paix*.

It was essential, as the Comité contre l'Antisémitisme put it in their letter, for Jews to conduct themselves 'not as Jews living in France, but as *citoyens français d'origine juive* whose rights were threatened . . .'.[2] Jews continued to seek refuge in the France of 1789, in the promise of emancipation which had never quite been kept. But while it had been natural for James Darmesteter, with little experience of an organized campaign of anti-Semitism, to articulate the simple faith and optimism of French Jewry, it was less easy to do the same in 1899. Jews, for the most part, had chosen to remain with France, but their attachment now involved less joyous enthusiasm, and more quiet desperation. Jews still thought of Armand Mayer as a martyr, but it was less clear that his death had any constructive meaning at all.

---

[1] See Gauthier, op. cit., p. 145.   [2] Collection Ochs, D 784.

CHAPTER IX

THE ZIONIST REVOLUTION

DURING the painful crisis precipitated by the Dreyfus Affair
Zionism emerged as the principal Jewish alternative to the politics
of assimilation. Jewish nationalism, as we noted in Chapter VII,
was a doctrine which directed attention to the positive aspects of
Jewish identity; developed in France by Bernard Lazare, it described the Jewish condition as being that of a proud but oppressed
people in desperate need of liberation. Zionism proposed the
means for that liberation. The Zionist solution was that the Jewish
nation should become aware of itself, should develop its own institutions, and, most importantly, should work for the establishment
of its own state. The Zionists, always a tiny minority within the
Jewish community in France, were on the margins of French
society, and had never fully become a part of it. Some of them
were but recently arrived, and could scarcely have been expected
to join with most French Jews in trumpeting their patriotism
before the French public. Others, like Bernard Lazare, refused to
become a part of a French society which for various reasons they
rejected. All of them, however, were in the process of refashioning
their identity in a manner which corresponded with their situation. All of them were in some sense a part of the *fin de siècle*
revolt of European youth against a liberal, rationalist culture
which was considered degenerate, without soul, and incorrigibly
bourgeois.[1] During the course of the Affair these Jews organized
Zionism into a movement in France, a movement which revolted
against the assimilationist ideas held by the vast majority of French
Jews, and which allied itself with similar movements developing
elsewhere in Europe.

[1] For a fascinating account of a similar development in Germany see George L.
Mosse, 'The Influence of the *völkisch* Idea on German Jewry', *Studies of the Leo
Baeck Institute* (1967), pp. 83–114.

The story of Zionist origins is extremely complex. Zionist organizations of sorts existed in France before the Dreyfus Affair, but they lacked a nationalist perspective. Jewish nationalism arose among some Jewish proletarian groups responding to the Dreyfus Affair, but without a Zionist focus. In the Dreyfus years, however, under the impact of severe anti-Semitic attacks, a coalescence occurred. Jewish nationalism and Zionism merged to form a single movement. This chapter begins by discussing how certain elements within the Jewish proletariat responded to the Dreyfus Affair with an assertion of Jewish nationalism, clearly in revolt against French society and the established community of French Jews, but as yet with no Zionist alternative. Next we shall digress somewhat, in order to trace the beginnings of Zionism in France, and the impetus given to the movement by Theodore Herzl's famous pamphlet of 1896—*Der Judenstaat*. Following this we shall sketch the formation of Zionist periodicals during the Dreyfus Affair, examining the way in which Jewish nationalism became associated with the Zionist cause. Consideration will be given to the work of specific leaders such as Bernard Lazare and Max Nordau, and the Zionist-oriented Université Populaire Juive which began at the time. Finally, we shall discuss the way in which the established Jewish community reacted to these developments, which were so contrary to its frequently stated policy.

At the time of the Dreyfus Affair, as we have seen, a substantial segment of the Jewish population of Paris, perhaps numbering as many as 20,000, could be called working class.[1] These Jews had no separate means to express their views, and had been generally neglected in discussions of French Jewry until 1898. From June of that year, however, a number of articles and discussions of the Jewish proletariat appeared in the French press.[2] The reason for the sudden interest was the publication of a detailed social and

[1] See pp. 45–7, above.
[2] See 'Le prolétariat juif', *L'Aurore*, 23 June 1898; Isidore Cahen, 'Un prolétariat méconnu', *A.I.*, 21 July 1898; Henri Dagan, 'Le prolétariat juif devant l'antisémitisme', *Les Droits de l'homme*, 24 Jan. 1899; Paul Pottier, 'Essai sur le prolétariat juif en France', *Revue des revues*, 1 Mar. 1899, pp. 482–92; Gaston Cogniard, 'Le prolétariat juif', *La Petite République*, 3 Mar. 1899.

economic study of the Jewish proletariat around the world, a doctoral dissertation presented at the University of Brussels by an eastern European Jew, Leonti Soloveitschik. This book was much discussed in Paris, where 'the Jewish question' was the order of the day, and where any new information became a matter of considerable public attention. Although the author did not treat the situation of Jewish workers in France, his observations were of importance for the French community. For Soloveitschik claimed, upon the basis of a careful statistical analysis, that Jews had proportionately a larger number of proletarians among themselves than any other people in the various countries examined. Far from being a people of bankers and merchants, as Drumont and many others had regularly contended, the Jews were a poor and often oppressed people in all of the countries in which they lived.[1]

About the same time, and in the wake of severe outbreaks of anti-Semitic violence, there appeared the first publicly articulated response to the Dreyfus crisis by working-class French Jews.[2] This was a short pamphlet, published by a body which called itself the Groupe des Ouvriers Juifs Socialistes de Paris. The form chosen for this purpose was an open letter from Jewish workers to the Parti Socialiste Français. In this combative and often bitter statement, the group maintained that the Dreyfus Affair had released powerful, dormant instincts in the French people. Exploited and robbed by capitalist interests, the French were renewing their anti-Semitic traditions. Instead of turning upon their oppressors, instead of attacking those who 'hold [the people] in slavery and exploitation', the latter were turning once again upon the Jews, who were in reality 'their fellow sufferers'. It was impossible to over-estimate the significance of what was happening or the terrible possibilities of such a course: '... the danger is great [that] the continuation of such a trend could end up with nothing less than a new attempt to exterminate a race, ... a new massacre of

[1] Léonti Soloveitschik, *Un prolétariat méconnu: étude sur la situation sociale et économique des ouvriers juifs* (Paris, 1898), pp. 121–2.
[2] *Le prolétariat juif: lettre des ouvriers juifs de Paris au Parti Socialiste Français* (Paris, 1898). Cf. Edmund Silberner, 'French Socialism and the Jewish Question, 1865-1914', *Historia Judaica*, vol. xvi, Apr. 1954, p. 15.

the weaker by the stronger'. Again and again the authors drove home the point that the Jews were a people of workers, 'the most proletarian people in the world':

> It is from our ranks that Lassalle and Karl Marx came; it is from among us that the first blow was struck against the old institution of the family; it is from among us that there arises today, in Russia, in America, and everywhere else, an enthusiastic youth which raises up the barricades of social justice throughout the world.

French socialists, it was argued, were not taking a principled stand on the issue of anti-Semitism, and were not offering the Jews the solidarity which they deserved. The pamphlet called upon socialists to aid the oppressed, to reassert their fraternal spirit, and to take the initiative in asserting the best of French traditions.

In addition to making this appeal to the French socialists, the pamphlet made a strong case for a Jewish peoplehood, for the existence of a bond which held together all Jews, irrespective of their backgrounds:

> ... in the midst of its suffering and hoping, our people dreams and is angry; and we have behind us, more than any other people, a chain of misery and suffering stretching back for centuries, penetrating our moral being with this bitter essence: the sense of man's injustice, the sense of our own humiliation. And we have before us a great valley of tears, as great as the entire world, where our brothers are dispersed and where, everywhere, in all climates, in all institutions ... in all nations, they are covered with injuries, humiliation, and misery. For we are cosmopolitans, not only by the fact of our bankers ... but even more so by our unfortunate families, which watch their children die in the four corners of the earth.

Recently, it was noted, Jews had been seized with 'a burning desire to escape this intolerable existence'. They were searching 'for a true light which will guide them. And this light begins to shine. Feebly and hesitantly, it appears nevertheless . . .' Suffering, then, was the basis of Jewish unity, a suffering which was common to all the Jews, wherever they lived. Yet the conclusion drawn from this general analysis, an analysis which might logically have ended with a call for Jewish separation, was simply that conventional revolutionary activity had to proceed. Here the pamphlet was singularly devoid of new ideas: '... it is indispensable', the work concluded, 'to overthrow this miserable social order [and] to replace it with a new order, conforming to universal well-being.' It would appear that a number of hands had prepared this brochure, which combined an element of Jewish nationalism with a phraseology and substance similar to various other socialist or anarchist groups.[1] According to one writer, the organization was probably anarchist, operating under a socialist guise to escape the anti-anarchist law of 1894. He seems correct in asserting that Bernard Lazare edited and helped with the pamphlet, for several passages are strongly reminiscent of the latter's own articles about this time.[2] In any case, Lazare's influence on the ideas expressed seems apparent. The point to be particularly noted, however, is that a Jewish proletarian group registered its dissatisfaction with French socialists who, it was held, were not responding to the needs of Jews in their struggle against anti-Semitism. Seeking an alternative, the Groupe des Ouvriers Juifs adopted some of the spirit of Jewish nationalism which Lazare and others had recently been articulating.

Little more is known about this group of Jewish working-class revolutionaries, who first made their existence known in Paris in 1898. It centred about a Jewish labour library on the Rue de Cécile where Jewish workers gathered in the evenings to read newspapers, but had no organ of its own, and little means for publicity. Neither the *Archives israélites* nor the *Univers israélite* carried notices of its activity. It would appear that its membership was made up in large part of eastern European immigrants, of Jews who felt some isolation from the established Jewish community in France.[3] These

[1] The pamphlet ended with this incongruous and unexplained anti-religious appeal to the French socialists: 'A vous de nous venir en aide pour travailler ensemble à la déjudaïsation et à la déchristianisation des peuples. A vous de nous venir en aide, afin que nous puissions jeter dans les masses juives la semence de l'avenir.' *Le Prolétariat juif*, p. 21.

[2] E. Tcher-ski, 'Die Dreyfus-Affare, die Arbeiter-Immigranten, un die fran-zosische-yiddische Firers' (in Yiddish), in E. Tcherikower (ed.), *Yidn in Frankraikh* (2 vols., New York, 1942), ii. 165-8.

[3] Ibid., p. 164; Pottier, 'Essai sur le prolétariat juif', p. 490; Dagan, 'Le prolé-tariat juif devant l'antisémitisme'.

Jews, moreover, believed that they were far more vulnerable to anti-Semitic attack during the Dreyfus Affair than were the wealthier members of the French Jewish community. One of them, in fact, was quoted as blaming Jewish financiers for the prejudice against the Jews. As with other socialists, the name Rothschild was a symbol of exploitation and excessive wealth. The Rothschilds, it was alleged, despite their charity, had brought much misery and suffering to the Jewish poor.[1]

It was probably this group of Jewish workers which organized, in September 1899, the only public Jewish protest meeting ever held against anti-Semitism during the entire Dreyfus Affair.[2] Jewish workers had to undertake the project themselves, it was felt, for one year after the open letter to French socialists the latter still did not provide the energy or leadership necessary to fight anti-Semitism. In announcing the meeting in the Dreyfusard newspaper *Les Droits de l'homme*, the group indicated that Jewish workers were forming an organization to defend themselves. Because the unions had failed to protect them, because the socialists remained unresponsive, Jews were forced to unite. Anti-Semites, the announcement warned, 'will find before them, not timid and irresolute people as in the Middle Ages, but men, steadfast and organized, determined to answer Force with Force'.[3]

At the meeting, held in a large hall in Montmartre, several hundred Jewish workers met to hear a series of turbulent speeches and to pass a resolution against those who were inciting a 'war of

---

[1] One Jewish worker declared the following to an interviewer in 1899: '. . . la charité de M. de Rothschild n'existe pas, il y a la charité de la maison Rothschild, c'est-à-dire le syndicat de la famille qui donne un peu de son or. Mais jamais un Rothschild, individuellement, n'ouvre sa bourse. Ah! leur charité! Vieux tambour qui ne résonne plus; non, il faut trouver autre chose. Ce sont eux qui nous ont fait haïr, ce sont eux qui nous empêchent de vivre et ont fait de nous des parias. S'il n'y avait pas de gros financiers juifs, il n'y aurait peut-être plus de haine contre la race juive, honnie partout. Ils s'en moquent de leurs victimes. Ce qu'ils distribuent? Leurs pauvres leur coûtent moins cher que leurs chevaux. . . .' Pottier, 'Essai sur le prolétariat juif', p. 492.

[2] The organizing body was referred to as 'Le Prolétariat juif de France' in *U.I.*, 8 Sept. 1899, p. 799; 'Le Groupe des Prolétaires juifs' in *L'Aurore*, 18 Sept. 1899; and 'Le Groupe des Ouvriers juifs de Paris' in *É.S.*, 20 Sept. 1899, p. 27.

[3] Maître Jacques, 'Prolétaires juifs', *Les Droits de l'homme*, 17 Sept. 1899.

races' in France. Much of the familiar socialist position was repeated at the meeting: the resolution, for example, declared 'that anti-Semitism is a prejudice inculcated in proletarians to make them forget ideas of liberation and to put them at the mercy of their cruellest enemies'; further, it proclaimed an international human fraternity 'without distinction of race'. But elements of Jewish nationalism were also intermingled with declarations of working-class solidarity. One of the speakers declared that the Jewish proletarians did not recoil from grouping themselves under the name of 'prolétaires juifs', for they were proud and not ashamed of that designation. Wealthier Jews, he implied, habitually insulted their own people by their insistence on assimilation; and even the socialists were following suit in this regard. But these assimilationists ignored the realities of the moment: 'On prêche aux juifs la fusion avec les autres races, la fraternisation. C'est parfait, mais que messieurs les assassins commencent.'[1]

This speaker, a contributor to anarchist newspapers named Henri Dhorr, put forward the position of Jewish working-class revolutionaries in a number of subsequent articles. Dhorr attacked the theory, which he said was shared by anti-Semites, by some revolutionaries, and even by some Jews, that anti-Semitism would disappear as the Jews themselves disappeared, as they became less and less visible in the community at large. As we have noted, this was roughly the position of Émile Zola, at least before the Affair, and also of a number of prominent Jewish assimilationists. But for Dhorr these people represented the enemy. Jews who believed in this general approach proposed, not murder, as did the anti-Semites, but in effect 'suicide'. In response to intolerance and restrictions on individual freedom, he argued, the worst policy imaginable for Jews would be one of assimilation and abjuration, the denial of their 'race'. Jews had to answer the anti-Semites 'by resistance, not by submission'. This implied a resistance to assimilationist forces as well as to more open attacks. Oppressed peoples such as the Jews could not escape from their oppression by assimilation, just as the proletariat could not change its

[1] 'Les réunions: meeting des prolétaires juifs', *Le Journal du peuple*, 18 Sept. 1899; *É.S.*, 20 Sept. 1899, p. 27. The meeting was not reported in *A.I.* or *U.I.*

condition by joining the bourgeoisie. Real resistance would come through the solidarity of the oppressed:

Just as the Poles refuse to assimilate into Russians, as Cubans refuse to assimilate into Spaniards, so the Jews affirm their race and, by showing solidarity in the face of persecution, carry on the work of revolution. I am pleased to be one of them and to say so. I claim to have the right to live although born a Jew. To live, one cannot live a lie. Since it is my right to be a Jew, it is my duty to say that I am one.

This assertion of Jewishness, it is clear, was not simply an effective tactical position for Dhorr. Like Bernard Lazare, he contended that the world could only thrive in diversity. Dhorr defended the need for Jews to remain Jews on the basis of what was best for humanity: '. . . it is salutary, for the purposes of liberty, that peoples, like individuals, preserve and develop their autonomy.' 'To renounce their way of life in order to comply with the common rule', he added, 'is for peoples, as for individuals, to run counter to the development of humanity.'[1]

When Dreyfus was pardoned and retired in peace to Carpentras in the autumn of 1899, and when the excitement caused by anti-Semitic outbreaks had fallen off considerably, Dhorr still censured French Jews for their optimism and their complacency. The end of the Dreyfus Affair, he wrote, 'is not the end of anti-Semitism'. On the contrary, he predicted that the struggle would become more dangerous and more decisive, for anti-Semitic attacks would now be launched against a whole category of people, and not simply Dreyfus himself. The government could never be counted upon to protect the Jews; it never took action, in effect, unless prompted to do so by 'the revolutionary element'. For Dhorr the failure of established authority (and the established Jewish community) to do anything about anti-Semitism was a confirmation of the need for a revolutionary perspective. The lesson which he drew from the Dreyfus experience was as critical of French society as it was of the established Jewish community in France:

In the same way that anti-Semitism is the most powerful diversion from the Revolution, so the Revolution is the sole barrier that one can

[1] Henri Dhorr, 'Le droit d'être juif', Le Libertaire, 24 Sept. 1899.

effectively oppose to anti-Semitism. Jews who are not revolutionaries
are traitors to their own cause. Let them only be able to perceive this in
time![1]

It is apparent that spokesmen for Jewish workers such as Dhorr
took a position during the Dreyfus Affair which differed sharply
from that of the majority of the Jewish community whose views
we examined in the previous chapter. While the latter emphasized
their patriotism and their Frenchness, the former stressed the old
community of suffering which bound Jews together throughout
the course of time. When the latter spoke of *la patrie*, the former
spoke of *la race*. A Jewish teacher, for example, a socialist, asked
that the Jew consult his 'moi supérieur' in order to perceive 'this
immortal pariah' which the Jew really was. At that moment the
Jew would recognize 'the socialist which lies in him' as an essential part of his being.[2] Jewish consciousness, a militant Jewish sense
of identity was to be encouraged and developed in the face of
adversity. But for these Jews, as for Bernard Lazare, the essence of
Jewishness was not religious affiliation, was not even an ethnic or
cultural identification, but was rather a social perspective on the
society in which the Jew found himself. Because they were basically
alienated from that society, they perceived their Jewishness in
terms of their alienation. For these Jews, Jewish nationalism was
thus an overwhelmingly negative phenomenon, a phenomenon
of protest and rebellion rather than one of affirmation. Zionism,
which required something other than, or something in addition
to, the overthrow of the existing order in France, was little discussed among this element of French Jewry.[3]

Among the Jewish workers discussed above we have seen Jewish nationalism without Zionism; among certain elements of the
Jewish community before the Dreyfus Affair one can detect the
existence of Zionism without Jewish nationalism. These elements
were made up in good measure of eastern or central European

[1] Henri Dhorr, 'Ohé! Les juifs!', *Le Journal du peuple*, 31 Oct. 1899.
[2] C. Wagner, 'Juif et socialiste', *Le Signal*, 1 Feb. 1899. Cf. Maurice Lauzel,
M. Édouard Drumont (Paris, 1898).
[3] Pottier, 'Essai sur le prolétariat juif', pp. 489–90.

Jews who had a strong sense of Jewish identity and who were anxious to promote Jewish settlement in Palestine as a solution to the problems of Jews.

The striking fact about most Zionist activity preceding the Affair is that it was carried out within the general framework of philanthropy. Little is known about the few, fitful Zionist organizations which were formed in Paris during the 1880s and early 1890s, succeeding one another with good intentions and indifferent success. The Alliance Israélite Universelle engaged in some important colonization activity in Palestine, occupying itself in part with the founding and operating of a few agricultural schools for the training of future colonists.[1] During this period a society called Hovevé Sion met in the French capital, attempting unsuccessfully to co-ordinate Zionist action there.[2] But rather than tending towards union, the early Zionist societies tended to multiply. The Société Mébassereth Zion was formed about 1895 or 1896, with the object of setting up a fund to send one of its members to Palestine annually in order to study future economic and colonial possibilities.[3] Similarly modest was the Société Ichoub Israël, a small body of interested Jews devoted to providing assistance for Jewish colonists already established in the Holy Land.[4] Within all of these organizations, the predominant spirit was one of dispensing charity. Most of the financial support for colonization at this time, and a good deal of its direction, came from the Baron Edmond de Rothschild, who had taken a personal interest in this field, and who poured substantial sums into a number of agricultural settlements in Palestine. But the Rothschild rule was distant and paternal; his colonies were strictly controlled by his own appointees, publicity about them was avoided, and anything like a mass movement on their behalf was strictly forbidden.[5]

[1] André Chouraqui, Cent ans d'histoire: l'Alliance Israélite Universelle et la renaissance juive contemporaine, 1860–1960 (Paris, 1965), part iii, passim.

[2] Alex Bein, 'Un siècle de préhistoire du sionisme français', La Terre retrouvée, 15 Nov. 1958, p. 6.

[3] Baruch Hagani, 'Les débuts du sionisme à Paris: souvenirs d'enfance', La Terre retrouvée, 25 May 1929, p. 3.

[4] J. W., 'Soirée à la Société "Ichoub Erez Israël" ', U.I., 11 Dec. 1896, p. 380.

[5] See Israël Margalith, Le Baron Edmond de Rothschild et la colonisation juive en

This kind of charitable activity, however, did not win support from the small number of Zionist students who took a more intellectual approach to the problems of persecution against the Jews. As we observed in Chapter III, as many as five hundred Jewish students from Russia and Poland were living in Paris about this time, and many of them still carried with them the consciousness and perspective of revolutionary activity within the Tsarist Empire.[1] Inclined, perhaps, to consider a drastic solution to a problem with which they were directly acquainted, they were prepared to envisage the formation of a Jewish state. Yet so far as we can tell, their Zionism involved no elaborate theory of Jewish nationhood such as Lazare was later to propound. According to Baruch Hagani, a Jew who was born in the Polish city of Vilna and who frequented student circles in Paris about this time, a conspicuous interest in Zionism existed among Jewish foreign students who were working and studying in Paris before the Dreyfus Affair. These young intellectuals had in many cases read Leo Pinsker's essay *Auto-Emancipation* (1882), and had thus some conception of the need to establish a Jewish state.[2] Their efforts, however, were largely theoretical, confined for the most part to discussions held at student cafés and the Société des Étudiants Israélites Russes. The latter was an important meeting-place for Zionist youth, established in 1892 with Zadoc Kahn as its honorary president. As an organization the Société provided social contact, some social welfare, but no significant activity in public affairs.[3] Zionism in this student milieu, therefore, was not yet a movement which could reach effectively beyond a small circle of initiates. In 1893 some attempt was made to launch a *Bulletin de l'Association des Étudiants Israélites*, a small periodical 'of poor

Palestine 1882–1899 (Paris, 1957), *passim*; Cohen, op. cit., p. 124; A. and M. Nordau, op. cit., p. 119; Max Nordau, *Écrits sionistes* (Paris, 1936), p. 107.

[1] See pp. 47–9, above.

[2] Baruch Hagani, 'Les débuts du sionisme à Paris: souvenirs d'enfance', *La Terre retrouvée*, 20 Mar. 1929, pp. 2–4; id., *Bernard Lazare, 1865–1903* (Paris, 1919), pp. 30–1. Hagani was deported and murdered by the Nazis during the Second World War. Pinsker was a Jewish doctor from Odessa whose pamphlet considered the need to implement a policy of Jewish nationalism as a response to anti-Semitic terror.

[3] *U.I.*, 16 Oct. 1892; *U.I.*, 16 Mar. 1893.

appearance' which did not achieve any success. Another journal, known as *Kadimah*, seems to have been published during part of 1896–7, and was apparently devoted to Zionist matters and other affairs of student interest. It too, however, did not succeed.[1] A movement, however, was about to take shape. In rapid succession came Herzl's explosive pamphlet, the intervention of Bernard Lazare, the dramatic anti-Semitic uprising in Algeria and then in France, and the First Zionist Congress. The Dreyfus Affair, of course, underlay each of these developments.

Theodore Herzl, an Austrian writer and journalist, was primarily responsible for the launching of the Zionist movement as an organized political enterprise.[2] His writing provided the theoretical basis with which to unite Jewish nationalists and those who had been occupied with the more modest work of colonization; his tireless organizational activity drew together the disparate elements which were to constitute an effective political force. Herzl developed the idea of a Jewish movement of this sort while living in France as a correspondent for an important Viennese newspaper, the *Neue Freie Presse*. Unquestionably the Dreyfus Affair, particularly its earliest stages, provided Herzl with the stimulus to sharpen his own thinking on the Jewish question, and the means to dramatize his case before the Jewish public. He reported on the case for Austrian readers, and quickly found himself drawn to speculate on the larger implications of the Affair.[3] In a resounding statement entitled *Der Judenstaat*, published in 1896, he advanced his scheme for 'the restoration of the Jewish state'. Support for Herzl's idea grew enormously during the next year, but not, appreciably,

[1] See A. Raskine, obituary of Bernard Lazare, *E.S.*, 15 Nov. 1903, p. 260. The author has been unable to find copies of either the *Bulletin* or the first journal known as *Kadimah*.

[2] On Herzl see Alex Bein, *Theodore Herzl: a Biography*, tr. Maurice Samuel (Cleveland, 1962); Israel Cohen, *Theodore Herzl: Founder of Political Zionism* (New York, 1959); André Chouraqui, *Théodore Herzl* (Paris, 1960).

[3] See Theodore Herzl, *L'Affaire Dreyfus: reportages et réflexions traduits par Léon Vogel* (Paris, 1958); Pierre van Passen, 'Paris, 1891–1895: a Study of the Transition in Theodore Herzl's Life', in Meyer W. Weisgal (ed.), *Theodore Herzl: a Memorial* (New York, 1929), pp. 37–9.

among the assimilated Jewry of western Europe. Eastern European Jews—from Galicia, from Russia, and from the eastern provinces of the Habsburg Empire—began to support the Zionist cause in large numbers; Russia alone sent eighty out of a total of two hundred delegates present at the Congress of 1897. In western Europe, however, Zionism developed no substantial mass support at this time.

And yet, even in France, the idea spread very rapidly among certain groups. Elements of Zionist thought were picked up by Jewish proletarian spokesmen, and most particularly by the students and intellectuals, who founded a number of periodicals during the Dreyfus years, taking issue with the position of most assimilated French Jews. With Herzl's pamphlet, a Zionist movement was made possible. It is therefore appropriate to pause for a moment in order to summarize the Zionist position as Herzl first presented it in France.

Herzl's explosive tract first appeared in French in a respected bi-monthly journal, the *Nouvelle Revue internationale*, published in Paris. It came out in two parts, in December 1896 and January 1897.[1] Central to his argument was a recognition that there *was* a 'Jewish question', and that that question turned upon the fact that Jews, virtually everywhere, were in distress. The problem was that for a number of reasons Jews were not admitted into full and equal membership in the societies in which they lived. Primarily this was because the Jewish question was a *national* question: the Jews were a nationality, and as such were looked upon with suspicion; as a nationality, moreover, the Jews had their own doubts, whether conscious or unconscious, about full assimilation into another nation. 'Nous sommes', the article declared, 'un peuple un.' For one reason or another, the Jews continued to retain their distinctiveness over the course of a long and troubled history: '. . . the Jewish personality does not want to, cannot, and must not disappear. It cannot, because its external enemies contribute to maintaining it. It does not want to, and this it has proven for two

---

[1] Theodore Herzl, 'L'État juif: essai d'une solution de la question juive', *La Nouvelle Revue internationale*, 31 Dec. 1896, pp. 842–60; ibid., 15 Jan. 1897, pp. 19–40.

thousand years, in the face of unspeakable suffering. It must not,
[and] this is what I am trying to show. . . .'¹

To be sure, there were some differences between the condition
of the emancipated Jewry of western Europe and that of their
eastern European co-religionists. But Herzl emphasized the essential similarities of the positions in which Jews found themselves.
Oppression, in fact, was *general*; it simply took different forms in
different places. Everywhere Jews lived among people who, in
one form or another, were anti-Semites. Indeed, emancipation
was the cause of the modern variety of anti-Semitism, for it permitted free competition between Christian and Jew, and provoked
the jealousy and hostility of the former against the latter. Even
where persecution was not overt as in Russia, it was as serious if
not more so, for the Jewish sensibility had increased ('The long
persecution has over-excited our nerves') and consequently the
pain which Jews felt was greater.²

Herzl proposed the establishment of a Jewish state as the solution to the Jewish question. His work provided the details for the
organization of this enterprise, and described the machinery necessary to set it in motion. He contended that only with the formation of this Jewish state and with the consequent migration of large
numbers of Jews would the curse of anti-Semitism ever be blotted
out.

It is difficult to judge the immediate impact of Herzl's tract upon
the French Jewish community.³ It is unlikely that many Jews read
the articles in the *Nouvelle Revue internationale* as they appeared,
and it is obvious that the effects in France did not match the sudden
enthusiasm which was felt in some parts of eastern Europe. But
the seeds of the Zionist idea did take root quickly among some
elements of the Jewish population in France, and in examining the
response of certain groups to the Dreyfus Affair we shall see its
first blooming on the soil of France.

Jewish nationalism and even Zionism, as we have seen, were
not unheard of in Paris when Herzl first published his tract and

---

¹ Herzl, 'L 'État juif', 31 Dec. 1896, p. 847.   ² Ibid., 15 Jan. 1897, p. 39.
³ This will be discussed in some detail at the conclusion of this chapter.

began preparation for the First Zionist Congress. Twelve delegates from France attended that meeting in Basel, which, in view
of the widespread interest in Jewish questions in that summer and
autumn of 1897, was extensively covered in the French press.[1]
With this congress, and with the dramatic anti-Semitic clashes of
the Dreyfus Affair, Zionist activity took on serious proportions.[2]
Four periodicals, each in some way responding to the Dreyfus
crisis, were primarily responsible for the dissemination of Zionist
ideas. Identifying both with Herzl and with Lazare, they based
their position upon a rejection of assimilation and a strong critique
of the established Jewish community in France.

The most significant fact associated with the upsurge of interest
and commitment on the part of Jews living in France was the
transformation of Zionism from a philanthropic venture into an
organized political movement. The significance of this change
cannot be overestimated. Numerous lectures and meetings devoted to Zionism and Jewish nationalism took place during the
Dreyfus years. These were often attended by several hundred
people, both men and women, predominantly of eastern European origin.[3] Communicating ideas and information through the
recently established Zionist press, and co-ordinating activity somewhat with similar groups in other European cities, the movement
took on an air of purposeful, effective political action. Each year
a small French delegation attended the international Zionist congress, and upon its return extensive reports were printed in the
existing Zionist journals. The period between 1897 and 1899 was
crucial in the development of this transformation.

Bernard Lazare provided the catalyst which precipitated political involvement on the part of a group of Jewish students and
intellectuals. His editorship of the review *Zion*, even before the
Dreyfus Affair reached its climax, led to the clarification of a number of issues which had been discussed in some Jewish circles, but

---

[1] Hayim Orlan, 'The Participants in the First Zionist Congress', in *Herzl Year-
book*, vol. vi (New York, 1964–5), pp. 133–52.
[2] See J. Tchernoff, *Dans le creuset des civilisations*, vol. iii, *De l'Affaire Dreyfus au
dimanche rouge à Saint-Pétersbourg* (Paris, 1937), p. 66.
[3] See M. Lazard, 'Sionisme', *U.I.*, 10 June 1898, pp. 371–3. Cf. *U.I.*, 20 May
1898, p. 281; S. Lubarski, 'Le sionisme à Paris', *U.I.*, 15 Sept. 1899, p. 827.

which had never received full public attention. *Zion* had begun in 1895 as a German-Jewish review published in Berlin; in 1897, the third year of its existence, a 'partie française' was added, with Lazare as editor.[1]

'Assimilation is not and cannot be a solution', he wrote.[2] Through the pages of this review Lazare elaborated extensively on this injunction, and developed a concrete theory of Jewish nationalism as the most effective and proper response to the condition in which Jews found themselves. Other collaborators followed suit, particularly in a number of articles leading up to the First Zionist Congress in the summer of 1897. Coming at this time, however, *Zion* reflected the fact that as yet neither Zionism nor Jewish nationalism was a well developed idea. 'We lack a principle which directs and regulates all activity,' complained one contributor, 'and without any programme we form simply a group or rather a heterogeneous mass in which are joined the most variegated and even sometimes contradictory elements. . . .'[3] But whatever the differences within the new circle of Zionist and nationalist thinkers in Paris, there seems to have been general agreement that French Jewry had shown itself incapable of self-defence. Continually, the politics of assimilation came under attack. When, for example, Joseph Reinach declared that attacks on Algerian Jews were attacks on the French government and upon European civilization, he was severely criticized for not daring openly to defend specifically Jewish interests.[4] The only proper response to

[1] Information on this review as well as microfilm of several numbers were obtained from Dr. Alex Bein and I. Philipp of the Zionist Central Archives in Jerusalem. See also Jean-Maurice Muslak, 'Bernard-Lazare', *R.E.J.*, vol. vi, no. 106 (1946), p. 51.

[2] Bernard Lazare, 'Solidarité', *Zion*, 31 May 1897, p. 26.

[3] A. Rokéach, 'Un programme sioniste', *Zion*, 30 June 1897, p. 41.

[4] Adolphe Raskine, 'L'Algérie', *Zion*, 30 June 1897, p. 51: 'Comme toujours, les juifs français n'ont pas osé défendre leurs intérêts franchement, ouvertement : c'est leur tactique habituelle de se cacher toujours derrière le gouvernement et leurs concitoyens catholiques.' In a lecture the following year Bernard Lazare referred to the Algerian situation and its implications. According to one report, 'M. Bernard Lazare demande à quoi sert aux juifs d'Algérie d'avoir été naturalisés. En vivent-ils plus tranquillement ? Mais ont-ils su profiter de l'avantage que leur conférait le décret de naturalisation ? Comment se fait-il qu'ils n'aient pu faire cesser les chantages perpétuels de certains journaux ? Sont-ils restés inertes ou

the growing current of anti-Semitism, it was felt, was an assertion of the Jewish personality; what Jews demand, declared one article in the autumn of 1897, is 'the right to develop freely', to cultivate 'our individuality', 'our national genius'. This position differed from that of the spokesmen for the Jewish proletariat in its emphasis upon the positive features of a specifically Jewish self-assertion. It was similar, however, in its combativeness and emphasis upon self-reliance. 'The time has passed', announced one student spokesman, 'when resignation, [and] the tacit agreement to accept submissively the domination of brute force, were exalted as indispensable virtues for the honest man.'[1]

Following the First Zionist Congress, and in the wake of the violent anti-Semitic uprisings occasioned by the Dreyfus Affair, a new periodical, the second to be known as *Kadimah*, appeared in February 1898.[2] This journal, which lasted only about seven months, was much more explicitly Zionist than its predecessor, and represented a much more clearly defined position with respect to Jewish nationalism. Its programme, the editors declared, had both a positive and a negative side: negatively the periodical attacked the 'juifs honteux', the Jews who were ashamed of their identity and who increasingly denied their Jewishness when faced with anti-Semitism; positively its aim was to cultivate the study of Jewish language, literature, and history, to renew the ties of solidarity among Jews, and to encourage the colonization of Palestine as a refuge for oppressed Jews the world over.[3] The Zionism of *Kadimah*, as one writer stressed, was not a philanthropic undertaking; Zionism was not just a movement to relieve the distress of the poorest among the Jews. Rather, he wrote, 'it is absolutely analogous with the aspirations of all oppressed nations. Material affliction is not the only or unique consequence of oppression; moral suffering counts for as much, if not more, in this respect. From this point of view the entire Jewish people is plunged into

bien se sont-ils vainement adressés aux tribunaux algériens?' R. T., 'Deux conférences', *U.I.*, 8 July 1898, pp. 486-7.

[1] Adolphe Raskine, 'Ce que nous demandons', *Zion*, Oct. 1897, pp. 77-8.
[2] '*Kadimah*' is a Hebrew word meaning 'forward to the east', and implying in addition an act of returning to roots.
[3] La rédaction, 'Notre programme', *Kadimah*, 15 Feb. 1898, pp. 1-3.

misery.'[1] From this point of view too, the salvation of the Jewish people was seen to lie as much in a proud assertion of the dignity of a people as in the physical betterment of the condition of the Jews through the establishment of a Jewish state. Jewish nationalism and Zionism were taken to be one.

For the contributors to *Kadimah* the Dreyfus Affair represented simply an intensification of the steady and unrelenting pressure against French Jews. As one of them put it, the Affair had 'lifted up one corner of the curtain which has been covering the situation of the Jews in France for a long time'.[2] The Affair served to expose the weakness of French Jewry, their isolation in the French community, and the strength of the hostile elements in French society.[3] And, finally, it provided the occasion for Jews to organize themselves, and to prepare the means for a truly effective emancipation.

These lessons were driven home with considerable force by the third Zionist periodical to appear during the Affair, a short-lived monthly called *Le Flambeau*. Founded early in 1899 by one of the French delegates to the First Zionist Congress, a brilliant journalist named Jacques Bahar, and with the help of Bernard Lazare, *Le Flambeau* viewed the Dreyfus crisis as a decisive moment in the history of French Jewry:

> The condition of the Jews in France has become intolerable. In the army, in the magistracy, and in the civil service, in commerce and in society, our condition no longer even resembles what it once was. . . .

[1] L. P., 'Pas d'exode', *Kadimah*, 15 Feb. 1898, p. 6.

[2] A. Rokéach, 'La quinzaine', *Kadimah*, 15 Feb. 1898, p. 10. At the Second Zionist Congress, in 1898, the Zionist leader Max Nordau put it this way: '. . . France, the France of the Great Revolution and of the Declaration of Human Rights, the country that first gave Europe the example of the legal emancipation of the Jews, France is today marching at the head of the anti-Semitic movement. Not yet in her official acts and utterances, justice commands us to state thus much: not yet avowedly, but none the less efficiently. . . . The Dreyfus Case has simply drawn aside veils and exposed moods of thought that had been hidden [until now]. It raises itself as an admonition and a lesson in the face of those Jews who still persist in believing themselves to be definitely and without reserve received into the national comradeship, at least of the most advanced Western countries.' Anna and Maxa Nordau, *Max Nordau: a Biography* (New York, 1943), pp. 141, 145–6.

[3] Ibid. Cf. J. D. M., 'L'antisémitisme devant l'opinion', *Kadimah*, 1 Aug. 1898, pp. 4–5.

The Algerian Jews are only guinea-pigs for the treatment which is being reserved for us.[1]

'... We are as oppressed [now] as during the time of the Pharaohs,' declared another writer somewhat extravagantly, 'and the Roths-childs themselves are as oppressed as we.'[2] Columnists found the passivity of French Jews contemptible, and condemned with little discrimination such Jewish leaders as Zadoc Kahn, Sylvain Lévi, and Alfred Neymarck. Arthur Meyer and Gaston Pollonnais, it was held, were simply acting in a manner consistent with the assimilationist position when they refused to defend Jewish rights.[3]

As an articulate representative of Zionist opinion, Le Flambeau confronted the question of assimilation directly. Its editor argued that Jews who were in the process of assimilation inspired distrust in the surrounding community: 'The Christians sense instinctively that those [Jews] are denying something in themselves in order to resemble them—and that makes them uneasy.' Thus the more the Jew assimilated, the more he was subject to attack; and for this reason French Jews, who were highly assimilated, were ex-periencing severe difficulties. Zionists, on the other hand, made no pretence of being Christians, or of subscribing to the latter's 'programme social religieux'. Zionists rejected assimilation as unnatural and as contributing to the climate of anti-Semitism in France.[4] But most of all the Zionists of Le Flambeau rejected

[1] La rédaction, 'Doctrine', Le Flambeau, Jan. 1899, p. 1. See Jacques Bahar, 'Autour du Flambeau', É.S., 10 Feb. 1913, pp. 40–1.
[2] Pinhas, 'La course au judaïsme', Le Flambeau, Feb. 1899, p. 20.
[3] L'Ami Schaddaï, 'Machiavélisme judéo-cafard', Le Flambeau, Mar. 1899, p. 16. Cf. Hassan Deslarts, 'Tintourin rabbinique', Le Flambeau, Mar. 1899, p. 21. In an earlier pamphlet, Jacques Bahar defined the policy of the Jewish leadership as the following: 'La politique des dirigeants juifs, nous la connaissons. Elle con-siste à faire la sourde oreille pour ne pas donner, par une riposte quelconque, l'éveil à ceux qui n'auraient peut-être pas entendu. C'est la localisation de l'attaque par la quarantaine du silence et de l'inertie. Avec cela et à grands renforts de l'ar-gent, on achète le mutisme des uns, l'apologie des autres. . . .' Jacques Bahar, 'Restons!' Réponse au projet d'exode des juifs (Paris, 1897), pp. 15–16.
[4] Jacques Bahar, 'Sionisme et patriotisme', Le Flambeau, Feb. 1899, pp. 13–15. 'La vérité est que, même au point de vue patriotique français, nous leur inspirons plus de confiance que les antisionistes. Les chrétiens sentent instinctivement que ces hommes-là renient quelque chose afin de leur ressembler — et cela les froisse. Ils ont raison dans leur inconscience, ces goyim!' Ibid., p. 13.

assimilation as necessarily involving association with a corrupt form of social organization. Jacques Bahar, like Lazare, made it clear that the essence of his Jewish nationalism was not an enthusiasm for the Jewish religion, at least in its institutional form.[1] When Bahar insisted that the Jews remain true to their 'race', when he spoke of the Jews' 'true, historical personality', which had to be maintained inviolate, he pointed to 'the essence of Judaism' as a set of *social* precepts: '. . . the essence of Judaism is nothing more than the most simple, the most practical, the most formidable and irresistible formula of social liberty and equality [and] which is realizable only through the impossibility of amassing monstrous fortunes and the consequent impossibility of pauperism [*sic*].'[2] The Jew, Bahar urged, should accept this 'essence' and should recognize that it formed a vital part of his being. Rejecting assimilation, the Jew would necessarily become engaged in a struggle against social inequality and injustice, and would thus fulfil the divine Jewish mission.[3] For Bahar and for his colleagues at *Le Flambeau*, Zionism was the revolutionary political organization through which the essence of Judaism could be realized and the Jews awakened to the fulfilment of their social mission.

Successor to *Le Flambeau* was *L'Écho sioniste*, a much more firmly established periodical which appeared bi-monthly, beginning in September 1899. By the autumn of 1899 the Dreyfus Affair was already slipping into the background; *L'Écho sioniste* therefore defined itself not in response to a particular crisis, but rather as an 'organe d'informations sionistes', a regular bulletin which continued through the First World War as a spokesman for a particular movement. The journal was devoted to 'Zionist discipline', and followed carefully the activities of the Zionist leadership.[4]

[1] See Jacques Bahar's letter in Albert Monniot, 'Le judaïsme contre la franc-maçonnerie et le protestantisme: un allié de Rome imprévu', *Revue internationale des sociétés secrètes*, June 1913, p. 1735.

[2] Jacques Bahar, 'La jeunesse juive et le judaïsme', *Le Flambeau*, Mar. 1899, p. 7.

[3] 'Et cela étant reconnu et observé chez soi, il est impossible, politiquement, de ne pas entrer en conflit avec les voisins, de ne pas les vaincre, de ne pas répandre ainsi la justice divine sur la terre en l'assurant à tout jamais.' Ibid.

[4] 'Notre programme', *É.S.*, n.d. [5 Sept. 1899], p. 1.

It reported Zionist meetings, printed articles on Zionist theory, and carried news events of related interest.

In the few short years of crisis, a movement had matured. From *Zion* to *L'Écho sioniste*, from a periodical founded by Bernard Lazare, who had recently awakened to Jewish nationalism, to a regular journal reporting the activities of a world-wide organization, the Zionist movement had grown, had become articulate, and had defined itself in relation to French society. By 1901, moreover, the *Écho sioniste* was able to announce a federation of all Zionist organizations in France, a long-sought unity which was scarcely possible in the days of *Zion*.[1] Only two years separated the founding of the two organs of opinion, but these two years had witnessed a critical upheaval in French society. Notably, all of the periodicals we have mentioned related in some way to the crisis wrought by the Dreyfus Affair. Zionism in France, more than in any other country, arose as a response on the part of a small minority to the anti-Semitic storm which raged over the fate of the Jewish officer between 1897 and 1899. Further, the Zionists believed that they were responding as much to the position taken by the Jewish majority as to that of the surrounding society.[2] Alienated both from the French community and from Jews who were assimilating into it, the minority of Zionists and Jewish nationalists struck out at the society which they believed was oppressing them and robbing them of their identity.

Each of these periodicals considered itself in some way as revolutionary; Zionism assumed, in its rhetoric and in its relationship to its opponents, the character of a movement in revolt. This was why Lazare described the Jews as 'the intractable rebel nation', and why Bahar defined the essence of Judaism as an ideal of social justice which was in permanent protest against all existing societies.[3] The Syndicalist leader Fernand Pelloutier, one of the few non-Jewish friends of the movement, reflected the thinking of

---

[1] D. J., 'La fédération des sionistes de France', *É.S.*, 20 July–5 Aug. 1901, pp. 237–8; Tchernoff, op. cit., p. 74.

[2] See L'Ami Schaddaï, 'Machiavélisme judéo-cafard', *Le Flambeau*, Mar. 1899, p. 16.

[3] Bahar, *Restons!*, p. 36.

Jewish nationalists in a lecture which dealt with 'the social and political organization of the Jewish people when it formed a free and independent nation'. 'The speaker concluded', said the account in *Kadimah*, 'that the rabbis [of the time] were veritable communists. The entire Talmud, he declared, was filled and penetrated with an anarchist or at least egalitarian spirit.'[1] Zionism, however, did not consider itself a reversion to that past, but rather a translation of this revolutionary spirit into the contemporary circumstances of oppression. Its vision was one in which the problems of the contemporary Jew would all find solution through the establishment of a revolutionary Jewish state. 'Zionism', wrote Alexander Marmorek, a Jewish scientist at the Institut Pasteur, 'does not want only to unite the poor; but, inspired by the spirit of our time, wants to prepare a better life for them and, through the protection of the poor and the weak, to create a true state of fraternity.'[2]

Another common element in Zionist periodical literature which appeared during the Dreyfus Affair was the unashamed profession of Jewish nationalism. On the surface, of course, this position was open to the charge that nationalism of any description was anachronistic, and that it was especially wrong to emulate the French nationalists who were the leading anti-Dreyfusards and anti-Semites.[3] Anticipating this challenge, Zionist writers took pains to distinguish their nationalism from French chauvinism, and constantly referred to it as an agency for the moral 'relèvement' of the

---

[1] J. D. M., 'L'antisémitisme devant l'opinion', *Kadimah*, Aug. 1898, p. 7.

[2] Dr. Al. Marmorek, 'Effets moraux du sionisme', *É.S.*, 5 Sept. 1899, p. 3.

[3] André Spire later recalled the serious reservations on this point: 'How could we French Jews at that moment come to have faith in a sort of homeopathic cure which proposed to eliminate the curse of nationalism [from] which we had suffered by a creation of a new nationalism? Nationalism was our sworn enemy; all nationalisms had to be destroyed. That is why we allied ourselves with all the parties of the Left—liberals, radicals, socialists—to defend the legality of individual rights for all citizens regardless of ethnic origins or religious convictions. Furthermore, we hoped that the example given by a victorious French liberalism would react sufficiently upon other European nations—Germany, Austria, Russia and other countries where we experienced ostracism and persecution—to make them adopt a more liberal attitude, not only in theory but in actuality vis-à-vis their Jewish populations.' André Spire, 'Herzl's Influence in France: the Growth of the Zionist Idea and its Effect on Judaism', in Weisgal (ed.), *Theodore Herzl*, p. 246.

Jewish people. Jewish nationalism, said one writer in *L'Écho sioniste*, differed from French nationalism which implied national supremacy; it was rather akin to the nationalism of the Greek people at the beginning of the nineteenth century, or the Hungarian people of 1848. It was a means for self-identification, the sentiment of a free people which was master of its own destiny.[1] Jewish nationalism, in short, was benign; it did not incite the hatred of other nations or peoples, but was an expression of the national liberation of Jews from the yoke of oppression.[2]

Among those who contributed most to the sense that the Dreyfus Affair required Jews to revolutionize their thinking was a writer of considerable European reputation, Max Nordau.[3] Born in Budapest in 1849, the son of a rabbi and a descendant of an old Spanish Jewish family, Nordau had studied medicine as a young man, and became famous as a psychologist whose works were widely read and translated into many languages. At the time of the Affair, Nordau had been living in Paris for almost twenty years, publishing several studies of the state of European civilization and gaining some notoriety as an eccentric but penetrating thinker. Still, as his daughter tells us, 'in Paris he remained the distinguished foreigner'; never truly becoming a part of French society, he held himself aloof from French social life, and in addition from a Jewish community with which he felt no ties, neither religious nor ethnic.[4] Like Theodore Herzl and like Bernard

---

[1] Henri Lev, 'Le mot et la chose', *É.S.*, 5 Oct. 1899, pp. 33–4. On this point see also A. Raskine, 'Notre nationalisme et le leur', *É.S.*, 5 Jan. 1901, 5 Mar. 1901; E. Dica, 'Nationalistes, internationalistes et antinationalistes', *É.S.*, 5 Jan. 1901, pp. 57–8.

[2] Cf. H. R. Trevor-Roper, 'Jewish and Other Nationalisms', *Commentary*, Jan. 1963, pp. 15–21.

[3] On Max Nordau see the biography by his wife and daughter, Anna and Maxa Nordau, *Max Nordau*; Meir Ben-Horin, *Max Nordau, Philosopher of Human Solidarity* (New York, 1956); George L. Mosse, introduction to the 1968 edition, Max Nordau, *Degeneration* (New York, 1968), pp. xv–xxxiv. Nordau's books set out to diagnose, from a psychologist's point of view, the deplorable condition of modern civilization in which France was leading the way towards a general level of depravity. The best-known of these works were *Die conventionellen Lügen der Kulturmenschlichkeit* (Leipzig, 1884), and *Entartung* (2 vols., Berlin, 1893).

[4] A. and M. Nordau, *Max Nordau*, p. 84.

Lazare, both of whom Nordau knew well, his views of the Jewish situation in France and in Europe underwent real change during the earliest stages of the Dreyfus Affair. Like them, he became a Zionist. Collaborating closely with Herzl, Nordau rose to particular prominence at the First Zionist Congress. There, in the opinion of one contemporary observer, he dominated the proceedings by the power of his eloquence and the force of his personality.[1]

Although he was disliked by many on account of his manner (Freud thought him 'vain and stupid'), he stood out as a leading spokesman for the Zionist cause in France, and helped to articulate the position of those Jews who were in revolt against the established Jewish community.[2] For example, while Jewish leaders tried, early in 1898, to put the most hopeful interpretation possible on the anti-Semitic tide which was sweeping France, Nordau told one interviewer that 'a general slaughter of Jews throughout the country' might well be imminent.[3] Such an alarmist position distinguished the Zionist minority from the rest of the Jewish community. Lecturing extensively in Paris, and contributing to the various Zionist reviews, he helped to spread the feeling of crisis and the sense of the need for a Jewish rebirth. As one who had made a great reputation for his studies of European degeneration and decline, Nordau won a ready attention among Jews inclined to resist assimilation into European nations.

Thus Nordau's often superficial prescriptions for the condition in which Jews found themselves were taken seriously in these circles. In addition to the cultivation of Jewish nationalism and the establishment of a Jewish home in Palestine, Nordau proposed that Jews should undertake a programme of gymnastics in order to instil a sense of discipline and to teach them 'to act with a single and collective goal in mind'.[4] In this as in other suggestions which

[1] Léon Baratz, 'Réalités et rêveries de ghetto: souvenirs sur Herzl et le IIIᵉ Congrès sioniste', *Revue juive de Genève*, July 1934, pp. 426–7.
[2] Ernest Jones, *The Life and Work of Sigmund Freud* (3 vols., New York, 1954–7), i. 205.
[3] R. H. Sherard, 'The Jews and their Fears: an Interview with Max Nordau', *Review of Reviews*, Feb. 1898, p. 138.
[4] Nordau, *Écrits sionistes*, p. 111. Cf. Tchernoff, op. cit., vol. iii, *Affaire Dreyfus*, pp. 67–70.

he offered, his object was a 'relèvement', a moral regeneration of a demoralized people:

> If the Jew sees himself honoured and possibly admired as a gymnast, as a fencer, etc., the good opinion which he will have of himself will help him all the more to lift himself up because his gymnastic exercises will have made him conscious of his dexterity, of his strength.[1]

Somewhat unfairly, Nordau charged that the Jewish leadership in France was largely responsible for the sad condition which Jews were forced to endure. This leadership had failed to provide a satisfactory ideal for its people, and it had created, in its zeal for assimilation, the basis for Jewish self-contempt. Its failure to speak out clearly in the face of anti-Semitism was an unforgivable error: 'This tragic Dreyfus Case', he said at the Second Zionist Congress in 1898, 'serves us as a fearfully exact measure of the degree to which we, in our feebleness, our pusillanimity, our callousness, our mutual estrangement have sunk.'[2] But Zionism, Nordau felt, would somehow provide the ideal which was missing, and would fortify Jews with the ability to resist: 'For the first time since the struggle of Bar-Kochba there exists among the Jews an inclination to show themselves and to show the world how much vitality they possess.'[3] Although the traditional leaders of the Jewish community opposed this new direction of affairs, their opposition would inevitably crumble, he felt, for they had been exposed, just as the false liberalism of the French Republic had been exposed.

This was largely rhetoric. Nordau employed his charisma in the service of the Zionist cause which, as we have seen, reflected the feelings of a small but significant segment of the Jewish community. His words struck fire, but created little light. It was left to others to probe more deeply, and to articulate with greater sensitivity the feelings of a saddened and demoralized people. Many of the writers who did so approached the problem through a revolutionary perspective, particularly through the identification of the Jewish people with an oppressed proletariat. We have observed that the publication in 1898 of Soloveitschik's study of the Jewish

---

[1] Nordau, *Écrits sionistes*, p. 118.   [2] A. and M. Nordau, *Max Nordau*, p. 145.
[3] Ibid., p. 146.

proletariat brought this question forward for general consideration. Another book, by a professor of Russian origin named
Chmerkine, appeared about the same time, arguing from the
Russian experience that anti-Semitism was not an attack on Jewish
capitalism, but primarily an attack upon the Jewish poor.[1] These
ideas were common currency in the Zionist press.

No one did more than Bernard Lazare to stress the revolutionary character of Zionism and the revolutionary cultural implications of the movement, particularly as it related to the Russian
experience. Lazare lectured to Jewish groups in Paris on this subject,
and corresponded with Russian revolutionaries. And when, in 1899,
he resigned from the Zionist central committee along with his
close associate Jacques Bahar, he took a public stand in favour of
this conception of the Zionist movement and against what he
judged to be that of Herzl. Lazare's stand was close to that of the
'Cultural Zionists', the followers of a Ukrainian Jew known as
Ahad Ha-am; his emphasis as a Frenchman and an anarchist, however, was upon the need for a revolution conceived of in western
European and libertarian terms. Central to his revolution was still
the overthrow of the bourgeoisie. In his letter of resignation
Lazare charged Herzl with attempting to lead a revolutionary
movement by authoritarian and middle-class methods. Essentially,
Lazare asserted, Herzl was a bourgeois:

> You are bourgeois in thought, bourgeois in feeling, bourgeois in ideas,
> and bourgeois in your social conceptions. And being such you want to
> lead a people, our people, which is a people of the poor, of the suffering,
> of proletarians. You can only do so in an authoritarian manner. . . . We
> must [rather] recreate our nation; that is for me a realistic task, a sound
> and above all a primary task. We must educate it, show it what it is,
> enrich it in its own eyes, in order to enrich it in the eyes of others, [and]
> to lift up its own heart and spirit. When it is such, it will be able
> to win its place. Jewish schools, that must be the first Zionist task, and
> schools where our proletariat can be lifted up democratically.[2]

[1] N. Chmerkine, *Les Conséquences de l'antisémitisme en Russie* (Paris, 1897);
Henri Dagan, 'Enquête sur l'antisémitisme: N. Chmerkine', *Les Droits de l'homme*,
25 May 1898.

[2] Edmund Silberner, 'Bernar Lazar v'Hatsionut' (in Hebrew), *Shivat Zion*, ii–iii
(1953), p. 358. Cf. Jacques Bahar, 'Explications', *Le Flambeau*, Apr. 1899, pp. 5–6.

Although Zionist organizations in France retained their allegiance to Herzl, there was considerable sympathy for Lazare's position in French Zionist circles at this time. Lazare himself remained on good personal terms with Herzl, and thus the rupture between the two was never made complete. Lazare's influence continued, and it did so even after his tragic death in 1903.

A Polish-born anarchist, Mécislas Golberg was one of those journalists who helped to give expression to this revolutionary tendency within the small band of French Zionists.[1] Golberg was born into a family of wealthy Jewish merchants from the small town of Plock, in Russian-occupied Poland, and he came to Paris in 1891 following medical studies in Switzerland. During the Affair, Golberg wrote for the Dreyfusard newspaper *Les Droits de l'homme*, organized public meetings, and was in constant difficulty with the Paris police owing to his association with revolutionary groups. Aligning himself with the Jewish nationalist cause largely because of his hostility to the society in which he lived, he made it clear that his nationalism was an antidote to the dehabilitating cultural effects of assimilation. Golberg felt that even the assimilated Jew, if he was a thoughtful person, found himself 'very uneasy in a milieu which was foreign to his destiny'. In fact, he wrote, the Jewish intellectual had become 'a renegade and a moral *déraciné*':

> He does not cease to be a Jew, but he is deprived of that which gives strength to his less assimilated brothers: the environment of his own people, his race and history which can be the foundation of and can sustain all intellectual effort.

When these Jews accepted the principles of Jewish nationalism, the strength returned:

> The Jew's modern nationalism furnishes him with the necessary environment. Assimilated to Western thought, he feels himself Oriental and a Jew, he accepts the responsibility of his race, he dreams of

[1] On Golberg see Pierre Aubery, 'Mécislas Golberg', *Les Lettres nouvelles*, July–Aug.–Sept. 1965, pp. 60–74; id., 'Qui était Mécislas Golberg?', *Les Nouveaux Cahiers*, Dec. 1965, pp. 42–5; Séverine, 'Notes d'une frondeuse: une victime', *La Fronde*, 19 Dec. 1898.

autonomy in the name of freedom of thought and the freedom to create. The intellectual uneasiness which leads to inhibition on the part of 'les assimilés' disappears [*la gêne intellectuelle qui aboutit à la bassesse cérébrale chez les « assimilés » disparaît*].[1]

For these reasons, Golberg claimed, Zionism was an ideology which was not just confined to the poor Jews of Russia, as had formerly been the case, but rather had become 'l'idée maîtresse de l'élite intellectuelle du judaïsme'.[2]

From this point of view, it should be noted, Jewish nationalism was not inconsistent with a certain degree of cultural assimilation. Indeed, Golberg seems to have assumed that the assimilated Jewish intellectual was potentially in the vanguard of the Zionist revolutionary movement.

The emphasis upon race which one can detect in Golberg's argument and elsewhere was a common theme in Zionist circles during the Dreyfus period.[3] In order to explain this emphasis it is inadequate to argue that the use of the term 'race' was often a semantic preference when referring to 'people'. Quite consciously, nationalist writers attacked those liberal Jews and non-Jews who, in their defence of French universalism against anti-Semitism, had contended that, biologically speaking, the Jews were not a race. Max Nordau, for example, felt uncomfortable with the refutations of the theory of a Jewish race. Even if the existence of a Jewish race were denied by some scholars, he noted, it was still true that the Jews constituted a physical type which was easily distinguishable.[4] In a highly critical article in *L'Écho sioniste*, one reviewer

---

[1] Mécislas Golberg, 'L'intellectualisme juif', *Le Flambeau*, Apr. 1899, pp. 7–10.

[2] Ibid., p. 7.

[3] 'L'éclosion de ces individualités [speaking of Borne, Heine, Marx, Lassalle] essentiellement juives, a fait naître le grand mouvement intellectuel du peuple juif. Les expériences sociales, les données scientifiques, la possibilité de vivre librement ont exalté le vieux sang, et, tout en prouvant que le peuple juif n'a cessé son rôle universel, ont montré que chaque juif n'a cessé d'appartenir à sa société et que son individualité épanouie n'est, au fond, que l'expression de la race.' Ibid., pp. 8–9.

[4] Max Nordau, 'Le sionisme', *Le Siècle*, 9 July 1899; J. D. M., 'L'antisémitisme devant l'opinion', *Kadimah*, 15 Aug. 1898, p. 4. In the pamphlet prepared by the Groupe des Ouvriers Juifs we find the following: 'Nous nous distinguons un peu partout par des particularités physiologiques. Nous sommes, en regard des autres

maintained that the attempt on the part of people like Salomon
Reinach to deny the existence of a Jewish race 'was the last and
supreme effort made by the proponents of assimilation to break
down every barrier between themselves and the non-Jewish
world'.[1] The most authoritative discussion of this point was made
in 1904 by a certain Dr. Jacobsohn who, in a series of five articles
for the same journal, reviewed the whole apparatus of cranial
measurements, eye and hair colour, and various other factors in
order to argue in favour of a distinct Jewish racial type.[2] The concept of *la race juive*, which, as we saw in Chapter II, was so deeply
rooted in the Jewish consciousness in France, was now mobilized
in the service of those Jews who argued for a degree of
Jewish exclusivism. In this respect, as in so many others, Zionists
rose to confront the liberal humanitarianism of assimilationist
ideology.

We can sense to some degree the character and the kind of support marshalled behind the growing Zionist movement by glanc-
ing for a moment at the Université Populaire Juive, begun in the
wake of the Dreyfus Affair in the spring of 1902. The Universités
Populaires were associations of working men and intellectuals
which drew upon the euphoria of the Dreyfus years in order to
construct small communities devoted to popular education. This
movement, which had a distinctly syndicalist flavour, flourished
briefly in the years following the Affair, only to fall into decline
and eventual extinction in the period of nationalist revival before
the First World War.

The Université Populaire Juive sprang from a milieu of Jewish
immigrants and working men; its primary supporters were Jewish
intellectuals who, like its president Alexander Marmorek, were of

nations, un peu moins débauchés, beaucoup moins meurtriers, beaucoup moins
voleurs, beaucoup plus nerveux, ce qui fait que nous avons parmi nous un peu
moins de Don Juan, beaucoup moins de Carrara, mais beaucoup plus de grands
commerçants, qui vident les poches, et de bas journalistes (tels que Drumont,
Arthur Meyer, Barrès — tous juifs) qui volent les consciences. Nous possédons
aussi une dose très forte et un peu anormale d'activité cérébrale.' *Le Prolétariat juif*,
p. 10.

[1] Reschef, 'M. Reinach et la race juive', *É.S.*, 15 Dec. 1903, p. 273.

[2] Dr. Jacobsohn, 'La race juive', *É.S.*, 15 Aug. 1904, pp. 155–7; 15 Sept. 1904, pp.
178–9; 15 Oct. 1904, pp. 195–6; 15 Dec. 1904, pp. 216–17; 15 Jan. 1905, pp. 16–17.

central or eastern European origin.[1] Zionism played a central role in these circles. At a speech delivered at the inauguration of new quarters for the Université in 1903 Marmorek declared that Zionism provided the bond between the diverse social groups which were participating:

> It is [Zionism] which has inaugurated this democratic undertaking, it is this which unites in this place young and old, workers and students, in a common love of our people and its past. Those who leave here will be more proud, more conscious of their personal dignity, and they will bear proudly the name of Jew.[2]

The programme of the Université, which was printed on the covers of *L'Écho sioniste*, represented an effort to cultivate a Zionist consciousness. Thus in addition to occasional talks by Bernard Lazare and the Zionist leader Max Nordau, and a visit from Herzl himself, there were regular lectures on Zionism, Palestine, Jewish history, and Jewish literature.[3] Courses were offered in conversational Hebrew, the Bible, and other more specialized topics. (Yet because of the immediate problems faced by the immigrant Jews

---

[1] 'A l'Université Populaire Juive', *É.S.*, 15 June 1902, p. 128. Marmorek was born in the town of Mielnick, Galicia, in 1865, and died in Paris in 1923. He studied medicine at the University of Vienna during the 1880s, and later specialized in bacteriology. After experiencing anti-Semitic attacks in the Austrian capital, he moved to Paris in 1893, where he became research director at the Institut Pasteur. See David Jacobson, *Alexandre Marmorek* (Paris, n.d.), and biographical article in *U.J.E.*

[2] 'L'inauguration de l'Université Populaire Juive', *É.S.*, 15 Mar. 1903, p. 54. According to the *Archives israélites* about five hundred persons participated in the ceremony. See 'Inauguration de l'Université Populaire Juive', *A.I.*, 5 Mar. 1903, p. 76. The goal of the Université Populaire Juive was declared to be 'de familiariser la masse juive avec l'histoire, la science et les pensées juives, la langue et la littérature hébraïques'. 'Université Populaire Juive à Paris', *É.S.*, 15 Mar. 1902, p. 73. At the founding of the Université Zadoc Kahn was quoted as saying: 'C'est au sionisme que nous devons le retour vers nous de la jeunesse studieuse qui menaçait de nous tourner le dos: c'est lui qui a éveillé le sentiment juif endormi. La même idée a guidé ceux qui ont fondé cette Université Populaire.' 'A l'Université Populaire Juive', *É.S.*, 15 June 1902, p. 128.

[3] See 'Le Dr. Herzl à l'Université Populaire Juive', *É.S.*, 15 May 1903, p. 97; 'Cours d'hébreu', *É.S.*, 15 May 1903, p. 99; J. Tchernoff, *Dans le creuset des civilisations*, vol. iv, *Des prodromes du bolchévisme à une société des nations* (Paris, 1938), pp. 279–81; A. and M. Nordau, *Max Nordau*, p. 157.

who attended, it should be noted that the Université Populaire, perhaps reluctantly, assumed some tasks of a more assimilationist nature: courses were given in conversational French, and special lectures were delivered on legal conditions and naturalization in France.)

Having considered the thought and activity of French Zionism as it was shaped in the fires of the Dreyfus crisis, it is clear that nothing could have been further from the spirit of assimilation which ran so strongly through the Jewish community. Nothing could have done more to undermine the persistent efforts on the part of French Jews to identify the spirit or essence of Judaism with that of France. Among the Zionist youth, and the politically conscious among the Jewish immigrants and poor, there was a profound feeling that the values of the European middle class, so loudly enunciated by assimilated Jews, had somehow proved to be a disaster for the Jewish people. This was the theme of an article written by one student, a delegate to the Third Zionist Congress in 1899. The article was entitled 'The Bankruptcy':

> The Jewish bourgeoisie which until now has claimed to lead the Jewish people has played its final card. Already its favourite theories, so cruelly tested by recent events throughout civilized Europe, are crumbling, and soon nothing will be left of them but a memory.[1]

But it was such 'favourite theories' upon which the majority of assimilated Jews in France had staked so much. The French ideals of universal fraternity and progress, symbolized in political rhetoric by the Revolution of 1789, had been so deeply revered that for many French Jews they were almost a religion in themselves, and had become practically accepted as a constituent part of Judaism. Assimilation had been defended as natural, as just, and as consistent with the fundamental principles of Jewish history and ideology. Now, as Zionists challenged all of this, the leaders of the established Jewish community in France delivered their own condemnation of the heresy in no uncertain terms, and renewed once again their protestations of loyalty and devotion to the France of 1789.

[1] Léon Paperin, 'La banqueroute', É.S., 5 Dec. 1899, p. 97.

Thus the two main Jewish periodicals were highly critical of Herzl's pamphlet when it first appeared, and scarcely even paused to take him seriously. A reviewer in the *Archives israélites* considered his whole idea 'a joke', although he contended, without bothering to give any explanation, that Zionism could put the interests of Judaism into grave peril, and 'give joy to our worst enemies'.[1] And similarly in the *Univers israélite* Louis Lévy abruptly affirmed that Herzl was 'a dangerous enemy for his co-religionists'.[2] However, these condemnations were followed in both journals by a much more thoughtful analysis, as the editors realized that, in some Jewish quarters at least, the idea of a Jewish state was awakening interest and excitement. Isaïe Levaillant devoted two articles to the subject in the beginning of 1897. At that time, as the Dreyfus Affair was beginning to have its repercussions for the Jewish community in France, Levaillant was fully prepared to agree that the situation of the Jews was perilous and required 'urgent solutions'. But Zionism, he argued, was a 'useless diversion' from these solutions. Levaillant noted critically that Herzl considered the problem of anti-Semitism to be 'irreparable'; that was why he resorted to dreams and to Utopias. Levaillant preferred to believe that France could return to the hallowed principles of 1789. Insuperable difficulties, moreover, prevented any possible establishment of a Jewish state: the European powers would never discuss such a question; the Jews had neither a common culture nor a common language with which to build a nation; and the financial obstacles to such a plan placed it beyond all foreseeable realization.[3]

What bothered these critics even more deeply than these objections, of course, was the way in which Zionism lent credence to the anti-Semitic charges of Jewish disloyalty to France. Levaillant pointed out, as did many others, that Drumont and his colleagues would surely exploit the work of Herzl.

[1] Ben Mosché, 'Le congrès de l'utopie', *A.I.*, 1 July 1897, p. 204.
[2] Louis Lévy, 'Point d'état juif, mais liberté de conscience', *U.I.*, 23 Oct. 1896, p. 133. Cf. 'Choses sionistes', *U.I.*, 21 June 1898, p. 432.
[3] B.-M., 'L'État juif', *U.I.*, 22 Jan. 1897, pp. 557–63; *U.I.*, 29 Jan. 1897, pp. 589–94. Cf. M. Lazard, Sionisme et Drumontisme', *U.I.*, 1 Oct. 1897, p. 54; 'Lettre de Bayonne', *U.I.*, 18 Feb. 1898, pp. 695–6; J. Lambert, 'S'il y a un patriotisme juif', *Le Journal du Loiret*, 17 Mar. 1898.

This last point was the theme of a widely-read article published in *La Grande Revue* in 1899, when Jewish opposition to the growing Zionist movement became extensive.[1] Alfred Berl, a Jew devoted to the assimilationist ideal and later involved in the Alliance Israélite Universelle, considered that the only possible defence of the Jewish people threatened by anti-Semitism lay, not in Zionism, but in a strengthening of the 'idée libérale', which he associated with the republican cause in France. Berl noted that in the absence of anti-Semitism (he meant up to 1894), 'the Jewish élite ... were directing and urging the masses of their co-religionists towards ideas of progress and sentiments of patriotism and fidelity'. With anti-Semitism, however, with the beginnings of persecution of the Jews in France at the time of the Dreyfus Affair, this leadership was challenged. Zionism arose in despair of such a hopeful and patriotic solution to the problem of Jewish exclusion; Zionism rejected the true solution, which consisted in viewing anti-Semitism as a part of a general assault upon the modern liberal state. Berl, of course, was correct in seeing liberalism as being at the heart of the issue; he perceived accurately that the same liberalism which was under constant attack from the forces of anti-Semitism and the Right had been largely rejected by the Zionist minority. The proper policy for Jews to follow, he argued, was to defend liberalism, to defend the France of 1789, and to stand by their rights to be Frenchmen like all others.

Joseph Reinach went so far as to declare that Zionism was 'a trap set by the anti-Semites for the naïve or thoughtless'.[2] In the autumn of 1897 *Le Figaro* carried an extensive interview on the subject with the well-known Jewish politician in which he emphasized the unpatriotic implications of the movement:

The sole result of this campaign, which in any case is destined for a pitiful failure, would be to give the impression . . . that those Frenchmen who belong to the Jewish faith are subordinating the idea of the

[1] Alfred Berl, 'Le mouvement sioniste et l'antisémitisme', *La Grande Revue*, 1 July 1899, pp. 13–51. Cf. id., 'Le sionisme', *Le Siècle*, 9 July 1899; id., 'L'éclipse des idées libérales', *La Grande Revue*, 1 May 1900, pp. 291–316; Louis Lévy, 'Le mouvement sioniste et l'antisémitisme', *U.I.*, 28 July 1899, pp. 587–90.

[2] Edmond LeRoy, 'Le royaume de Palestine: l'opinion de M. Reinach', *Le Figaro*, 7 Sept. 1897.

fatherland to I cannot imagine what sort of ethnic solidarity, which existed in a vague way during barbarous times, which was prevalent no doubt at the origin of civilized societies, but which in modern societies is an anachronism. . . .[1]

This 'idea of the fatherland', Reinach contended, was 'the most elevated, the most noble, and the most worthwhile which could organize mankind'. Reinach denied that the Jews formed a nation apart or that they wished in any way to reject their French nationality: 'The French fatherland was given to the Jews by the Revolution—the anti-Semites will not take it away from them, and the Zionists at Basel will not determine any Jew to renounce it.' Both the Zionists and the anti-Semites, then, were trying to destroy the work of the Revolution. Assimilated Jews like Reinach and Berl felt obliged to denounce Zionism energetically, and once again to assert their patriotic devotion to the country which had given them citizenship. 'We are French, and French we shall remain', Reinach concluded. 'All our efforts, all our intellectual activity, all our love, the last drop of our blood belongs to France, and to her alone.'

Yet as the seriousness of the Zionist leaders became apparent, and as the movement made an impressive showing during the first few congresses at Basel, some French writers conceded that Zionism might have a certain significance for the oppressed Jews of eastern Europe.[2] One frequent distinction was that proposed by Louis Lévy in the *Univers israélite*. Lévy asserted that he was in favour of 'le sionisme économique, philanthropique ou colonisateur', because it was concerned with helping to support the deprived and the destitute among the Jewish people.[3] But this had to be separated in the public image from 'le sionisme nationaliste' which reflected poorly on the patriotism of the Jews in France.[4]

[1] LeRoy, op. cit.
[2] See Salomon Lubetzki, 'Le congrès sioniste et l'antisémitisme', *U.I.*, 15 Oct. 1897, pp. 105–8.
[3] Louis Lévy, 'M. Max Nordau et le sionisme', *U.I.*, 31 Mar. 1899, p. 46; id., 'Choses sionistes', *U.I.*, 21 June 1898, p. 432. Cf. H. Prague, 'Les sionistes à l'œuvre', *A.I.*, 9 Sept. 1897, p. 283.
[4] 'Sur le dernier congrès sioniste', *U.I.*, 16 Sept. 1898, pp. 831–2. Cf. Tchernoff, op. cit., vol. iii, *Affaire Dreyfus*, p. 76.

The one was simply benevolent humanitarianism, the other was dangerous and subversive. Such a distinction revived the older view of Zionism as a philanthropic undertaking, an enterprise to which the assimilated Jews of western Europe could lend gracious support, following the example of the Rothschild family, but which was devoid of any nationalist or revolutionary implications. This Zionism would be safe.

Concern about the ominous revolutionary dimension of the movement became increasingly prevalent, particularly as the political situation in France made men conscious of social upheaval. The fact that it was largely eastern European Jews who joined Zionist groups in Paris meant that the movement was to be regarded immediately with a certain *méfiance*. Not only were these unassimilated (or at least un-French) Jews mistrusted because they called attention to the Jew as a foreigner, not only did they greatly embarrass French Jews at a moment when a demonstration of patriotism was considered essential, they also contained among them communists and anarchists, the kind of Russians who struck terror into middle-class hearts at the end of the nineteenth century.[1] Zionism was said to tend 'to precipitate the Jewish masses . . . into the worst adventures'; 'Zionist dreams' were likened to 'the excitations of communism and nihilism', which could only exacerbate the condition of the persecuted.[2] According to Hippolyte Prague, the future Zionist state would live in constant disorder, and 'revolution would exist permanently'.[3]

[1] See Margalith, op. cit., p. 179. The following was Alfred Berl's description of the Zionist leadership: 'Il se compose d'une grande masse ignorante, et d'intellectuels non pourvus d'emploi: ingénieurs, médecins, avocats encore inoccupés.' 'Mouvement sioniste', p. 37.
[2] H. Prague, 'Le sionisme', *A.I.*, 15 Sept. 1898, p. 298; I. Cahen, 'Un prolétariat méconnu', *A.I.*, 21 July 1898, p. 225; H. Prague, 'Les sionistes à l'œuvre', *A.I.*, 9 Sept. 1897, p. 283.
[3] H. Prague, 'Les sionistes', *A.I.*, 2 Sept. 1897, p. 275. When a Russian Zionist attempted to assassinate Max Nordau in 1903, Prague displayed common assumptions about Russian Zionists in an article on the subject. Of the accused assailant Prague wrote: 'Ayant grandi dans les ténèbres du Territoire, la civilisation s'est révélée à lui subitement comme un enchantement. C'est comme un coup de soleil que ce malheureux reçoit sur la tête à peine remise des émotions, des angoisses et des terreurs du régime muscovite, et il peut arriver aisément que les impressions

The Zionist movement presented an extremely delicate issue to French rabbis. On the one hand they were servants of the French State, and patriotically devoted to the fatherland. Their congregations, in very large measure, were vigorously opposed to the Zionist cause. On the other hand the rabbinate, particularly under the leadership of Zadoc Kahn, had tried to instil in French Jewry some feeling of responsibility for the more unfortunate among their co-religionists. French Jews, the rabbis had tended to say, had a special mission to improve the situation of eastern European Jews. Moreover, in an increasingly secular and even irreligious environment, the rabbis saw the Zionists attempting to infuse the Jewish masses with a practically forgotten Jewish literature and culture. While French Jews were rapidly becoming completely French, Zionists were attempting to become more Jewish. For the rabbis there was obviously some attraction to the latter.

Unlike the situation in Germany, where many rabbis came out violently against the Zionist enterprise while others supported it, the French rabbinate adopted the somewhat neutral position which was carefully defined by Zadoc Kahn in 1897. In the autumn of that year, as the First Zionist Congress was assembling in Basel, it became imperative to have some statement on the subject from the Grand Rabbi of France. No French rabbis attended the meeting, and an interview with J.-H. Dreyfuss in *Le Figaro* appeared to have given the impression that religious authorities were hostile to the proceedings.[1] Zadoc Kahn therefore prepared a long statement on the subject which, after being altered slightly to appear as an interview, was published in the Paris daily *Le Journal* on 11 September 1897.[2]

qu'il ressent, et auxquelles il n'était guère préparé, lui dictent des actes où la réflexion cède le pas à l'impulsion, car c'est un être tout vibrant, tout palpitant que l'israélite slave, dont les nerfs tendus à l'excès, sous l'état de sa condition humiliée, éprouvent, à un moment donné, le besoin de se détourner, de se soulager en un cri, en un geste, par où son âme comprimée se débonde, pour ainsi dire.' 'Le sionisme au révolver', *A.I.*, 24 Dec. 1903, p. 409.

[1] Émile Berr, 'Un nouveau parti: les sionistes', *Le Figaro*, 4 Sept. 1897.

[2] M. Liber, 'Zadoc Kahn et le sionisme', *É.S.*, 10 May 1913, p. 94. Cf. 'Le congrès de Bâle et le Grand Rabbin de France', *U.I.*, 24 Sept. 1897, pp. 5-8; 'Interview de M. le Grand Rabbin de France', *U.I.*, 24 Sept. 1897, pp. 11-13; 'Le sionisme et le rabbinat français', *A.I.*, 23 Sept. 1897, p. 300.

The Grand Rabbi of France took a cautious view of the meeting at Basel.[1] In his opinion anti-Semitism was indeed the cause of Zionism as Herzl had contended, but he felt that anti-Semitism was destined to pass away and that progress in terms of human fellowship was bound to continue after a slight interruption. French Jews, he said, were for this reason not unduly alarmed by the anti-Semitic agitation:

They consider it to be like a temporary relapse, one of those momentary recessions such as have always been recorded in the ebb and flow of history. They realize that these retrograde movements can only retard and not stop the continuous progress which France is making in the direction of right and reason.

And thus, for French Jewry, the Zionist solution was entirely inappropriate to the situation at hand. French Jews would rely upon French legislation and upon the anticipated return to republican principles for the betterment of their condition. In France, moreover, Zadoc Kahn declared that Jews no longer believed in the ancient Jewish concept of Messianism which flowed so readily into the Zionist stream. 'For a large number of Jews', the Grand Rabbi indicated, 'the Messiah had become the symbol of progress, of human fraternity finally realized, of the triumph of the great moral and religious truths that Judaism has declared and has spread. . . . Zionism has [therefore] lost its *raison d'être*.' Still, he refrained from direct criticisms of Zionist activities such as others had offered. Zionism had some meaning for the downtrodden Jews of Russia, he felt; Zionism could force Europe 'to effect a return to itself and thus undertake an examination of its conscience'. But for French Jews Zadoc Kahn ventured to propose a slogan which summed up their reliance upon their own country: 'Neither to Jerusalem nor to Basel.'

The journalist who assembled Zadoc Kahn's statement in the form of an interview closed the article with the following words: '. . . I took leave of Monsieur Zadoc Kahn, without yet knowing

[1] 'A propos du sionisme', *Le Journal*, 11 Sept. 1897. Cf. Zadoc Kahn's similar views almost a decade before; L. W., 'La Palestine aux Juifs', *U.I.*, 16 Jan. 1889, pp. 265–6.

his true feelings on the matter [*le fond de sa pensée*], and if he considered Zionism a chimerical or a realizable conception.' Zadoc Kahn was never to clear up this ambiguity. Although he would often mention the immense practical difficulties of the Zionist scheme, and although he protested the patriotism of French Jews with great enthusiasm, the Grand Rabbi of France generally retained friendly relations with the Zionists and, within the real limits of his position, supported them as well as he could. For doing so he was often criticized by members of the Jewish community.[1] In effect, Zadoc Kahn ensured, through his delicately balanced position, that the French rabbinate would not become mobilized in opposition to the Zionist cause. The prestige of his office, along with the dignity with which he argued his case, helped to moderate the general thrust of the attack upon Zionism which arose within the Jewish community in France.

For the most part, French Jewry tended to take a positive approach to the difficulties which beset it. Its emphasis was less upon attacking the Zionist minority (which, after all, remained such) than upon affirming its patriotism. This was the note struck by the well-known Jewish historian, Maurice Bloch, as he discussed the Zionist question in 1907. Bloch too was for Zionism, he said, as were most Jews of the West, but for a Zionism which was 'more expansive, more open, which would unite not only Jews, but all the people of the earth'. There was little to quarrel with in such a conception. When that Messianic dream was to be fulfilled, he added, the triumph would be due as much to France as to the ancient Hebrew faith; when Zionism finally achieved realization, the 'new Jerusalem' so long awaited would be a monument to French Republican principles:

The new Jerusalem will exist everywhere that the Declaration of the Rights of Man prevails. The new Jerusalem will be where the French Revolutionary will triumph. The new Jerusalem will be there with the

[1] See Liber, 'Zadoc Kahn et le sionisme', *É.S.*, 10 May 1913, p. 96; Julien Weill, *Zadoc Kahn, 1839–1905* (Paris, 1912), p. 186; H. Prague, 'Les sionistes', *A.I.*, 2 Sept. 1897, p. 275. Cf. Tchernoff, op. cit., vol. iii, *Affaire Dreyfus*, pp. 76–7; Theodore Herzl, *Theodor Herzls Tagebücher 1895–1904* (3 vols., Berlin, 1922), i. 312.

principles of 1789. And before this new Jerusalem people will be able to say once again: *'Gesta dei per Francos!'*[1]

Between this spirit and that of the small minority we have been discussing there stretched the unbridgeable gulf of disagreement over the fundamental question of assimilation. The Dreyfus Affair had occasioned this sharp division of opinion within the Jewish community, but its causes ran deep in the social perspectives of the two sides. With the Zionists, the Jewish nationalists, and the opponents of assimilation went those who in some way felt estranged from the community at large. These were the young militants from eastern Europe, articulate spokesmen for a Jewish proletariat, and intellectual critics like Lazare, Nordau, and Bahar. These Jews had always considered themselves on the fringes of French society, for various reasons, and had never asked to be a part of it. Now, as that society was being swept by a storm of unparalleled ferocity, and as it floundered in a great gust of anti-Jewish hostility, they abandoned all remnants of deference, and declared their emancipation from all that they had despised in French life. Their splendid creations, in the forms of a Zionist Utopia in Palestine, or a Jewish nationalist ideal, or a virile, heroic Jewish resistance, were rooted in their fundamental antipathy to the France in which they found themselves. They opposed assimilation as a capitulation to that society, an acceptance of inferiority, and a fatalistic servility bordering on self-contempt. On the other side the élite of French Jewry, the members of high society, the business and professional men who had made a place for themselves in the France of the Third Republic, the men, in short, who had benefited from assimilation—these men clung with a sometimes desperate energy to the nation which they believed had befriended them. To their fellow Jews who suffered oppression (and to Dreyfus on Devil's Island) they could occasionally respond with generosity and benevolence; but the politics of assimilation proved to be stronger even than their philanthropy, and the Zionist revolution was no match for their patriotism.

[1] Maurice Bloch, 'La société juive en France depuis la Révolution', *R.E.J.*, vol. xlviii (1904), p. xli. Cf. Maurice Kahn, 'Quelques réserves', *Pages libres*, 29 Oct. 1904, pp. 355–9; Spire, 'Herzl's influence in France', p. 246.

CHAPTER X

CONCLUSION

THE Jewish community studied here did not undergo significant changes during the Dreyfus period. There was no mass defection of Jews in favour of Catholicism, and neither was there, as some hoped, a reinvigoration of the Jewish community. Instead, it remained practically unchanged, and the most important anti-Semitic crisis of nineteenth-century France appeared as only a ripple in the smooth course of Jewish life in that country.

This lack of important change stands out against a background of expectation generated during the darkest hours of anti-Semitic violence. Jews believed then, as men tend to believe in moments of great upheaval, that the world which was so familiar to them would never really be the same again. In the autumn of 1898, for example, when anti-Semitic attacks struck at the heart of French Jewry, Hippolyte Prague anticipated that Jews could never again remain indifferent to their community, and would thenceforth rise from their torpor to reform and strengthen Jewish life in France.[1] Throughout the period Zadoc Kahn had urged that Jews seize the occasion given by the shocking events of the day to end religious stagnation and to instil in young people a Jewish consciousness which they had previously lacked.[2] And even Isaïe Levaillant, who was always ready to criticize French Jews for their excessive optimism, believed in 1899 that the Affair had seen a rebirth of 'le sentiment juif' which could awaken Jews from their previous quiescence.[3]

Everywhere these expectations were disappointed. Commenting upon the condition of the Jewish community in 1900, Prague observed that there had been no visible progress in the directions

[1] H. Prague, 'Vers la justice', *A.I.*, 22 Sept. 1898, p. 307.
[2] See H. Prague, 'Un devoir urgent', *A.I.*, 5 Oct. 1899, pp. 317–19.
[3] B.-M., 'La crise ministérielle et l'Affaire Dreyfus', *U.I.*, 23 June 1899, pp. 426–7. Cf. Louis Lévy, 'Des effets bienfaisants de l'Affaire', *U.I.*, 30 June 1899, pp. 461–2; R. T., 'La vitalité d'Israël', *U.I.*, 16 Dec. 1898, p. 391.

which he had outlined: 'No effort has been made ... to remedy the situation,' he wrote. 'Youth continues to grow up in ignorance of its religious duties and without understanding of our noble traditions.'[1] Although one writer felt that the Affair had slowed the course of Jewish assimilation somewhat, the general impression was that the trend towards 'fusion' with other Frenchmen would only be 'momentarily' diminished.[2]

Several years after the Affair, however, there did develop something of a Jewish literary renaissance. A number of writers, in particular André Spire, Edmond Fleg, and Henri Franck, attempted to create a literary mode which was at once Jewish and French, which cultivated a Jewish consciousness, and which at the same time resisted assimilationist pressures.[3] Though they frequently evoked the experience of the Affair, most of these Jews were too young to have been provoked by it directly; their inspiration came rather from the French literary currents of the moment, from the quickening pace of nationalist revival, the search for cultural roots and religious enthusiasm which preceded the First World War. Celebrating a return to Jewish tradition, a pride in the Jewish people, and a Jewish consciousness that was overwhelmingly nationalist, they were in some sense the Jewish analogues to Maurice Barrès, Charles Maurras, and Léon Daudet.[4] And thus even here, even in the vigorous assertion of a Jewish identity, the influence of France was predominant.[5]

This stability, even lethargy, of the Jewish community during the Dreyfus crisis testifies to the strength of the assimilationist

[1] H. Prague, 'Revue de l'année israélite 5660–5661', *Annuaire 5661* (1900–1), p. 378.
[2] I. Déhalle, 'L'assimilation des israélites français', *U.I.*, 9 Aug. 1901, p. 659.
[3] See Rabi (pseud.), *Anatomie du judaïsme français* (Paris, 1962), pp. 86–94; C. Lehrmann, *L'Élément juif dans la littérature française*, vol. ii, *De la Révolution à nos jours* (Paris, 1961), pp. 84–5; Cécile Delhorbe, *L'Affaire Dreyfus et les écrivains français* (Paris, 1932), p. 336; Pierre Aubery, *Milieux juifs de la France contemporaine à travers leurs écrivains* (Paris, 1957), p. 176.
[4] On the influence of Barrès see André Spire, *Quelques juifs et demi-juifs* (2 vols, Paris, 1928), i. vi–vii, 156; Lehrmann, op. cit., pp. 84, 104; Frédéric Empaytaz, 'Barrès et les juifs', *Revue littéraire juive*, May 1928, pp. 408–13; Aubery, op. cit., pp. 306–7.
[5] See, for example, Edmond Fleg, *Pourquoi je suis juif* (Paris, 1939), pp. 50–3.

tradition. For over a hundred years Jews felt the powerful attraction of French culture; since the end of the eighteenth century they had basked in the warmth of a society which recognized not primarily men's right to be different, to be left alone, but rather men's right to be French. 'The unity of France', wrote Prague, 'is constructed, and well constructed, with an absolute homogeneity, for all the elements which compose it are completely dissolved into the great soul of the fatherland.'[1] There was no pluralist tradition in France, and the Jewish community was unused to expressing its unique and distinct contribution to French life. Jews indeed became French. Their community was weakened by the corrosive effects of assimilation; their politics were shaped in the image of French patriotism. By the end of the nineteenth century their Frenchness was so pronounced that, with Darmesteter and others, they frequently contemplated the very essence of Judaism in terms of the *tricolore*. By the time of the Dreyfus Affair the Jews in France had lost most sense of their community, and had fashioned their political perspective in a cautious attempt to accentuate their respectability.

This was why the Jewish community was caught so unawares by the anti-Semitic crisis, with its violent denunciation of Jewish 'foreigners', and why Jewish leaders were generally unable to respond except with the most orthodox assertions of patriotism. From the Jewish point of view, this response was facilitated by the small size and the weakness of their community. But mostly it was made possible by the cultural ideal which Jews had built for themselves, following a pattern drawn by French culture; having emphasized for so long that they were French, they could scarcely assert with any vigour their right to be Jews. In this, as in everything else they did, they showed themselves truly to be the Frenchmen they claimed to be. And none was more French than Alfred Dreyfus, the Jew who bore his suffering with a firm and undiminished love for the fatherland.

Yet within the Jewish community a small group of Jews, unimpressed with the assimilationist politics of their co-religionists, and undaunted by a powerful opposition, chose the darkest moment

[1] H. Prague, 'Causerie', *A.I.*, 2 June 1892, p. 171.

to declare their Jewishness. Led by the pugnacious journalist
Bernard Lazare, they answered wild attacks with determined
resistance, and insult with a proud affirmation of their distinctiveness. With an energy drawn from their own estrangement from
French society, and with a disgust directed at their fellow Jews,
they denounced the politics of assimilation in favour of Jewish
nationalism, and in many cases the Zionist programme. Religious
differences played no part in their protest; like assimilationist
Jews, and like the majority of politically active Frenchmen of the
time, they accepted the premises of the secular society which
France was coming to be. For them the issue was rather one of
social perspective; the question to be answered was whether Jews
should embrace French society, its ideals and social organization,
or whether they should liberate themselves from that society, and
in so doing reclaim their identity as Jews. For this reason the Zionists and the Jewish nationalists attracted those Jews consciously
alienated from French society—anarchists, revolutionaries, and
foreigners dissatisfied with life in France.

For the majority, however, the appeal to a Jewish personality
was meaningless in the face of the powerful attraction of France.
Throughout adversity, French Jews have tended to fall back upon
the protection afforded by the ideals of the French Revolution and
the allure of *la patrie*. *Civis gallicus sum*. This brief slogan, fashioned
by the distinguished Jewish sociologist Georges Friedmann as his
response to the horror which surrounded him during the terrible
winter of 1940–1, has always been the response of French Jews
when France seemed to be on the verge of betraying them.[1]
Unhappily, France has not always responded in kind.

[1] Georges Friedmann, *Fin du peuple juif?* (Paris, 1965), p. 9. Cf. Josué Jéhouda,
Les Cinq Étapes du judaïsme émancipé (Geneva, 1942), pp. 74–5; Rabi (pseud.),
'Notre fondamentale ambiguïté', *Confluences*, vol. vii, nos. 15–17 (n.d.), pp. 54–76.

BIBLIOGRAPHICAL NOTE

MUCH of the material which might have been useful for a study such as this did not survive the Second World War. The dossier in the archives of the Alliance Israélite Universelle dealing with the Dreyfus Affair, a dossier which would have revealed much about the reactions of the Jewish community in France, was destroyed. Many private papers of Jewish contemporaries were lost, including those of Narcisse Leven, and apparently those of Zadoc Kahn. Following the defeat of the Germans many books, periodicals, and documents which had been taken by the Nazis found their way to the Central Zionist Archives in Jerusalem. It is possible that a thorough investigation of these archives might uncover valuable material for further study of the Jewish community in France. The archives of the Consistoire Central and the Consistoire de Paris, which were hurriedly transported to the south of France to escape the Nazis, have survived, and are in the process of reclassification. These archives are located in the offices of the Société Consistoriale de Paris, 17 rue Saint-Georges, Paris IXe. Very little remains of the private papers of Bernard Lazare. A number of his letters and other documents may be found in the archives of the Alliance, and several other dossiers remain in the possession of his niece, Mlle Jacqueline Bernard.

The library of the Alliance, located at 45 rue La Bruyère, Paris IXe, is the best single source of published works on the Jews of France. Many items not available in the Bibliothèque Nationale may be found there, along with a fairly complete collection of contemporary Jewish periodical literature. The Collection Ochs, probably the largest existing collection of Dreyfusiana, is housed in the Bibliothèque Historique de la Ville de Paris, 29 rue de Sévigné, Paris IIIe. Particularly useful in this collection is the excellent assemblage of newspaper clippings, dealing largely with anti-Semitism, but containing much material on the Jewish community taken from the French press.

There are a number of useful bibliographical sources which may be mentioned here. Pierre Aubery's *Milieux juifs de la France contemporaine à travers leurs écrivains* (Paris, 1957) is the best place to begin a search for books on French Jewry, both fiction and non-fiction. There is, in addition, a bibliography by Bernhard Blumenkranz, *Bibliographie des juifs en France* (Paris, 1961), published by the École Pratique des Hautes Études. Useful bibliographical references are appended to the articles in the *Jewish Encyclopaedia* (12 vols., New York, 1901–6), and the *Universal Jewish Encyclopaedia* (10 vols., New York, 1939–43). Another helpful source is Edmund Silberner, *Western European Socialism and the Jewish Question: a Selective Bibliography* (Jerusalem, 1955). Details on Jewish periodical literature are available from the article 'Periodicals' in the *Jewish Encyclopaedia*, ix. 616–39, and the article 'A la Bibliothèque Nationale: les périodiques juifs français du XIXe siècle', *Archives juives*, vol. ii (1965–6), no. 4, pp. 7–8. There is also a bibliography of the Jewish press of France and the French colonies (in Yiddish) in E. Tcherikower (ed.), *Yidn in Frankraikh* (2 vols., New York, 1942), i. 236–308.

Material in this book has been drawn largely from the two main Jewish periodicals, the *Univers israélite* and the *Archives israélites*. These journals, which appeared weekly during most of our period, contain articles and news items on all subjects relevant to the Jewish community. The monthly *La Famille de Jacob*, published in Avignon, is a periodical with some discussion of questions of interest to the Jewish communities of the south of France. Observations on various aspects of the Jewish community and often a record of Jewish achievement in public life may be found in the year-book *Annuaire des Archives israélites*. A number of other publications appeared within the Jewish community, but were generally related to specific issues. Thus the *Vraie Parole* or the *Or et Argent* were published immediately before the Dreyfus Affair, offering the viewpoint of those Jews actively engaged against anti-Semitism. Some discussion of these journals may be found on pages 146–51, above. During the Affair a series of Zionist journals appeared, as spokesmen for a militant minority within the Jewish community. These journals, known as *Zion, Kadimah, Le Flambeau*, and *L'Écho sioniste*, are discussed in detail on pages 257–63, above.

Other published sources on the Jewish community in France are scarce, often contain little information, and must be searched out with considerable perseverance. In addition to the sources considered above, it may be useful to outline some of the published works which are of particular importance for an understanding of French Jews at the end of the nineteenth century.

A number of general studies of the Jews in France will familiarize the reader with some of the problems associated with a highly assimilated Jewish community. Foremost among these are three recent books which investigate some of the philosophical dimensions of Jewish assimilation: André Neher, *L'Existence juive: solitude et affrontements* (Paris, 1962); Albert Memi, *Portrait d'un juif* (2 vols., Paris, 1962); and Robert Misrahi, *La Condition réflexive de l'homme juif* (Paris, 1963). Probably still the most brilliant discussion of this genre, however, is Jean-Paul Sartre, *Réflexions sur la question juive* (Paris, 1946). Léon Berman's *Histoire des juifs de France des origines à nos jours* (Paris, 1937) provides a survey of the Jewish experience in France, but is far too superficial to be of great use. On the other hand, the excellent book by Rabi (pseud.), *Anatomie du judaïsme français* (Paris, 1962), is extremely suggestive, and has a comprehensive discussion of both the structural and the cultural aspects of the Jewish community. A fascinating, though sometimes obscure, picture of the Jewish condition in nineteenth-century France and western Europe may be found in Hannah Arendt, *The Origins of Totalitarianism* (Cleveland, 1958). Her work abounds with penetrating generalizations, but often lacks a sure grounding in historical fact. Details on the social and economic life of the Jewish community in Paris may be found in the useful work of Michel Roblin, *Les Juifs de Paris: démographie, économie, culture* (Paris, 1952), and in Zosa Szajkowski, *Poverty and Social Welfare among French Jews, 1800–1880* (New York, 1954). A good sense of the experience of Algerian Jews may be gleaned from a study by Claude Martin, *Les Israélites algériens de 1830 à 1902* (Paris, 1936), and the more recent and more sympathetic Michel Ansky, *Les Juifs d'Algérie: du décret Crémieux à la libération* (Paris, 1950).

A number of Jews have contributed to our understanding of the period by publishing their memoirs and recollections. Most noteworthy in this respect is Jehudah Tchernoff, *Dans le creuset des civilisations* (4 vols., Paris, 1936–8), whose observations of the Jewish community have frequently been cited in the chapters above. These impressions may be compared with those of the worldly and fashionable editor of *Le Gaulois*, Arthur Meyer, in his *Ce que mes yeux ont vu* (Paris, 1911) and *Ce que je peux dire* (Paris, 1912). In addition, there are the books by Julien Benda, *La Jeunesse d'un clerc* (Paris, 1936); André Spire, *Souvenirs à bâtons rompus* (Paris, 1962); Jules Isaac, *Expériences de ma vie*, vol. i, *Péguy* (Paris, 1959); and Edmond Fleg, *Pourquoi je suis juif* (Tunis, 1939), which contain differing personal experiences of Jewishness. For the Dreyfus crisis itself there are the memoirs of Léon Blum, *Souvenirs sur l'Affaire* (Paris 1935), and Daniel Halévy, *Apologie pour notre passé*, in *Cahiers de la quinzaine* (Paris, 1910). For an interesting account of the experiences of a Jewish foreign student in Paris during the Affair see Sam Lévy, 'Mes mémoires: l'Affaire Dreyfus', *Tresoro de los Judios Sefardies: estudios sobre la historia de los Judios Sefardies y su cultura*, vol. xxii, no. 3, July 1960, pp. 131–58. Not to be neglected in this connection are the observations of a non-Jewish participant who was close to Bernard Lazare and a number of other Jews—Charles Péguy. His *Notre Jeunesse* (1910), in *Œuvres complètes*, vol. iv (Paris, 1916), includes some important passages describing the political disposition of French Jews at this time.

Biographical notes on important figures within the Jewish community may be found in the text. For the notes on James Darmesteter see page 101; on Joseph Reinach see page 137, note 1; on Bernard Lazare see page 164. Of the various other biographical studies available, several particularly deserve mention. Julien Weill's *Zadoc Kahn, 1839–1905* (Paris, 1912) is indispensable, both for a knowledge of the life of the Grand Rabbi of France, and also for an understanding of some of the relationships among Jewish community leaders. Max Nordau's wife and daughter, Anna and Maxa Nordau, have written *Max Nordau: a Biography* (New York, 1943), which contains long excerpts from Nordau's writings and speeches. This book is far more useful to the historian than Meir Ben-Horin, *Max Nordau: Philosopher of Human Solidarity* (New York, 1956), which does not adequately relate its subject to the historical context. Alain Silvera's recent *Daniel Halévy and his Times: a Gentleman-Commoner in the Third Republic* (Ithaca, New York, 1966) is the life of a highly assimilated Jew, as is Robert J. Niess, *Julien Benda* (Ann Arbor, Michigan, 1956).

Jean Bouvier's *Les Rothschild* (Paris, 1960) is an excellent introduction to a study of the role of the Rothschild family.

Finally, we may mention a number of books and articles of particular value in studying various aspects of the Jewish community in France. A contemporary article by Simon Debré, 'The Jews of France', *Jewish Quarterly Review*, vol. iii, April 1891, pp. 367–435, offers a good picture of the institutions of the Jewish community. For a bibliographical note on the administrative structure of the community see page 69, note 1, above. Jules Bauer, *L'École rabbinique de France, 1830–1930* (Paris, n.d.), gives a fair impression of the educational background of French rabbis, while Benjamin Mossé (ed.), *La Révolution française et le rabbinat français* (Paris, 1890), is a mine of rabbinical statements on questions of assimilation. The sermons of the Grand Rabbi of France and the Grand Rabbi of Paris at this time have been published and contain much of interest to the historian. See Zadoc Kahn, *Sermons et allocutions* (3 vols., Paris, 1894) and *Souvenirs et regrets: recueil d'oraisons funèbres prononcées dans la communauté israélite de Paris, 1868–1898* (Paris, 1898), and J.-H. Dreyfuss, *Sermons et allocutions* (2 vols., Paris, 1908–13). André Chouraqui's recent book, *Cent Ans d'histoire: l'Alliance Israélite Universelle et la renaissance juive contemporaine, 1860–1960* (Paris, 1965), gives a sympathetic description of the workings of that institution. This book, which stresses the positive contributions of the Alliance, should be compared with some of the articles by the more hostile Zosa Szajkowski, such as 'How the Mass Migration to America Began', *Jewish Social Studies*, vol. iv, no. 4, October 1942, pp. 291–310, or 'Jewish Diplomacy: Notes on the Occasion of the Centenary of the Alliance Israélite Universelle', *Jewish Social Studies*, vol. xxii, no. 3, July 1960, pp. 131–58. A survey of the Jewish 'image' as established by French writers is to be found in Earle Stanley Randall, *The Jewish Character in the French Novel, 1870–1914* (Menasha, Wisconsin, 1941), and C. Lehrmann, *L'Élément juif dans la littérature française*, vol. ii, *De la Révolution à nos jours* (Paris, 1961). The latter also contains discussion of literary currents within the Jewish community itself.

INDEX

Abraham, Pierre, 62–3.
Adam, Paul, 166.
Ahad Ha-am (Asher Ginzberg), 268.
Alexander III, Tsar, 155, 157.
Alger, Consistoire d', 236.
Algeria, 30, 81, 163, 208, 209, 233, 234–7, 258, 261, 288.
Algerian *consistoires*, see *Consistoires*, Algerian.
Algiers, 235.
Alliance Israélite Universelle, 5, 16, 17, 28, 286, 289; and anti-Semitism, 147, 238–9, 241; and assimilation, 116; and East European Jews, 159, 160, 170; membership of, 16, 76, 82, 124, 137, 217, 241, 275; philanthropic activities, 81–2, 252; and Zionism, 252; *Bulletin de l'*, 239.
Almeida, Baron d' (Jewish nobleman), 36.
Alsace, Jewish community of, *see* Ashkenazim.
Amicale d'Odessa, 47.
Amicale Russe, 47.
Amis Solidaires, 47.
Anarchists and anarchism, 108, 126, 135, 145, 183, 247, 264, 285; *see also* Lazare, Bernard and anarchism.
Angoulême, 209.
Annuaire des Archives israélites, 44, 56n, 287.
Anthropological Society of Paris, 13, 20.
Anti-clericalism, 128–31, 135, 154–5, 169; *see also* Separation of Church and State.
Anti-Juif, L', 125.
Antijuif, L', 236.
Anti-Semitism, 49–50, 99, 122, 124–5, 286; German, 99, 124–5; Russian, 3, 46, 48, 99, 125, 154–5, 188; Jewish reactions to, *see especially* Alliance

Israélite Universelle; *Archives israélites*; Cahen, Isidore; Comité contre l'Antisémitisme; Consistoire Central; Kahn, Rabbi Zadoc; Lazare, Bernard; Levaillant, Isaïe; Prague, Hippolyte; Reinach, Théodore; *Univers israélite*; manifestations of, *see especially* Boulangism; Dreyfus Affair; Duels and Duelling; Mayer, Armand; Panama Scandal; Violence; proponents of, *see especially* Drumont, Édouard.
Archives israélites, 44, 53, 94, 98, 156, 247, 249n, 272n, 287; on anti-Semitism, 53, 145, 198, 218, 219, 222, 233, 238; and the *consistoires*, 70, 81; on the Dreyfus Affair, 211–13, 218–19, 227; on French politics, 134, 135; on Herzl, 274; on Lazare, 185; readership, 148; *Annuaire des*, 44, 56n, 287; *see also* Cahen, Isidore; Prague, Hippolyte.
Arendt, Hannah, 6–7, 126, 209, 215, 287.
Aristocracy, Jewish, 36–7, 79; *see also* headings beginning with Rothschild.
Army, Jews in, 41, 71, 197, 206; *see also* Dreyfus, Alfred.
Aron, Henri, 71, 72, 241.
Aron, Joseph, 149–53, 162, 213.
Ashkenazim, 32–4, 35, 54, 74, 75, 100.
Assimilation, 87, 261–2; defined, 2; *see also* Conversions; Franco-Judaism; Intermarriage; Lazare, Bernard and assimilation; Patriotism; repudiation of, *see* Jewish nationalism; Zionism.
Association des Étudiants Israélites, Bulletin de l', 253–4.
Association of Jewish Students from Russia, 76, 80.
Astruc, Rabbi Élie-Aristide, 93n.

Duels and duelling, 153-4, 182, 196, 197.
Dumas, Alexandre (fils), 39.
Durkheim, Émile, 99.

East European Jews, 3, 80, 236, 247, 256; immigration, 34, 46-7, 83, 157-62; religious practices, 31, 56, 59-60; and Zionism, 251-2, 255, 257, 272, 277, 278, 281; see also Lazare, Bernard on East European Jews; Orthodox Jews.
Écho sioniste, L', 262, 263, 265, 270-1, 272, 287.
École de Travail, 79.
École Rabbinique de France, 34, 54, 70, 72, 74, 75, 128.
Entretiens politiques et littéraires, 166, 167, 169.
Ephrussi, Jules, 38.
Ephrussi, Mme Jules, 80.
Épinal, Consistoire d', 69.
Estafette, L', 159.
Esterhazy, Major C. Ferdinand Walsin, 197.

Famille de Jacob, La, 287.
Ferry, Jules, 16.
Fiancée de Corinthe, La, 168.
Figaro, Le, 132, 145, 166, 171, 275, 278.
Financial Post, 150.
Financiers, Jewish, 35-9, 71.
First Zionist Congress of 1897, 254, 255, 257, 266, 278.
Flambeau, Le, 260-2, 287.
Fleg, Edmond, 283, 288.
Fleurs de l'histoire, Les, 234.
Fouillé, Alfred, 14.
Fould, Achille, 123.
France, Anatole, 39.
France catholique, La, 207-8.
France juive, La, see Drumont, Édouard, La France juive.
Franck, Adolphe, 82, 112-13, 130, 131, 143.
Franck, Henri, 283.
Franco-Egyptian Bank, 38.
Franco-Judaism, 88, 90, 105-21; de-

fined, 100; see also Darmesteter, James; Patriotism.
Franco-Prussian War, 98, 99.
French National Anti-Semitic League, 132.
French Revolution, see Revolution of 1789.
Freud, Sigmund, 266.
Friedmann, Georges, 285.

Gambetta, Léon, 61, 81, 134, 137, 138, 154, 155, 198, 220.
Gaulois, Le, 145n, 154, 228, 230, 288; see also Meyer, Arthur.
German-speaking Jews, see Ashkenazim.
Geschichte der Juden, 88.
Ghetto, The, 9, 10, 19, 35, 46, 49, 51, 94, 95, 105, 178-9.
Ghetto, Das (later Das neue Ghetto), 179.
Gobineau, Count Arthur de, 12.
Golberg, Mécislas, 269, 270.
Goudchaux, Michel, 38, 123.
Government, Jews in, 38, 41, 123-4, 135, 206.
Graetz, Heinrich, 88.
Grand Rabbi of France, 34, 56, 69, 72, 73; see also Isidor, Rabbi Lazare; Kahn, Rabbi Zadoc.
Grand Rabbi of Paris, 73, 76; see also Dreyfuss, Rabbi Jacques-Henri; Kahn, Rabbi Zadoc.
Grand Rabbis, 72, 73.
Grande Revue, La, 275.
Grande Encyclopédie, 20, 114.
Grave, Jean, 167-8.
Groupe des Ouvriers Juifs Socialistes de Paris, 245-9, 270n.
Grünebaum-Ballin, Paul, 41.
Guérin, Jules, 163.
Guesde, Jules, 210.
Guide du croyant israélite, Le, 117.
Günzberg, Baron Horace de, 36.
Günzberg, Baroness Horace de, 80.
Guyot, Yves, 86.

Hadamard, Mme (mother-in-law of Alfred Dreyfus), 215.